Routledge Qu

English Legal System
2013–2014

Routledge Q&A series

Each Routledge Q&A contains approximately 50 questions on topics commonly found on exam papers, with comprehensive suggested answers. The titles are written by lecturers who are also examiners, so the student gains an important insight into exactly what examiners are looking for in an answer. This makes them excellent revision and practice guides. With over 500,000 copies of the Routledge Q&As sold to date, accept no other substitute.

New editions publishing in 2013:

Civil Liberties & Human Rights
Company Law
Commercial Law
Constitutional & Administrative Law
Contract Law
Criminal Law
Employment Law
English Legal System
Equity & Trusts
European Union Law

Evidence
Family Law
Jurisprudence
Land Law
Medical Law
Torts

Published in 2012:
Business Law 2012–2013
Intellectual Property Law 2012–2013

For a full listing, visit **http://cw.routledge.com/textbooks/revision**

Routledge Questions & Answers Series

English Legal System

2013–2014

Gary Slapper, LLB, LLM, PhD, PGCE(Law)
Global Professor at New York University, and Director of New York University in London; Door Tenant, 36 Bedford Row, the Chambers of Frances Oldham QC; Visiting Professor of Law at The Open University, and The Chinese University, Hong Kong

AND

David Kelly, BA, BA (Law), PhD
Previously Principal Lecturer in Law, Staffordshire University

Additional Content supplied by:

Karen Davies, LLB (Wales), LLM (European Law)
Programme Director for the Graduate Diploma in Law (GDL/CPE) and lectures on a number of undergraduate and postgraduate courses

Routledge
Taylor & Francis Group

LONDON AND NEW YORK

Tenth edition published 2013
by Routledge
2 Park Square, Milton Park, Abingdon, Oxon OX14 4RN

Simultaneously published in the USA and Canada
by Routledge
711 Third Avenue, New York, NY 10017

Routledge is an imprint of the Taylor & Francis Group, an informa business

© 2013 Gary Slapper and David Kelly

First edition published by Cavendish Publishing 1993
Ninth edition published by Routledge 2011

British Library Cataloguing in Publication Data
A catalogue record for this book is available from the British Library

Library of Congress Cataloging in Publication Data
Slapper, Gary
  English legal system/Gary Slapper, David Kelly. – 10th ed
    p.cm. — (Q&A, Routledge questions & answers series)
  ISBN 978-0-415-50356-3 (pbk) — ISBN 978-0-203-12914-2 (ebk)
  1. Law—England—Examinations —study guides.   2. Law—England—Problems, exercises, etc.   I. Kelly,
  David, 1950–   II. Title.
  KD663.S58 2013
  349.42—dc23

2012024445

ISBN: 978–0–415–50356–3 (pbk)
ISBN: 978–0–203–12914–2 (ebk)

Typeset in TheSans
by RefineCatch Limited, Bungay, Suffolk

Printed and bound in Great Britain by the MPG Books Group

Contents

Preface		vii
Table of Cases		ix
Table of Legislation		xv
Guide to the Companion Website		xxi
	Introduction	1
1	Sources of Law and Legal Reform	4
2	The Courts and the Appellate Process	45
3	Judicial Reasoning	79
4	Judges and Juries	105
5	The Criminal Process	132
6	Civil Process and Legal Services	185
7	Alternative Dispute Resolution	218
8	The Rule of Law, Judicial Review and Human Rights	244
	Index	271

Preface

This book has been written to assist students in their study of the English legal system. It has been composed for students of this subject in general and for undergraduates and those studying for professional examinations, in particular. The text is not a substitute for course books, law reports and legal journals, but aims to complement them by showing how typical examination and assignment questions can be answered.

The subject matter of the English legal system requires students to be familiar with our legal institutions and procedures, the criminal and civil processes, some substantive law, legal theories and debates in the realms of morals and politics. One thread running through all these topics is the requirement that students be evaluative and critical in their approach to the issues. It is also essential that answers take account of recent developments. Our answers in this book aim to show examples of such techniques.

These answers will, perhaps, be most appreciated by students who have already acquired a good working knowledge of the relevant issues, principles and law and who desire clarification on the techniques that can be used to best present their knowledge in response to typical questions. The questions are modelled on those from a variety of English legal system courses, including the University of London (External) LLB. We have chosen a mix of essay and 'problem' questions and concentrated on issues which have current significance.

There have been many changes made to the apparatus and processes of the English legal system since the ninth edition of this book was published in 2011. There have been changes to civil and criminal process, the court system, the funding of legal services, the jury, human rights law, and several important common law decisions in the Court of Appeal, the Supreme Court, and the European Court of Human Rights. These have all been digested in this edition.

We would like to thank Karen Davies for her excellent work on the diagrams and annotations found in this new edition.

We have endeavoured to state the law as at May 2012.

Gary Slapper
David Kelly
June 2012

Table of Cases

A and others v Secretary of State for the
Home Department [2004] UKHL 56,
[2005] 3 All ER 169 **28, 268**

A v Secretary of State for the Home
Department (2002) (2004) **115, 251, 256,
270**

ABC case (1978) The Times, 18 November
127

Addy and Sons v Dumbreck [1929] AC 358
50

Adler v George [1964] 1 All ER 628 **91**

Agar [1990] 2 All ER 442, CA **178**

Algar [1954] 1 QB 279 **69**

AM&S Europe Ltd v EC Commission (1983)
Case 155/79 **205**

Angry Brigade see R v Greenfield

Antaios Compania Naviera SA v Salen
Redereiarna AB [1985] AC 191; [1984] 3
All ER 229 **237**

Associated Provincial Picture Houses Ltd
v Wednesbury Corporation [1948] 1 KB
223; [1947] 2 All ER 680 **188, 190, 191, 260**

Attorney-General's Reference (No 3 of
1999) [2000] 4 All ER 360 **103**

Austin v Mayor and Burgesses of the
London Borough of Southwark [2010]
UKSC 28; [2009] EWCA Civ 66 **49**

Aziz [1996] AC 41; [1995] 3 All ER 149 **142**

B v Auckland District Law Society [2003]
UKPC 38; [2004] 4 All ER 269 **205**

Badham [1987] Crim LR 202 **155, 157, 158**

Bellinger v Bellinger [2003] 2 WLR 1174 **24**

Belmarsh case see A and others v Secretary
of State for the Home Department

Bentley v Brudzinski [1982] Crim LR 825
159, 160

Bird [1977] 67 Cr App Rep 203 **178**

BLCT (13096) Ltd v J Sainsbury plc [2003]
EWCA Civ 884; [2004] 2 P & CR 32 **237**

Boardman v DPP [1974] 3 All ER 887; [1975]
AC 421 **100**

Bolitho v City and Hackney Health
Authority [1998] AC 232; [1997] 4 All ER
771 **215**

Breslin & Ors v McKenna & Ors (Omagh
Bombing Case) [2008] IEHC 122 **135**

Brogan v UK (1989) **254, 256**

Bromley LBC v GLC [1983] 1 AC 768; [1982] 1
All ER 129 **261**

Broome v Cassell [1972] AC 1027; [1972] 1 All
ER 801 **81**

Brown [1988] 87 Cr App Rep 52 **103**

Burmah Oil Co Ltd v The Lord Advocate
[1965] AC 75 **97**

Cain [1976] Crim LR 464, CA **176**

Campbell v UK (1992) 15 EHRR 137 **205**

Chaffers, Re, ex parte A-G (1897) 45 WR 365,
76 LT 351 **59**

Chandler [1976] 1 WLR 585, CA **150, 152, 154**

Chorherr v Austria (1994) **256**

Christie v Leachinsky [1947] AC 573 **165**

Churchill [1989] Crim LR 226, CA **158**

CILFIT Srl v Minister of Health (No 283/81)
[1982] ECR 3415 **37**

Civil Service Unions v UK (1988) **256, 260**

CMA CGM SA v Beteiligungs KG [2002]
EWCA Civ 1878; [2003] 3 All ER
330 **237**

Coombes (1960) 45 Cr App Rep 36, 125 JP
139 **99**

Corkery v Carpenter [1950] 2 All ER 745;
[1951] 1 KB 102 **91**

Council of Civil Service Unions v Minister
for the Civil Service (GCHQ Case) [1984]
1 WLR 1174, CA **260**

Culver (infant) v Beard [1938] 2 KB 292n;
[1937] 1 All ER 301 **73**

Curry v DPP (1994) 144 NLJ 498 **85, 88**

D v M [1983] Fam 33; [1982] 3 All ER 897 **73**

Danvers [1982] Crim LR 680 **126**

Davidson [1988] Crim LR 442 **146**

Davis (1959) 43 Cr App Rep 215 **150**

Dellow's Will Trusts, In re [1964] 1 WLR 451,
455 **138**

Dimes v Grand Junction Canal (1852) 3 HL
Cas 759 **118, 120**

Donnelly v Jackman [1970] 1 WLR 562, CA
160, 161

Doolan [1988] Crim LR 747 **103**

DPP v Hawkins [1988] 1 WLR 1166 **165**

DPP v Schildkamp [1970] 2 WLR 279; [1969]
2 All ER 835n **95**

Duncan (1981) 73 Cr App Rep 359 **142**

Dunford (1990) 91 Cr App Rep 150; [1991]
Crim LR 370, CA **147**

Dunnett v Railtrack plc (2002) EWCA Civ
302 **242–3**

Eagil Trust Co Ltd v Pigott Brown [1985] 3
All ER 119 **73**

Earl of Oxford's Case (1615) 1 Rep Ch 1, 21 ER
485 **14**

Emmerson (1990) 92 Cr App Rep 284, [1991]
Crim LR 194 **143**

European Parliament v Council [1990] ECR
I-2041 **37**

Factortame Ltd v Secretary of State for
Transport (No 1) [1989] 2 All ER 692 **35**

Fennelley [1989] Crim LR 142 **159, 162**

Fisher v Bell [1961] 1 QB 394; [1960] 3 All ER
731 **90**

Fitzpatrick v Sterling Housing Association
Ltd [1999] 4 All ER 705 **265**

Ford [1989] 3 WLR 762 **126**

Francisco v Diedrick (1998) TLR 218 **137**

Fulling [1987] 2 WLR 923, CA **143**

Gallie v Lee [1971] AC 1004 **82**

GCHQ case see Council of Civil Service
Unions v Minister for the
Civil Service

Goldenberg (1988) 152 JP 557, CA **140, 142,
143**

Golder v United Kingdom (1979–80) 1 EHRR
525 **62**

Goodwin v UK (2002) **257**

Greenough v Gaskell (1833) 1 My & K 98;
[1824–34] All ER Rep 767 **204**

H and R, Re (Child Sexual Abuse:Standard
of Proof) [1995] 1 FLR 643 **137, 139**

Halford v Brookes and another (1991) The
Times, 9 October 1998 **137**

Hall (Arthur JS) & Co v Simms and Others
[2000] 3 WLR 543 **206**

Halsey v Milton Keynes General NHS Trust
[2004] EWCA (Civ 576) **243**

Handyside v United Kingdom (1979–80) 1
EHRR 737 **62**

Harper-Taylor, Baker and Bakker [1991] RTR
76n, [1988] NLJR 80; (1988) The Times, 3
March **178**

Herrington v British Railways Board [1972]
AC 877 **48, 50**

Heydon's case (1584) 3 Co Rep 7a **91**

HM Treasury v Mohammed Jaber Ahmed
(2010) UKSC 2 **28**

Home Secretary v Wainright [2002] 3 WLR
405 **97**

Horton v Sadler [2006] UKHL 27 **48, 50–1**

Hurnam v DPP of Mauritius [2005] UKPC
49; [2007] UKPC 24 **168**

Hurst v Leeming [2001] EWHC 1051 Ch **243**

Inze v Austria (1988) 10 EHRR 394 **62**

IRC v Frere [1969] 3 WLR 1193, CA **98**

Ireland v United Kingdom (1979–80) 2
EHRR 25 **62**

Jose da Conceicao Guerreiro v Portugal
(2002) App No 00045560/99 (G Ress P),
31 January **198**

Kenlin v Gardiner [1967] 2 QB 510; [1967] 2
WLR 129 **160**
Kjeldson and others v Denmark (1979–80) 1
EHRR 711 **62**

L (1994) **143**
Lemsatef [1977] 1 WLR 812, CA **160**
Lewis (John) & Co Ltd v Tims [1952] AC 676
164, 167
Linton v Ministry of Defence (1983) 133 NLJ
1103 **68**
Locabail (UK) Ltd v Bayfield Properties Ltd
and Another [2000] 2 WLR 870; (1999)
149 NLJ 1793, CA **117, 119, 121**
London Tramways Co Ltd v London County
Council [1898] AC 375 **49**
London Transport Executive ex p GLC
[1983] QB 484 **261**

McCay [1991] 1 All ER 232 **161**
McIlkenny and Others (1991) The Times, 1
April **72**
McIvor [1987] Crim LR 409 **144, 145**
Marks v Beyfus (1890) 25 QBD 494 **103**
Marshall v Southampton and West
Hampshire AHA [1993] 3 WLR 1054, CA **37**
Mason [1987] 3 All ER 481; [1988] 1 WLR 139
139, 140, 141
Maynard (1979) 69 Cr App Rep 309 **68**
Meering v Grahame-White Aviation Co Ltd
(1919) 122 LT 44; [1918–19] All ER Rep Ext
1490 **164**
Melluish (Inspector of Taxes) v BMI (No 3)
Ltd [1995] 4 All ER 453 **96**
Mendoza v Ghaidan [2002] EWCA Civ 1533;
[2003] 2 WLR 478 **88, 93, 265**
Miliangos v George Frank (Textiles) Ltd
[1975] 3 WLR 758, CA; [1976] AC 443 **81**
Miller [1986] 1 WLR 1191 **103, 140**
Momodou [2005] EWCA 177 **180, 181, 182**

Moy v Pettmann Smith [2005] UKHL 7 **212**

North Range Shipping Ltd v Seatrans
Shipping Corporation [2002] EWCA Civ
405 **237**

Omagh Bombing case; Breslin & Ors v
McKenna & Ors (Omagh Bombing
Case) [2008] IEHC 122 **135**

P [1991] 2 AC 447; [1992] Crim LR 41 **100**
Paris (1992) 97 Cr App Rep 99, [1994] Crim
LR 320 **143**
Parkes [1976] 3 All ER 380 **150, 152**
Parris [1989] Crim LR 214, CA **144, 146**
Pepper v Hart [1993] 1 All ER 42, CA **92, 94,
96**
Pinochet case see R v Bow Street
Metropolitan Stipendiary Magistrate ex
p Pinochet Ugarte
Pitman [1991] 1 All ER 468, CA **174, 177**
Powell v Kempton Park Racecourse [1899]
AC 143 **98**
Price v Leeds City [2006] UKHL 10 **82, 264**

Quintavalle v Secretary of State for Health
[2003] 2 WLR 550 **92**

R (1991) (Rape: Marital Exemption) [1992] 1
AC 599; [1991] 4 All ER 481 **9, 40, 87**
R (on the application of Gillan) v (1)
Commissioner of Police for the
Metropolis (2) Secretary of State for the
Home Department [2004] EWCA Civ
1067; [2005] QB 388 **60–1, 62–3**
R (on the application of Greenpeace Ltd)
v Secretary of State for Trade and
Industry [2007] EWHC 311 (Admin) **188,
189, 192**
R (on the application of Jackson) v Attorney
General [2005] 3 WLR 733 **22**
R (on the Application of Quintavalle) v
Secretary of State for Health [2003] 2
WLR 692 **92**

R (on the Application of Rottman) v Commissioner of Police [2002] 2 WLR 1315 **96**

R v A [2001] UKHL 25; [2002] 1 AC 45 **88, 93**

R v (1) Abdroikov (2) Green (3) Williamson [2005] EWCA Crim 1986; [2006] 1 Cr App Rep 1 **123, 128, 129**

R v Argent [1997] 2 Cr App Rep 27 **152**

R v Beycan [1990] Crim LR 185, CA **144, 148**

R v Bow Street Metropolitan Stipendiary Magistrate ex p Pinochet Ugarte (No 2) [2000] 1 AC 119; [1999] 1 All ER 577 **117, 118, 120, 121**

R v Camborne Justices ex p Pearce [1955] 1 QB 41; [1954] 2 All ER 850 **120**

R v Clinton [1993] 1 WLR 1181 **210**

R v Condron [1997] 1 Cr App Rep 85 **152**

R v Cooper [1969] 1 QB 267; [1968] 3 WLR 1225 **154**

R v Cowan [1996] QB 373; [1995] 4 All ER 939, CA **152**

R v Cox and Railton (1884) 14 QBD 153; [1881–5] All ER Rep 68 **203, 205**

R v Gough [1993] AC 646; [1992] 4 All ER 481 **117, 120**

R v Greenfield (The Angry Brigade) [1973] 1 WLR 1151 **126, 127**

R v Inhabitants of Sedgley (1831) 2 B & Ad 65 **98**

R v John K (2007) **64**

R v Kansal [2001] All ER (D) 311 (May) **97**

R v Lambert [2001] 1 All ER 1014 **97**

R v Nottingham Justices ex p Davies [1980] 3 WLR 15 **173**

R v Rand LR 1 QBD 230 **120**

R v Secretary of State for the Home Department ex p Brind [1991] 2 WLR 588, CA **262**

R v SH [2010] EWCA Crim 193 **75**

R v Sussex Coroner ex p Homberg [1924] 1 KB 256 **56**

R v Sussex JJ ex p McCarthy [1924] 1 KB 256; [1923] All ER Rep 233 **118**

Ras Behari Lal v King-Emperor (1933) 102 LJPC 144 **52**

Rice v Connolly [1966] 3 WLR 17 **150, 151**

Ricketts v Cox [1982] Crim LR 184 **150, 151**

Rogers (1994) 158 JP 909; [1995] Crim LR 148 **101**

Rondel v Worsley [1967] 3 WLR 1666, CA; [1969] 1 AC 191 **68, 207**

Roquette Frères SA v Council (1980) ECR 3333 **189, 192**

Royal College of Nursing v DHSS [1981] 2 WLR 279, CA **95**

Samuel [1988] 2 WLR 920, CA **103, 144, 146**

Sang [1980] AC 402; [1979] 3 WLR 263, CA **139, 140, 143**

Secretary of State for the Home Department ex p Hickey and Others [1995] 1 WLR 534 **133**

Secretary of State for the Home Department v JJ and Others [2007] All ER (D) 489 (Oct); [2007] UKHL 45 **269**

Secretary of State for the Home Department v MB and AF [2007] All ER (D) 01 (Nov) **269**

Self [1992] 1 WLR 657, CA **164, 166**

Selvey v DPP [1970] AC 304; [1968] 2 All ER 497 **100**

Shah v Gale [2005] EWHC 1087 QB **139**

Sharp [1988] 1 All ER 65 **140, 142**

Smith v Eric S Bush [1988] QB 743; [1987] 3 All ER 179 **144, 145**

Sparks v R [1964] AC 964 **101**

Spencer [1987] AC 128; [1986] 2 All ER 928 **82**

Spicer v Holt [1977] Crim LR 364 **164**

Stafford v DPP [1974] AC 878; [1973] 3 All ER 762 **68**

Straffen [1952] 2 QB 911 **100**

Sutcliffe (1981) The Times, 23 May 762 **177**

Sweet v Parsley [1969] 2 WLR 470, CA; [1970] AC 132, HL **97**

Taylor v Chief Constable of Cheshire [1987] 1 All ER 225; [1986] 1 WLR 1479 **101**

Three Rivers DC v Bank of England (No 2)
    [1996] 2 All ER 363 **96**
Townsend [1987] Crim LR 411 **101**
Turner [1970] 2 WLR 1093, CA **174, 176**

Wadman [1996] EWCA Crim 1540 **149**
Walkley v Precision Forgings Ltd [1979] 2 All
    ER 548 **51, 52, 53**
Walsh (1990) 12 Cr App Rep (S) 243
    147
Walters v WH Smith & Son Ltd [1914] 1 KB
    595 **164, 165, 166**
Webster & Ors v Ridgeway Foundation
    School [2010] EWCA 318 QB **212,
    213, 217**

Wednesbury case *see* Associated Provincial
    Picture Houses Ltd v Wednesbury
    Corporation
Weekes (1993) 97 Cr App Rep 222 **103**
Wingrove v UK [1996] ECtHR (No 17419/90)
    255

Young, James and Webster v United
    Kingdom (1981) 4 EHRR 38 **62**
Young v Bristol Aeroplane Co Ltd [1944] KB
    718 **81, 83**

Z [1990] 2 QB 355; [1991] Fam Law 137 **101**
Zavekas [1990] 2 QB 355; [1991] Fam Law
    137 **139, 141**

Table of Legislation

STATUTES

Abortion Act 1967 **20**
Access to Justice Act 1999 **187, 199, 222**
Anti-Terrorism Crime and Security Act 2001
        28, 115, 251, 254–5, 256, 267–8
  s 21 **268**
  s 21(1) **267**
  s 23 **115, 268**
  s 23(1) **268**
Arbitration Act 1950
  Part 1 **233**
Arbitration Act 1975 **233**
Arbitration Act 1979 **233**
Arbitration Act 1996 **232–7, 239**
  Part 1 **234**
  s 1 **233**
  s 5 **234**
  s 5(3) **234**
  ss 9–11 **236**
  s 15 **234**
  s 17 **234**
  s 18 **236**
  s 20(4) **234**
  s 24 **236**
  s 28 **234**
  s 29 **234**
  s 30 **235**
  s 33 **235**
  s 35 **235**
  s 39 **235**
  s 43 **236**
  s 45 **236**
  s 46 **235**
  s 48 **235**
  s 49 **235**
  s 50 **235**

  s 58 **235**
  s 66 **235**
  s 67 **236**
  s 69 **237**

Bail Act 1976 **168, 171, 174**
  s 3 **173**
  s 4 **169**
  s 6 **172**
  s 7 **172**
  s 9 **172**
  s 154 **172**
  Sched 1 **169, 170**
Bail (Amendment) Act 1993 **168, 173**

Civil Evidence Act 1968 **68**
Companies Act 1985 **23**
Constitutional Reform Act 2005 **107, 108**
  s 1 **245, 250**
  s 17(1) **250**
  s 23 **108**
  s 23(3) **109**
  s 23(4) **109**
  s 23(6) **109**
  s 24 **109**
  s 25 **109, 112**
  s 26 **109**
  s 26(4) **109**
  s 27 **109, 110, 112**
  s 27(2) **110**
  s 27(3) **110**
  s 27(8) **110**
  s 27(9) **110**
  s 28 **109, 110**
  s 28(1) **110**

s 29 **110–11**
s 30 **109**
s 30(1) **111**
s 30(3) **112**
s 31 **109**
Sched 8 **109, 112**
Contracts (Rights of Third Parties) Act 1999
    41
Coroners and Justice Act 2009 **55, 57**
County Courts Act 1984 **26**
Courts and Legal Services Act 1990
    s 71 **54**
Criminal Appeal Act 1968 **69**
    s 1 **69**
    s 2 **68**
    s 4 **70**
    s 12 **69**
    s 23(1) **70**
    s 23(1)(c) **70**
    s 23(2) **70**
Criminal Appeal Act 1995 **47, 154**
    s 1 **69**
    s 2 **69**
    s 19 **71**
Criminal Evidence Act 1898 **99**
    s 1 **100**
Criminal Justice Act 1982 **173**
Criminal Justice Act 1988 **102, 123, 126**
    s 155 **173**
Criminal Justice Act 1991
    s 34 **101**
    s 52 **101**
Criminal Justice Act 2003 **41, 42, 123, 128,**
    171
    Part 2 **171**
    Part 9 **72**
    ss 13–21 **171**
    ss 43–50 **133**
    s 177 **124, 130**
    ss 227 and 228 **124, 130**
    s 321 **129, 133**
    Sched 33
        Para 2 **123, 128**
        Para 3 **125, 131**

Criminal Justice and Immigration Act 2008 **133**
Criminal Justice and Public Order Act 1994
        123, 134, 152, 173
    s 25 **168, 169, 170, 171**
    ss 25–30 **168**
    s 27 **168, 169**
    s 28 **169**
    s 29 **169**
    ss 32–33 **134**
    s 34 **152, 153, 154**
    ss 34–37 **134**
    ss 34–38 **152, 154**
    s 34(1) **153**
    ss 36 and 37 **153**
    s 38 **154**
Criminal Law Act 1977
    s 62 **148**

Dangerous Drugs Act 1965
    s 5(b) **97**
Domestic Violence
    Crime and Victims Act 2004
    ss 5 and 6 **42**

Employment Rights Act 1996 **220**
European Communities Act 1972
    s 2(2) **7**
    s 3 **82**
    s 3(1) **82, 264**

Human Fertilisation and Embryology Act
    1990 **92**
Human Rights Act 1998 **6, 19, 23–4, 25, 28, 81,**
        85, 88, 113, 114, 115, 117, 128, 245, 257–67
    s 2 **88, 93, 264, 270**
    s 3 **88, 97, 265, 266, 267, 270**
    s 4 **265, 266, 267**
    s 4(6) **270**
    s 6 **265**
    s 7 **265**
    s 10 **270**
    s 19 **264**
    s 22(4) **97**
    Sched 1 **263**

Hunting Act 2004 **22**

Interpretation Act 1978 **92, 95**

Judicature Acts 1873–75 **17, 18**
Juries Act 1974 **123, 127**
    s 9 **125, 131**
    s 9(1) **125, 131**
    s 9AA **131**
    s 12(6) **125**

Land Registration Act 2002 **41**
Law Commission Act 1965 **39**
Law Commission Act 2009 **39, 43, 44**
Law Practitioners Act 1982
    s 101(3)(d) **205**
Legal Services Act 2007 **187**
Licensing Act 1872
    s 12 **91**
Limitation Act 1980
    s 11 **50, 51**
    s 33 **50, 51, 52**
Limited Liability Partnership Act 2000
    ss 14 and 15 **26**
Local Government Act 1972 **26**
Local Government Act 1974 **228–9**

Magistrates' Courts Act 1980 **26**
Merchant Shipping Act 1988 **36**

Offences Against the Person Act 1861
    s 38 **166**

Parliament Act 1911 **22**
Parliament Act 1949 **22**
Parliamentary Commissioner Act 1967
    227–32
    s 12(3) **229**
Partnership Act 1890 **23**
Police Act 1964
    s 51 **155, 158**
    s 51(3) **151**
Police and Criminal Evidence Act 1984
    Part IV **169**

s 1 **134, 159, 161**
s 1(7)(b)(i) **161**
s 1(8)(a) **161**
s 2 **134, 159, 162**
s 2(3) **162**
s 2(3)(c) **162**
s 2(9) **163**
s 8 **134**
s 10(1)(a) **158**
s 15 **134**
s 16 **134**
s 18 **134, 155, 156, 157, 158**
s 19 **155, 157**
s 20 **155**
s 24 **134, 156, 165**
s 24(1)(b) **144, 145**
s 24(4) **166**
s 24(5) **166**
s 25 **134, 165**
s 28(3) **165**
s 32 **134, 155, 157, 158**
s 38 **169**
s 38(1)(a) **169**
s 47 **169**
s 54 **134**
s 56 **148**
s 56(5) **148**
s 56(6) **148**
s 58 **144, 146, 147**
s 58(1) **145**
s 58(8) **148**
s 64 **104**
s 64(1) **103**
s 67 **159**
s 67(11) **155, 157, 161**
s 76 **70, 103, 139, 140, 142, 153**
s 76(2) **140, 141**
s 76(2)(a) **142**
s 76(2)(b) **141, 142, 149**
s 78 **103, 139, 140, 141, 143, 147, 149, 153,**
    154, 155, 156, 158, 159, 161, 162
s 78(1) **104**
s 82 **140, 141, 143**
s 82(1) **139, 142**

s 116 **144**
s 116(6)(e) **145**
s 116(6)(f) **145**
s 117 **155, 158**
Sched 5 **145**
Powers of Criminal Courts (Sentencing) Act
      2000
    ss 27 and 28 **124**
    s 91 **124, 130**
    s 177 **124**
Prevention of Terrorism Act 2005 **268–70**
Prevention of Terrorism (Temporary
      Provisions) Act 1989 **256, 268–70**
Proceeds of Crime Act 2002 **205**
Prosecution of Offences Act 1985
    s 6(1) **135**
    s 6(2) **135**

Rent Act 1977 **265**
Royal Assent Act 1967 **22**

Sale of Goods Act 1893 **23**

Serious Organised Crime and Police Act 2005
      175
Sex Discrimination Act 1975 **37**
Solicitors Act 1974 **26**
Statute of Gloucester 1278 **12**
Sunday Entertainments Act 1932 **190**
Supreme Court Act 1981 **26**
    s 42 **59**

Terrorism Act 2000 **205, 256**
    s 44 **60–1**
    ss 44–47 **61**
    s 45 **61**
Treasure Act 1996 **54**
Tribunals, Courts and Enforcement Act 2007
      219, 223–7
Tribunals and Inquiries Act 1971
    s 12 **222**
Trustee Act 2000 **41**

War Crimes Act 1991 **97**
War Damage Act 1965 **97**

SECONDARY LEGISLATION

Civil Procedure Rules 1998 **74, 75, 192, 196,**
      198
    Part 1 **196**
    Part 6, s 38 **214**
    Part 27 **240**
    Part 35 **214**
    Part 36 **192, 193, 196**
    Part 44.3 **196**
    Part 45, s VI **203**
    r 1.1(1) **186**
    r 1.2 **187**
    r 24.2 **208**
    r 26.4 **242**
    r 35 **215**
    r 35.7(3) **215**
    r 44.3 **196**
    r 44.3(2) **242**
    r 44.3(4) **242**

    r 44.3(5) **242**
    r 44.5 **242**
Civil Procedure (Amendment) Rules 2020 (SI
      2010/621) **203**
Criminal Procedure Rules **215**
Human Rights Act 1998 (Designated
      Derogation) Order 2001 **268**
Limited Liability Partnership Regulations
      2001 **26**
Magistrates Courts' (Remands in Custody)
      Order 1991 (SI 1991/2667) **173**
Police and Criminal Evidence Act 1984
    Code A **159, 161–2, 163**
      para 1.6(a) **162**
    Code B **155, 157, 158**
    Code C **140, 141, 147, 148**
      Annex B
      Note B4 **144, 147**

Note C1 146

Annex C 143

para 1.5 143

para 1.6(a) 162

para 1.7(aa) 162

para 3.1 144

para 3.1(ii) 148

para 6.3 148

para 6.6(d) 148, 149

para 10 153

para 10.1 153

para 10.3 153

para 11.1 143

para 11.1(a) 153

para 11.14 143

para 11.3 142

para 12.7 143

Code D 154

para 10.3 153

Rules of the Supreme Court

INTERNATIONAL INSTRUMENTS

Charter of Fundamental Rights of the
    European Union 30

EC Treaty 1957 30

    Arts 85 and 86 32

    Art 234 35, 36

    Art 249 30

Equal Treatment Directive 76/207/EEC
    37–8

European Convention on Human Rights 1950
    6, 61, 62, 63, 81, 88, 113, 115, 129, 171,
    198, 237, 254, 257, 262–3

    Art 1 263

    Art 2 263, 264

    Art 3 263, 264

    Art 4 263, 264

    Art 5 60, 256, 263, 268, 269

    Art 6 63, 129

    Art 6(1) 198, 263

    Art 7 263, 264

    Art 8 61, 254, 263, 264, 269

    Art 9 254, 263, 264

Art 10 61, 254, 263, 264, 269

Art 10(2) 255

Art 11 254, 263, 264, 269

Art 11(2) 254, 264

Art 12 263

Art 14 263, 264, 265, 268

Protocol 1 263

Protocol 6 263

Lisbon Treaty 9, 30–1, 32, 34

Maastricht Treaty 1992 29

Nice Treaty 2001 29

Single European Act 1986 (SEA) 32

Treaty on European Union (TEU)

    Art 1 29

Treaty on the Functioning of the European
    Union (TFEU)

    Art 2 29

    Art 3 30

    Art 267 35, 36

    Art 288 30

    Arts 105 and 106 (formerly 85 and 86) 32

Guide to the Companion Website

http://cw.routledge.com/textbooks/revision

Visit the Routledge Q&A website to discover even more study tips and advice on getting those top marks.

On the Routledge revision website you will find the following resources designed to enhance your revision on all areas of undergraduate law.

The Good, The Fair, & The Ugly

Good essays are the gateway to top marks. This interactive tutorial provides sample essays together with voice-over commentary and tips for successful exam essays, written by our Q&A authors themselves.

Multiple Choice Questions

Knowledge is the foundation of every good essay. Focusing on key examination themes, these MCQs have been written to test your knowledge and understanding of each subject in the book.

Bonus Q&As

Having studied our exam advice, put your revision into practice and test your essay writing skills with our additional online questions and answers.

Don't forget to check out even more revision guides and exam tools from Routledge!

Lawcards

Lawcards are your complete, pocket-sized guides to key examinable areas of the undergraduate law.

Routledge Student Statutes

Comprehensive selections; clear, easy-to-use layout; alphabetical, chronological, and thematic indexes; and a competitive price make *Routledge Student Statutes* the statute book of choice for the serious law student.

Introduction

This book is intended to be of help to students studying the English legal system where they feel that they have acquired a reasonable body of knowledge and skills, but do not feel confident about using them effectively in exams. This book sets out to demonstrate how to apply the knowledge to the question and how to structure the answer. Students, especially first-year students, often find the technique of answering problem questions particularly hard to grasp, so this book contains a number of answers to such questions.

It is hoped that this book will be particularly useful at exam time, but it may also prove useful throughout the year. The book provides examples of the kind of questions that are usually asked in end-of-year examinations, along with suggested solutions. Each chapter deals with one of the main themes covered in legal system courses and contains typical questions on that area. The aim is not to include questions covering every aspect of a course, but to pick out the areas that tend to be examined because they are particularly contentious or topical. Many courses contain a certain amount of material that is not examined, although it is important for providing background knowledge.

PROBLEM AND ESSAY QUESTIONS

Some areas tend to be examined only by essays, some mainly – although not invariably – by problems, and some by either. The questions chosen reflect this mix, and the introductions at the beginning of each chapter cover the themes commonly examined. It is important not to choose a topic and then assume that it will appear on the exam paper in a particular form unless it is in an area where, for example, a problem question is never set. If it might appear as an essay or a problem, revision should be geared to either possibility; a very thorough knowledge of the area should be acquired, but also an awareness of critical opinion in relation to it.

LENGTH OF ANSWERS

The answers in this book are about the length of an essay that a good student would expect to write in an exam. Some are a little longer and that will be of assistance in explaining the topic during the course.

ADDITIONAL NOTES

Some essays are followed by additional notes exploring areas of the answer in more depth, which should be of value to the student who wants to do more than cover the main points.

EXPRESSING A POINT OF VIEW

Students sometimes ask, especially in an area such as English legal system which can be quite topical and politically controversial, whether they should argue for any particular point of view in an essay. It will be noticed that some of the essays in this book do this. In general, the good student does argue for one side but he or she always uses sound arguments to support his or her view. Further, a good student does not ignore the opposing arguments; they are considered and, if possible, their weaknesses are exposed. Of course, it would not be appropriate to do this in a problem question or in some essay questions but, where an invitation to do so is held out, it is a good idea to accept it rather than sit on the fence.

EXAMINATION PREPARATION

There are very few universally applicable tips for examination preparation and revision because people like to do these things in their own way.

If you are preparing for an examination you should however:

❖ Plan your revision programme so that you can tell, weeks from the examination, on what days you will be revising which subjects and topics. Allocating your time to revising different subjects on a random or intuitive basis is not good idea.
❖ Have a system for testing your powers of recall, e.g. see if you can recite the topic you have learnt to an imaginary audience and re-start this exercise if you falter on any point.
❖ Ensure with as many topics as you can that you know not only the law and its ambiguous points but also what critical commentary exists in the area.

In the examination:

❖ Stick rigidly to the time for each question, e.g. if you have to write four answers in three hours, do not exceed 45 minutes for any answer. It will be hard to pick up *extra* marks by slogging away at an answer to which you have already devoted 45 minutes; it will be significantly easier to gain *the first ten marks* awardable for the next answer.
❖ Focus on the precise question asked and frame your response to answer that question. Avoid simply reproducing in the script (however accurately) everything you have learnt about the relevant theme.

Common Pitfalls

The most common mistake made when using Questions & Answers
books for revision is to memorise the model answers provided and try to
reproduce them in exams. This approach is a sure-fire pitfall, likely to result
in a poor overall mark because your answer will not be specific enough to
the particular question on your exam paper, and there is also a danger that
reproducing an answer in this way would be treated as plagiarism. You must
instead be sure to read the question carefully, to identify the issues and
problems it is asking you to address and to answer it directly in your exam.
If you take our examiners' advice and use your Q&A to focus on your
question-answering skills and understanding of the law applied, you will
be ready for whatever your exam paper has to offer!

Sources of Law and Legal Reform

INTRODUCTION

There are different interpretations of the phrase 'source of law'. It can, in jurisprudence, refer to what it is in our nature or society that necessitates law. More generally, however, the expression refers to the procedural origin of the law which is applied in the courts. There are three main sources: Parliamentary legislation, delegated legislation and the common law. Used in this sense, the latter phrase 'common law' connotes all judge-made law and therefore includes equity.

If you are covering this theme, you should be very familiar with the origins and modern role of both common law and equity. You should also understand the details of the process of enacting legislation from the stage before the publication of Green Papers to the final stage, the Royal Assent. However, the English legal system cannot be treated as static; it is continuously responding to changes that take place in society as a whole. To deny the relevance of European law in an English legal system course would not only be restrictive, it would be wrong to the extent that it ignored an increasingly important factor in the formation and determination of UK law.

You should also have a good knowledge of the different bodies associated with reform: permanent institutions, that is, the Law Reform Committee, the Criminal Law Revision Committee and the Law Commission, and *ad hoc* bodies, such as Royal Commissions. You should also understand how the system resolves the interplay of several competing interest groups in order to produce legislation. This is a subject area where it is especially useful to have a sound knowledge of recent examples.

Checklist ✔

You should be familiar with:

- the origin and modern operation of the common law;
- the origin and modern operation of equity;
- the stages of promulgation of legislation;

- Parliamentary sovereignty and types of legislation;

- the types of delegated legislation and its advantages and disadvantages;

- the major institutions of the European Union (EU) particularly the European Court of Justice of the European Union (CJEU);

- the institutions of law reform, the Law Commission, *ad hoc* bodies, etc.

QUESTION 1

What are the main sources of law today?

How to Answer this Question

This is, apparently, a very straightforward question, but the temptation is to ignore the European Union (EU) as a source of law and to overemphasise custom as a source. The following structure does not make these mistakes:

Answer Structure

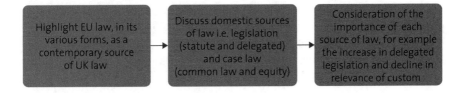

ANSWER

EUROPEAN LAW

Since the UK joined the European Economic Community (EEC) (now, following the Lisbon Treaty, the European Union EU), it has progressively but effectively passed the power to create laws which are operative in this country to the wider European institutions. The UK is now subject to Community law, not just as a direct consequence of the various treaties of accession passed by the UK Parliament, but increasingly, it is subject to the secondary legislation generated by the various institutions of the EU.

European law takes three distinct forms: regulations, directives and decisions. Regulations are immediately effective without the need for the UK Parliament to produce its own legislation. Directives, on the other hand, require specific legislation to implement their proposals, but the UK Parliament is under an obligation to enact such legislation as will give effect to their implementation. Decisions of the CJEU are binding throughout the EU and take precedence over any domestic law.[1]

PARLIAMENTARY LEGISLATION

Under UK constitutional law, it is recognised that Parliament has the power to enact, revoke or alter such and any law it sees fit to deal with and no one Parliament can bind its successors. The extent of this sovereignty may be brought into question with respect to the EU for such time as the UK remains a member, but within the UK, Parliament's power is absolute. This absolute power is a consequence of the historical struggle between Parliament and the Stuart monarchy in the seventeenth century. Parliament arrogated to itself absolute law-making power, a power not challenged by the courts, which were in turn granted an independent sphere of operation. It should be remembered, however, that the **Human Rights Act (HRA) 1998** has, for the first time, given the courts the power to question, although not strike down, primary legislation as being incompatible with the rights protected under the **European Convention on Human Rights (ECHR)**. It also allows the courts to declare secondary legislation to be invalid for the same reason.[2]

Parliament makes law in the form of legislation, that is, Acts of Parliament. There are various types of legislation. Whereas public Acts affect the public generally, private Acts only affect a limited sector of the populace, either particular people or people within a particular locality. Within the category of public Acts, a further distinction can be made between Government Bills and Private Member's Bills. The former are usually introduced by the Government, whilst the latter are the product of individual initiative on the part of particular MPs.

Before enactment, the future Act is referred to as a Bill and many Bills are the product of independent commissions, such as the Law Commission, or committees, such as the Law Reform Committee and the Criminal Law Revision Committee. Without going into the details of the procedure, Bills have to be considered by both Houses of Parliament and have to receive Royal Assent before they are actually enacted.

Delegated legislation has to be considered as a source of law, in addition, but subordinate, to general Acts of Parliament. Generally speaking, delegated legislation is

---

1   Highlighting EU law as a source of UK demonstrates an awareness of contemporary sources. It also demonstrates an understanding of how EU law is incorporated into UK law (either automatically, called 'direct application', or through enactment by one of the UK's legislative authorities). Discussion of the impact of EU law is also relevant, in particular the knowledge that where EU and domestic sources of law conflict, EU law will take precedence (known as supremacy).
2   This demonstrates an understanding not only of the power of the UK parliament as a legislator, and the relevance of statute as the main source of UK law, but also of contemporary pressures on the constitutional principle of parliamentary sovereignty.

law made by some person or body to whom Parliament has delegated its general law-making power. In statistical terms, it is arguable that at present, delegated legislation is actually more significant than primary Acts of Parliament. The output of delegated legislation in any year greatly exceeds the output of Acts of Parliament and, each year, there are over 3,000 sets of rules and regulations made in the form of delegated legislation, compared to fewer than 100 public Acts of Parliament. Delegated legislation can take the form of Orders in Council, which permit the Government to make law through the Privy Council. This power is usually considered in relation to impending emergencies, but perhaps its widest effect is to be found in relation to EU law, for under **s 2(2)** of the **European Communities Act 1972**, ministers can give effect to provisions of the Community which do not have direct effect. Most delegated legislation, however, takes the form of statutory instruments, through which government ministers exercise the powers given to them by general enabling legislation to make the particular rules which are to apply to any given situation within its ambit. A third type of delegated legislation is the bylaw, through which local authorities and public bodies are able to make legally binding rules within their area of competence or authority.

Delegated legislation has developed for a number of reasons. One such reason is the increased pressure on Parliamentary time, with the consequent hiving off of detailed and time-consuming work to ministers and their specialist departments. Another reason for the growth in the output of delegated legislation is the highly technical nature of the subject matter to which it tends to be addressed and the concomitant need for such rules themselves to be highly technical. Any piece of delegated legislation is only valid if it is within the ambit of the powers actually delegated by Parliament. Any law made outside that restricted ambit of authority is void, as being *ultra vires*, and is open to challenge in the courts under the process of judicial review.[3]

COMMON LAW

The next source of law that has to be considered is case law, the effective creation and refinement of law in the course of judicial decisions. It should be remembered that the UK's law is still a common law system and, even if legislation in its various guises is of ever increasing importance, the significance and effectiveness of judicial creativity should not be discounted. Judicial decisions are a source of law, through the operation of the doctrine of judicial precedent. This process depends on the established hierarchy of the courts and operates in such a way that generally, a court is bound by the *ratio decidendi*, or rule of law implicit in the decision of a court above it in the hierarchy and

3   The discussion on delegated legislation demonstrates not only knowledge of its increasing use and importance but also an understanding of how it is enacted and its limits, as compared to statute.

usually by a court of equal standing in that hierarchy. Where statute law does not cover a particular area, or where the law is silent, it will be generally necessary for a court deciding cases relating to such an area to determine what the law is and, in so doing, that court will inescapably and unarguably be creating law. The scope for judicial creativity should not be underestimated and it should be remembered that the task of interpreting the actual meaning of legislation in particular cases also falls to the judiciary and provides it with a further important area of discretionary creativity. As the highest court in the land, the Supreme Court has particular scope for creating or extending the common law, and a relatively contemporary example of its adopting such an active stance can be seen in the way in which it overruled the long-standing presumption that a man could not be guilty of the crime of rape against his wife (see *R* (1991)). It should, of course, always be remembered that Parliament remains sovereign as regards the creation of law and any aspect of the judicially created common law is subject to direct alteration by statute.[4]

An extension of the doctrine of judicial precedent leads to a consideration of a further possible source of law, for when the court is unable to locate a precise or analogous precedent, it may refer to legal textbooks for guidance and assistance. Such books are sub-divided, depending on when they were written. In strict terms, only certain venerable works of antiquity are actually treated as authoritative sources of law. Amongst the most important of these works are those by Glanvill from the twelfth century, Bracton from the thirteenth century, Coke from the seventeenth century and Blackstone from the eighteenth century. Legal works produced after *Blackstone's Commentaries of 1765* are considered to be of recent origin, but although they cannot be treated as authoritative sources, the courts on occasion will look at the most eminent works by accepted experts in particular fields in order to help determine what the law is or should be.

CUSTOM

The final source of law that remains to be considered is custom. The romantic view of the common law is that it represented a crystallisation of common customs, distilled by the judiciary in the course of its travels around the land. Although some of the common law may have had its basis in general custom, a large proportion of these so-called customs were invented by the judges themselves and represented what they wanted the law to be, rather than what people generally thought it was.

There is, however, a second possible customary source of law and that is rules derived from specific local customs. Here, there is the possibility that the local custom might differ from the common law and thus limit its operation. Even in this respect, however,

....

4   Discussion here centres on how common law is created (i.e. it is law emanating from the courts) and its impact and importance (i.e. through the doctrine of judicial precedent). Legal authority is also provided, in support, in the form of a case example.

reliance on customary law as opposed to common law, although not impossible, is made unlikely by the stringent test that any appeal to it has to satisfy. Amongst these requirements are that the custom must have existed from 'time immemorial' (that is, since 1189) and must have been exercised continuously within that period and without opposition. The custom must also have been felt as obligatory, have been consistent with other customs and, in the final analysis, must be reasonable. Given this list of requirements, it can be seen why local custom does not loom large as an important source of law.[5]

Common Pitfalls

The temptation is to concentrate on only one source such as legislation or the common law, and to go into far more detail than is necessary for such a general question. Remember that each subtopic in this answer can be asked as a question topic in its own right. So remember to cover most, if not all, of the potential sources.

Aim Higher

It is essential to be aware of the EU as a source of modern law and reference to the **Lisbon Treaty** will show an up to date awareness of that particular source. In relation to legislation, reference could be made to examples of legislation introduced by the new coalition Government.

QUESTION 2

Explain the emergence of the common law as a distinct historical category of legal regulation.

How to Answer this Question

A suggested plan for answering this question is as follows:

- ❖ introduction – the range of contributory factors;
- ❖ 'tradition expressed in action' (Simpson, *Legal Theory and Legal History*, 1987);
- ❖ the role of Henry II's clerics – itinerant royal justice;
- ❖ royal justice in competition with other sorts of justice;
- ❖ Pollock and Maitland's six principles (in *History of English Law*, 1911);
- ❖ conclusion – evaluating the role of an individual in legal history.

---

5   The discussion of custom as a source of law demonstrates an awareness that, although EU law, legislation and common law are the main sources of UK law, there are other sources. It also demonstrates an understanding that the importance of a source of law can change with time.

Answer Structure

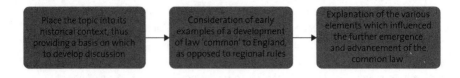

Place the topic into its historical context, thus providing a basis on which to develop discussion → Consideration of early examples of a development of law 'common' to England, as opposed to regional rules → Explanation of the various elements which influenced the further emergence and advancement of the common law

ANSWER

Before the Norman conquest in 1066, the English legal system involved a mass of oral customary rules, which varied according to region.[6] Most writers agree with Pollock and Maitland's view that the common law had been largely established by the accession to the throne of Edward I in 1272. Certainly, the three courts of King's Bench, Common Pleas and Exchequer were operational by this time. It is true that Henry II, who reigned 1154–89, did much of significance to enhance the development of the common law, for instance, by popularising the King's court with the introduction of the Petty Assizes. However, we are not really familiar with how the *Curia Regis* acted during the Norman period before Henry II, because the earliest plea rolls date from his reign, so it would perhaps be over-presumptuous to credit too much to Henry II. In any event, the development of the common law was contributed to by many factors of a general historical nature and it might be more meaningful to speak of the various parties which helped nurture the common law from its first green shoots to its full bloom rather than to try and find a 'father'.

Unlike continental civil law, the English system does not originate from any particular set of texts or digests but from what Simpson has called 'tradition expressed in action'. It began as customary law used in the King's court to settle disputes and conflicts which touched the monarch directly. To begin with, these only included the graver crimes which became Pleas of the Crown. After the Norman invasion, there were still many different types of court apart from the royal court: for example, the stannary courts of Devon and Cornwall, but, most importantly, in their potential rivalry with the royal court in terms of power and income, were the feudal and manorial courts. The era running from the Norman invasion to the accession of Edward I in 1272, saw the struggle to administer justice between the royal judges and the tribunals of feudal lords, the shires and the hundreds which had survived from Anglo-Saxon times.

During Henry II's reign (1154–1189), the clerics in his court began specialising in legal business and acting in a judicial capacity. These clerics developed a range of writs and establishing procedures which, perhaps very significantly, afforded them greater

---

6   An introduction 'sets the scene' and demonstrates an understanding of what the common law developed *from*, that is a mass of often disparate regional rules.

importance and provided them with a generous income.[7] These practices developed into the common law of England, the law which was available throughout the realm. Henry II may be regarded as the 'father of the common law' in that he was largely responsible for the regional and itinerant royal justice, through which (by sending his judges up and down the country) the law truly became common. Henry sent officials from the royal household to the counties and the travelling judges formed a nucleus of *iusticiarii totius Angliae* who had no local roots. They were thus much less susceptible to the corruption which had spoilt a similar attempt, earlier in the twelfth century, in which the royal judges had actually been based in the local communities. It was under Henry II that judges were for the first time sent on 'circuits', hearing pleas in the major places they visited and taking over the work of the local courts. In this travelling mode, the royal representatives were *iusticiae errantes* (wandering justices) or *iusticiarii in itinere* (justices in eyre, that is, law French for journey). The judges were periodically sent on a 'general eyre', which included the whole country. Baker has argued, however, that it was the smaller circuit which was to prove 'the essence of the common law system', by bringing royal justice regularly to the counties.

The efforts of the royal judges were significantly assisted by the works of the text writers Glanvill and Bracton. Glanvill's *Tractatus de Legibus Angliae* (published under Henry II) was the first clear statement of the law, administered throughout the procedure of the royal courts. Glanvill was a senior royal judge. The writer's preface (it was probably not actually written by Glanvill, but by Hubert Walter or by Henry II's Chief Justiciary) divides the pleas into criminal and civil and the body of the work is mostly practical.

With only a few principles of general application before them and by virtue of some particular advantages of the evolving system, the royal judges had established the supremacy of their courts over all competing jurisdictions by the time of Edward I's reign. Pollock and Maitland formulated six principles upon which was founded the usurpation of general jurisdiction by the *Curia Regis*.

First, the King's court was a court to go to in default of justice. Under the Norman kings, the litigant who wished to proceed in the ordinary court obtained the King's 'Writ of Right Patent' which contained the threat *quod nisi feceris vicecomes meus faciet* (if you do not do this, my sheriff will). Complaints and petitions for justice were numerous and these cases formed the basis of the growth of the common law throughout the development of the Register of Writs (added to each time a judge accepted a new writ as suitable to be used again in similar cases).

Secondly, the Writ of Right issued by the Royal Chancery became compulsory for all pleas relating to freehold land, according to an apparently lost ordinance of Henry II. This was

----

7   This demonstrates an understanding of not only how but also of why the 'common law' was developed.

so, even where the case was to be tried in the seigniorial court and so gave the King power over manorial courts.

Thirdly was the introduction by Henry II of the Grand Assize as an alternative to trial by battle in the proceedings on the Writ of Right. As these cases were decided by impartial neighbours, it became much more popular than trial by battle and was only available in the royal court.

Fourthly was Henry II's introduction of the Petty Assizes, also only obtainable in the King's court. These assizes were for trying disputes concerning *disseisin* of land. They did not actually infringe the feudal rights of the lord to try actions relating to the title to the freeholds of his tenants. They did, however, become very popular because of their summary nature and were frequently used by dispossessed owners to recover *seisin*, since the opponent rarely took any further action if his claim was weak.

The fifth factor accounting for the usurpation of jurisdiction by the King's court was the expansion of the 'King's Peace' (the monarch's as opposed to a lord's right to deal with any local disorder, crime, etc). Pleas of the Crown increased rapidly at this time and included many claims that would eventually evolve into torts.

Finally, Pollock and Maitland mention the important series of writs which began with the word *praecipe*, where the sheriff was commanded to investigate a matter and give any wrongdoer the right to give satisfaction, or else face the royal judges for their judgment. This was among the Pleas of the Crown and again quickly became quite popular on account of its efficiency.[8]

Kiralfy (in *English Legal History*, 1958) has advanced another factor significant in the acquisition of jurisdiction by the royal courts, namely, the construction given to the **Statute of Gloucester 1278** by the royal judges. This statute provided that no cases involving an amount of less than 40 shillings should be brought in the royal courts, but that they should be tried before local tribunals. The judges interpreted this to mean that no personal actions to recover a sum greater than 40 shillings could be commenced in the local courts, thus reserving all important legislation for themselves. It is relevant here that the judges were anxious to attract litigants because their fees varied with the amount of business done.

Apart from the advantageous nature of the remedy in the recovery of land provided by the Petty Assizes, the growth in popularity of the royal courts is connected with

....

8   These paragraphs provide an insight into how the common law afforded an improved system of justice and also reasons for its emerging popularity.

the progressive move towards strong, centralised government and its accompanying ability to compel attendance at court and enforce execution of its judgments. By contrast, we can look at the diminution in power of the feudal lords, their dilatory procedures and the inadequate powers to make defendants appear in their courts and to enforce judgments. Additionally, only the royal courts could give litigants the novel and desirable method of proof, the *recognitio* or jury, as it came to be called.

In conclusion, although Henry II may be seen as instrumental in making a number of important innovations which promoted the development of the common law, these policies were part of a wide and complex struggle for the power and revenue to be enjoyed by whoever controlled and administered justice. There were many other important figures involved, such as the clerics, the judges and the writers, whose own behaviour and interests it is important to appreciate in developing a proper understanding of the origins of the common law.

Common Pitfalls

Do not adopt the overly-romantic, not to say misguided, approach of those who mistakenly see the progress of the judiciary round the country as a way of seeking out the existing common laws and bringing them together to establish a body of rules to be applied generally. The common law was to be common *to* all in application, but certainly was not common *from* all.

Aim Higher

The emergence of the common law has to be placed in its immediate historical context. The common law emerged as the product of a particular struggle for political power. Prior to the Norman Conquest of England in 1066, there was no unitary, national legal system. The emergence of the common law represents the imposition of such a unitary system under the auspices and control of a centralised power in the form of a sovereign king; in that respect, it represented the assertion and affirmation of that central sovereign power. The role of the legal writers, such as Glanvill and Bracton, should not be ignored in the development of the common law.

QUESTION 3

Account for the emergence and development of equity.

How to Answer this Question

In response to this question, you should:

- ❖ define the concept of equity;
- ❖ outline the origins of the system of equity;
- ❖ examine defects in the common law: expense, delay, corruption, single remedy, etc;
- ❖ note trusts;
- ❖ note the advantages of equity – no formality, enforceable judgments, mobility of court, varied remedies, etc;
- ❖ include some mention of the 1873–75 legislation;
- ❖ comment on the irony of modern equity being slow and rule-bound.

Answer Structure

ANSWER

In his *Nicomachean Ethics*, Aristotle argued that law operates through general rules in the pursuit of justice and is thus imperfect because it will fail to deal fairly with all eventualities. It is impossible for those who draft law to anticipate the infinite variety of circumstances which could arise in the future. Thus, if we are to have justice, we must use not simply a system of rules but also a power to depart from the rules in certain cases. Aristotle referred to *epieikia*, 'equity' as it was later known in its English form, as the absolute justice which corrects law in particular cases. In the light of the many problems encountered by litigants at common law, and the concerns of many Chancery personalities, equity developed to 'soften and mollify the extremity of the law': *per* Lord Ellesmere in *The Earl of Oxford's Case* (1615).[9]

The establishment of the common law courts in the early medieval period did not represent the full extent of the Crown's jurisdiction. The monarch as the 'fountain of justice' retained a residuary power 'to do equal and right justice and discretion in mercy and truth' (Coronation Oath). The King received many petitions for justice from dissatisfied litigants and, by the fourteenth century, there were so many that they were

....

9 This demonstrates an understanding of what equity is and what it was developed to provide, in terms of supporting the common law system.

being dealt with by the King's Council. By the end of the century, most were being sent directly to the Chancellor, the most senior officer of the Council.[10]

The Chancery originated as the royal secretariat (its name comes from the chancel or latticed screen behind which the clerks worked) and the Chancellor was responsible for authenticating writs in ordinary cases. The earliest judicial work in Chancery was concerned with settling disputes within the department. Petitions to the King for legal redress against the Crown also began here. These proceedings were recorded in Latin, but it was the so-called 'English side' of Chancery, which grew to meet the more mundane needs of litigants, that hatched the Court of Chancery.

By the late fourteenth century, the Chancellor was dealing with a high number of petitions which could not properly be heard on the 'Latin side' of Chancery. By 1460, the Court of Chancery was as established as the common law courts. The ordinary ways of obtaining justice were not feasible options for many prospective litigants because they were too poor to afford the expensive process entailed in an action through the Court of Common Pleas. The claimant had to take care that the writ he chose was the appropriate one and that all the particulars were correct, otherwise the case might be lost as a result of the procedural defect.

A greater problem was that the common law only provided the remedy of damages, whereas a claimant might really wish for the defendant to desist from carrying out some activity (for example, a nuisance) or force him to carry out an obligation (for example, to sell a particular area of land). Additionally, the common law did not recognise simple breaches of common law as actionable. Actions for breaches of agreement could only be brought if they could be framed as writs for debt or detinue (wrongful detention of another's goods). The common law courts did not recognise actions for breaches of contract *per se*.

Local corruption also thwarted many claims. There is even evidence, mentioned by Baker (in *An Introduction to English Legal History*, 1971), that some supplicants complained of witchcraft.

The common law had been quite well developed and was, as Simpson has argued, passed down as an essentially oral tradition amongst a very small legal profession (not many more than 50 judges and important lawyers in about 1450). This group, however, had a very conservative conception of law. The response of the common law to the development of trusts, for example, illustrates how its conservatism led to the need for equity. The practice of making trusts (for example, a father giving property to two trusted friends to hold, on trust, for his son until the son reached a certain age) was becoming

----

10 This begins the discussion on the defects of the common law and demonstrates an understanding of the need for equity to 'fill the gaps' created by the defects.

more popular by the end of the fourteenth century, especially amongst those who were going off to battle and were uncertain of whether they would return. The common law courts, though, did not recognise such an arrangement. The property had been given to the trustees and it was theirs, thought the common law, to do with as they pleased. The intended beneficiary, the son, could have no legal remedy if the trustees abused their position. The Chancellor could, and did, act in such circumstances to order the trustees to fulfil the trust reposed in them.

The law was no respecter of persons and afforded no justice to those who came a cropper of a technicality. By contrast, equity acts *in personam*, that is, it is concerned with the conscience of the individual. In one fifteenth-century case, Fortescue CJ rebuked counsel for advancing a legal point: 'We are here to argue conscience not the law!'

There were, principally, two theoretical justifications used by the Chancellors who developed the doctrines of equity. The first was that they were administering not law, but *conscience*. Thus, those who abused their position as trustee or who sought to take an unconscionable advantage of another's mistake in a contract were corrected by equity. In the fifteenth century, the Chancellor's court was called a court of conscience. The use of the term 'equity' in this context, and its Aristotelian meaning, became more popular in the sixteenth century.

There were great advantages in the early forms of Chancery action. Unlike the actions at common law, the petition required no formality and the *subpoena* which was issued was much more effective than the common law *capias*. The former commanded the respondent to appear in Chancery and answer the petition under a fixed pain, often £100. There were none of the sort of problems involved at common law, where litigants were defeated by errors on the face of the writ because no cause of *subpoena* was stated on the petition. The hearings were not hampered by rules of evidence like those which required debts to be proven with deeds, and the Chancellor – who acted without a jury – could take evidence from the parties themselves. Unlike the common law courts, Chancery was not in a fixed place and followed the Chancellor. The court could even convene in his private house. A number of discretionary remedies were developed by Chancery. Specific performance was an order to compel a defendant to perform a specified activity, usually involving the sale of land. The injunction was an order used to prevent defendants from taking some specified action.[11]

By the sixteenth century, the distinct approaches and procedures of law and equity had become clear. Law was concerned with a body of rules applicable to certain facts, whereas the Chancellor was concerned with individual cases which were dealt with

11   This discussion clearly indicates not only knowledge of how equity was applied but also an understanding of its advantages over the defects of the common law.

according to the dictates of 'conscience'. Equity was consolidated during the seventeenth and eighteenth centuries, but difficulties were still experienced by litigants who had to seek legal and equitable remedies in separate courts. This could be problematic (slow and expensive), where a case required consideration from both legal and equitable perspectives. The administration of law and equity was achieved through the **Judicature Acts 1873–75**, after which equity could be obtained in any division of the High Court.[12]

It was a problem for equity that, on the one hand, its justice flowed from its not being a rule-bound system, but one operating on discretion whilst, on the other hand, uncontrolled discretion could itself become oppressive by its unpredictability. Conscience varied from man to man. It was Selden (in *A Brief Discourse Touching the Office of Lord Chancellor of England*, 1617) who remarked that if the measure of equity was the Chancellor's conscience, then one might as well make the standard measure of one foot the Chancellor's foot. Chancellors began to give reasons for their decisions in the seventeenth century and these were reported and gradually formed into a set of rules. Some maxims of equity were published in 1727 by Richard Francis, and have been relied on by courts ever since. They include the propositions 'he who comes to equity must have clean hands'; 'equity is equality'; 'equity does nothing in vain'; and 'equity regards the substance not the form'. However, the improved system of reporting during the eighteenth century helped a system of equity precedents to develop and by then, as Baker puts it, *rigor aequitatis* had set in. It is an irony of legal history that as equity developed, it became less discretionary and was often as rigid as law.

Not long after its emergence, the Court of Chancery, with its cheap, quick and effective procedures, became attractive to the wealthy as well as the poor. Avery (in 'The history of the equitable jurisdiction of the Court of Chancery before 1460' (1969)) has shown that between 1432 and 1450, the total number of petitions to the court increased sixfold and over 90 per cent of the cases were, by this time, disputes about land.

From the seventeenth century, Chancery became notorious for delay and expense, a theme given a wonderfully biting and humorous exposure in Dickens' *Bleak House*. The court was insufficiently staffed with judges and had no effective appeal system. Estimates of cases pending in Chancery at this time went as high as 20,000. Some cases were still pending after 30 years. The court was also plagued with corruption. Gifts of gold or silver to court officials could often expedite proceedings and, by long usage, many of the gifts became 'fees' which could be demanded as of right. Fees could be demanded at each distinct stage of the proceedings, so Masters procured rules of court which extended court cases beyond any reasonable length.

....

12 Reference to the **Judicature Acts** demonstrates knowledge of the reform of the court system which allowed common law and equitable rules to be applied in the same courts, thus linking the 'old' system with the modern application of equity.

What had begun as a system based on speed, cheapness, informality and a concern to assist the poor had collapsed by the nineteenth century into an incredibly protracted, rule-bound, expensive system for the wealthy.

This irony can, however, be overstated. There were several more positive contributions made by equity to the legal system. Its discretionary remedies of the injunction and specific performance, the law of trusts and the equity of redemption should all be cited in this regard.[13]

Common Pitfalls

It is important to note that this question requires a historical approach to the topic and consequently requires an explanation of why equity was developed as a counterbalance to the strictures of the common law. The development of the two distinct systems with separate rules and courts should be considered, together with their eventual coming together under the Judicature Acts 1873–75.

Aim Higher ★

To explain the development of equity requires a consideration of the shortcoming to be found in the operation of the common law, so time should be spent in dealing with those weaknesses; the cost of actions, the formality of the process with the consequent need to fit clams within the writs actions, the lack of remedies other than damages.

The development of the classic equitable form of the trust should be considered together with the remedies available in equity.

The irony of the way in which equity itself developed from a way of avoiding the conservatism/formalism of the common law, into a rule bound system in its own right should be mentioned.

A sound conclusion would emphasise the unification of the systems under the Judicature Acts since when all courts have been courts of law and courts of equity.

---

13 This discussion demonstrates an understanding of how, although the rules have not been merged, the modern-day legal system can apply both common law and equitable principles and the manner in which equity may still exert influence in areas of law such as tort and contract.

QUESTION 4

Explain how legislation is enacted and distinguish between primary and secondary legislation.

How to Answer this Question

This is a wide-ranging question that requires a fairly close knowledge of the workings of Parliament. A suggested structure is as follows:

❖   distinguish statute law from judge-made common law;
❖   consider where the actual proposals for legislation come from – for example, government policy, Green Papers, White Papers;
❖   mention the limited scope for individual MPs to generate legislation;
❖   set out the actual process that legislation has to pass through to be enacted;
❖   make reference to the various types of legislation, emphasising the role of delegated legislation; mention should also be made of the potential impact of the **Human Rights Act (HRA) 1998**.

Answer Structure

ANSWER

Although the courts retain an essential function in the interpretation of statutes, it has to be recognised that legislation is the predominant form of law making in contemporary times and is superior to the common law in that it can overrule decisions of the courts. The process through which an Act is passed by Parliament is itself a long one, but before concentrating on that process, some attention should be focused on the pre-Parliamentary process through which the substantive content of the Act is generated.[14]

SOURCES OF LEGISLATION

There are various sources of legislative proposals.[15]

The majority arise from government departments, in pursuit of their policies in relation to their allocated area of responsibility. Actual policy will, of course, be a consequence of

14 A brief introduction allows legislation to be put into context and contrasted with 'judge-made' law.
15 Discussion of the background to a decision to create a statute demonstrates the variety of influences impacting on new legislation.

the political persuasion and imperatives of the Government of the day and as, by convention, the Government is drawn from the majority party, it can effectively decide what legislation is to be enacted through its control over the day to day procedure of the House of Commons, backed by its majority voting power. The decision as to which Bills are to be placed before Parliament in any session is under the effective control of a cabinet committee known as the Legislation Committee, which draws up the legislative programme announced in the Queen's Speech, delivered at the opening of the Parliamentary session.

In some cases, the Government will set out its tentative plans for legislation in the form of a Green Paper and will invite interested parties to comment on the proposals. After considering any response, the Government may publish a second document, in the form of a White Paper, in which it sets out its firm proposals for legislation.

If the Government is the source of most legislation, the role of the individual MP, acting through the process for the enactment of Private Member's Bills, should not be forgotten. There are, in fact, three ways in which an individual MP can propose legislation. These are through the ballot procedure, by means of which backbench MPs get the right to propose legislation on the 10 or so Fridays specifically set aside to consider such proposals, under Standing Order 39 and under the 10-minute rule procedure. Of these procedures, however, only the first has any great chance of success and, even then, success will depend on securing a high place in the ballot and, in practice, must not incur Government disapproval. If such a proposal is looked upon with favour by the Government, it has an especially good chance of being enacted, since the Government may provide additional time to allow it to complete its passage. Perhaps the most famous Private Member's Bills have related to the provision of abortion. The original **Abortion Act 1967** was introduced by the Liberal MP David Steel, and has been subject to numerous attempts to amend it by further Private Member's Bills.

Alternative sources for proposed legislation are the recommendations of independent commissions and committees, such as the Law Commission, or the Law Reform Committee, which considers alterations in the civil law, and the Criminal Law Reform Committee, which performs similar functions in relation to the criminal law.

It is always open to pressure groups to lobby political parties and individual MPs in an attempt to have their particular interests made concrete in legislation. However, some concern has been expressed at the growing number of professional lobbyists who are paid to make sure that their clients' cases are prominently placed before the appropriate people within the legislature.

THE LEGISLATIVE PROCESS

Before any legislative proposal (known at that stage as a Bill) can become an Act of Parliament, it must proceed through, and be approved by, both Houses of Parliament and must receive the Royal Assent.[16] A Bill must be given three readings in both the House of Commons and the House of Lords before it can be presented for the Royal Assent. It is possible to commence the procedure in either House, although 'money Bills' (containing only financial provisions) must be placed before the Commons in the first instance.

When a Bill is introduced in the Commons, it undergoes five distinct procedures:

(a) it receives its first reading. This is purely a formal procedure in which its title is read and a date set for its second reading;

(b) after this comes the second reading; this is the time when its general principles are subject to extensive debate. The second reading is the critical point in the process of a Bill. At the end, a vote may be taken on its merits and if it is approved, it is likely that it will eventually find a place in the statute book;

(c) if the Bill passes its second reading, it is sent for consideration by a standing committee which will consider its provisions in detail. The function of the standing committee, which, if it is successfully proposed, may be replaced by a Select Committee or committee of the whole House, is to go through the Bill clause by clause and to amend it to bring it into line with the general approval given by the House at its second reading;

(d) the next stage is the report stage, at which the standing committee reports the Bill back to the House for the consideration of any amendments made by it;

(e) the final stage in the process is the third reading, during which further debate may take place, although on this occasion, it is restricted strictly to matters relating to the content; matters relating to general principles cannot be raised.

When a Bill has passed all these stages, it is passed to the House of Lords for its consideration, which is essentially similar, if less constrained by the pressures of time. After consideration by the Lords, the Bill is passed back, with any amendments, to the Commons, which must then consider such amendments. Where one House refuses to agree to the amendments made by the other, Bills can be repeatedly passed between them, but it should be remembered that Bills must complete their passage within the life of a particular parliamentary session and that a failure to reach agreement within that period might lead to the total loss of the Bill. Given the fact that the House of Lords is a non-elected institution and that the Members of the House of Commons are the democratically elected representatives of the voters, it has been apparent since 1911 that the House of Lords should not be in a position to block the clearly expressed wishes of the Commons. The **Parliament Act** of that year and of **1949** restricted the blocking power of the Lords. The situation now is that a money Bill can be enacted without the approval of the House of Lords after only one month's

---

16 The question specifically asks for a descriptive account of the process which must be undertaken in order to create statute. Consequently, the various stages must be clearly set out.

delay and any other Bill can only be delayed by one year by the House of Lords' recalcitrance.[17]

The most recent use of the **Parliament Acts** occurred in relation to the **Hunting Act 2004,** which in turn led to the Court of Appeal's determination of the legality of the later **Parliament Act**, which itself was introduced through the earlier **Act of 1911**. In *R (on the application of Jackson) v Attorney-General* (2005) the Court of Appeal concluded that the **1949 Act** was properly introduced and consequently the **Hunting Act** could not be challenged. However, the Court of Appeal also suggested that the **1949 Act** might not be capable of being used to introduce major constitutional reforms, such as completely doing away with the House of Lords, for example.

Subsequently an augmented nine-member panel of the House of Lords unanimously held that the reasoning of the Court of Appeal could not be sustained. In reaching that conclusion the House of Lords rejected the argument that the **Parliament Act of 1911** was an exercise in the *delegation* of powers from Parliament to the House of Commons, which could not later be used to extend those powers. Rather as Lord Bingham stated:

> The overall object of the **1911 Act** was not to delegate power: it was to restrict, subject to compliance with the specified statutory conditions, the power of the Lords to defeat measures supported by a majority of the Commons . . .

The House of Lords, however, did differ in their assessment of the extent of the power extended to the House of Commons under the **Parliament Acts**. It is clear that a majority of the House of Lords were of the view that the House of Commons could use the powers given to it under the **Parliament Acts** to force through such legislation as it wished, but a number of the judges were of the view that the Commons could not extend its own lifetime through such a procedure, as that would be in direct contradiction to the provisions of the **Parliament Act 1911**.

No statute becomes law unless it has received the Royal Assent and although in the unwritten constitution of the UK, no specific rule expressly states that the monarch has to assent to any Act passed by Parliament, there is, by now, a convention to that effect and any monarch would place their constitutional status in extreme jeopardy by a refusal to grant the Royal Assent to legislation passed by Parliament. The procedural nature of the Royal Assent was highlighted by the **Royal Assent Act 1967**, which reduced the process of acquiring Royal Assent to a formal reading out of the short titles of any Act in both Houses of Parliament.

---

17 The two Houses of Parliament (Commons and Lords) do not enjoy equal power in terms of enacting legislation, which is highlighted here.

An Act of Parliament comes into effect on the date of the Royal Assent, unless there is any provision to the contrary in the Act itself. It is quite common for newly enacted statutes to contain commencement clauses which provide for the Act to become operational at some date in the future. Difficulty and an inevitable lack of certainty is produced, however, by the now common occurrence of passing general enabling Acts which delegate powers to a government minister to introduce specific parts of the Acts in question at some later date, through the means of statutory instruments.[18]

TYPES OF LEGISLATION

There are two distinct types of legislation: the public Act and the private Act. The former relates to questions which affect the general public, whereas the latter relates to the powers and interests of particular individuals or institutions. Public Bills can be further categorised into Government Bills and Private Member's Bills, to which reference has already been made.

Acts of Parliament can also be distinguished on the basis of their function. Some are designed to initiate new legislation to cover new areas of activity, previously not governed by legal rules, but other Acts are aimed at rationalising or amending existing legislative provisions. Examples of the latter type of legislation are the consolidating Act and the codifying Act. The purpose of any consolidating Act is to bring together the various statutory provisions contained in a number of discrete pieces of legislation, without altering them, for the main part. Company law is a classic example of this procedure, in that it has evolved through the enactment of numerous Acts of Parliament which have, every so often, been brought together under one large consolidating Act. The **Companies Act 2006** is just such an Act, it does make many important substantive changes to company law.

Codifying Acts seek not just to bring existing statutory provisions under one Act, but also look to give statutory expression to common law rules. The classic examples of such legislation are to be found in the commercial sector; amongst them are the **Partnership Act 1890** and the **Sale of Goods Act 1893**.

THE HRA 1998

Traditionally, by virtue of the operation of the doctrine of Parliamentary sovereignty, Parliament could pass whatever laws it thought proper, without the courts being able to challenge the legality of such legislation. Although the **HRA 1998** has not directly challenged this relationship, it has nonetheless altered it significantly. Even where a court holds that a piece of primary legislation does not comply with the provisions of the

---

18 This introduction to delegated or secondary legislation allows for further discussion of how primary and secondary legislation can be distinguished.

ECHR, that court cannot declare the legislation invalid: the court has no such power to strike down primary legislation. However, the court can issue a declaration of incompatibility stating that the Act breaches the provisions of the **Convention** (see, for example, *Bellinger v Bellinger* (2003)). Although changing the incompatible Act remains solely the power of Parliament, it is highly likely that a judicial declaration of incompatibility would lead to an alteration of the Act in question. The **HRA 1998** provides for a fast-track procedure for changing any Act subsequently found to be in breach of the **Convention**.[19]

Common Pitfalls

Answers should ensure that the all aspects of the question are covered. This is a function of the essential examination skill of time management. There is so much than could be written in answering this question that the focus has to be on covering the essential materials.

The question specifically refers to the enactment of legislation. It is consequently not an invitation to consider the rules of statutory interpretation (see question 17 below).

Aim Higher

Marks will be gained not just by setting legislation in contrast to the judge-made common law, but also by explaining its superiority and the source of that superiority in the democratic process.

The different powers of the courts, under the **Human Rights Act 1998**, in relation to primary and secondary legislation are important and consideration of that aspect will be credited.

QUESTION 5

What do you understand by 'delegated legislation'? Consider its advantages and disadvantages and explain how it is controlled by Parliament and the courts.

---

19   The enactment of the **HRA** has, in effect, introduced an important new 'stage' in the process of enacting primary legislation, which is highlighted here.

How to Answer this Question

This question focuses more closely than the previous one on delegated legislation. It is suggested that the increased importance of delegated legislation makes it a likely question topic. A good answer plan will do the following:

❖ give an explanation of what is meant by delegated legislation;
❖ emphasise the large amount of delegated legislation that is produced annually;
❖ provide examples of the various types of delegated legislation;
❖ list and consider in some detail the various advantages and disadvantages;
❖ mention Parliamentary scrutiny of delegated legislation;
❖ consider the powers of the courts to control delegated legislation, through judicial review and under the **Human Rights Act (HRA) 1998**;
❖ weigh the advantages and disadvantages and offer a conclusion in favour or against its use.

Answer Structure

ANSWER

Modern legislation tends to be of the enabling type, which simply states the general purpose and aims of the Act and lays down a broad framework, whilst delegating to ministers of the state the power to produce detailed provisions in pursuit of those general aims.

Generally speaking, delegated legislation is law made by some person or body to whom Parliament has delegated its general law-making power. In statistical terms, it is arguable that at present, delegated legislation is actually more significant than primary Acts of Parliament. The output of delegated legislation in any year greatly exceeds the output of Acts of Parliament and each year there are over 3,000 sets of rules and regulations made in the form of delegated legislation, compared to fewer than 100 public Acts of Parliament.

Any piece of delegated legislation has the same legal force and effect as the Act of Parliament under which it is enacted, but equally only has effect to the extent that it is authorised by its enabling Act.

Delegated legislation can take the form of Orders in Council which permit the Government, through the Privy Council, to make law. The Privy Council is nominally a non-party political body of eminent Parliamentarians, but in effect, it is simply a means through which the Government, in the form of a committee of ministers, can introduce legislation without the need to go through the full Parliamentary process. Although legal textbooks tend to use situations of state emergency as exemplifying occasions when the Government will resort to the use of Orders in Council, in actual fact, a great number of Acts are brought into operation through these provisions. Perhaps the widest scope for Orders in Council is to be found in relation to EU law, for under **s 2(2)** of the **European Communities Act 1972,** ministers can give effect to provisions of the Community which do not have direct effect.

Statutory instruments are the means through which government ministers introduce particular regulations under powers delegated to them by Parliament by enabling legislation. As with Orders in Council, such provisions do not have to undergo the full rigour of Parliamentary procedure involved in the passing of Acts of Parliament. The relative and, indeed, the absolute importance of statutory instruments can be seen by the fact that in 2004, Parliament enacted 3,459 statutory instruments, as compared to only 38 general public Acts. There is such a range of powers delegated to ministers and such a range of Acts of Parliament which are given practical effect by statutory instruments, that it is almost pointless to give examples, but it is certainly worth pointing out that such regulations tend to be of a highly specific and technical nature. One example of the way in which statutory instruments were used, if not abused, may be found in the **Limited Liability Partnership Act 2000.** Although the Act established this new form of legal entity, it stated very little about how it was to operate and be regulated. **Sections 14 and 15** of the Act simply stated that appropriate regulations would be made in the future and introduced through statutory instruments (the **Limited Liability Partnership Regulations 2001**).

Bylaws are the third type of delegated legislation, by means of which local authorities and public bodies are empowered by Parliament to make legally binding rules within their area of authority. Bylaws may be made by local authorities under such enabling legislation as the **Local Government Act 1972.**

In addition to the foregoing, the various Court Rule Committees are empowered to make the rules which govern procedure in the particular courts over which they have delegated authority, under such Acts as the **Supreme Court Act 1981,** the **County Courts Act 1984** and the **Magistrates' Courts Act 1980.**

The final source of delegated legislation is to be found in the power given to certain professional bodies to regulate the conduct of their members. An example of this type of delegated legislation is the power that the Law Society has been granted under the **Solicitors Act 1974** to control the conduct of practicing solicitors.

Parliament delegates its law-making powers for a number of reasons. Amongst these is the fact that it simply does not have the time to consider every detail that might be required to fill out the framework of enabling legislation. A related point is the fact that given the highly specialised and extremely technical nature of many of the regulations that are introduced through delegated legislation, the majority of MPs simply do not have sufficient expertise or the technical knowledge to consider such provisions effectively.

These reasons why there has been an increased reliance on delegated legislation also suggest its potential advantages over the more traditional set-piece public Acts. For example, the fact that Parliament does not have to spend its time considering the minutiae of specific regulations permits it to focus its attention more closely, and at greater length, on the broader but no less important matters of principle in relation to the enactment of general enabling legislation. The use of delegated legislation also permits far greater flexibility in regulation, permitting rules to be changed quickly in response to changes in the situations they are aimed at regulating. It can also be appreciated that the use of delegated legislation not only permits an *ad hoc* response, but also a quicker response to emergencies or unforeseen problems. With regard to bylaws, it practically goes without saying that local and specialist knowledge should give rise to more appropriate rules than reliance on the general enactments of Parliament.

There are, however, distinct disadvantages in the prevalence of delegated legislation as a means of making legal rules. The most important of these relates to a perceived erosion in the constitutional role of Parliament, to the extent that it does not actually consider provisions made in this way. To the extent that Parliament, as a body, is disempowered, other people, notably government ministers and the civil servants who work under them in order to produce the detailed provisions of delegated legislation, are given more power than might be thought constitutionally correct. The foregoing, which inevitably involves the question of general accountability and the need for effective scrutiny, is compounded by the difficulty which ordinary MPs face in keeping abreast of the sheer mass of technically detailed legislation that is enacted in this form. Also, the point must be raised that if Parliamentarians cannot keep up with the flow of delegated legislation, how can the general public be expected to do so?

These difficulties and potential shortcomings in the use of delegated legislation are, at least to a degree, mitigated by the fact that specific controls exist in relation to it. These controls are twofold: Parliamentary and judicial. Parliament exercises general control, to the extent that ministers are always responsible to Parliament for the regulations they actually make within the powers delegated to them by Parliament. Additionally, it is a usual requirement that such regulations be laid before Parliament. This laying before Parliament can take two forms, depending on the provision of the enabling legislation. The majority of Acts simply require that regulations made under their auspices be placed before Parliament and automatically become law after a period of 40 days, *unless a resolution to annul them is passed.* Other regulations, on the other hand, require a positive resolution of one or both of the Houses of Parliament before they become law. Also, since 1973, there has been a Joint Select Committee on Statutory Instruments, whose function is to consider statutory instruments. It has to be remembered, however, that this committee merely scrutinises statutory instruments from a technical point of view as regards drafting, and therefore has no power as regards any question of policy in the regulation.

Previously, judicial control of delegated legislation was limited, but not unimportant. It was always possible for delegated legislation to be challenged, through the procedure of judicial review, on the basis that the person or body to whom Parliament has delegated its authority has acted in a way that exceeds the limited powers delegated to them. Any provision found to be outside this authority was *ultra vires* and consequently void. Additionally, there is a presumption that any power delegated by Parliament is to be used in a reasonable manner and the courts may, on occasion, hold particular delegated legislation to be void on the basis that it is unreasonable. The **HRA 1998** fundamentally alters the courts' power over delegated legislation. As secondary legislation, rather than primary legislation such as Acts of Parliament, delegated legislation may be declared ineffective by the courts where it is found not to comply with the provisions of the **HRA 1998**, so ministers must be extremely careful to ensure that any delegated legislation is in fact compatible with the **ECHR**. An example of the courts quashing secondary legislation can be seen in *A v Secretary of State for the Home Department* (2005), in which the House of Lords quashed a derogation order wrongly made in relation to the **Anti-Terrorism Crime and Security Act 2001**. For a later example, see *HM Treasury v Mohammed Jaber Ahmed* (2010) (UKSC 2), the first substantive case heard by the Supreme Court. The court quashed fully the **Terrorism (United Nations Measures) Order 2006** and quashed parts of the **Al-Qaida and Taliban (UN Measures) Order 2006** as being *ultra vires* the powers of the Treasury extended to them under the **United Nations Act 1946**.

QUESTION 6

The English legal system can no longer be considered on its own, but has to be understood within the context of the European Union and its institutions.

What are the institutions referred to and what is their impact on the English legal system?

How to Answer this Question

Again, it has to be emphasised that the English legal system can only be understood in the context of the EU. This straightforward question ensures that a candidate is at least aware of that context. Such an awareness can be shown by covering the following points:

❖ a short history of the EU – consideration of its present status after the **Lisbon Treaty**, perhaps, its future;

❖ a detailed account of the various types of EU legislation, that is, treaties, regulations and directives, and how they are each brought into effect;

❖ a description of the essential institutions of the EU and their relationships and particular roles and functions;

❖ a focus on the relationship between the CJEU and the domestic courts of the UK, with examples where possible.

Answer Structure

ANSWER

The European Community was set up by the **EEC Treaty** (known as the Treaty of Rome and later re-named the **EC Treaty**) in 1957, and the UK joined the Community in 1973.

On joining the Community, now called the European Union, the UK and its citizens became subject to EU law. This subjection to European law remains the case, even where the parties to any transaction are themselves both UK subjects. In other words, in areas where it is applicable, European law supersedes any existing UK law to the contrary.

Community law consists primarily of the **EC Treaty** and any amending legislation such as the **Single European Act (SEA)** to which the UK acceded in 1986, the **Maastricht Treaty 1992** and the **Treaty of Nice 2001**. However the most recent reform was introduced by the **Lisbon Treaty**, signed by all the members in 2007 and subsequently ratified by them individually by the autumn of 2009. The necessary alterations to the fundamental treaties governing the EU, brought about by the **Lisbon Treaty**, was published at the end of March 2010. As a result there are three newly consolidated treaties:

❖ The **Treaty on European Union (TEU)**
Article 1 of this treaty makes it clear that 'The Union shall be founded on the present Treaty and on the Treaty on the Functioning of the European Union (hereinafter referred to as 'the Treaties'). Those two Treaties shall have the same legal value. *The Union shall replace and succeed the European Community.'*

❖ The **Treaty on the Functioning of the European Union (TFEU)**
Article 2 of this treaty provides that:

'When the Treaties confer on the Union exclusive competence in a specific area, only the Union may legislate and adopt legally binding acts, the Member States being able to do so themselves only if so empowered by the Union or for the implementation of Union acts.'

Article 3 specifies that the Union shall have exclusive competence in the following areas:

(a)   customs union;
(b)   the establishing of the competition rules necessary for the functioning of the internal market;
(c)   monetary policy for the Member States whose currency is the euro;
(d)   the conservation of marine biological resources under the common fisheries policy;
(e)   common commercial policy.

Additionally **Article 3** provides that the Union shall also have exclusive competence for the conclusion of an international agreement when its conclusion is provided for in a legislative act of the Union or is necessary to enable the Union to exercise its internal competence, or in so far as its conclusion may affect common rules or alter their scope.

❖   *The* **Charter of Fundamental Rights of the European Union (CFREU)**
Many member states, including the UK, have negotiated opt outs of some of the provisions of the charter.

The **EC Treaty**, as subsequently amended by the **Treaty on the Functioning of the European Union**, provides for two types of legislation: regulations and directives:

(a)   Regulations under **TFEU Art 288** (formerly **Art 249** of the **EC Treaty**) apply to, and within, member states generally without the need for those states to pass their own legislation. They are binding and enforceable, therefore, from the time of their creation within the European context and need no further validation by national Parliaments.
(b)   Directives, on the other hand, are in theory supposed to state general goals and leave the precise implementation to individual member states in the form that they consider appropriate. In practice, however, directives tend to state the means, as well as the ends, to which they are aimed and the ECJ will give direct effect to directives which are sufficiently clear and complete.

The major institutions of the EU are: the Council; the European Parliament; the Economic and Social Committee; the Commission; and the ECJ.

THE COUNCIL

The **Lisbon Treaty** established two new offices:

❖   President of the European Union, a position currently held by Herman Van Rompuy of Belgium; and

❖   High Representative for Foreign Affairs, effectively that of EU foreign minister, a position held by Baroness Ashton from the UK.

However, it should be recognised that, although significant, neither of these new posts carries any real executive power as against that of the Union's main sources of political power, pre-eminently the Council of Ministers.

The Council is made up of ministerial representatives of each of the 27 member states of the Union. Thus, when considering economic matters, the various states will be represented by their finance ministers or, if the matter relates to agriculture, the various agricultural ministers will attend. The Council of Ministers is, in essence, the supreme organ of the EU and, as such, it has the final say in deciding upon Community matters, although the **Treaty of Lisbon** has given the parliament powers of co-determination in some areas. Although it acts on recommendations and proposals made to it by the Commission, it does have the power to instruct the Commission to undertake particular investigations and to submit detailed proposals for its consideration.

THE EUROPEAN PARLIAMENT

The European Parliament is the directly elected European institution and, to that extent, it can be seen as the body which exercises democratic control over the operation of the EU. As in national Parliaments, Members are elected to represent constituencies, the elections being held every five years. Membership is divided amongst the 27 member states in proportion to the size of their various populations. The Parliament's general secretariat is based in Luxembourg and although the Parliament sits in plenary session in Strasbourg for one week in each month, its detailed and preparatory work is carried out through 18 permanent committees which usually meet in Brussels.

The powers of the European Parliament, however, should not be confused with those of national Parliaments, for the European Parliament is not a legislative institution and, in that respect, it plays a subsidiary role to the Council of Ministers. Originally, its powers were merely advisory and supervisory.

In pursuance of its advisory function, the Parliament always had the right to comment on the proposals of the Commission and, since 1980, the Council has been required to wait for the Parliament's opinion before adopting any law. In its supervisory role, the Parliament scrutinises the activities of the Commission and has the power to remove the Commission by passing a motion of censure against it by a two-thirds majority.

The legislative powers of the Parliament were substantially enhanced by the **SEA 1986**. Since that enactment, it has had a more influential role to play, particularly in relation to the completion of the internal market. For one thing, it can now negotiate directly with the Council as to any alterations or amendments it wishes to see in proposed legislation. It can also intervene to question and, indeed, to alter any 'joint position' adopted by the

Council on proposals put to it by the Commission. If the Council then insists on pursuing its original 'joint position', it can only do so on the basis of unanimity.

The **SEA 1986** also required the European Parliament's assent to any international agreements to be entered into by the Community. As a consequence, it has ultimate control, not just in relation to trade treaties, but also as regards any future expansion of the Union's membership. The **Lisbon Treaty** has subsequently further increased the powers of the parliament, effectively giving it equal power of co-decision with the Council for most legislation, including the budget and agriculture.

THE COMMISSION

The Commission is the executive of the EU, but it also has a vital part to play in the legislative process. To the extent that the Council can only act on proposals put before it by the Commission, the latter institution has a duty to propose to the Council measures that will advance the achievement of the Union's general policies.

Another of the key functions of the Commission is the implementation of the policies of the Union and to that end, it controls the allocation of funds to the various common programmes within the Union. It also acts, under instructions from the Council, as negotiator between the Union and external countries.

A further executive role of the Commission is to be found in the manner in which it operates to ensure that Treaty obligations between states are met and that Community laws relating to individuals are enforced. In order to fulfil these functions, the Commission has been provided with extensive powers, both in relation to the investigation of potential breaches of Community law and the subsequent punishment of offenders. The classic area in which these powers can be seen in operation is competition law. Under **Arts 105** and **106** of the **TFEU** (formerly **Arts 85** and **86** of the **EC Treaty**), the Commission has substantial powers to investigate and control potential monopolies and anti-competitive behaviour and it has used these powers to levy what, in the case of private individuals, would amount to huge fines where breaches of Community competition law have been discovered. For example, in 2004 Microsoft were fined €497m and in 2009 Intel were fined €1.06bn. If the individual against whom a finding has been made objects to either the result of the investigation or the penalty imposed, the course of appeal is to the ECJ.

THE COURT OF JUSTICE

The ECJ is the judicial arm of the EU and, in the field of Community law, its judgments overrule those of national courts. It consists of 27 judges, assisted by eight advocates general, and the Court sits in Luxembourg. The role of the advocates general is to investigate the matter submitted to the Court and to produce a report, together with a recommendation for the consideration of the Court. The actual court is free to accept the report, or not, as it sees fit.

The jurisdiction of the ECJ involves it in two key areas in particular:

(a) determining whether any measures adopted, or rights denied, by the Commission, Council or any national government are compatible with Treaty obligations. Such actions may be raised by any Union institution, government or individual. A member state may fail to comply with its Treaty obligations in a number of ways. It might fail or indeed refuse to comply with a provision of the Treaty or a regulation; alternatively, it might refuse to implement a directive within the allotted time provided. Under such circumstances, the state in question will be brought before the ECJ, either by the Commission or another member state or, indeed, individuals within the state, as being in dereliction of its responsibility;

(b) determining, at the request of national courts, the interpretation of points of Community law. This procedure can take the form of a preliminary ruling where the request precedes the actual determination of a case by the national court. The point that has to be remembered, however, is that it is the ECJ's role to determine such issues and in relation to those issues, it is superior to any national court.

THE GENERAL COURT (FORMERLY THE COURT OF FIRST INSTANCE)

The Court of First Instance, separate from the existing Court of Justice, was introduced **SEA 1986**. Under the **Treaty of Lisbon** it was renamed the General Court. It has jurisdiction in first instance cases, with appeals going to the CJEU on points of law.

CIVIL SERVICE TRIBUNAL

The former jurisdiction of the Court of First Instance, in relation to internal claims by EU employees was transferred to this distinct institution in 2004.

The above three distinct courts together constitute the *Court of Justice of the European Union*.

> **Common Pitfalls** ✗
>
> It is an almost unforgivable error to confuse the European Union and the European Council and their respective courts the European Court of Justice and the European Court of Human Rights. They are distinct and must always be dealt with as such.

QUESTION 7

Explain the structure and powers of the Court of Justice of the European Union (CJEU), paying particular regard to its relationship with UK courts.

How to Answer this Question

Particular attention should be paid to the relationship of the CJEU to the domestic courts within the UK. In answering it, students could usefully apply the following structure:

❖ reference must be made to the three distinct legal forums that constitute the CJEU as well as the a court that goes by that name;

❖ describe the overall structure and the interrelationship between the several individual courts within that structure;

❖ detail the role and powers of the CJEU;

❖ explain the way in which references can be made to the CJEU from domestic courts under **Art 267** (formerly **Art 234**);

❖ provide some examples of cases decided by the CJEU that have had particular impact on the UK.

Answer Structure

Introduce the CJEU and outline its structure → Outline the jurisdiction and powers of the CJEU → Discuss the links which exist between the CJEU and the Member States, in particular **Art 267 TFEU** → Highlight the relationship between the CJEU and the UK courts using decided cases in support

ANSWER

Prior to the **Lisbon Treaty**, it was accurate to refer to European Community law, but this reference has now been replaced by European Union law. The Court of Justice of the European Union (CJEU) is the judicial arm of the EU and, in the field of European Union law, its judgments overrule those of national courts. Prior to the Lisbon treaty this court was known as the European Court of Justice (ECJ)

The current CJEU consists of 27 judges, assisted by eight advocates general, and sits in Luxembourg. The role of the advocates general is to investigate the matter submitted to the Court and to produce a report, together with a recommendation for the consideration of the Court. The actual Court is free to accept the report or not, as it sees fit.

A Court of First Instance, separate from the CJEU was introduced by the **Single European Act 1986**. Under the **Treaty of Lisbon** it was renamed the General Court. It has jurisdiction in first instance cases, with appeals going to the CJEU on points of law.

The former jurisdiction of the Court of First Instance, in relation to internal claims by EU employees was transferred to to a newly created European Union Civil Service Tribunal in 2004. Together the three distinct courts together constitute *the Court of Justice of the European Union*. The aim of introducing the two latter courts was to reduce the burden of work on the CJEU, but there is a right of appeal, on points of law only, to the full CJEU.[20]

The CJEU performs two key functions:[21]

(a) It decides whether any measures adopted, or rights denied, by the Commission, Council or any national government are compatible with Treaty obligations. Such actions may be raised by any EU institution, government or individual. A member state may fail to comply with its Treaty obligations in a number of ways. It might fail or, indeed, refuse to comply with a provision of the Treaty or a regulation; alternatively, it might refuse to implement a directive within the allotted time provided for. Under such circumstances, the state in question will be brought before the CJEU, either by the Commission or another member state or, indeed, individuals within the state concerned.

(b) It provides authoritative rulings, at the request of national courts under **Art 267**[22] of the **Treaty on the Functioning of the European Union (TFEU)** (formerly **Art 234** of the **EC Treaty**), on the interpretation of points of Union law. When an application is made under **Art 234**, the national proceedings are suspended until such time as the determination of the point in question is delivered by the CJEU. Whilst the case is being decided by the CJEU, the national court is expected to provide appropriate interim relief, even if this involves going against a domestic legal provision, as in *Factortame Ltd v Secretary of State for Transport (No 1)* (1989). The Common Fishing Policy established by the EEC had placed limits on the amount of fish that any member country's fishing fleet was permitted to catch. In order to gain access to British fish stocks and quotas, Spanish fishing boat owners formed British companies and reregistered their boats as British. In order to prevent what it saw as an abuse and an encroachment on the rights of indigenous fishermen, the British Government

---

20 This introduction provides a helpful overview of the CJEU, in particular its structure and composition.

21 In order to answer the question set, the jurisdiction and powers of the CJEU need to be carefully considered.

22 **Art 267 TFEU** provides the only direct link between the CJEU and courts within the member states. As the question specifically asks for consideration of the relationship between the European Court and the UK courts, no answer would be considered complete without such discussion.

introduced the **Merchant Shipping Act 1988**, which provided that any fishing company seeking to register as British would have to have its principal place of business in the UK and at least 75 per cent of its shareholders would have to be British nationals. This effectively debarred the Spanish boats from taking up any of the British fishing quota. Some 95 Spanish boat owners applied to the British courts for judicial review of the **Merchant Shipping Act 1988**, on the basis that it was contrary to Community law. The case went from the High Court, through the Court of Appeal, to the House of Lords which referred the case to the CJEU. There, it was decided that the **EC Treaty** required domestic courts to give effect to the directly enforceable provisions of Community law and, in doing so, such courts are required to ignore any national law that runs counter to Community law.

This procedure can take the form of a preliminary ruling where the request precedes the actual determination of a case by the national court. **Article 267** (formerly **Art 234**) provides that:

> The Court of Justice shall have jurisdiction to give preliminary rulings concerning:
>
> (a)   the interpretation of treaties;
> (b)   the validity and interpretation of acts of the institutions of the Union and of the European Central Bank;
> (c)   the interpretation of the statutes of bodies established by an act of the Council, where those statutes so provide.
>
> Where such a question is raised before any court or tribunal of a member state, that court or tribunal may, if it considers that a decision on the question is necessary to enable it to give judgment, request the Court of Justice to give a ruling thereon.
>
> Where any such question is raised in a case pending before a court or tribunal of a member state against whose decision there is no judicial remedy under national law, that court or tribunal shall bring the matter before the Court of Justice.

It is clear that it is for the national court, and not the individual parties concerned, to make the reference. Where the national court or tribunal is not the 'final' court or tribunal, the reference to the CJEU is discretionary. Where the national court or tribunal is the 'final' court, then reference is obligatory. However, there are circumstances under which a 'final' court need not make a reference under **Art 267** (formerly **Art 234**). These are:

(a)   where the question of Community law is not truly relevant to the decision to be made by the national court;
(b)   where there has been a previous interpretation of the provision in question by the CJEU, so that its meaning has been clearly determined;

(c)   where the interpretation of the provision is so obvious as to leave no scope for any reasonable doubt as to its meaning. This latter instance has to be used with caution given the nature of Union law; for example, the fact that it is expressed in several languages using legal terms which might have different connotations within different jurisdictions. However, it is apparent that where the meaning is clear, no reference need be made. In undertaking such a task, a purposive and contextual approach is mainly adopted, as against the more restrictive methods of interpretation favoured in relation to UK domestic legislation. The clearest statement of this purposive/contextualist approach adopted by the CJEU is contained in its judgment in the *CILFIT* case:

Every provision of Community law must be placed in its context and interpreted in the light of the provisions of Community law as a whole, regard being had to the objectives thereof and to its state of evolution at the date on which the provision in question is to be applied.

CILFIT Srl v Minister of Health (No 283/81) (1982)

Another major difference between the CJEU and courts within the English legal system is that the former is not bound by the doctrine of precedent[23] in the same way as the latter are. It is always open to the CJEU to depart from its previous decisions where it considers it appropriate to do so. Although it will endeavour to maintain consistency, it has on occasion ignored its own previous decisions, as in *European Parliament v Council* (1990), where it recognised the right of the Parliament to institute an action against the Council.

The manner in which European law operates to control sex discrimination, through the **Equal Treatment Directive**, is of significant interest and in *Marshall v Southampton and West Hampshire AHA* (1993)[24] a number of the points that have been considered above were highlighted. Ms Marshall had originally been required to retire earlier than a man in her situation would have been required to do. She successfully argued before the CJEU that such a practice was discriminatory and contrary to **Council Directive 76/207/EEC** on the equal treatment of men and women.

The present action related to the level of compensation she was entitled to as a consequence of this breach. UK legislation, the **Sex Discrimination Act 1975**, had set limits on the level of compensation that could be recovered for acts of sex discrimination. Marshall argued that the imposition of such limits was contrary to the **Equal Treatment Directive** and that in establishing such limits, the UK had failed to comply with the **Directive**.

....

23   The matter of precedent is significant as, although the CJEU is not bound by its own decisions, its decisions are binding on national courts, including those of the UK.

24   This case is an excellent example of not only the impact of EU law but also of the manner in which co-operation between the CJEU and the national courts ensures that rights emanating from EU law are made available to individuals within the UK and other member states.

The House of Lords (now the Supreme Court) referred the case to the CJEU under **Art 264** (formerly **Art 234**) and the latter determined that the rights set out in relation to compensation under **Art 6** of the **Directive** were directly effective, and that as the purpose of the **Directive** was to give effect to the principle of equal treatment, that could only be achieved by either reinstatement or the awarding of adequate compensation. The decision of the CJEU, therefore, overruled the financial limitations placed on sex discrimination awards and effectively overruled the domestic legislation.

Common Pitfalls

❖   Do not confuse the CJEU with the ECtHR.
❖   Ensure that reference is to the current titles of the courts.
❖   Ensure that references are to the current treaties.

Aim Higher

❖   It is a requirement of the question, but the functions of the three different judicial forums will be welcomed by examiners.
❖   Many textbooks will not, even yet, have been updated in time to include the new Article numbers in the two new treaties. Clearly good marks are available for anyone who knows the changes.

QUESTION 8

Critically examine the role of the Law Commission in the development of law in England.

How to Answer this Question

This question requires an analysis of the role of, and the work undertaken by, the Law Commission. As is usually the case, the word 'critically' indicates that what is required is, not merely a description of the Law Commission and its role, but an examination of its position, as a source of legislative proposals, within the wider constitutional framework together with an assessment of its effectiveness or any reasons for its lack of effectiveness.

Particular points to cover are:
❖   the limitations inherent in the roles of parliament and the courts in formulating new legal proposals;
❖   the creation, structure and procedure of the Law Commission should be considered in some detail;
    ❖   reference should be made to the content of current (11th) programme;
    ❖   reference should also be made to previous commission recommendations that have been implemented;

❖ rejected recommendations and as yet unimplemented recommendations should be mentioned;

❖ the provisions of the **Law Commission Act 2009** should be considered.

Answer Structure

ANSWER

According to strict legal practice, law reform is either a product of parliamentary or judicial activity. Parliament tends, however, to be concerned with particularities of law reform, and the judiciary are constitutionally and practically disbarred from reforming the law in anything other than an opportunistic and piecemeal way. Therefore, there remains a need for the question of law reform to be considered generally and a requirement that such consideration be conducted in an informed but disinterested manner.

That need is met particularly by the Law Commission.[25]

The Law Commission was established under the **Law Commission Act 1965**. It was set up under the auspices of Lord Gardiner LC, with the specific aim of improving the previous *ad hoc* consideration of law reform by charging it with the duty of keeping the law *as a whole* under review and making recommendations for its *systematic* reform. Under the **Act of 1965**, the Law Commission was constituted as an independent body with full-time members. It was given duties with regard to the revision and codification of the law, but its prime duty was, and remains, law reform.

It is estimated that at any one time, there are some 25 law reform projects being actively considered by the Commission, and it only ever recommends reform after it has undertaken an extensive process of consultation with informed and/or interested parties. It is this process of general and disinterested consultation, as the basis for the formulation of a genuinely informed recommendation, which distinguishes the procedure of the Commission from the reforms of the judiciary and the partial reforms advocated by interested parties. Although it is certainly true that it was the judiciary who altered the

....

25 This introduction sets the scene for the rest of the answer by immediately clarifying the need for the Law Commission.

common law rule relating to rape within marriage (*R* (1991), but it is perhaps worthy of mention that the Law Commission had already issued a working paper, entitled *Rape Within Marriage* in 1990, and its report of the same name was issued in 1992 (Law Com No 205). The Commission continues to consider whether this particular matter, and other important related matters concerning the relationships of married couples, such as the question of compelling a wife to give evidence against her husband, should be subject to legislative reform. The point to be made is that judges can only change the common law with regard to the problem encapsulated in the case that comes before them: the Commission, on the other hand, is at liberty to consider all matters relating to a specific issue.

The scope of the Commission is limited to those areas set out in its programme of law reform, but its ambit is not unduly restricted, as may be seen from the range of matters covered in its eleventh programme,

Although the scope of the Commission is limited to those areas set out in its programme of law reform, its ambit is not unduly restricted, as may be seen from the range of matters covered in its eleventh programme set out in July 2011.[26]

Among the areas to be covered in the new programme are:

❖ Charity law, examining a range of issues concerning the constitution and regulation of charities and their activities;

❖ Conservation covenants, investigating the case for a new statutory interest in land that would enable a conservation obligation to be enforcable against a landowner by someone who is not a neighbour;

❖ Contempt, reviewing the law on contempt to take into account use of the internet and other technologies and to ensure courts have the powers they need to deal with contempt in the face of the court;

❖ Data sharing between public bodies, clarifying the existence and nature of legal obstacles to data sharing;

❖ Electoral law, rationalising the complicated framework of rules governing electoral processes and take account of advances in technology;

❖ Electronic communications code, considering whether the Code can be made more transparent, user-friendly and efficient in resolving disputes;

❖ European contract law, assessing the impact of the EC-generated optional instrument that sets out which laws apply to contracts made between businesses (and between businesses and consumers) from different member states;

❖ Family financial orders, considering how court orders for financial provision following divorce or the end of a civil partnership and orders concerning financial arrangements for children are enforced;

----

26 Discussion of its present, and extensive, programme of work highlights the relevant and important nature of the Law Commission's work and demonstrates a more than superficial knowledge of its role.

❖ Misconduct in a public office, simplifying and clarifying this common law offence, and ensuring the law takes into account the fact that functions traditionally considered to be public in nature are now often discharged by private individuals and volunteers;

❖ Offences against the person, restructuring the law, probably by creating a new hierarchy of offences, and modernising and simplifying the language used to define offences against the person;

❖ Rights to light, assessing whether this area of law correctly balances a right to receive light against the right of neighbours affected by it to develop their land; including examining the relationship with planning law and the range of remedies available where a right is interfered with;

❖ Taxis and private hire vehicles, reviewing and simplifying the existing complex and separate regulatory systems, removing geographical inconsistencies and modernising to reflect advances in technology;

❖ Trademark and design litigation, unjustified threats, considering whether to repeal, reform or extend four provisions that impose liability to pay damages on the makers of an unjustified threat of intellectual property litigation;

❖ Wildlife, modernising the law on wildlife management, simplifying it and making it easier to understand.

In addition to these programme projects, ministers may refer matters of particular importance to the Commission for its consideration. For example, it was just such a referral by the Home Secretary, after the Macpherson Inquiry into the *Stephen Lawrence* case, that gave rise to the Law Commission's recommendation that the rule against double jeopardy be removed in particular circumstances. An extended version of that recommendation was included in the **Criminal Justice Act 2003.**[27]

Annual reports list all Commission publications. The Law Commission claims that, in the period since its establishment in 1965, over 100 of its law reports have been implemented. Examples of legislation following from Law Commission reports are: the **Contracts (Rights of Third Parties) Act 1999**, based on the recommendations of the Commission's Report No 180, *Privity of Contract;* and the **Trustee Act 2000**, based on the Commission's Report No 260. In February 2002 the **Land Registration Act** was passed, which has had a major impact on the land registration procedure. The Act implemented the draft Bill which was the outcome of the Commission's largest single project.

Current judicial review procedures are very much the consequence of a 1976 Law Commission report, and a review of their operation and proposals for reform was issued in October 1994.

....

27 Provision of details relating to some of its noteworthy achievements again allows depth of knowledge to be demonstrated.

In the area of criminal law, the preparatory work done by the Commission on several aspects of the criminal justice system (bail, double jeopardy and the revelation of an accused person's bad character) was incorporated into the **Criminal Justice Act 2003**.

In addition, **ss 5** and **6** of the **Domestic Violence, Crime and Victims Act 2004** reflect the recommendations of an earlier Commission report. The issue investigated related to situations where a child is non-accidentally killed or seriously injured, and it is apparent that one or more of a limited number of defendants must have committed the crime, but there is no evidence that allows the court to identify which of the defendants actually committed the offence. The **Domestic Violence, Crime and Victims Act 2004** also contains provisions reflecting the Commission report relating to the prosecution of people charged with multiple offences.

In August 2004 the Commission published its *Report on Partial Defences to Murder*, recommending the reform of the defence of provocation, with particular reference to murders committed in the context of domestic violence. That report also included a recommendation that the Home Office undertake a wholesale review of the law of murder, including sentencing regimes, and subsequently in December 2005 the Commission published its proposals for reforming the law of murder, *Bringing the Law of Murder into the 21st Century*. Its initial conclusion was that the current law on murder 'is a mess' and in an attempt to remedy that situation it provisionally recommended that there should be three tiers of homicide:

❖ In the top tier would be cases where there is an intention to kill. This is the worst category and would retain the mandatory life sentence.
❖ In the second tier would be cases of killing through reckless indifference to causing death and intention to do serious harm but not to kill. This tier would also include revised versions of provocation, diminished responsibility and duress. The sentence would depend on the details of the case.
❖ In the third tier (manslaughter) would be cases of killing by gross negligence or intention to cause harm but not serious harm.

In November 2006 the Law Commission published its final report setting out recommendations for reform of the law of homicide proposing the adoption of the three-tier structure, comprising first degree murder, second degree murder and manslaughter.

Although the recommendations on partial defences were implemented to a substantial extent in the **Coroners and Justice Act 2009**, as yet there has been no move to implement the Commission's wider recommendation in regard to the law relating to murder. However, such a dilatory response to Commission reports is not unusual. In its report covering 2005/06, its 40th anniversary year, the then chairman Sir Roger Toulson expressed some regret, not to say frustration, at the limited impact that the Commission could make in the area of law making and reform. As he stated:

> Today, as in 1965, our principal objective is to seek to achieve a body of law that is accessible to those who are affected by it. The task that faced our predecessors in 1965 was great, but the inexorable increase in the pace of legislation and the increasing readiness of government to seek legislative solutions to problems has made it much greater. In a legislative programme that is so full of priority government measures, it is increasingly difficult for our work to find the time it needs to be made into law. We continue to be told that some reports issued more than 10 years ago will be implemented 'when Parliamentary time becomes available'. This is a source of very real concern to us. Our process is thorough, involving wide consultation and careful analysis.
>
> The public money spent on enabling us to help provide the citizen with laws that are understandable and relevant to the 21st century can only be justified if the government is able to find time to implement those proposals it accepts.

In response to this failure to implement Law Commission reports, the former Law Lord, Lord Lloyd of Berwick, introduced the Law Commission Bill 2008–09 in the House of Lords. In support of the Bill Lord Kingsland pointed out that: 'Over the years . . . [the Law Commission] has been tasked with many seemingly intractable problems, has grappled with them and produced a solution, only to find that solution spurned by the political classes.'

The resultant Act[28] contains provisions to amend the **Law Commission Act 1965** so as to:

* require the Lord Chancellor to prepare an annual report, to be laid before parliament, on the implementation of Law Commission proposals;
* require the Lord Chancellor to set out plans for dealing with any Law Commission proposals which have not been implemented and provide the reasoning behind decisions not to implement proposals;
* allow the Lord Chancellor and Law Commission to agree a protocol about the Law Commission's work. The protocol would be designed to provide a framework for the relationship between the UK Government and the Law Commission, and the Lord Chancellor would have to lay the protocol before parliament.

The Commission's annual report for 2010/11 states that currently only 15 reports remain to be implemented.

....

28 The **Law Commission Act 2009**, is important as it strengthens the influence of the Law Commission and encourages Government to look carefully at its proposals

Common Pitfalls

In regard to this topic, the temptation is to undertake an answer without sufficient information. The assumption, and probably the fact, is that the writer knows something about the role and function of the Law Commission, but such general, superficial, knowledge soon runs out. It is for that very reason that a good plan/structure is necessary, to ensure that the answer will cover sufficient ground to generate good marks.

It is also essential to make sure that reference is made to the appropriate, and by definition the most up to date, sources of information relating to the Law Commissions' programmes and it latest successes, or otherwise, in implementation

Aim Higher

References to specific investigations, outside of the general programme, which may have been approved, should be referenced, as should any legislation introduced as a result of previous Commission recommendations.

Ensure that reference is made to the **Law Commission Act 2009**.

The Courts and the Appellate Process

THE COURTS

A sound knowledge of the civil and criminal court structure is essential for a proper understanding of many aspects of the English legal system. You should be aware of the jurisdiction of each court (that is, which types of cases each court is competent to deal with), how its workload compares with other courts, how it is organised and what criticisms have been made of these features. The courts in question are the county courts, magistrates' courts, the Crown Court, the High Court, the Court of Appeal, the Supreme Court and the Judicial Committee of the Privy Council.

The court system of 2012 is significantly different from that of 20 years earlier. It has undergone many changes to fit in more with the interests and conveniences of litigants and less with the interests of lawyers. A charter for the civil courts now states, for example, that anyone telephoning a court between 9 am and 5 pm on a weekday will get a prompt and helpful answer. It also says that within 10 working days of a court receiving a letter, the sender will get a reply by letter or telephone.

The Judicial and Court Statistics (published in June 2011 and revised in July 2011) give the following profile of court activity for 2010:

KEY FINDINGS

APPEALS

A total of 80 appeals were entered, and 33 disposed of by the Judicial Committee of the Privy Council during the year, compared to 65 and 47 for 2009 respectively.

250 appeals were presented to the Supreme Court, of which 220 were disposed of: 130 of these were refused outright.

Of the 7,250 applications for leave to appeal filed with the Court of Appeal Criminal Division, 21% were appeals against conviction and 76% were appeals against sentence. Of these 13% of the appeals against conviction were allowed and 27% of the appeals against sentence were allowed.

In the Civil Division of the Court of Appeal 1,180 appeals were set down, of which 45% were allowed.

In the Administrative Court (a division of the High Court Queen's Bench Division), there were 16300 applications for permission to claim judicial review, a 24% increase from 2009. Of the 460 substantive applications for judicial review disposed of in 2010, 42% (194) were allowed.

COUNTY COURT

The total number of civil (non-family) cases started in 2010 was 1,617,000, a 14% decrease compared with 2009.

The number of 'money' claims with specified claim amounts in 2010 was 1,041,000, a decrease of 19% from 2009. 36% of these claims had a claim value of up to £500, down from 38% in 2009.

The total number of 'money' claims with unspecified claim amounts was 191,000 in 2010, an increase of 6% compared with 2009.

The number of mortgage repossession claims issued in 2010 was 75,000, a decrease of 19% from 2009. The number of landlord possession claims decreased by 1% compared with 2009.

The number of defences was 8% lower and the number of allocations to track 6% lower than in 2009.

There were 20,000 trials, a 2% rise on 2009, and 43,000 small claim hearings, a 9% decrease on 2009.

Trials took place on average 50 weeks following issue, up from 48 weeks in 2009, while small claim hearings took place 31 weeks following issue, the same as in 2009.

MAGISTRATES' COURTS

An estimated 1.68 million defendants were proceeded against in criminal cases in magistrates' courts in 2010.

Magistrates' courts recorded 180,000 trials in 2010 (unchanged from 2009). Of those trials, 39% were recorded as cracked (up by one percentage point from 2009), with 19% recorded as ineffective (down by one percentage point from 2009).

The estimated time from offence to charge in 2010 was 85 days. Sexual offences took the second longest time between offence and charge (285 days), while drink driving offences took the shortest (15 days).

The estimated average time taken from offence to completion in 2010 was 138 days for defendants in completed criminal cases in magistrates' courts (down from 141 days in 2009).

The estimated average time taken from charge to completion in 2010 for adult charged cases, excluding cases sent or committed to the Crown Court, was 6.7 weeks (down from 6.9 weeks in 2009).

Enforcement of financial penalties: the amount paid in England and Wales in 2010 was £281 million (a 12% increase from 2009).

CROWN COURT

The number of cases committed/sent for trial to the Crown Court in 2010 was 97,700, the same as in 2009. The number of disposals for cases committed/sent for trial increased by 6% to 100,100.

The number of cases committed to the Crown Court for sentence increased by 6% to 40,800, while the number of appeals decreased by 4% to 13,800. Guilty pleas as a proportion of all cases where a plea was entered fell from 71% in 2009 to 70% in 2010.

The cracked and ineffective trial rates both rose by one percentage point to 43% and 14% respectively.

The average waiting time for defendants committed for trial on bail was 15.6 weeks and 19.4 weeks for those held in custody. The average waiting time for defendants sent for trial on bail was 23 weeks and 15.5 weeks for those held in custody.

THE APPELLATE PROCESS

You should be familiar with:

❖ what rights of appeal exist and what conditions, if any, apply in relation to all courts (civil and criminal);
❖ the findings and recommendations of the Runciman Commission on Criminal Justice (1993) about criminal appeals;
❖ appeals procedure: what powers the appellate courts have;
❖ the systems for references to be made to the Court of Appeal (Criminal Division) by the Home Secretary and the Attorney-General;
❖ how the **Criminal Appeal Act 1995** changed the system of criminal appeals, and changes made from 1998 to the work of the Court of Appeal (Civil Division) as a result of the Bowman Report;
❖ the recommendations of the Royal Commission on Criminal Justice, under the chairmanship of Viscount Runciman, which reported in July 1993. Many of its 352 recommendations address matters relating to the courts, juries and the appellate

process. Wherever appropriate, the relevant proposals have been incorporated into answers here;

❖ the findings and recommendations of the Auld Review of the Criminal Courts of England and Wales.

QUESTION 9

State and explain in what circumstances the Supreme Court can overrule one of its own previous decisions, and illustrate your answer with an example.

How to Answer this Question

A good answer will:

❖ Set the historical and legal theory context, and say why the matter is important within the English legal system.

❖ Explain in some detail the provisions of the 1966 Practice Statement.

❖ Explain something of the meaning of the 1966 formula as given in subsequent case law like *Herrington v British Railways Board* (1972).

❖ Illustrate the principle being used to change the law, for example in *Horton v Sadler* (2006).

❖ Conclude with some evaluation or appraisal of the power being used in this case, perhaps revisiting the essay's opening paragraph's coverage of the finality/flexibility issue, and examining that issue in relation to the case.

Answer Structure

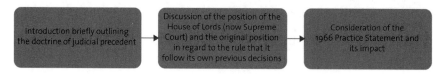

Introduction briefly outlining the doctrine of judicial precedent → Discussion of the position of the House of Lords (now Supreme Court) and the original position in regard to the rule that it follow its own previous decisions → Consideration of the 1966 Practice Statement and its impact

ANSWER

One expected quality of the court at the apex of a pyramidal court structure is finality of judgment. What is laid down as the law by such a court will be certain and reliable because there is no court above it to which a dissatisfied side can appeal for another decision on the law. Historically, before the Supreme Court was established in 2009, the House of Lords for a long time would not overrule its earlier decisions even if they later seemed wrong. Since 1966, however, it was able to overrule its earlier rulings. It seldom did so, but did so in 2006, and thereby conduced to greater justice for litigants.

House of Lords' decisions are binding on all other courts in the legal system, except, today, the Supreme Court. The House of Lords was bound by its own previous decisions until it changed this practice in 1966. The historical practice of always sticking faithfully to whatever it had earlier ruled was the law that had been established by the nineteenth century and was reaffirmed in a famous case in 1898 – *London Tramways Co Ltd v London County Council.*

However, this approach did not appear to create certainty and had become very rigid by the end of the nineteenth century. Several areas of law fossilised because rules laid down by the Lords remained fixed, while social developments rendered them archaic and Parliament did nothing to modernise them using legislation. The practice was eventually changed in July 1966 when Lord Gardiner, the Lord Chancellor, made a statement on behalf of himself and his fellow Law Lords. This *Practice Statement* says:

> Their Lordships regard the use of precedent as an indispensable foundation upon which to decide what is the law and its application to individual cases. It provides at least some degree of certainty upon which individuals can rely in the conduct of their affairs as well as a basis for orderly development of legal rules.

> Their Lordships nevertheless recognise that too rigid adherence to precedent may lead to injustice in a particular case and also unduly restrict the proper development of the law. They propose, therefore, to modify their present practice and, while treating former decisions of this House as normally binding, to depart from a previous decision when it appears right to do so. In this connection they will bear in mind the danger of disturbing retrospectively the basis on which contracts, settlements of property, and fiscal arrangements have been entered into and also the special need for certainty as to the criminal law. This announcement is not intended to affect the use of precedent elsewhere than in this House.

> [1966] 3 All ER 77

> The House of Lords 1966 Practice Statement on departure from its own previous decisions applies equally to the Supreme Court.
>
> *Austin v Mayor and Burgesses of the London Borough of Southwark* (2010)
> Lord Hope, paras [24]–[25]

The current practice enables the Supreme Court to adapt English law to meet changing social conditions. It was also regarded as important at the time (in 1966) that the House of Lords' practice be brought into line with that of superior courts in other countries, like the United States Supreme Court and state supreme courts elsewhere which are not bound by their own previous decisions.

The possibility of the Supreme Court changing its previous decisions is a recognition that law, whether expressed in statutes or cases, is a living, and therefore changing, institution which must adapt to the circumstances in which, and to which, it applies if it is to retain practical relevance.

Since 1966, the House used this power quite sparingly. Today, the Supreme Court will not refuse to follow its earlier decision merely because that decision was wrong. A material change of circumstances will usually have to be shown.

In *Herrington v British Railway Board* (1972), the House of Lords overruled *Addy and Sons v Dumbreck* (1929). In the earlier case, the House of Lords had decided that an occupier of premises was only liable for the injury to a trespassing child if that child was injured by the occupier intentionally or recklessly. In its later decision, the House of Lords changed the law in line with the changed social and physical conditions since 1929. Their Lordships felt that even a trespasser was entitled to some degree of care, which they propounded as a test of 'common humanity'. In imposing a duty of care on occupiers, and arguing for the overruling of the 1929 decision, Lord Pearson said:

> It seems to me the rule in *Addie v Dumbreck* has been rendered obsolete by changes in physical and social conditions and has become an incumbrance impeding the proper development of law. With the increase in population and the larger proportion living in cities and towns and the extensive substitution of blocks of flats for rows of houses with gardens or back yards and quiet streets, there is less playing space for children and so a greater temptation to trespass. There is less supervision of children so they are more likely to trespass . . . Also with the progress of technology there are more and greater dangers for them to encounter . . .
>
> [1972] 1 All ER 749 at 785–786

The rarely used power of the House of Lords was utilised in *Horton v Sadler* in 2006 (below). Under the **Limitation Act 1980**, certain time-limits are imposed on people who want to bring legal actions for compensation. For actions concerning personal injuries, a claimant must sue within three years of the injury being caused, or whenever the injury or illness became apparent (**s 11**). By virtue of **s 33** of the Act, however, that three-year time-limit can be disapplied by the courts (so that the claimant *can* sue) but only if the time-limit would, if applied, 'prejudice' the claimant, and if suspending the three-year rule would be 'equitable' in the all the circumstances. If, for example, the claimant's solicitors make the claim one day late beyond the three-year limit, and the defendant does not really suffer any disadvantage by virtue of that very slight rule violation, the courts will probably use **s 33** to disapply the three-year limit.

Horton v Sadler (2006) was a case about a traffic accident in Salford. The claimant was seriously injured, and the driver at fault was not insured.

The claimant had initially issued proceedings before the three-year time-limit had expired. That claim was not properly made by the claimant's lawyers, so new proceedings were issued, but after the end of the original three-year period. It was ultimately held by the Lords that the court *could* use its discretion under the **Limitation Act 1980 s 33** to disapply the three-year time-limit. In reaching that decision, it overruled its earlier decision in *Walkley v Precision Forgings Limited* (1979). The 1979 decision had deprived many claimants of a right that Parliament had intended them to have, and had given rise to much unsatisfactory jurisprudence.

In the 2006 case, the appellant, Mr Horton (H) appealed against a decision applying the ordinary three-year time-limit under the **Limitation Act 1980 s 33** in his road traffic claim against the respondents (S). The Motor Insurers' Bureau (MIB), which is liable to make payments where the defendant is uninsured, nominated insurers and made an interim payment to H.

H issued proceedings two days before expiry of the three-year limitation period, but failed to comply with a condition precedent of the MIB's liability, namely the requirement to give them notice.

When it was later sued, the MIB served a defence that denied its liability because of the claimant's failure to comply with the notice condition, and counterclaimed for the return of its interim payment to the injured man. H then issued duplicate proceedings against S, giving the correct notice to the MIB who were again joined as a party to the second action. The MIB had defended the claim arguing that it was now statute-barred under the **Limitation Act 1980 s 11**. H responded seeking an order disapplying the ordinary three-year time-limit under **s 33** of the Act.

The judge indicated that had it been permissible for him to disapply the time-limit under **s 33** then he would have exercised his discretion in favour of H. H's subsequent appeal had been dismissed based on binding authority, in particular *Walkley v Precision Forgings Ltd* (1979). H submitted that the reasoning in *Walkley* could not be supported; the Court of Appeal had in various subsequent cases sought to rely on 'fine distinctions' (that is minutely nuanced differences) to enable it to disapply *Walkley* in any case where it was not strictly constrained to apply it. The law was unfair and judges had to try to find ways around it. H also argued that the decision was inconsistent with the wide and unfettered discretion which the legislation had intended to give the court.

The House of Lords held that the appeal by Mr Horton would be allowed. It reasoned in this way:

> The true question for the court under **s 33** of the Act was always whether it was equitable or inequitable as between the parties to override the time bar, which, if relied on by the defendant and unless disapplied by order of the court, would defeat the action that a claimant (here H) had brought out of time. That analysis could not be reconciled with *Walkley*, which had held that **s 11** could not prejudice a claimant who had commenced proceedings within the three-year period, and so it was only in exceptional circumstances that such a claimant could have the time bar disapplied. *Walkley* was therefore overruled.

While the House of Lords had exercised its power to depart from its own precedent rarely and sparingly, and it had never been thought enough to justify doing so that a later generation of Law Lords would have resolved an issue or formulated a principle differently from their predecessors, too rigid an adherence to precedent might lead to injustice in a particular case and unduly restrict the development of the law. The House would depart from a previous decision where it appeared right to do so. The instant case was not one in which contracts, settlements of property or fiscal arrangements had been entered into on the faith of a settled legal rule. The criminal law, where certainty was particularly important, would be unaffected if the House departed from *Walkley*. There would be no detriment to public administration. While injustice might bear more hardly on individuals, that concept was not to be regarded as inapplicable to judgments affecting corporations with competing interests. In the result, *Walkley* should be departed from as it unfairly deprived claimants of a right Parliament intended them to have; it had driven the Court of Appeal to draw distinctions which were so fine as to reflect no credit on the instant area of law; and it subverted the clear intention of Parliament.

It held that the case would be remitted to the county court for the judge to resolve the application under **s 33**.

One of the main reasons that the House of Lords decided to overrule the legal analysis it had given in the 1979 case was that the decision had caused great unfairness ever since. Every so often, car accident victims whose lawyers issued claims within the three-year period were barred from suing when there was something wrong with the claim, and then another claim issued after the three years was struck down as time-barred. When such defeated litigants tried to get the courts to utilise the discretion to override the three-year rule, the courts refused because they said the litigant had 'not been prejudiced by the *three-year* rule', he had not been dilatory, as he *had* issued claim within the time, albeit an ineffective one.

That is an odd argument because when the same claimant came to issue a second claim in respect of the same harm, the reason he would *then* fail was precisely because of the three-year rule (because he usually issued the second claim more than three years after the accident) so he *was* being prejudiced by it! To give justice to injured claimants who would otherwise fall foul of the 1979 House of Lords' decision, subsequent courts had to make all sorts of dubious distinctions. The House of Lords was right to change its mind. The authority and 'finality' of the 1979 decision created many human difficulties, and as Lord Atkin once observed (*Ras Behari Lal v King-Emperor* (1933)): 'Finality is a good thing, but justice is a better.'

Common Pitfalls
The 1966 Practice Statement is a multifactor formula. It is a common fault to omit one or more elements of the formula. Its contents should be learnt in full.

QUESTION 10

Describe the work of the coroners' courts and explain what social role this part of the legal system is expected to perform.

How to Answer this Question

You should:

- ❖ explain the historical setting of coroners' courts;
- ❖ note current numbers and duties of coroners;
- ❖ consider verdicts and purpose of classifications;
- ❖ consider patterns of death;
- ❖ discuss the problems posed by the meaning of the word 'how' in the requirement for inquests to decide 'how' someone died.

Answer Structure

Introduce the coroners' courts, their development and place in the court system → Outline the work of modern coroners' courts → Explain the social role of the coroners' courts

ANSWER

The coroners' courts are one of the most ancient parts of the English legal system, dating back to at least 1194. They are not, in modern function, part of the criminal courts, although, for historical reasons, they have an association with that branch of the justice system.

Coroners were originally appointed as *custos placitorum coronae*, keepers of the pleas of the Crown. They had responsibility for criminal cases in which the Crown had an interest, particularly if this interest was financial. By development of their role, however, and particularly through the pioneering work of the nineteenth-century coroner Dr Thomas Wakley, the coroner became, in Wakley's phrase, 'the people's judge'. The coroner is the ultimate public safeguard in an area of unmatched importance: the official documenting of how people die. Marilyn Lannigan, an authority on the history of the coroner, has pointed to the fact that it was Wakley who originally campaigned for all suspicious deaths, deaths in police custody or prison, and deaths attributable to neglect, to be brought within the jurisdiction of the coroner. He was an energetic reformer, who was also an MP and the founder of the medical journal *The Lancet*.

Today, there are 157 coroners' courts, of which 21 sit full-time. Coroners are usually lawyers (with at least a five-year qualification within **s 71** of the **Courts and Legal Services Act 1990**), although about 25 per cent are medical doctors with a legal qualification. The main jurisdiction of the coroner today concerns unnatural and violent deaths, although treasure troves are also something occasionally dealt with in these courts. However, the **Treasure Act 1996** which came into effect in 1997 introduced new rules relating to the reporting of finds and how they should be dealt with. The number of inquests into treasure troves will eventually fall away to zero.[1]

The classifying of types of death, of which there are about 500,000 each year in England and Wales, is clearly of critical importance, not just to the state, politicians and policy makers, but also to the sort of campaign groups that exist in a constitutional democracy to monitor suicides, drug-related deaths, deaths in police custody and prison, accidental deaths, deaths in hospitals and through industrial diseases. About 40 per cent of deaths each year are reported to coroners as unnatural, or violent, or as reportable from certain industries, or are from an unknown cause.

In 2009, there were 500,100 registered deaths in England and Wales. The number of these reported to coroners was 229,900, resulting in 105,400 post-mortem examinations and 31,000 inquests. Having a reliable system for charting who is dying, and in what circumstances, is of considerable social value. It is important for us to know, for example, that there were 3,800 suicides in England and Wales in 2009, as this should inform public policy related to the health service, community services, custodial policy and the emergency services.[2]

Most inquests (96 per cent) are held without juries, but the state has been insistent that certain types of case must be heard by a jury in order to promote public faith in government. When in 1926, legislation, for the first time, permitted inquests to be held without juries, certain types of death were deliberately marked off as still requiring jury scrutiny and these included deaths in police custody, deaths resulting from the actions of a police officer on duty and deaths in prison. This was seen as a very important way of fostering public trust in potentially oppressive aspects of the state. In 1971, the Brodrick Committee Report (Cmnd 4810) on the coronial system saw the coroner's jury as having a

---

1   Introductory paragraphs provide an interesting overview of the original coroners' courts and also then moves on to place the courts into a modern-day context.
2   Rather than being purely descriptive answer in terms of the role of the coroners' courts, the essay recognises the importance of getting to grip with the main issue of their 'social role'.

symbolic significance and thought that it was a useful way to legitimate the decision of the coroner.

The coroner's court is unique in using an inquisitorial process. There are no 'sides' in an inquest. There may be representation for people like the relatives of the deceased, insurance companies, prison officers, car drivers, companies (whose policies are possibly implicated in the death) and train drivers, etc, but all the witnesses are the coroner's witnesses. It is the coroner who decides who shall be summoned as witnesses and in what order they shall be called.

Historically, an inquest jury could decide that a deceased had been unlawfully killed and then commit a suspect for trial at the local assizes. When this power was taken away in 1926, the main bridge over to the criminal justice system was removed. There then followed, in stages, an attempt to prevent inquest verdicts from impinging on the jurisdictions of the ordinary civil and criminal courts. Now, an inquest jury is exclusively concerned with determining who the deceased was and 'how, when and where he came by his death'. The court is forbidden to make any wider comment on the death, and must not determine or appear to determine criminal liability 'on the part of a named person'. Nevertheless, the jury may still now properly decide that a death was unlawful (that is, a crime). The verdict of 'unlawful killing' is on a list of options (including 'suicide', 'accidental death' and 'open verdict') made under legislation and approved by the Home Office.

Under the **Coroners and Justice Act 2009**, the coronial system was reorganised.[3] The Act establishes a Chief Coroner to lead the coroners service, with powers to intervene in cases in specified circumstances, including presiding over an appeals process designed specifically for the coroner system. The Act establishes a senior coroner for each coroner area (previously known as coroner districts) with the possibility of appointing area coroners and assistant coroners to assist the senior coroner for the area (in place of the existing deputy coroners and assistant deputy coroners). A senior coroner who is made aware that the body of a deceased person is within that coroner's area must as soon as practicable conduct 'an investigation' into the person's death if there is evidence that –

(a)   the deceased died a violent or unnatural death;
(b)   the cause of death is unknown; or
(c)   the deceased died while in custody or otherwise in state detention.

Some of the legal questions vexing the coronial process are quite significant when one considers the general role of the coroner system to plot national patterns of death. It is, as

---

3   Including consideration of the most recent legislation demonstrates up-to-date knowledge and adds weight and authority to the answer.

noted above, the purpose of an inquest to determine, among other things, how the deceased died, and 'how' in this context means, according to one view, simply by what physical cause and in what immediate circumstances. According to another proposition however, one needs to take a much broader interpretation of the word 'how', in order to give a sufficiently thorough investigation to the issue (in some cases) of whether there was an unlawful killing.

Among the possible scenarios covered by the phrase 'unlawfully killed' is manslaughter through gross negligence committed by a company. The problem here is that in a case involving a member of the public, or an employee who has been killed in an event arising from a company's operations, one often cannot properly tell whether the death has resulted from 'gross negligence' on the company's part, unless and until one has found out the answers to all sorts of questions about how the company ran its business prior to the death. But to ask such questions can be objected to, on the basis that such an explorative exercise involves an excursus into matters beyond the proper scope of the inquest, according to the Divisional Court in *R v Sussex Coroner ex p Homberg* (1994).

The meaning of the word 'how' in a coroner's court was addressed in *Homberg*. Simon Brown LJ stated that although the word 'how' is to be widely interpreted, it means 'by what means' the death came about, rather than 'in what broad circumstances'. Thus, a coroner or counsel at an inquest can object to any line of inquiry which seeks to find out about 'the broad circumstances of the death'. On the other hand, unless the court knows something about the broad circumstances of a company's operations, it is impossible to determine whether there has been 'gross negligence'. Questions from counsel designed to elicit information from witnesses about the past practices of a company, its record on safety, or who in the company knew what and at what time, could thus be objected to on the basis of *Homberg*, while being perfectly defensible on the basis of testing whether the principle of 'gross negligence' manslaughter is applicable.

It is not always possible to identify suspicious deaths, and the recent case of Dr Harold Shipman highlighted the need to have a system which generally identifies cases which require further investigation, before the cause of death is officially certified and the matter closed. In 2002, it became apparent, following the report of Dame Janet Smith, that Dr Shipman was able, while practising as a GP, to kill over 215 people without the system detecting this homicidal conduct.

Not all of the work of coroners is as riddled with intrigue as a day in the life of the American medical examiner, as portrayed in contemporary fiction and television. Nonetheless, the importance of the system in maintaining an open society and acting as a buttress against sinister conduct is immense.

Common Pitfalls

Under the Coroners and Justice Act 2009, there are clear rules governing when an inquest should be held. Ignorance of these rules is a common feature of poorer answers.

Aim Higher

High credit can be gained by demonstrating a good knowledge and understanding of the social importance of the coronial system – for example, why it is important for a society to know how many people commit suicide each year.

NOTES

Under the **Coroners and Justice Act 2009**, the coronial system was reorganised. The Act establishes a Chief Coroner to lead the coroners' service, with powers to intervene in cases in specified circumstances, including presiding over an appeals process designed specifically for the coroner system. The Act establishes a senior coroner for each coroner area (previously known as coroner districts) with the possibility of appointing area coroners and assistant coroners to assist the senior coroner for the area (in place of the existing deputy coroners and assistant deputy coroners). A senior coroner who is made aware that the body of a deceased person is within that coroner's area must as soon as practicable conduct 'an investigation' into the person's death if there is evidence that:

(a) the deceased died a violent or unnatural death,

(b) the cause of death is unknown, or

(c) the deceased died while in custody or otherwise in state detention.

The general rule is that an inquest must be held without a jury. There are, though, some exceptions. A jury must be summoned where the deceased died while in custody or otherwise in state detention, and the death was violent or unnatural, or of unknown cause; where the death was as a result of an act or omission of a police officer or member of a service police force in the purported execution of their duties; or where the death was caused by an accident, poisoning or disease which must be reported to a government department or inspector. This includes certain deaths at work. Although a jury is not required in any other case, the coroner will be able to summon one in any case where he or she believes there is sufficient reason for doing so. Coroners sit with juries of between 7 and 11 people.

QUESTION 11 --

In what ways does the English legal system seek to balance interests? Using examples, discuss the challenges faced by the system in doing this effectively.

How to Answer this Question

A good answer will:

- ❖ give some general examples (like freedom of speech) to put the question in a context;
- ❖ give an example of the English legal system itself having to balance interests, as where, even before arguments about balancing interests over freedom of speech, it has to decide questions like who to let into court and how long litigants get to put their cases;
- ❖ look at an example from beyond the formal legal system (like the NHS) where the same considerations apply;
- ❖ show considerations of time and resources;
- ❖ explore a concrete case example, *Re G* (2004);
- ❖ put the question into a political context.

Answer Structure

Introduction explaining the issues of 'interests' and the need for 'balance' → Provision of examples as expressly asked for in the question → Consideration of the 'difficulties' in achieving a balance of interests

ANSWER --

One of the important functions of the legal system is to balance interests. This it does in hundreds of different ways. One person's right to 'free speech' must be balanced against another person's right to be protected against being defamed by lies, or being attacked because of incitements to racial hatred. One person's right to play loud music or operate an airport near a residential area needs to be balanced against the rights of others not to be badly disturbed. People have the right to bring legal actions in the civil courts but it is in the interests of society that we are protected against being bothered by serial litigants who want to use the legal system in an obsessive way and, therefore, such people can be barred from the courts as 'vexatious litigants'.[4]

....

4   By providing appropriate examples, the answer immediately 'sets the scene', clearly demonstrating *why* the English legal system (ELS) needs to balance interests. This indicates, to the examiner, an understanding of the issues and satisfies the specific instruction to provide examples contained in the question.

These issues often raise questions of fundamental social and political importance. For example, consider the question of at exactly what point we should exclude an intending litigant from the courts. Someone might have a genuine case against a part of the central or local governmental machinery. He or she might have been the real victim of repeated unfairness, or of a miscarriage of justice, or malice or prejudice. History shows that such things can happen. Such victims might then find themselves in an awful legal battle, like the case in Franz Kafka's novel *The Trial*, trying to use the law to fight parts of some huge organisation (like a governmental department, or a large telecom company, or financial institution) only to then be branded as a 'vexatious litigant' and excluded from the very processes of justice that exist to examine alleged wrongs.

Like the legal system, the health system also has to balance interests. It must be disposed to treat all sorts of patients because you do not cease to be entitled to civilised care just because you are an irritating person, or an eccentric, or have incurred ill health or injury in the course of some reproachable conduct. In 2006, for example, over 3,000 people under 16 years old were treated in hospital accident and emergency departments for excessive alcohol intake or alcohol-related injuries. Their folly did not debar them from treatment. There is, though, a limit to those who will be given the provision of health care. In May 2004, Norman Hutchens, 53, from York, became the first person to be banned by a magistrates' anti-social behaviour order, from entering or calling any National Health Service premises in the country. The court had been told Hutchens, who has a fetish for surgical masks, had verbally and physically abused NHS staff 47 times in the previous five months. In the juridical weighing scales, the interests of NHS staff eventually tip the balance against the interest of the man who was hassling staff.

The legal system can also exclude from all its own law courts a litigant who has 'habitually and persistently and without reasonable cause' instituted vexatious proceedings. In 1897, it was ruled that a court can consider the number and general character of a serial litigators' cases, and can make an exclusion order even if there may have been reasonable grounds for the proceedings in each case considered separately: *Re Chaffers, ex parte A-G* (1897). The **Supreme Court Act 1981 s 42** prevents a vexatious litigant from commencing any further proceedings without the permission of the High Court.

Similarly, the time taken in court by litigants and their lawyers needs to be controlled. It might well be that given an extra few weeks in court, a claimant or defendant might (in his or her own view) be able to make their case much more persuasively through their lawyer. If, however, they have been afforded a reasonable time, and time in line with general practice, it will commonly be seen as fair that their period for argument is curtailed. Their right to talk at inordinate length must be balanced with other considerations like that of allowing a good flow of cases through the courts. With limited resources (judges, courtrooms, court staff), a court will usually be doing better to hear, say, 10 cases in a month in a time-managed way as opposed to one case in an unlimited way. Sometimes, the exceptional nature of a case will warrant the court being generous with its time. On 30 June 2004 Gordon Pollock QC finished his opening speech in the unprecedented litigation taken against the Bank of England by the liquidators of the Bank of Credit and Commerce International (BCCI). He had begun his introduction, the longest opening courtroom speech in English legal history, on 13 January. In 2005, that record was broken again, in the same case, by Nicholas Stadlen QC, the barrister for the other side. This, though, was a case in which 80,000 investors lost money, and where a body as august as the Bank of England is alleged to have acted wrongly – so, in allowing this unusually long speech, the balancing scales were tipped in favour of the interests of the numerous creditors, and the huge sums of money involved, as against the other smaller and less momentous cases that might otherwise be before the court.

Another recent example[5] of the courts balancing interests can be found in a case from the Civil Division of the Court of Appeal. In times of heightened awareness of terrorist threats, a balance must be made between civil liberty and public safety. The scales could be weighted entirely in favour of public safety by giving the police the unlimited authority to do anything they saw fit in order to counter possible terrorist threats: to arrest anyone and question him for months or years without having to give a reason for the suspect having been arrested. Tens of thousands of people could be imprisoned on the basis of suspicion as evidenced by their clothes or ethnicity or religion; traffic could be outlawed from whole sections of cities; and the population could be put under an 8 pm curfew. That might reduce the risk of terrorist acts but there would be a high price to pay in the dimension of civil liberty.

By contrast, the police could be asked to prevent and detect terrorism without being given any extra powers. That would allow a high degree of civil liberty but would arguably make life easier for terrorists. These issues were considered in the following case. The Court of Appeal decided that the disadvantage of the intrusion imposed on individuals by being stopped and searched by police officers under the **Terrorism Act 2000 s 44** was outweighed by the advantage of the possibility of a terrorist attack being avoided or deterred by use of that power.

In *R (on the application of Gillan) v (1) Commissioner of Police for the Metropolis (2) Secretary of State for the Home Department* (2004), the Court of Appeal addressed these issues. The applicants (G and Q) appealed against the dismissal of their claim for judicial review of the lawfulness of their being stopped and searched by police officers. In September 2003, G, a student, was on his way to demonstrate at an arms fair in London when he was stopped and searched under the **Terrorism Act 2000 s 44** for articles

....

5   The inclusion of up-to-date examples demonstrates impressive *current* knowledge and awareness.

concerned in terrorism. G was allowed to go after 20 minutes. Q was stopped and searched under the same provisions at the same event. She was at the fair to film the protests. She felt distressed by the search. Nothing incriminating was found on G or Q and they later complained. The police officers relied on an authorisation made under **s 44** of the **2000 Act** by the Assistant Commissioner and its subsequent confirmation by the Secretary of State to justify their actions.

The authorisation ran for 28 days and had then been further authorised twice for two further periods of 28 days. G and Q stated that the evidence showed that the rolling programme of authorisations had become part of day-to-day policing, contrary to the intention of the **2000 Act**. G and Q argued that the court erred in: (a) concluding that the authorisation under **s 44** was lawful; (b) concluding that the use of stop and search powers under the authorisation against G and Q did not frustrate the legislative purpose of the **2000 Act**; (c) failing to construe **ss 44** to **47** of the **2000 Act** in accordance with the principle of legality or in accordance with the requirements of the **Human Rights Act 1998 s 3** so that it would be compatible with rights under the **European Convention on Human Rights 1950**; and (d) concluding that the authorisation and the use of the powers there under were prescribed by law. They argued that the use of the powers was not a proportionate means of achieving the legislative purpose of preventing acts of terrorism.

The Court of Appeal held that:

(1)   The **2000 Act** was to be given its ordinary meaning. It was entirely consistent with the framework of the legislation that a power to stop and search should be exercised when a senior police officer considered it advantageous for the prevention of terrorism. Interpreted as such, **ss 44** and **45** could not conflict with the provisions of the European Convention. The courts would respect the authorities' view on matters of security but the court did have a role as to proportionality. The ultimate determination of what was proportionate rested with the court.

(2)   The stop and search powers did not constitute an infringement of **Art 5** (right to liberty and security) as the search was usually of a limited nature and its aim was not to deprive an individual of his liberty but to effect a verification. **Article 8** did apply to the stop and search process. However **Arts 10** and **11** could not be invoked as the powers were limited to searching for articles of a kind used in connection with terrorism.

(3)   The procedure complained of was prescribed by law. The law that was under criticism was the statute and not the authorisation. Further, the statute contained controls on the powers.

(4)   As to the authorisations, the disadvantage of the intrusion imposed on individuals by being stopped and searched was outweighed by the advantage of the possibility of a terrorist attack being avoided or deterred by use of the power. The rolling programme was justified in the current situation and there was nothing to support the suggestion that the powers were used for day to day policing.

(5)   The police commander had been entitled to decide to use the **s 44** powers at the arms fair, given the nature of the fair, its location close to an airport and the site of a previous terrorist incident. However, the respondents had not provided sufficient evidence that police officers had received careful instruction on the use of the powers. It was important that, when the police were given exceptional powers, they were prepared to demonstrate that they were being used with appropriate circumspection. The onus was on the first respondent to show that the interference with G's and Q's rights was lawful. On the evidence, it was not possible to say that that onus had been discharged.

(6)   The court's provisional view was the judgment was best left to speak for itself and there be no order on the appeal as to the merits.

This case is a good illustration of the way a law court can be engaged in the evaluation of social or political issues in the process in deciding what is the appropriate balancing (or imbalance) of oppositional interests. Several cases have sought to balance the interests of the individual and those of the state, especially in respect of issues, as in the *Gillan* case above, arising from the **European Convention on Human Rights**.

In *Human Rights and Criminal Justice* (Ben Emmerson QC and Andrew Ashworth QC, 2001), the authors note (p 60, para 2–03), that the principal object and purpose of the **European Convention on Human Rights** is the protection of individual rights from infringement by the contracting states (*Ireland v United Kingdom* (1979–80) 2 EHRR 25 at para 239). The convention seeks to achieve this objective through the maintenance and promotion of 'the ideals and values of a democratic society' (*Kjeldsen and others v Denmark* (1979–80) 1 EHRR 711 at para 53). The authors observe that particularly important features of a democratic society in the context of criminal cases are 'pluralism, tolerance and broadmindedness' (*Handyside v United Kingdom* (1979–80) 1 EHRR 737 at para 49) and 'the rule of law' (*Golder v United Kingdom* (1979–80) 1 EHRR 525 at para 34). The authors note (2–05) that it is important to distinguish between 'democratic values' and the protection of majority sentiment. The duty to protect inalienable rights sometimes requires the Court to set standards, even where these do not meet with majority approval. They then cite *Inze v Austria* (1988) 10 EHRR 394 at para 44, where the Court considered that support amongst the local population for measures discriminating against illegitimate children merely reflected 'the traditional outlook'. The authors conclude this point with an apposite quotation from the Court that ruled that 'although the interests of the individual must on occasion be subordinated to those of a group, democracy does not simply mean that the views of the majority must always prevail: a balance must be achieved which ensures the fair and proper treatment of minorities and avoids any abuse of a dominant position' (*Young, James and Webster v United Kingdom* (1981) 4 EHRR 38 at para 63).

In *Gillan*, the Court of Appeal makes a comparably 'political' point when it ruled that the disadvantage of individuals by being stopped and searched by police officers was outweighed by the advantage of the possibility of a terrorist attack being avoided or deterred by use of that power.

One thing that this case illustrates, along with the other issues examined in this essay, is that, ultimately, the balancing of interests is an exercise that must be carried out according to large political or social principles that are above and beyond clinical legal questions.[6]

QUESTION 12

Explain and assess the effectiveness of cross-examination as a method of getting to the truth in court.

How to Answer this Question

The court case – the civil and criminal trial – is at the heart of the English legal system. Within such trials, the process of cross-examination is a key mechanism for producing the truth, or at least of producing a just result. The answer should make it clear how, in general terms, the system works and why it is used.

- ❖ Introduce the procedure.
- ❖ Explain its basic purpose.
- ❖ Explain the balance of power between advocate and witness.
- ❖ Illustrate effective use of questioning: e.g. Isaacs and Seddon.
- ❖ The use of sustained questioning: e.g. Cadbury's case.
- ❖ Conclusion – effective unless one too many questions are asked.

Answer Structure

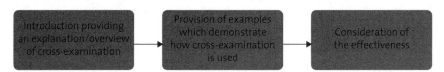

Introduction providing an explanation/overview of cross-examination → Provision of examples which demonstrate how cross-examination is used → Consideration of the effectiveness

ANSWER

Cross-examination is an important feature of criminal and civil trials. It has been recognised by the Court of Appeal that an unwarranted restriction of an advocate's opportunity to cross-examine a witness can render a trial unfair under **Art 6** of the **European Convention on Human Rights**, and therefore be a reason for ordering a re-trial:

---

6   The provision of a brief conclusion not only brings discussion to an end but, importantly, allows the question to be referenced and a succinct overview of the main thrust of the answer to be provided.

R v John K (2007). The simple point of significance decided in this case in the context of the English legal system is the indispensable value of cross-examination.

In court, cross-examination is where an advocate questions a witness who is part of the other side of the case. The questions cross from one side's lawyer to the other side's witness.[7]

The aim of the exercise is to weaken the opponent's case, and to help establish facts which are favourable to the side of the cross-examiner. It is an opportunity to expose any unreliability in an opposing witness's testimony. Cross-examination can be done politely and without hostility. Sir John Mortimer QC notes (*Clinging to the Wreckage*, 1982, p 106) that his late father (also a distinguished barrister) used to say 'the art of cross-examination is not the art of examining crossly'.

When a prosecuting advocate has finished questioning (called 'examining') a witness called by the prosecution, defence counsel can cross-examine that witness. Later the prosecution has the same chance to discredit the evidence of defence witnesses. In a civil case, similarly, the claimant and the defendant (usually through advocates) can cross-examine each other, and each other's witnesses. The procedure has a long history. The noun 'cross-examination' was first recorded in a case in 1729, although the technique itself is much older, appearing in one case involving a will in Norwich at the beginning of the thirteenth century. Cross-examination is an excellent method of clarifying the facts of a disputed matter. It is a serious intellectual contest fought in the threat of grave consequences. It is people at the peek of rational truth-finding.

The advocate has many advantages over the witness, such as knowing the rules of evidence, and choosing the line of inquiry in cross-examination. But the advocate does not always get the upper hand. A barrister in Ireland once began a cross-examination of an Irish Prelate with the words: 'Am I wrong in thinking you are the most influential man, and decidedly the most influential Prelate or Potentate, in the Province of Connaught?' The witness replied: 'Well, you know, they say these things, but it is in the sense that they would say that you are the very light of the Bar of Ireland: these are children's compliments'.

Cross-examination can involve counsel taking a witness through a sequence of propositions he will have to agree with until he is eventually cornered into agreeing with one final deadly point. But, equally, advocates sometimes pivot quickly to a riveting question. In opening the cross-examination of Frederick Seddon (who was on trial for the murder of his lodger, Miss Eliza Barrow), Sir Rufus Isaacs, Attorney General, began thus:

....
7   Sets the scene by explaining cross-examination, what it involves and its uses.

ISAACS: Miss Barrow lived with you from July 26, 1910, to September 14, 1911?
SEDDON: Yes.
ISAACS: Did you like her?

This flummoxed Seddon and he did not regain his composure. He could see that if he said he had liked her he would be asked why he had put her in a pauper's grave, whereas if he said he had not liked her he would tilt the case further against himself. Decidedly, this was a killer question. Seddon was eventually executed for the murder.

One masterful cross-examination was that in 1909 by Sir Edward Carson KC of the witness William Cadbury, director of the chocolate company (see Richard Du Cann, *The Art of the Advocate*, 1964, ch. 7). Between 1901 and 1908, Cadbury's chocolate obtained half their cocoa from islands off Angola which exploited forced slave labour. Cadburys knew about the slavery, and profited hugely from it for years but did not reveal it to the public. Instead, it traded on its reputation as a model employer, and the benevolent treatment of its workers at Bourneville in England. Meanwhile, people were snatched as slaves and forced to march up to a thousand miles to the plantations, and killed if they did not keep up. *The Evening Standard* published an article critical of Cadburys, and the firm sued saying it made them look like 'a bunch of canting hypocrites'. In a brilliant cross-examination lasting five hours, Carson dismantled the case of William Cadbury and the firm. The final exchange was a dramatic dénouement. After hours of quizzing about how much slave blood and suffering was involved in the production of the chocolate, and the complicity of Cadbury, there was this question:

CARSON: Have you formed any estimate of the number of slaves who lost their lives in preparing your cocoa from 1901 to 1908?

That is a bit like asking 'have you stopped beating your wife?' – a question which, answered either way, condemns the quizzed person. In answer to the question whether he had quantified the suffering on which he had sold chocolate, the director replied meekly:

CADBURY: No, no, no.

The jury found Cadburys had been libelled but awarded damages of one farthing.[8]

Sir Henry Curtis-Bennett KC (1879–1936) was famous for maintaining that in cross-questioning an advocate should never ask a question if he did not already know the answer. A modern case in point was recounted by Sir Oliver Popplewell (*Benchmark*, 2003, p 130). As a young barrister defending a man charged with careless driving, Mr Popplewell was

---

8   Provision of appropriate examples clearly demonstrates the effectiveness of carefully crafted cross-examination questions.

cross-examining a prosecution witness who had testified that the defendant had been speeding. The witness was repeatedly pressed to estimate the speed of the car but declined. Having satisfactorily established the witness's incompetence in car-speed estimation, Mr Popplewell did not sit down but asked one final fatal question: 'Why are you telling the court you cannot estimate the speed of my client's car?' The witness's response was calm and clear: 'Because I have never seen a car go as fast as that in all my life!'[9]

QUESTION 13

What general principles (if any) can be deduced from the existing appeal structure in England and Wales? Is any extension or limitation on existing rights of appeal desirable?

How to Answer this Question

You should include:

- ❖ changes in criminal appeals;
- ❖ recommendations from the Runciman Commission and the Auld Report;
- ❖ changes in civil appeals;
- ❖ the *Practice Direction on Civil Appeals* (2000).

Answer Structure

Introduction and overview of the Anglo-Welsh appeal structure → Highlight principles of current appeal structure → Consideration of perceived problems of the present system change → Arguments for/against possible changes

ANSWER

Several general principles emerge from a study of the current appeal structure, principles which relate to the evolved purposes of the appeal process. These purposes include:

(a) the opportunity for a litigant to have more than one occasion to put his case – an idea based upon the premise that people and processes are fallible;

(b) the opportunity to reconsider a problem in the light of new evidence; and

(c) the need for an appellate body to standardise the legal response to particular sorts of problem.

Research undertaken for the Royal Commission on Criminal Justice (1993) revealed that of 300 appeals in 1990, just over one-third were successful. Almost two-thirds of defendants appealed against conviction on the ground that the trial judge had made a critical

---

9   Once examples have been provided, it will then allow an opportunity to move on and evaluate how effective the process can be/is in ascertaining the truth, as specifically required by the question.

mistake and of these, 43 per cent succeeded in having their convictions quashed. In about 80 per cent of cases where convictions were quashed, there had been an error at the trial, usually by the judge.

In general, the Anglo-Welsh system of appeals avoids 'finality' after just one appeal hearing. There is for most cases (subject to the approval of the first appeal court or the next intended forum) more than one possible appeal hearing. An appeal from the civil jurisdiction of the magistrates' court, for example, could be taken to the Divisional Court of the Family Division and thence to the Court of Appeal Civil Division and finally, within the UK, to the Supreme Court. Additionally, both the Civil and Criminal Divisions of the Court of Appeal can order retrials where the interests of justice so require.[10]

The appeal structure puts great emphasis on the principle of extempore judicial wisdom.[11] In the USA, the appeal system relies more upon reserved, written judgments, and most appellate judges enjoy the services of 'law clerks' (accomplished graduates from law school, paid from public funds), who assist the judges with research work and discussion of complex and contentious points of law. The English system makes much use of unreserved judgments in the Court of Appeal, after listening to oral argument, again in contrast to the American preference for appellate judges considering long, written submissions in respect of the appeals. This principle of orality was reaffirmed by Sir John Donaldson MR (as he then was) in an article in 1982; he said that 'the conduct of appeals by way of oral hearing lies at the heart of the English tradition' ((1982) 132 NLJ 959).

Another principle clearly governing the operation of the appeal system is that of carefully controlled accessibility. Probably as a deterrent against what might be regarded as overuse of the system by all convicted defendants, there are several obstacles placed in front of anyone contemplating an appeal. Leave must be obtained in all appeals, for example, from the Crown Court to the Court of Appeal (Criminal Division), unless the matter is concerned only with a point of law. The Court of Appeal also has a power to order that time spent appealing will not count towards the sentence. Shortly after this policy was introduced in 1970, the number of applications for leave to appeal in such cases was reduced by about half.

Accessibility to the appeal courts is also restricted by the poor record of trial proceedings in magistrates' and county courts.[12] Additionally, appeals can be based upon fresh evidence, but the courts have sometimes taken a very narrow view of what is within this term. In criminal cases, the Court of Appeal has discretion whether to admit new evidence if it

....

10 Provision of an overview of the present appeal system demonstrates both knowledge and understanding of an important element of the ELS.
11 Consideration of 'principles' demonstrates that the question has been carefully analysed and its requirements recognised.
12 Highlighting perceived problems provides a helpful link between the discussion of 'general principles' and the requirement of considering the need for change to the system.

thinks it 'necessary or expedient in the interests of justice' (**Criminal Appeal Act 1968**). The court 'shall' admit the new evidence, that is, it *must*, where it: (a) affords a ground for appeal; (b) looks credible; (c) would have been admissible at the trial; and (d) the court is satisfied of a reasonable explanation as to why the evidence was not adduced at the trial.

Similar rules apply in respect of civil appeals. If the new evidence is something that could, with 'reasonable diligence', have been obtained for use in the trial, then it will not be permitted as the foundation of an appeal. In *Linton v Ministry of Defence* (1983), the House of Lords upheld this principle and denied a fresh trial to the appellant in circumstances where it was clear that his case would be very much stronger than in the original trial. This principle also applies to points taken by counsel; if they could have been put at trial, then they cannot form the basis of an appeal. In *Maynard* (1979), Roskill LJ said that if the rule were otherwise, it would enable counsel to keep a point up their sleeve at trial and then, if the case went against them, try to raise the point for the first time on appeal, thus having a second bite at the 'forensic cherry'.

If an appellant has not succeeded in the ordinary appeal process, he cannot get around the problem indirectly by taking an action for negligence against his lawyers (*Rondel v Worsley* (1969)). Neither may a convicted person re-open the trial by suing for defamation anyone who says he was rightly convicted (**Civil Evidence Act 1968**).

Access to the final appellate court, the Supreme Court, is very limited, since it will only hear cases with leave, and in criminal appeals, there must also be a certificate from the Court of Appeal that the case involves a point of law of general public importance.

Even when access to the appeal process has been granted to the appellant, a constellation of rules is set to prevent technical abuse of the system. Thus, the 'proviso' to **s 2** of the **Criminal Appeal Act 1968** allows the court to agree with the ground for the appeal, but to keep the conviction if no substantial miscarriage of justice has occurred.

SUGGESTED EXTENSIONS AND LIMITATIONS

CRIMINAL APPEALS

It was argued by Lord Devlin that it is wrong whenever judges, rather than juries, try to decide whether a defendant/appellant is guilty. There are still cases, however, where this happens. In cases involving new evidence, Viscount Dilhorne said (*Stafford v DPP* (1974)) that even if there was a chance that a jury might have come to a different view had it heard the new evidence, the conviction should not be quashed if the appeal court was satisfied that there was no reasonable doubt about the guilt of the accused.

An abandonment of this policy would bring appeal practice more in line with the theoretical constitution.

The **Criminal Appeal Act 1995** introduced significant changes to the law. **Section 1** amends the **Criminal Appeal Act 1968** so as to bring an appeal against conviction, an appeal against a verdict of not guilty by reason of insanity and an appeal against a finding of disability, on a question of law alone, in line with other appeals against conviction and sentence (that is, those involving questions of fact, or mixtures of law and fact). Now, all appeals against conviction and sentence must first have leave from the Court of Appeal, or a certificate of fitness for appeal from the trial judge, before the appeal can be taken. Before the new Act came into force, it was possible to appeal without the consent of the trial judge or the Court of Appeal on a point of law alone. In Parliament, the reason for this change was given as the need to 'provide a filter mechanism for appeals on a ground of law alone which are wholly without merit' (HC Official Report, *SCB (Criminal Appeal Bill)*, 1995, 21 March, col 6).

Section 2 changes the grounds for allowing an appeal under the **1968 Act**. Under the old law, the Court of Appeal was required to allow an appeal where:

(a)   the conviction, verdict or finding should have been set aside, on the ground that, under all the circumstances, it was unsafe or unsatisfactory; or

(b)   the judgment of the court of trial or the order of the court giving effect to the verdict or finding should be set aside, on the ground of a wrong decision of law; or

(c)   there was a material irregularity in the course of the trial.

In all three situations, the Court of Appeal was allowed to dismiss the appeal if it considered that no miscarriage of justice had actually occurred. The new law requires the Court of Appeal to allow an appeal against conviction under **s 1** of the **1968 Act**, an appeal against a verdict under **s 12** (insanity) or an appeal against a finding (disability) if it thinks that the conviction, verdict or finding is 'unsafe' (as opposed to the old law, which used the 'unsafe or unsatisfactory' formula).

During the Parliamentary passage of the Act, there was much heated debate about whether the new provisions were designed to narrow the grounds of appeal. That would amount to a tilt in favour of the state, in that it would make it harder for (wrongly) convicted people to appeal. Government ministers insisted that the effect of the new law was simply to restate or consolidate the practice of the Court of Appeal. One government spokesman said that:

> In dispensing with the word 'unsatisfactory', we agree with the Royal Commission on Criminal Justice that there is no real difference between 'unsafe' and 'unsatisfactory'; the Court of Appeal does not distinguish between the two. Retaining the word 'unsatisfactory' would imply that we thought there was a real difference and would only lead to confusion.

There were many attempts during the legislation's passage to insert the words 'or may be unsafe' after the word 'unsafe'. The Law Society, the Bar, Liberty and Justice called on the Government to make such a change. Also opposed to the use of the single word 'unsafe' was the eminent criminal law expert Professor JC Smith. He has argued cogently that there are many cases where a conviction has been seen as 'unsatisfactory' rather than 'unsafe', so that there is a need for both words. Sometimes, the Court of Appeal might be convinced that the defendant is guilty (so the conviction is 'safe'), but still wish to allow the appeal because fair play according to the rules must be seen to be done. Accepting improperly extracted confessions (violating **s 76** of the **Police and Criminal Evidence Act 1984**) simply because it might seem obvious that the confessor is guilty will promote undesirable interrogation practices, because police officers will think that even if they break the rules, any resulting confession will nevertheless be allowed as evidence.

Professor Smith has given an example (see (1995) 145 NLJ 534) of where there has been a serious breach of the rules of evidence: see *Algar* (1954). In that case, the former wife of the defendant testified against him regarding matters during the marriage. The Court of Appeal allowed his appeal against conviction, but Lord Goddard said: 'Do not think that we are doing this because we think that you are an innocent man. We do not. We think that you are a scoundrel.' The idea underpinning such remarks is that rules are rules, and the rules of evidence must be obeyed in order to ensure justice. Once you start to accept breaches of the rules as being justified by outcome (ends justifying means), then the whole law of evidence could begin to collapse.

The proposal to include 'or might be unsafe' was rejected for the reason probably best summarised by the former Lord Chief Justice, Lord Taylor, who argued in the Lords that there was no merit in including the words 'or may be unsafe', as the implication of such doubt is already inherent in the word 'unsafe'.

Section 4 provides a unified test for the receipt of fresh evidence in the Court of Appeal. Under the old law, the Court of Appeal had a discretion, under **s 23(1)(c)** of the **1968 Act**, to receive fresh evidence of any witness if it was thought necessary or expedient in the interests of justice. **Section 23(2)** added a duty to receive new evidence which was relevant, credible and admissible, and which could not reasonably have been adduced at the original trial. There was often much argument about whether new evidence should be received under the court's discretion or its duty. Gradually, the 'duty' principles came to be merged into the 'discretion' principles. The aim of the latest amendment is to reflect the current practice of the court. The general discretion under **s 23(1)** has been retained, but the 'duty' principle has been replaced with a set of criteria which the court must consider. These are:

(a) whether the evidence appears to the court to be capable of belief;

(b) whether it appears to the court that the evidence may afford any ground for allowing the appeal;

(c) whether the evidence would have been admissible at the trial on the issue under appeal; and

(d) whether there is a reasonable explanation for the failure to adduce the evidence at trial.

The **1995 Act** also legislated for the new Criminal Cases Review Commission (CCRC). The CCRC has taken over the Home Secretary's power to reinvestigate already unsuccessfully appealed cases, and refer back to Court of Appeal cases of suspected miscarriages of justice. The wide power to reinvestigate cases where there appears to be a 'real possibility' (**s 13**) of miscarriage has been generally greeted with approval, but it is a matter of regret in some quarters that those reinvestigating cases will not be CCRC investigators but, usually, police officers (**s 19**). As many allegations of injustice involve accusations against the police, there is a school of thought suggesting that a manifestly impartial, outside body should be responsible for the reinvestigation. In order to establish that there is a real possibility of an appeal succeeding regarding a conviction, there has to be:

❖ an argument or evidence which has not been raised during the trial or at appeal; or
❖ exceptional circumstances.

In order to establish that there is a real possibility of an appeal succeeding against a sentence, there has to be:

❖ a legal argument or information about the individual, or the offence, which was not raised in court during the trial or at appeal.

Other than in exceptional circumstances, the Commission can only:

> . . . consider cases in which an appeal through the ordinary judicial appeal process has failed, and once a decision is taken to refer a case to the relevant court of appeal, the Commission has no other involvement.
> Criminal Cases Review Commission, *Annual Report*, 2000

The Commission cannot overturn a conviction or change a sentence. In those cases where the criteria above are met, the Commission can refer a case to the Court of Appeal (in the case of Crown Court convictions) or the Crown Court (in the case of magistrates' court convictions). Only about 5 per cent of new cases received by the Commission since 1997 have been against summary convictions.

Since its inception, the CCRC has had some notable, high profile 'successes', in the sense that important cases it has referred have resulted in the Court of Appeal allowing appeals.

In 1997, for example, in one of its first referrals, the Commission referred the case of Derek Bentley to the Court of Appeal. Mr Bentley, although hanged for murder in 1953, eventually had his conviction quashed in August 1998 by the Court of Appeal.

The Auld Report (2001) recommended some changes in this area. It argued (para 18) that there should be the same tests for appeal against conviction and sentence at all levels of appeal, and suggested there should be a single line of appeal from the magistrates' courts and above to the Court of Appeal in all criminal matters. That would involve the abolition of the appeal from the magistrates' courts to the Crown Courts by way of rehearing, and its replacement with an appeal to a single judge in the Crown Court. It would also involve the abolition of the appeal from the magistrates' courts and the Crown Court to the High Court by way of 'case stated', or a claim for judicial review, and their replacement by an appeal to the Court of Appeal. The Report also suggested (para 19) that there should be provision for appeal by the defence or the prosecution against a special verdict of a jury which is 'perverse'. Other suggestions included the idea that procedures in the Court of Appeal should be improved to enable it to deal more efficiently with appeals touching on matters of general public importance or of great complexity. **Part 9** of the **2003 Criminal Justice Act** institutes an interlocutory prosecution right of appeal with leave, against rulings that would terminate a trial.

CIVIL APPEALS

The civil work of the Court of Appeal continues to increase. Figures available in 1995 show that 1,338 appeals were set down in 1989; by 2007, this had risen to 3,006. The House of Lords, however, saw a fall in the number of appeals, from 72 to 62, over the same period. There is less clamour for the machinery and rules here to be revised. In part, this follows from the fact that civil appeals are different in nature from criminal appeals. This difference was highlighted by the Court of Appeal in quashing the convictions of the Birmingham Six (*McIlkenny and Others* (1991)). It said that in a civil appeal, there is a rehearing of the whole case and the appeal court is concerned with fact as well as law, so that it may take a different view of the facts from the court below. In a criminal case, on the other hand, primacy is enjoyed by the jury, so that the appellate court is really just a 'court of review'. It is thus easier for the Court of Appeal (Civil Division) to reverse the decision of a civil trial court than for the criminal courts to do the same.

The Report of the Review of the Court of Appeal (Civil Division), undertaken by Sir Jeffrey Bowman (1997), contains important recommendations for reducing the number of cases coming to the Court of Appeal and for improving practice and procedure in the Civil Appeals Office and in the Court of Appeal itself.

Based on averages, the time between setting down and final disposal of 70 per cent of appeals in 1996 had increased to 14 months. The corollary is that 30 per cent of appeals took over 14 months and at the end of 1996, some appeals had been outstanding for over five years. The Review's major recommendations include:

(a) that certain appeals which now reach the Court of Appeal (Civil Division) should be heard at a lower level – the largest category of such cases being appeals against decisions in fast-track cases;

(b) it should still be possible for appeals which would normally be heard in a lower court to reach the Court of Appeal (Civil Division) in certain circumstances. In particular, an appeal could be considered if it raises an important point of principle or practice, or one which, for some other special reason, should be considered by the Court of Appeal (Civil Division);

(c)   the requirement for leave to appeal should be extended to all cases coming to the Court of Appeal (Civil Division), except for adoption cases and child abduction cases;

(d)   an increasing role for appropriate judicial case management;

(e)   more focused procedures – cases should be better prepared, at a much earlier stage in the process, and realistic timetables should be set, which must be strictly observed;

(f)   the Court of Appeal (Civil Division) should impose appropriate time-limits on oral argument – on appeal, the balance of judicial time should lean more towards reading and less towards sitting in court;

(g)   the greater use of IT to support the other recommendations of the review;

(h)   information for litigants in person about the appeal process and what it can deliver must be available at an early stage. The information must be easily understandable and delivered in a range of different ways.

Some of the Report's more controversial recommendations include the following:

(a)   there should be a power to appoint lawyers of outstanding distinction as academics or practitioners to sit as members of the Court of Appeal on occasions;

(b)   there should be a discretion to list cases before a single member of the Court of Appeal;

(c)   where specialist knowledge of law, procedure or subject matter is an advantage, the constitution of the Court of Appeal (Civil Division) should usually include one or two members with the appropriate specialist knowledge, but the constitution should not usually consist solely of specialist members.

One problem still remaining, however, with the civil appeal process is whether or not the Court of Appeal should 'correct' the discretionary decision of a trial court which it believes has made an error of judgment. As this matter is unsettled, advice to prospective appellants can be very difficult to give. The traditional rule, expressed by the Court of Appeal in *Culver v Beard* (1937), is that the appeal court should not interfere with a discretionary decision, unless it can be shown to be 'wrong in principle'. A decision can, therefore, be reversed if it has been based on a mistake of law or of fact or took into account legally irrelevant matters. This approach has been affirmed by the Court of Appeal in *Eagil Trust Co Ltd* (1985), where it was said that lawyers should not use the discretionary decision of a High Court judge as a mere 'conduit pipe' to the Court of Appeal. This is quite clear, but there are other decisions of the Court of Appeal (for example, *D v M* (1982)) which interpret its role as being to arrive at the correct, proper, just decision, even if this means contradicting the discretion of the trial judge – not to do so would be to perpetuate injustice. Legislation, perhaps, should settle this matter.

Finally, it is important to note evidence given by Adrian Zuckerman to the Woolf inquiry in 1995. Sometimes, it was pointed out, if a claim or defence is amended, the fate of the amendment may take two appeal hearings to decide. In one case, the issue of whether a writ had been properly served on the opposing side had to be considered by a Master and, on appeal, by a judge, and then by the Court of Appeal. The process is so protracted that the pre-trial dispute can take on a life of its own.

An attempt was made to streamline and rationalise the civil appeals system in the wake of the new Civil Procedure Rules. The contents of a Practice Direction from Lord Woolf (*Court of Appeal (Civil Division): Leave to Appeal and Skeleton Arguments*, November 1998) have now been digested in a consolidating Practice Direction about civil appeals (*Practice Direction for the Court of Appeal (Civil Division)*, 16 May 2000). The Direction states (para 2.1.3) that:

> The experience of the Court of Appeal is that many appeals and applications for permission to appeal are made which are quite hopeless. They demonstrate basic misconceptions as to the purpose of the civil appeal system and the different roles played by appellate courts and courts below. The court below has a crucial role in determining applications for permission to appeal. This guidance indicates how applicants, and courts, should approach the matter.

In answer to the following question 'From which court should permission to appeal be sought?', the Direction articulates the following two key propositions. First (para 2.2.1), it notes that:

> The court which has just reached a decision is often in the best position to judge whether there should be an appeal. It should not leave the decision to the Court of Appeal. Courts below can help to minimise the delay and expense which an appeal involves. Where the parties are present for delivery of the judgment, it should be routine for the judge below to ask whether either party wants permission to appeal and to deal with the matter then and there. However, if the court below is in doubt whether an appeal would have a realistic prospect of success or involves a point of general principle, the safe course is to refuse permission to appeal. It is always open to the Court of Appeal to grant it.

The Direction then states (para 2.2.2) that:

> The advantages which flow from permission being considered by the court of first instance are lost if the application cannot be listed before the judge who made the decision which is the subject of the application.

It states that where it is not possible for the application for permission to be listed before the same judge, or where undue delay would be caused by so listing it, the Court of Appeal will be sympathetic to applicants who claim that it was impracticable for them to make their application to the court below, and will not require such an application to be made. The new directions will clearly assist in the introduction of a more nationally uniform response to appeals and to greater expedition in their processing, factors which will, arguably, improve the experience of all those using the system.

QUESTION 14

'Government cuts are not fair.' Discuss how the legal system is being affected by the economic recession.

How to Answer this Question

- ❖ Evidence of the recession on the legal system (*R v SH* [2010] EWCA Crim 193, para 5).
- ❖ Judge Paul Collins' comments.
- ❖ Cutbacks in family justice system.
- ❖ Tribunal Service.
- ❖ Crown Prosecution Service.
- ❖ Judges threaten industrial action.
- ❖ What is meant by 'fair'.
- ❖ Conclusion.

Answer Structure

It is clear that the legal system is under an economic strain. The state of the economy has even been commented upon judicially. A judge in a Crown Court trial concerning a charge of 'causing racially aggravated fear or provocation of violence' told the court we do not have the luxury of trying such cases because 'This country is next to broke'.

That was in 2010 (*R v SH* [2010] EWCA Crim 193, para 5),[13] and since then things have deteriorated. Recent governmental plans will see the Ministry of Justice's budget cut by 23 per cent. The staffing of courts is already desperately inadequate but 14,250 of these frantically demanding jobs will go leaving the residual workforce to toil in an awful, Sisyphean challenge.

....

13 The use of appropriate, supporting legal authority is always valuable, as it can add weight to any argument and/or assist with explanation

Judge Paul Collins, London's most senior county court judge, said in 2007 that low pay and high turnover among staff meant that serious errors were commonplace and routinely led to incorrect judgments in court. He said that with further cuts looming 'we run the risk of bringing about a real collapse in the service we're able to give to the people using the courts'.

The law is everybody's law but historic and prospective legal aid cuts have now decitizenised huge swathes of the population. Ministers now plan to cut the legal aid bill by £600 million a year, and family cases will bear the brunt, with 246,000 cases a year taken out of public funding.

In 2011, Stephen Cobb, QC, chairman of the 2,500-strong Family Law Bar Association, said that the proposals going through Parliament in the Legal Aid, Sentencing and Punishment of Offenders bill would have a 'serious and damaging effect'. Some 54,000 fewer people would be represented in the family courts a year, affecting some 68,000 children at the centre of family breakdowns, he said (Frances Gibb, *The Times*, 29 September 2011).

In 2010, the Tribunal Service reported an increase of 56 per cent in the number of claims in the year up to March against employers in England, Scotland and Wales. This is the highest ever: the total is 236,000, up from 151,000.

In 2012, it was reported that errors by Crown prosecutors are leading to about 63,000 criminal cases a year across England and Wales being wrongly dropped or unjustifiably brought to trial. It is estimated that the mistakes are being made in 7 per cent of the 900,000 Crown Court cases each year. The court performance of Crown Prosecution Service advocates has also shown an overall decline over two years. In the bulk of cases, where defendants plead not guilty, CPS advocates are often ill-prepared and fail to challenge prejudicial evidence (see Frances Gibb, *The Times*, 30 March, 2012, and Her Majesty's Crown Prosecution Service Inspectorate 2012).

In 2012, some 400 judges took an unprecedented first step towards suing the Government over changes to their pensions that effectively amounts to a pay cut (Frances Gibb, *The Times*, 9 March, 2012).

The judges sent a letter to the Lord Chancellor, Kenneth Clarke, warning that if he proceeds with the controversial plans, they will challenge him in the courts.

The action by the judges, who instructed the international law firm Clifford Chance to send the 'letter before action', gave ministers 14 days to respond before legal proceedings were launched but the Government did respond in time. A Ministry of Justice spokesman added: 'These changes will see judges contribute towards their own pension for the first time, creating up to £7 million in savings for taxpayers.'

In 2011, the former Lord Chief Justice Lord Woolf warned that the Government must amend its proposals to overhaul the £2.1 billion legal aid system so as to protect access to justice. Lord Woolf said that the proposals risk, some of which have already been implemented, breach fundamental principles of the rule of law because people will be denied access to the courts.[14]

Can the Government's cuts be fair? There are 60 million people in the UK and most did not do anything wrong in places like Lehman Brothers to cause the near collapse of western capitalism. So, according to one principle, it is not fair that the majority will now have to suffer painful cuts in their standard of living and reduced access to legal justice.

Unfairness can be a visceral and hard-wired feeling. Long before they hear or read anything about theories of justice, young children can say 'it's not fair' if they are the victims of inequity.

Defining what is 'fair', though, in a serious and rational way is as impossible as defining what is the best political party or the best music. Different people have different ideas about what is fair.

So, saying that the cuts to the justice system are unfair begs the question 'according to what definition of fairness?' The debate then fragments into a hundred shards of opinion.

What can be shown, however, is that if the cuts are implemented, they will prevent the proper functioning of the legal system.

It is only after a society secures law and due process that it can move on to debate what is economically fair. In the phrase of the pre-eminent 20th-century jurist Herbert Hart, we should be primarily concerned with 'social arrangements for continued existence, not with those of a suicide club'.

Law is the foundation of civilised society. The legal system has greater first-order importance than education and health in one key respect: unless you have guaranteed order and peaceful ways of settling disputes and punishing rule-breakers, there is little point in investing in classrooms and hospital wards.

The Chancellor George Osborne has said that in adjusting to the world of new hardships, the heavy burdens should fall on the broadest shoulders. If the Government is serious

---

14 Discussion not only highlights a number of cuts resulting from financial cutbacks but, importantly, also assesses the impact of such cuts on the legal system.

about that it should consider making the multi-billion pound businesses worldwide which use the English courts as their favoured litigation forum pay much more than they do for that privilege.

Poets and philosophers might show how it is unfair that the financial acts of a reckless few have impoverished the lives of the blameless many. More urgent is the stark truth that without clemency, the axe set to fall on justice will break the legal system.

Judicial Reasoning

INTRODUCTION

This chapter examines the way in which judges reach decisions in particular cases. Central to the common law is the doctrine of judicial precedent. This means that, depending on the level of the court in the hierarchy, previous 'decisions' of one court are supposed to be binding on later courts. The implication of the traditional approach to precedent is that it is a strictly applied, highly rational and almost scientific process. However, as will be demonstrated, the mechanisms deployed by judges in deciding cases allow them a large degree of discretion in reaching decisions. This introduction of the possibility of discretion necessarily opens the question of the accountability of the judges, which will be addressed directly in the following chapter.

Whilst the common law is, by definition, judge made, the extent to which judges can influence the operation of statute law through interpreting it in particular ways should not be underestimated.

It is obvious, but no less important for that, that the outcome of cases to a large extent depends upon what evidence the parties to the action can put before the court. That in turn is dependent upon the rules of evidence which apply in the courts.

Checklist ✔

You should be familiar with:

- the nature of legal reasoning, as opposed to reasoning in general;
- the hierarchy of the courts;
- the doctrine of binding precedent;
- how judges avoid the strict operation of precedent;
- the rules of, and presumptions relating to, statutory interpretation;
- the rules of evidence.

QUESTION 15

Consider how the doctrine of binding precedent operates in the English courts, having particular regard to its advantages and disadvantages.

How to Answer this Question

This is a very straightforward, traditional question. It requires the following:

❖ define what binding precedent is in such a way as to explain how it is supposed to operate, with appropriate reference to *ratio decidendi* and *obiter dictum/dicta*;

❖ emphasise the authoritative hierarchy of the court structure in the UK legal system, although mention should be made of the Court of Justice of the European Union (CJEU) and the European Court of Human Rights (ECtHR);

❖ highlight the fact that the Supreme Court has now replaced the House of Lords as the highest court in the UK;

❖ consider the relationship between the various courts within the hierarchy, and also the extent to which they are governed by their own previous decisions;

❖ establish the difference in status between decisions of the European Court of Justice and the European Court of Human Rights;

❖ consider the difference between the criminal and civil law at the level of the Court of Appeal;

❖ refer to the process of distinguishing cases on the basis of their facts;

❖ consider advantages and disadvantages – it is essential to note that some of the supposed advantages are, in fact, problematic, not to say contradictory.

Answer Structure

| Introduction to the concept of precedent, including Latin terminology | → | Explanation of the relevance of court hierarchy and law reports | → | Consideration of the impact of EU law and of the **ECHR/HRA**, plus discussion on 'avoiding' binding precedent | → | Evaluation of advantages and disadvantages |

ANSWER

The doctrine of binding precedent, or *stare decisis*, lies at the heart of the English legal system. In essence, the doctrine refers to the fact that within the hierarchical structure of the English courts, a decision of a higher court will be binding on a court below.[1]

---

1   An introduction allows the scene to be set and the basics of the topic to be outlined.

Since September 2009 the Supreme Court[2] has replaced the House of Lords so the Supreme Court now stands at the summit of the English court structure and its decisions are binding on all courts below it in the hierarchy (all future references to the Supreme Court will include the previous court where appropriate). It always has to be borne in mind, as regards European Union (EU) law, that the CJEU is superior to the Supreme Court, and its decisions are binding on all UK courts. Also, as a consequence of the **Human Rights Act (HRA) 1998**, the decisions of the ECtHR[3] are now part of the jurisprudence of the UK courts. This latter factor means that it is possible that the superior courts will find it necessary to alter previous precedents where they have been generated without reference to the **European Convention on Human Rights (ECHR)**. Those issues apart, as regards its own previous decisions, up until 1966, the Supreme Court, regarded itself as bound by its previous decisions. In the *Practice Statement (Judicial Precedent)* of that year, however, Lord Gardiner indicated that the Supreme Court would in future regard itself as free to depart from its previous decisions[4] where it appeared right so to do. It should be noted that, given the potentially destabilising effect on existing legal practice based on previous decisions of the Supreme Court, this is not a discretion that the Supreme Court exercises lightly. However, there have been a number of cases in which it has elected to exercise this discretion (for example, *Miliangos v George Frank (Textiles) Ltd* (1976), in which it decided that damages in English court cases did not have to be awarded in sterling).

The next court in the hierarchical structure is the Court of Appeal, but in order to consider its place within the doctrine of binding precedent, it is necessary to consider its civil and criminal jurisdiction separately.

In a civil case, the situation is that, as an inferior court, the Court of Appeal is generally bound by previous decisions of the Supreme Court. Although the Court of Appeal, notably under the aegis of Lord Denning, attempted on a number of occasions to escape from what it saw as the constraints of *stare decisis*, the Supreme Court repeatedly reasserted the binding nature of its decisions on the Court of Appeal in such cases as *Broome v Cassell* (1972) and *Miliangos v George Frank (Textiles) Ltd* (1976).

The Court of Appeal is generally also bound by its own previous decisions. As explained, however, by Lord Greene MR in *Young v Bristol Aeroplane Co Ltd* (1944), there are a limited number of exceptions to this general rule. These exceptions arise where:

....

2   The hierarchy of the courts is a basic element of the system of binding precedent and consequently has to be discussed in detail.

3   The impact of the **HRA**, in regard to decisions of the **ECHR**, and of the UKs membership of the EU, have both had an impact of the doctrine of precedent and shouldn't therefore be ignored.

4   Mention of the various means of departing from – or avoiding – seemingly binding precedent should not be ignored as they allow the courts discretion.

(a)   there is a conflict between two previous decisions of the Court of Appeal, in which case, the later court must decide which decision to follow and, as a corollary, which to overrule;

(b)   a previous decision of the Court of Appeal has been overruled, either expressly or impliedly, by the Supreme Court, in which case, the Court of Appeal is required to follow the decision of the Supreme Court;

(c)   one of its previous decisions has been given *per incuriam* or, in other words, that previous decision was taken in ignorance of some authority that would have led to a different conclusion, in which case, the later court can ignore the previous decision in question.

In addition to the above, there is also the possibility that as a consequence of **s 3** of the **European Communities Act 1972**, the Court of Appeal can ignore a previous decision of its own which is inconsistent with EC law or with a later decision of the ECJ. In *Price v Leeds City* (2006) the Supreme Court distinguished between decisions of the European Court of Justice and those of the European Court of Human Rights: the former are binding, while the latter are not. As Lord Bingham put it:

> The mandatory duty imposed on domestic courts by **s 2** of the **1998 Act** is to take into account any judgment of the Strasbourg Court and any opinion of the Commission. Thus they are not strictly required to follow Strasbourg rulings, as they are bound by **s 3(1)** of the **European Communities Act 1972** and as they are bound by the rulings of superior courts in the domestic curial hierarchy.

As a consequence the Supreme Court decided that the normal rules of precedent should apply, and lower courts should follow the Supreme Court, even when their decisions have been overturned by the ECtHR. This does not apply, however, where the previous authority had been set without reference to the **Human Rights Act 1998**.

Once again, there was an attempt by the Court of Appeal under Lord Denning to widen these exceptions in *Gallie v Lee* (1971), but again, the Supreme Court reaffirmed the limited nature of these exceptions and reasserted the strict operation of the doctrine of *stare decisis*.

Although, on the basis of *Spencer* (1987), it would appear that there is no difference in principle between the operation of the doctrine of *stare decisis* between the criminal and civil divisions of the Court of Appeal, it is generally accepted that in practice, precedent is not followed as strictly in the former as it is in the latter. Courts in the criminal division are not bound to follow their own previous decisions which they subsequently consider to have been based on either a misunderstanding or a misapplication of the law. The reason for this increased measure of apparent laxity is the fact that the criminal courts deal with matters involving individual liberty and therefore require a wider ambit of discretion to prevent injustice.

Further down the hierarchy, the Divisional Court is bound by the doctrine of *stare decisis* in the normal way and must follow decisions of the Supreme Court and of the Court of Appeal. It is also normally bound by its own previous decisions, although in civil cases, it may avail itself of the exceptions open to the Court of Appeal (in *Young v Bristol Aeroplane Co Ltd* (1944)), and in criminal appeal cases, the Queen's Bench Divisional Court may refuse to follow its own earlier decisions where it feels the earlier decision to have been wrongly made.

As regards the High Court, decisions by individual High Court judges are binding on courts inferior in the hierarchy. Such decisions are not binding on other High Court judges, although they are of strong persuasive authority and tend to be followed in practice. Although subject to binding precedent from superior courts, Crown Courts cannot create precedent and their decisions can never amount to more than persuasive authority. The decisions of county courts and magistrates' courts are never binding.

The operation of the doctrine of binding precedent is, of course, dependent on the existence of an extensive reporting service to provide access to judicial decisions. However, it should not be thought that the doctrine is as hard and fast as it originally appears. The technique of 'distinguishing' cases on their facts provides judges with scope for declining to follow precedents by which they would otherwise be bound. The legal decision in any case is an abstraction from the immediate facts of the case. If a judge decides, for some reason, that the facts in the case before him are so different from those of a case setting a precedent, he is at liberty to ignore the precedent and treat the case in question as not being covered by it. He can then decide the case as he thinks fit, without being bound by the otherwise binding precedent.

Scope for further uncertainty is introduced by the necessary distinction between *ratio decidendi* and *obiter dicta*.[5] The only part that is binding in any judgment previously decided is the *ratio* of the case: the actual legal reason for the decision. Anything else in the judgment is by the way, or *obiter*. Difficulty arises from the fact that judges do not label their judgments in this way. They do not actually nominate the *ratio* of the case. Additionally, their judgments may be of great length, or there may be as many as five judges delivering individual judgments on the case, and there is no requirement that all the judgments should agree on the principle of law governing the decision in the case. In any event, it is later judges who, in effect, determine what the particular *ratio* of any case was. The problem in relation to binding precedent is that it is open to later judges to avoid precedents by declaring them to be no more than *obiter* statements.

....

5   Both the *ratio* (binding element) and what is said *obiter* ('by the way') are recorded and are often difficult to differentiate, as they are not highlighted in a way which distinguishes them.

There are numerous *advantages*[6] to the doctrine of *stare decisis*. Amongst these are the following:

(a) it saves the time of the judiciary, lawyers and their clients, since cases do not have to be re-argued – this also has the benefit of saving the money of potential litigants;

(b) it provides a measure of certainty to law – thus, lawyers and their clients are able to predict what the outcome of a particular legal question is likely to be in the light of previous judicial decisions;

(c) it provides for a measure of formal justice, to the extent that like cases are decided on a like basis;

(d) it provides an opportunity for judges to develop the common law in particular areas without waiting for Parliament to enact legislation.

There are, however, corresponding *disadvantages* in the doctrine. Amongst these are the following:

(a) the degree of certainty provided by the doctrine is undermined by the absolute number of cases that have been reported and can therefore be cited as authorities – this uncertainty is compounded by the ability of the judiciary to select which authority to follow, through use of the mechanism of distinguishing cases on their facts;

(b) law may become ossified on the basis of an unjust precedent, with the consequence that previous injustices are perpetuated – an example of this is the long delay in the recognition of the possibility of rape within marriage, which has only recently been recognised;

(c) in developing law, it might be claimed that the judiciary is, in fact, overstepping its constitutional role by making law rather than simply deciding its application.

Common Pitfalls

It is simply not acceptable not to be aware of the Supreme Court, nor should it be referred to as additional to the House of Lords.

It is a also important to explain in clear terms the meaning and difference between the *ratio decidendi* of a judgment and *obiter dicta* within that judgment.

----

6   In order to answer the specific question set, both the advantages and disadvantages of the system of precedent must be discussed. Confusingly, the advantages and disadvantages are sometimes seen as overlapping!

Aim Higher ★

❖ Although the Supreme Court merely replaces the House of Lords and is not the same as other Supreme Courts in jurisdictions with written constitutions, it is valuable to consider the potential for future developments in the that area, especially given the increased powers of the courts under the **Human Rights Act**.

❖ It is important to be able to cite some of the decisions made by the Supreme Court since it started in 2009.

❖ A good explanation of how 'distinguishing' works is likely to be well rewarded.

QUESTION 16

How can the common law progress if judges are bound by precedent?

How to Answer this Question

A question of this type requires the following approach:

❖ consider what is meant by the common law;

❖ explain what is involved in the declaratory view of the role of the judiciary;

❖ analyse the operation of the system of *stare decisis* as it is supposed to operate;

❖ highlight some of the loopholes in the traditional version of *stare decisis*, for example, *Curry v DPP* (1994);

❖ provide some examples where the judges have continued to create new law;

❖ consider the constitutional role of the judiciary in the UK, and whether it should or should not be allowed to go on making new law.

Answer Structure

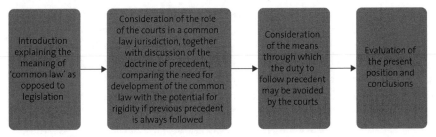

| Introduction explaining the meaning of 'common law' as opposed to legislation | → | Consideration of the role of the courts in a common law jurisdiction, together with discussion of the doctrine of precedent, comparing the need for development of the common law with the potential for rigidity if previous precedent is always followed | → | Consideration of the means through which the duty to follow precedent may be avoided by the courts | → | Evaluation of the present position and conclusions |

ANSWER

This question requires a consideration of the scope of judges to avoid the consequences of *stare decisis* in order to reach their own subjective decisions, and the dangers inherent in so doing. In answering the question, it is necessary to consider the place and function of the judiciary within the constitution of the UK and to consider its role in the creation and development of the common law.

Within the constitutional division of powers in the UK, it is the function of the legislature to make law and it is merely the function of the courts to apply that law. The declaratory view of the function of the English judiciary accepts this constitutional division of power and portrays it as not making law, but merely deciding cases in accordance with existing legal rules. The doctrine of binding precedent operates in such a way that judges, in deciding particular cases, are not merely referred to earlier decisions for guidance, but are actually bound to apply the rules of law contained in those decisions. The operation of this principle depends on the established hierarchy of the court structure: all courts standing in a definite relationship of superiority/inferiority to every other court. Usually, a court is bound by decisions of a court of equal standing, or of higher authority than itself in the court structure. Allowing for the fact that the doctrine of *stare decisis* is supposed to have binding force within this hierarchical framework, two questions still arise.

First, it is axiomatic that legal rules cannot be subject to infinite regression; every rule of the common law must have had an origin. If one rejects as untenable the proposition of natural law – that it is possible for law to exist as an entity outside of, and distinct from, social practice – then it follows that if a particular law was not created by statute, it must have been created by a judge; even if this creative activity is no more than recognising the legitimacy, or otherwise, of the practice in question. As a matter of course, it follows that where there is no established precedent, the doctrine of *stare decisis* breaks down and the courts are faced with the alternatives of either refusing to decide a case, or stating what the law should be. Even in modern times, courts are still required on occasions to consider situations for the very first time without access to precedent. These cases, described as cases of first impression, inevitably involve judges in the establishment of new law.

Second, the question arises as to how the law is to develop and change to cater for changed circumstances if cases are always to be decided according to ageless precedent. In practice, flexibility is achieved through the possibility of previous decisions being either overruled or distinguished, or the possibility of a later court extending or modifying the effective ambit of a precedent. At this stage, it must be emphasised that, strictly speaking, it is wrong to speak of a decision being binding, just as it is technically incorrect to refer to a decision being overruled. It is not the actual decision in a case that sets the precedent, but the rule of law on which that decision is founded. This rule, which is an abstraction from the facts of the case, is known as the *ratio decidendi* of the case. Thus, the *ratio decidendi* of a case may be understood as the statement of the law applied in deciding the legal problem raised by the concrete facts of the case. Moreover, not every statement of law in a judgment is binding; only those which are based on the particular facts of the case, as found and upon which the decision was based, are binding. Any other statement of law is, strictly speaking, superfluous and any such statement is termed *obiter dictum*, that is, said by the way. It is significant that although *obiter dicta* do not form part of the binding precedent of the case in which they occur, and therefore do not have to be followed by judges deciding later similar cases, they do amount to persuasive authority and can be taken into consideration in later cases if the judge in the later case considers it appropriate to do so. This apparently small measure of discretion, in relationship to whether later judges are minded to accept the validity of *obiter* statements in precedent cases, opens up the possibility that judges in later cases have a much wider degree of discretion than is originally apparent in the traditional view of *stare decisis*, when it is realised that it is the judges in the later cases who actually determine the *ratio decidendi* of previous cases. In delivering judgments in cases, judges do not separate and highlight the *ratio decidendi* from the rest of their judgment, and this can lead to a lack of certainty in determining the *ratio decidendi*. This uncertainty is compounded by the fact that reports of decisions in cases may run to considerable length and where there are a number of separate judgments, although the judges involved may agree on the decision of a case, they may not agree on the legal basis of the decision reached. This difficulty is further compounded where there are a number of dissenting judgments. In the final analysis, it is for the judge deciding the case in which a precedent has been cited to determine the *ratio* of the authority and thus to determine whether he is bound by the precedent or not. This factor provides the courts with a considerable degree of discretion in electing whether to be bound or not by a particular authority.

It is somewhat anomalous that within the system of *stare decisis*, precedents gain increased authority with the passage of time. As a consequence, courts tend to be reluctant to overrule long-standing authorities, even though they may no longer accurately reflect contemporary practices or morals. Allied to the wish to maintain a high degree of certainty in the law, the main reason for judicial reluctance to overrule old decisions would appear to be the fact that overruling operates retrospectively. Overruling a precedent might therefore have the consequence of disturbing important financial arrangements previously settled in line with what were thought to be settled rules of law. It might also in certain circumstances lead to the imposition of criminal liability on previously lawful behaviour. It has to be emphasised, however, that the courts will not shrink from overruling authorities where they see them as no longer representing an appropriate statement of law. The legal recognition of the possibility of rape within marriage is simply one example of this process (see *R* (1991)).

In comparison to the mechanism of overruling, which is rarely used, the main device for avoiding binding precedents is that of distinguishing. As has been previously stated, the *ratio decidendi* of any case is an abstraction from, and is based upon, the material facts of the case. This opens up the possibility that a court may regard the facts of the case before it as significantly different from the facts of a cited precedent and thus not binding. The cases have been distinguished on their facts and the court is at liberty to ignore the precedent in the prior case.

Judges use the device of distinguishing where, for some reason, they are unwilling to follow a particular precedent. The law reports provide many examples of strained distinctions, where a court has quite evidently not wanted to follow an authority that it would otherwise have been bound by. An example is *Curry v DPP* (1994), in which the Court of Appeal attempted to remove the previous presumption that children between the ages of 10 and 14 charged with a criminal offence do not know that their actions are seriously wrong and the requirement that the prosecution provide evidence to rebut the presumption. Mann LJ justified reversing the presumption by stating that although it had often been assumed to be the law, it had never actually been specifically considered by earlier courts. On such reasoning, he felt justified in departing from previous decisions of the Court of Appeal which otherwise would have bound him. The House of Lords, as it then was, subsequently restored the original presumption. Although their Lordships recognised the problem, they thought it was a matter more for Parliamentary action than judicial intervention.

A further way in which judges have a creative impact on the law is in the way in which they adapt and extend precedent in instant cases. Judicial reasoning tends to be carried out on the basis of analogy, and judges have a large degree of discretion in selecting what are to be considered as analogous cases. They also have a tendency continuously to extend existing precedents to fit new situations, as the historical evolution of the tort of negligence will show.[7]

The **Human Rights Act 1998**, which incorporated the **European Convention on Human Rights** into United Kingdom law, has had profound implications for the operation of the English legal system. For example **s 2** of the Act requires courts to take into account any previous decision of the European Court of Human Rights. This provision impacts on the operation of the doctrine of precedent within the English legal system, as it effectively sanctions the overruling of any previous English authority that was in conflict with a decision of the ECtHR. In addition, **s 3** requires all legislation to be read, so far as possible, to give effect to the rights provided under the Convention. This power has the potential to permit the courts to overrule previous precedents that were made without reference to the **ECHR** (see *Mendoza v Ghaidan* (2003)). Moreover, **s 3** extends this power to previously accepted interpretations of statutes, which were made, by necessity, without recourse to the Convention (*R v A* (2001) is a case in point).

> ## Common Pitfalls
> It is common either to underestimate, but more likely to overestimate, the extent to which judges can manipulate the rules of precedent to develop law.

---

7   The discussion set out above provides clear evidence of both knowledge and understanding of the doctrine of precedent, together with its application and effects. Such consideration also demonstrates skills such as analysis and evaluation.

QUESTION 17

To what extent and why has there been a shift away from the traditional judicial approach to statutory interpretation?

How to Answer this Question

This question recognises the change that has taken place in the way judges interpret, or perhaps more correctly, justify their interpretations of, statutes. Students must know the traditional rules of statutory interpretation, but they must also show that they are fully aware that there has been a shift from the literal to the purposive approach to statutory interpretation. They are not all compatible, nor do they form a clear hierarchy. Judges therefore have a measure of freedom to select which ones they wish to follow. Answers should:

- ❖ address the point that interpretation is creative by its very nature;
- ❖ note that statutes may partake of the general uncertainty inherent in language;
- ❖ set out the three rules of statutory interpretation and highlight the use of each with reference to cases;
- ❖ refer to the cases which indicate a shift towards the purposive approach to statutory interpretation;
- ❖ refer to the **Human Rights Act (HRA) 1998**, citing cases in support of the analysis.

Answer Structure

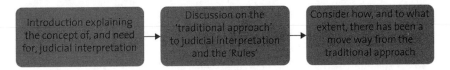

Introduction explaining the concept of, and need for, judicial interpretation → Discussion on the 'traditional approach' to judicial interpretation and the 'Rules' → Consider how, and to what extent, there has been a move way from the traditional approach

ANSWER

According to the traditional theory of the division of powers, the role of the judiciary is simply to apply the law that Parliament has created. This view is, however, simplistic in so far as it denies, or at least ignores, the extent to which the judiciary has a measure of discretion and creative power in the manner in which it interprets the legislation that comes before it.[8]

Contrary to common-sense views, communication is not a passive, receptive process. Language necessarily involves the listener in a process of active interpretation, in order to determine the content and meaning of what is actually being communicated to him. Legislation can be seen as a form of communication. It represents and passes on to the judiciary and society at large what Parliament has determined should be the law governing a particular situation. To that extent, legislation shares the general problem of uncertainty inherent in any mode of communication. The conflicting aims of legislation, however, give rise to particular problems of interpretation; these conflicting aims are the need to be clear whilst at the same time being general. Clarity and precision tend to be achieved only in inverse proportion to generality, but legislation must, by and large, endeavour to be of general applicability. There is therefore in all legislation a penumbra of uncertainty that can only be illuminated and made certain by judicial interpretation. That interpretation is a creative process and inevitably involves the judiciary in the process of creating law.

The question arises, therefore, as to how judges actually interpret legislation that comes before them and the traditional answer was that in determining the actual meaning of legislation, they make use of the three primary rules of statutory interpretation and a variety of other secondary aids to construction.[9]

The three rules of statutory interpretation are: (a) the literal rule; (b) the golden rule; and (c) the mischief rule. Before any detailed consideration of these rules of interpretation is undertaken, however, it must be emphasised that they are not really rules, but, as will be shown, they may best be considered as *post hoc* justifications for decisions taken in line with judicial preference.

THE LITERAL RULE

Under this rule, the judge is required to consider what the legislation *actually* says, rather than considering what it *might mean*. In order to achieve this end, the judge should give words in legislation their literal meaning, that is, their plain, ordinary, everyday meaning, even if the effect of this is to produce what might be considered as an otherwise unjust or undesirable outcome. A classic example of this approach from the area of contract law is *Fisher v Bell* (1961). In this case, a shopkeeper who had put a flick-knife in his shop

8   The introductory paragraphs 'set the scene', providing evidence of knowledge and understanding of why judicial interpretation is necessary to the appropriate application of law.

9   In order to assist the courts in ensuring that they interpreted statute in accordance with the intention of Parliament, a system of 'rules' was developed by the courts to aid them in their task. Without discussion of these 'traditional approaches' it would not be possible to evaluate whether there had been a 'shift away', in addition to the 'rules'.

window, together with a price tag, was charged under a particular statute with 'offering the knife for sale'. The charge was dismissed on the basis that in line with the general contract law principles, the placing of an article in a window did not amount to an offer, but was merely an invitation to treat and, therefore, the charge was inaccurate. There was no doubt that the flick-knife was an offensive weapon and that the legislation was aimed at controlling the sale of such weapons, nor was there any doubt that the shopkeeper would have sold the knife, but the court stood by the literal interpretation of the Act in question and refused to extend the usual legal interpretation of the word 'offer'.

THE GOLDEN RULE

This rule is used when application of the literal rule will result in what appears to the court to be an obviously absurd result. An example of the application of the golden rule is *Adler v George* (1964). Under the **Official Secrets Act 1911** in operation at the time, it was an offence to obstruct HM Forces *in the vicinity of* a prohibited place. George had in fact been arrested whilst obstructing such forces *within* such a prohibited place. The court found no difficulty in applying the golden rule to extend the literal wording of the statute to cover the action committed by the defendant.

THE MISCHIEF RULE

This rule is of venerable age, being clearly established in *Heydon's case* (1584). It gives the court a justification for going behind the actual wording of a statute in order to consider the problem that the particular statute was aimed at remedying. At one level, the mischief rule is clearly the most flexible rule of interpretation, but it is limited by being restricted to using previous common law to determine the particular mischief the statute in question was designed to remedy. In *Heydon's Case*, it was stated that in making use of the mischief rule, the court should consider the following four matters:

(a)   What was the common law before the passing of the statute?
(b)   What was the mischief in the law with which the common law did not adequately deal?
(c)   What remedy for that mischief had Parliament intended to provide?
(d)   What was the reason for Parliament adopting that remedy?

An example of the use of the mischief rule is clearly found in *Corkery v Carpenter* (1951), where a person was arrested for being drunk in charge of a bicycle. He was subsequently charged under **s 12** of the **Licensing Act 1872** with being drunk in charge of a carriage, as the legislation made no actual reference to cycles. It is certainly arguable that a cycle is not a carriage, but in any case, the court elected to use the mischief rule to decide the matter. The purpose of the Act was to prevent people from using any form of transport on the public highways whilst in a state of intoxication. The cycle was clearly a form of transport and therefore its user was correctly charged.

It is usually suggested that the above three rules are ranked in a hierarchical order, the first being the preferred rule only giving way to the second in certain circumstances, and the third rule only being brought into use in a perceived failure of the other two to deliver an appropriate result. On consideration, however, it becomes obvious that there is no such hierarchy. The literal rule is to be used unless it leads to a manifest absurdity, in which case, it will give way to the golden rule; but what determines whether any particular result is an absurdity, other than the view of the judge deciding the case? The rules are contradictory, at least to a degree, and there is no way in which the outsider can determine in advance which of them the courts will mobilise to decide the meaning of a particular statute. In reality, it may be seen that the three rules are simply different rules which are no more than devices, by means of which the judges justify their particular decisions.

The foregoing represents the traditional approach to judicial interpretation, however, it has to be recognised that for some time there has been a move away from the over-reliance on the literal approach to statutory interpretation to a more purposive approach. As Lord Griffiths put it in *Pepper v Hart* (1993):[10]

> The days have long passed when the court adopted a strict constructionist view of interpretation which required them to adopt the literal meaning of the language. The courts now adopt a purposive approach[11] which seeks to give effect to the true purpose of legislation and are prepared to look at much extraneous material that bears on the background against which the legislation was enacted.

Such a shift has been necessitated, to no little degree, by the need for the courts to consider matters that were not within the original contemplation of Parliament at the time when the legislation was passed, but which have since been brought into play by the effect of technological advances.

Thus in *Quintavalle v Secretary of State for Health* (2003) the House of Lords held that embryos created by cell nuclear replacement (CNR), a form of human cloning involving a human egg and a cell from a donor's body, were regulated under the **Human Fertilisation and Embryology Act (HFE) 1990**, which had been passed at a time when embryos were only ever created by fertilisation of an egg by a sperm. The House of Lords held that CNR organisms were, in essence, sufficiently like other embryos to be considered as belonging

....

10 In addition to the traditional rules of interpretation, the courts have access to a number of aids which can be internal to the legislation, such as other sections of legislation, and external, such as dictionaries, the **Interpretation Act** and, since the case of *Pepper v Hart Hansard* (account of Parliamentary debate). These are discussed in the next question.

11 The purposive method of interpretation is the method favoured by the Court of Justice of the EU and is used by the courts, amongst other times, when interpreting law emanating from the EU. It is consequently a good example of the courts 'shifting away' from tradition.

to the same 'genus of facts'. Parliament could not rationally have been assumed to have intended to exclude such embryos from the regulation.

In reaching his decision, Lord Bingham considered the purpose and procedure of statutory interpretation and concluded that:

> The basic task of the court is to ascertain and give effect to the true meaning of what Parliament has said in the enactment to be construed. But that is not to say that attention should be confined and a literal interpretation given to the particular provisions which give rise to difficulty. Such an approach not only encourages immense prolixity in drafting, since the draftsman will feel obliged to provide expressly for every contingency which may possibly arise. It may also (under the banner of loyalty to the will of Parliament) lead to the frustration of that will, because undue concentration on the minutiae of the enactment may lead the court to neglect the purpose which Parliament intended to achieve when it enacted the statute . . . The court's task, within the permissible bounds of interpretation, is to give effect to Parliament's purpose. So the controversial provisions should be read in the context of the statute as a whole, and the statute as a whole *should be read in the historical context of the situation which led to its enactment.*[12]

The **Human Rights Act 1998** has also had profound implications for the operation of the English legal system. **Section 2** of the Act requires courts to take into account any previous decision of the European Court of Human Rights.[13] This provision impacts on the operation of the doctrine of precedent within the English legal system, as it effectively sanctions the overruling of any previous English authority that was in conflict with a decision of the ECHR. This has implications for precedents relating to cases in which statutes were interpreted without reference to the ECtHR jurisprudence.

More immediately for this question, however, **s 3** requires all legislation to be read so far as possible to give effect to the rights provided under the Convention. This power has the more obvious potential to invalidate previously accepted interpretations of statutes, which were made, by necessity, without recourse to the Convention (*R v A* (2001) and *Mendoza v Gaihddan* (2002) are cases in point).

QUESTION 18

Explain the resources and presumptions that judges may use in their interpretation of legislation.

---

12 The *dicta* in this case provide an excellent example of why the courts have needed to move away from more traditional methods.

13 An important and self-evident example of and reason for changes to the 'traditional approach'.

How to Answer this Question

This fairly narrow, knowledge-based, question asks students to explain the sources, other than the statute itself, to which judges can make reference in search of the actual meaning of legislation. It also requires a consideration of the presumptions that the judges will operate under. As usual, case authorities should be cited in support of all the references made.

In addition to the three main rules of interpretation, there are a number of secondary aids to construction. These can be categorised as either intrinsic or extrinsic in nature:

In particular:

- ❖ Candidates should explain the distinction between *intrinsic* and *extrinsic* assistance.
- ❖ Reference should be made to the decision in *Pepper v Hart*, which is important for the fact that it replaced the long-standing rule denying judges the right to use Parliamentary debates to decide the meaning of legislation.
- ❖ The presumptions that the judges will normally apply should then be dealt with in some detail.

Answer Structure

Introduction, providing background to statutory interpretation and the 'rules' of interpretation → Discussion of the use of intrinsic and extrinsic aids to interpretation → Consideration of the use of presumptions, including rules of language in regard to statutory interpretation

ANSWER

In addition to the three main rules of interpretation,[14] there are a number of secondary aids to construction to which the judges will refer in an endeavour to find the meaning of particular pieces of legislation. These specifically relate to sources to which the judges may make reference, but in addition to these there are a number of presumptions that the judges will accept as normally operating. These latter *may* be overturned by legislation, but in order to do so the legislation in question must be specific to that intent.

As regards to the sources to which judges may resort, these may be divided into intrinsic and extrinsic sources of assistance as below.

14 The rules of interpretation have already discussed in the precious question. (If this had not been so, a very brief overview may have been helpful here.) This introduction is also helpful as it places the resources and presumptions into context, demonstrating understanding as well as knowledge.

INTRINSIC ASSISTANCE

Intrinsic assistance is derived from the statute which is the object of interpretation; the judge uses the full statute to understand the meaning of a particular part of it. The *title*, either long or short, of the Act under consideration may be referred to for guidance (*Royal College of Nursing v DHSS* (1981)). It should be noted, however, that a general intention derived from the title cannot overrule a clear statement to the contrary in the text of the Act.

It was a feature of older statutes that they contained a *preamble*, which was a statement, preceding the actual provisions of the Act, setting out its purposes in some detail and to which reference could be made for purposes of interpretation. Again, however, any general intention derived from the preamble could not stand in the face of express provision to the contrary within the Act.

Whereas preambles preceded the main body of an Act, schedules appear as additions at the end of the main body of the legislation. They are, however, an essential part of the Act and may be referred to in order to make sense of the main text.

Some statutes contain section headings and yet others contain marginal notes relating to particular sections. The extent to which either of these may be used is uncertain, although *DPP v Schildkamp* (1969) does provide authority for the use of the former as an aid to interpretation.

Finally, in regard to intrinsic aids to interpretation, it is now recognised that punctuation has an effect on the meaning of words and can be taken into account in determining the meaning of a provision.[15]

EXTRINSIC ASSISTANCE

Extrinsic assistance, that is, reference to sources outside of the Act itself, may on occasion be resorted to in determining the meaning of legislation; but which sources? Some external sources are unproblematic. For example, judges have always been entitled to refer to *dictionaries* in order to find the meaning of non-legal words. They also have been able to look into *textbooks* for guidance in relation to particular points of law, and in using the mischief rule, they have been able to refer to *earlier statutes* to determine the precise mischief at which the statute they are trying to construe is aimed. The **Interpretation Act 1978** is also available for consultation with regard to particular difficulties. Unfortunately, its title is somewhat misleading in that it does not give general instructions for interpreting legislation, but simply defines particular terms that are found in various statutes.

....

15   This discussion on intrinsic aids to interpretation is particularly good because it clearly demonstrates that even within a statue there may be a number of different sources to consider. In addition, it provides all-important important legal authorities in support of what has been proposed.

Until fairly recently, however, *Hansard*, the verbatim record of Parliamentary procedure, literally remained a closed book to the courts, but in the landmark decision in *Pepper v Hart* (1993), the House of Lords held that where the precise meaning of legislation was uncertain or ambiguous, or where the literal meaning of an Act would lead to a manifest absurdity, the courts could refer to *Hansard*'s reports of Parliamentary debates and proceedings as an aid to construing the meaning of the legislation.

The operation of the principle in *Pepper v Hart* was extended in *Three Rivers DC v Bank of England (No 2)* (1996) to cover situations where the legislation under question was not in itself ambiguous, but might be ineffective in its intention to give effect to some particular EC directive. Applying the wider purposive powers of interpretation open to it in such circumstances the court held that it was permissible to refer to *Hansard* in order to determine the actual purpose of the statute.

The *Pepper v Hart* principle only applies to statements made by ministers at the time of the passage of legislation, and the courts have declined to extend it to cover situations where ministers subsequently make some statement as to what they consider the effect of a particular Act to be (*Melluish (Inspector of Taxes) v BMI (No 3) Ltd* (1995)).[16]

PRESUMPTIONS

In addition to the rules of interpretation, the courts may also make use of certain presumptions. As with all presumptions, they are rebuttable. The following presumptions operate:[17]

❖ *Against the alteration of the common law.* Parliament is sovereign and can alter the common law whenever it decides to do so. In order to do this, however, Parliament must expressly enact legislation to that end. If there is no express intention to that effect, it is assumed that statute does not make any fundamental change to the common law. With regard to particular provisions, if there are alternative interpretations, one of which will maintain the existing common law situation, then that interpretation will be preferred (see *R (Rottman) v Commissioner of Police* (2002)).

❖ *That a mental element is required for criminal offences.* It is a general requirement of the criminal law that, in order for a person to be convicted of a crime, he is proved not only to have committed the relevant act or conduct but also to have done this with a blameworthy state of mind known as *mens rea*. However, in some areas of social concern, such as traffic offences or underage drinking, Parliament has seen fit

---

16 Again, this discussion is particularly good because not only does it demonstrate in-depth knowledge but it is also very well supported by appropriate legal authority and includes reference to the important case of *Pepper v Hart* (1993).

17 This provides in-depth consideration of the presumption, again well supported by appropriate authority, and also highlighting the rebuttable nature of the presumptions.

to pass what are known as 'strict liability' offences. These are criminal offences for which it is *not* necessary for the prosecution to prove that the defendant had a particular attitude towards the crime in question, for example, that he intended to commit it, but merely that the relevant conduct took place. When, someone comes before the criminal law courts accused of an offence created by statute the courts must decide whether the words of the statute imply that it is necessary for the prosecution to prove the defendant had a mental element. The general rule is that Parliament will be presumed not to have wanted to create a strict liability criminal offence unless it has been explicit about wanting to do so. In *Sweet v Parsley* (1970), the accused had a house which she rented out and visited only occasionally. She was convicted of being concerned in the management of premises used for the purpose of smoking cannabis, contrary to **s 5(b)** of the **Dangerous Drugs Act 1965**; however, she had had no knowledge that the house was being used in this way. The House of Lords held that her conviction should be quashed, since it had to be proved that it was the accused's 'purpose' that the premises were used for smoking cannabis. In the case, Lord Reid said that:

> ... whenever a section is silent as to *mens rea* there is a presumption that ... we must read in words appropriate to require *mens rea*.

❖ *Against retrospective effect of new law*. The courts operate a presumption of interpretation that statutes will not operate retrospectively. The presumption against retrospective effect was considered by the Court of Appeal in *Home Secretary v Wainwright* (2002). Two relatives visiting a prisoner were strip-searched as a condition of entry to the prison, and subsequently claimed a violation of their right to respect for private life. The court held that since the events in question had happened before the **HRA 1998** came into force, **s 3** of that Act could not be relied on. As Parliament had expressly made **s 22(4)** of the Act retroactive, its failure to do the same for **s 3** must be taken to have been intentional. See also *R v Lambert* (2001) and *R v Kansal* (2001).

As Parliament is supreme, it can pass retrospective legislation if it wishes, but it must do so using express words to achieve this end. The **War Damage Act 1965** was passed specifically to overrule the decision of the House of Lords in *Burmah Oil Co Ltd v The Lord Advocate* (1965), and to deprive Burmah Oil of the results of having won that case. An example of modern legislation which has been made expressly retrospective is the **War Crimes Act 1991**.

❖ *Presumption against deprivation of liberty*. The law courts work on the assumption that Parliament does not intend to deprive a person of his liberty unless it is explicitly making provision for such a punishment.

❖ *Against application to the Crown*. Unless the legislation contains a clear statement to the contrary, it is presumed not to apply to the Crown.

❖ *Against breaking international law*. Where possible, legislation should be interpreted in such a way as to give effect to existing international legal obligations.

❖   *In favour of words taking their meaning from the context in which they are used.*[18] This presumption appears as three distinct sub-rules, each of which carries a Latin tag:

> The *noscitur a sociis* rule is applied where statutory provisions include a list of examples of what is covered by the legislation. It is presumed that the words used have a related meaning and are to be interpreted in relation to each other. (See *IRC v Frere* (1969), in which the House of Lords decided which of two possible meanings of the word 'interest' was to be preferred by reference to the word's location within a statute.)

> The *ejusdem generis* rule applies in situations where general words are appended to the end of a list of specific examples. The presumption is that the general words have to be interpreted in line with the prior restrictive examples. Thus, a provision which referred to a list that included 'horses, cattle, sheep and other animals' would be unlikely to apply to domestic animals such as cats and dogs. (See *Powell v Kempton Park Racecourse* (1899), in which it was held that, because a statute prohibited betting in a specified number of indoor places, it could not cover an outdoor location.)

> The *expressio unius exclusio alterius* rule simply means that where a statute seeks to establish a list of what is covered by its provisions, then anything not expressly included in that list is specifically excluded. (See *R v Inhabitants of Sedgley* (1831), where rates expressly stated to be payable on *coal* mines were held not to be payable in relation to *limestone* mines.)

QUESTION 19

Evidence must be sufficiently relevant to be admissible, but sufficiently relevant evidence is only admissible in so far as it is not excluded by any rule of the law of evidence. The consequence . . . is that some relevant evidence is excluded.

Keane, A, The Law of Evidence, 4th edn, 1996

▸   **Explain the exclusionary rules of evidence and assess how far they are successful in promoting a fair trial.**

How to Answer this Question

A good approach to this discussion and assessment would be to:

❖   introduce the different types of excluded evidence;

18   The rules of language can help make the meaning of words and phrases clear where particular sentence construction is used and this answer makes this important point.

- ❖ consider evidence unduly prejudicial to the defendant – **Criminal Evidence Act 1898**, *Selvey v DPP* (1968), *Boardman v DPP* (1974), *P* (1991);
- ❖ include discussion of inherently unreliable evidence – children's evidence, hearsay evidence (with exceptions; discuss *Rogers* (1994));
- ❖ deal with evidence against the public interest – legal professional privilege, confessions obtained by oppression;
- ❖ conclude with some discussion of the need to balance the interests in question.

Answer Structure

ANSWER

The exclusionary rules of evidence are a characteristic of the common law tradition and are not favoured by continental jurisdictions. There are three main types of evidence which can be excluded from a trial, even though containing information relevant to the case: (a) evidence which might be unduly prejudicial to the defendant; (b) evidence which is inherently unreliable; and (c) evidence which it would be against the public interest to admit into the hearing.[19]

It is generally unduly prejudicial to the defendant for the court to learn, during the trial, of his previous convictions. He must be judged according to the evidence relating to the crime in question (*Coombes* (1960)). This exclusionary rule, however, does not apply if the defendant asserts his own good character. Here, the prosecution can rebut the assertion with the defendant's criminal record. A defendant's past misconduct can also be disclosed if he attacks a co-accused, even a co-accused not charged with the same offence. The defendant who is attacked may cross-examine the attacker about his criminal record.

There are two further exceptions to the 'unduly prejudicial' exclusion rule. The defendant's record can be admitted if he attacks a prosecution witness, or where there is

19 This introduction places the topic into context and introduces the main issues requiring further discussion.

a marked similarity of facts between the crimes under consideration and earlier ones for which the defendant has been convicted. Both these exceptions have proved problematic in practice.

Section 1 of the **Criminal Evidence Act 1898** states that a defendant's record can be admitted where the 'nature or conduct of the defence is such as to involve imputations on the character of the prosecutor or the witnesses for the prosecution'. The rationale of the rule is that in circumstances of a simple quarrel on evidence between the sides, where the defence explains the prosecution's story by alleging that the prosecution witness is lying, it is proper for the court to know of any evidence that the defendant is a liar, so as best to judge which side is telling the truth. The problem here is for an innocent defendant who does have a criminal record and against whom there is being put some dishonest evidence. He cannot attack the prosecution's improper case without exposing his criminal record and thus probably damaging his defence. Additionally, as Zander has argued, if it is regarded as generally correct to withhold evidence of past misconduct from the court because it is unduly prejudicial, it does not become any the less prejudicial simply because the accused has impugned a prosecution witness (*Cases and Materials on the English Legal System*, 7th edn, 1996).

In *Selvey v DPP* (1968), the House of Lords ruled that where previous convictions of a defendant are admitted, they are to be treated by the court only as evidence of the defendant's creditworthiness, not of his propensity to commit the offence in question. This, however, is a rather pious hope. Once jury members learn of the defendant's convictions, they are likely to draw unfavourable conclusions about the person and probably do just what the House of Lords have declared should not be done.

As to the 'similar fact' exception, it was held in *Straffen* (1952) that previous convictions can be admitted where the facts in a case are so strikingly similar to the facts in previous cases for which the defendant has been convicted as virtually to rule out coincidence. The test for when the exception can be used was relaxed by the House of Lords in *Boardman v DPP* (1974), where it was suggested that the similarity did not need to be 'striking'. In *P* (1991), the House of Lords held that the real test was whether the 'probative force' of the evidence to be admitted was great enough to justify the prejudice given to the accused. Thus, in a charge of rape and incest against P, it was acceptable for the evidence of one of two victimised daughters to be used in the same hearing as her sister's evidence. Both girls had testified about prolonged misconduct and the probative value of each girl's evidence outweighed the prejudice to the father in using one allegation to fortify another.[20]

---

20 This discussion of the rule relating to unduly prejudicial evidence is good as it explains the rational behind the rule, is supported by appropriate legal authority and also highlights circumstances in which it will not apply, demonstrating sound knowledge and understanding of the issues.

Another category of evidence which English law excludes from the trial is that which is inherently unreliable. Thus, a judge can exclude the evidence of a proposed witness who does not have the mental capacity to testify. Two more problematic types of evidence in this class are children's evidence and hearsay evidence.

Traditionally, there was an assumption that young children were not reliable witnesses. Children could give sworn testimony if the judge believed that they appreciated the solemnity of the occasion and understood the importance of the oath. There was a more relaxed rule in criminal cases, where unsworn evidence could be taken from a child who was sufficiently intelligent. Evidence has been heard from children as young as six (Z (1990)). Psychological research (for example, Davies, Tarrant and Flin, 'Close encounters of the witness kind' (1989) 80 British Journal of Psychology 415) has now shown, however, that children are more reliable witnesses than was earlier thought. Now, **s 52** of the **Criminal Justice Act 1991** requires that all witnesses under 14 years of age are to give unsworn evidence, unless a judge rules that such a person is incompetent. Another reform was made by **s 34** of the Act, which abolished the requirement for the unsworn evidence of children to be corroborated and provided that the unsworn evidence of children could corroborate any other witness' testimony. The law, prior to these reforms, had made it extremely difficult to get convictions in serious cases of sexual abuse.

Hearsay evidence – that of someone not actually present in court – is regarded as inherently unreliable because the person who actually saw or heard something relevant cannot be tested by cross-examination in court. A document is hearsay unless its author is also present to testify. In Sparks v R (1964), a white man was convicted for sexual assault on a three-year-old girl. When asked just after the event by her mother 'who had assaulted her', the girl allegedly said 'It was a coloured boy', but the Privy Council ruled that the mother could not give this as part of her evidence, as it would be hearsay. There are now so many exceptions to this exclusionary rule that it has been described by Zander as being in 'an advanced state of disintegration'.

The hearsay rule only applies if the statement is to be introduced in order to establish the truth of its contents. It is not counted as hearsay if it is to be introduced as 'direct evidence'. The law on this is somewhat erratic, for example, it was held in Taylor v Chief Constable of Cheshire (1987) that a video recording was not hearsay but direct evidence, whereas in Townsend (1987), a robbery victim had scribbled down the registration number of the defendant's car. The pen was defective and made only indentations which the police had managed to boost, but they lost the original note. The technical evidence was ruled to be hearsay. Hearsay evidence is admissible where the original statement was made as a dying declaration, or as part of the res gestae (a statement made so close to the incident in question that it can be regarded as part of the event).

An interesting decision is Rogers (1994). The appellant had been convicted of possession of heroin with intent to supply. He had sought to have admitted as evidence a statement made by the wife of an old associate of his who had died before the trial. The wife's statement was a report of what she said her husband, L, had told her before he died. The statement began: 'L said there were a number of guys after him for the money for the heroin that the police had found.' It continued to the effect that L had been supplying the appellant with heroin for his personal use only and that the appellant knew nothing of the larger stock (which the prosecution alleged he did control). The appellant submitted that Mrs L's evidence fell within an exception to the hearsay rule – that statements made by a deceased were admissible if they were against his pecuniary interest (the rationale being that no one would acknowledge an obligation against his pecuniary interests unless it was true) – in that, the first sentence was such a statement as the deceased was acknowledging that he owed money and the remainder of the statement was admissible as collateral evidence. The appeal was dismissed. It was held that on the facts, the first sentence was not against the deceased's pecuniary interests, since he was not saying that he actually owed anyone any money and so was not acknowledging any obligation. Furthermore, even if that sentence was admissible, the rest of the statement, which was the part on which the defence wished to rely, was not admissible as collateral evidence as it would only be so admissible if further information was needed to explain the nature of the transaction in question, which was not the case.

Documentary hearsay evidence has been admissible in civil cases since 1938 and, in 1968, the rule was widened to include oral evidence with the consent of the other side. In 1991, the Law Commission recommended that the hearsay rule should be abolished in civil proceedings to bring the rules of evidence in line with the recent changes facilitating pre-trial exchange of witness statements. Many erosions of the hearsay rule in criminal cases have also been made, for example, statements of the dead, people who have (since they made the statement) become unfit, the untraceable, business documents and expert evidence are all admissible under the **Criminal Justice Act 1988**. Zuckerman (in *The Principles of Criminal Evidence*, 1989) has argued that these examples of 'non-hearsay' are just convenient ways of avoiding the rule, where it is thought that a certain type of statement will be reliable.[21]

The third category of relevant evidence excluded from trial is that which it would be against the public interest to admit. There are several types of evidence which fall under this heading. Legal professional privilege means that any communications between a client and his legal adviser (arising from an existing or contemplated case, or to enable advice to be given) generally cannot be adduced in evidence by the lawyer without the permission of the client. The privilege is afforded to promote openness between the client and the lawyer. The privilege is not absolute, however, where the material sought

----

21   The discussion of the rule relating to hearsay evidence is very good as it again explains the rational behind the rule, is supported by appropriate legal authority and also highlights circumstances in which it will not apply, demonstrating sound knowledge and understanding of the issues.

to be produced in court would help to establish someone's innocence. This has arisen in cases with several co-accused and the judge must decide whether the legitimate interest of the defendant, who wants to keep the privilege, outweighs that of the client, who wants to breach it.

Since *Marks v Beyfus* (1890), it has been accepted by the courts that it is in the public interest that the identity of police informers should be kept secret. Nonetheless, this principle can be superseded by the principle that the defendant should not be unfairly impeded from establishing his innocence. In *Brown* (1988), convictions were quashed where the trial judge had refused to allow police officers to be questioned about their surveillance operation.

Section 76 of the **Police and Criminal Evidence Act (PACE) 1984** allows for the exclusion of evidence of a confession which has or might have been obtained by 'oppression' or in consequence of anything said or done which was likely to render it unreliable. 'Oppression' is defined as including torture, inhuman or degrading treatment and the use or threat of violence. There have been very few successful appeals using this section and the courts appear to have taken the contentious view that whether police questioning is oppressive or not depends upon the intention of the interrogating officers, rather than the actual effect the questions have on the defendant. This reasoning was adopted in *Miller* (1986).

Much more effectively used has been **s 78** of **PACE**. Under this, the court can refuse to admit evidence if it appears to the court that in all the circumstances, the evidence would have such an adverse effect on the fairness of proceedings that the court ought not to admit it. The majority of cases where the section has been successfully used have concerned breaches of **PACE** or its Codes of Practice with facts involving wrongful refusal to provide legal advice or the failure to record interviews (see, for example, *Samuel* (1988) – defendant denied access to solicitor; *Doolan* (1988) – defendant not cautioned; *Weekes* (1993) – defendant not provided with appropriate adult).

In *AG's Reference (No 3 of 1999)* (2000), the House of Lords gave a ruling which shows how subtle in their reasoning the courts should be when balancing: (a) the interests of the accused not to have prejudicial evidence used against him; and (b) the interests of the public in convicting offenders. In this case, a man was accused of burglary and rape. He was alleged to have broken into the house of a 66-year-old woman and raped her anally. He was arrested and prosecuted after a DNA sample taken from the victim was found to match his DNA taken from a sample he had provided in the investigation of an earlier unconnected burglary. According to **s 64(1)** of **PACE**, the sample he gave at the time of the first burglary should have been destroyed because he was tried for, but acquitted of, that crime. If that sample had been destroyed, then the police would not have had it, so, when the DNA sample was taken from the woman in the later burglary, it would not have matched any sample in the police records. In the second case, the police had, once they apprehended the defendant, taken a new sample from him to match with that found on the victim. But, they would not have done that had they not identified him as a suspect in the first place, which they only did because of the first, improperly held, sample. The Lords held that in future cases, where there were exceptional circumstances, the courts could, by analogy with **s 78(1)**, admit evidence apparently rendered inadmissible by **s 64** (which deals with the destruction of fingerprints and other samples if a person is cleared of an offence or is told that no prosecution will take place).

In conclusion, it can be noted that the real difficulty in this area is the familiar legal problem of balancing the interests of two sides.[22] English law has taken the view that the judge should be the gatekeeper of much evidence brought to court by lawyers, deciding whether the jury can hear it and make up their own minds. The judge is given guidance by the law on how to decide these matters but ultimately, many of his decisions are matters of personal opinion, for example, whether a child is fit to give evidence, or whether the defendant is imputing the character of a prosecution witness or simply asserting his own innocence.

---

22 The account helpfully concludes by highlighting the problem of balancing the needs of the two sides involved in a court case, demonstrating thoughtfulness.

Judges and Juries

JUDGES

Judges obviously occupy a central role in the legal system with regard to both civil and criminal law and, for that reason, questions about the judiciary are found in most examination papers on English legal system courses. There are, across all the ranks, 3,800 judges in England and Wales, and 30,000 magistrates. It is frequently claimed that judges represent the views of a highly limited section of society, being mainly white, middle-aged men. The point to consider, however, is whether this social placement has a deleterious effect on the decisions that the judges make. If judges are simply the mouthpieces of the law and their decisions represent no more than the automatic outcome of a strictly logical process of reasoning, then the actual social situation and background of the judge is immaterial, for the decisions are contained in the law itself. If, on the other hand, legal reasoning is not as prescriptive as outsiders generally consider it to be and judges actually have a substantial measure of discretion in the way in which they reach their decisions, then the social placement of the judiciary does become a matter to be critically analysed with regard to the decisions that they reach. Law becomes not the expression of some imminent authority, but the expression of individual and, perhaps more importantly, group prejudice.

For the above reasons, it is important to avoid reliance on superficial and anecdotal assertions as to the lack of awareness of judges, in favour of a reasoned and well supported critique of the nature of legal reasoning, before attention is focused on the social background of the judiciary. The answers offered in this chapter locate weaknesses in the process of legal reasoning as of central importance and, indeed, as prior to any critical understanding of how judges operate.

JURIES

The role of the jury in the English legal system is the subject of contentious debate. You should be familiar with recent research on this theme and some particular questions which have been addressed by researchers; for instance, how often do juries return 'perverse' verdicts and are such practices desirable? Are juries capable of properly following the details of complex trials? Be careful to observe how much the question you are answering requires a factual account or explanation of procedure, as opposed to evaluative, argumentative material. In any event, you will need a good knowledge of the legal and historical aspects of the jury in order to be able to rehearse the controversial parts of this topic.

In 2010, a major empirical study found that juries virtually always acted in a fair way. The research, conducted by Professor Cheryl Thomas at University College London, *Are Juries Fair?*, is the most in-depth study into the issue ever undertaken in the UK (available at: www.justice.gov.uk/publications/are-juries-fair.htm).

The study involved a two-year survey of more than 1,000 jurors at Crown Courts and a separate study of over 68,000 jury verdicts. In the report, sensitive issues about jury decision-making were examined for the first time.

The report reveals that:

❖ all-white juries do not discriminate against defendants from black and minority ethnic backgrounds;
❖ juries almost always reach a verdict and convict two-thirds of the time;
❖ there are no courts where juries acquit more often than convict.

The study also shows that:

❖ jurors want more information about how to do their job;
❖ written instructions improve jurors' legal understanding of cases;
❖ some jurors use the internet to look for information about their case; and
❖ some jurors find media reports of their case difficult to ignore.

The study recommends that all sworn jurors be issued with written guidelines explaining what improper conduct is, including use of the internet, and how and when to report it. The study also recommends that judges consider issuing jurors with written instructions on the law to be applied in each case.

The **Criminal Justice Act 2003** contained provisions allowing for trials in cases of serious crime to take place without juries. The provision was to act as a safeguard against 'jury nobbling' – where jurors are intimidated or bribed into voting for an acquittal. Non-jury trials had been used in Northern Ireland in the 1970s during a period of civil strife when there were fears of jury nobbling, but outside of that situation cases of serious crime had been tried by juries for over four centuries. The power provided for in the **2003 Act** was not used until February 2010.

Peter Blake, John Twomey, Barry Hibberd and Glen Cameron were tried for a violent £1.75 million armed robbery at Heathrow in 2004. The decision to allow the juryless trial was taken by the Court of Appeal in 2009 after an investigation by the police found that 'approaches' had been made to two members of the jury in the third trial of the men. The court decided that a serious attempt at jury tampering had taken place. It was also found that there was a real and present danger that jury tampering would recur if there were a further jury trial. In deciding to order a juryless trial, the Court of Appeal noted that the alternative of providing the jury with round-the-clock protection would still leave their families vulnerable and that such protection would cost £6 million as opposed to the £1.6 million for a judge-only trial.

In the juryless trial, the judge acts as both judge and jury: he resolves matters of law and has to do 'mental gymnastics' (*The Times*, 1 April 2010) as one barrister put it, if he excludes evidence as inadmissible – trying to put it out of his mind and to pretend that he has never seen it. In a jury trial, the jury is sent out by the judge when there are technical legal arguments about controversial evidence and does not hear any evidence that has been excluded or even know that it has been excluded. After less than three months (about half the time a jury trial for such a complex case would have lasted) the defendants were found guilty by the single judge and given a range of sentences from life imprisonment to 15 years.

Checklist ✔

You should be familiar with:

- the way in which judges are appointed and the role of the Lord Chancellor in their appointment;
- how judges can avoid the strict operation of precedent and their powers in relation to the interpretation of statutes;
- the difference between individual and corporate prejudice;
- the social background of the judiciary;
- possible ways of diminishing perceptions of judicial bias;
- the historical justification for trial by jury;
- the rules concerning eligibility (including disqualification and excusal);
- the powers of the prosecution and defence to alter the composition of the jury;
- the practice of jury vetting and issues of selection procedure and impartiality;
- the arguments for and against retaining the jury for criminal trials.

QUESTION 20

Examine the need for a new Supreme Court to replace the House of Lords and evaluate the procedure for appointing members of the Supreme Court under the **Constitutional Reform Act 2005**.

How to Answer this Question

This question requires candidates to evaluate the provisions in the **Constitutional Reform Act 2005** in relation to the appointment of judges to the new Supreme Court. It consequently requires candidates to show some knowledge and understanding of the nature of that new court and why it was introduced, before they go on to describe the procedure for appointing its members. However, it should be noted that the key requirement in the question is 'evaluation'. It is not therefore simply a matter of describing the appointments procedure, some assessment of how it might function is also required, which in turn necessitates some critique of the system that is being replaced.

A possible structure for dealing with the issues might be as follows:

- ❖ explain why it was thought necessary to introduce a new Supreme Court, and how it differs from the House of Lords;
- ❖ set out what were the perceived problems in the previous appointments procedure;
- ❖ describe the structure of the new Supreme Court;
- ❖ detail the appointments procedure of the new system, focusing in particular upon the role of the Lord Chancellor;
- ❖ offer some evaluation, even if limited, of the new system.

Answer Structure

ANSWER

It has long been considered an anomaly, and contrary to the doctrine of the separation of powers,[1] that the highest court within the United Kingdom has been located within the upper legislative body, the House of Lords. In summer 2004 the then Government, somewhat surprisingly, announced its intention to bring the United Kingdom constitution into line with a more clearly delineated separation of powers. To that end the **Constitutional Reform Act (CRA) 2005** provided for the establishment of a new, independent Supreme Court, separate from the House of Lords.

Section 23 of the **CRA 2005** established the Supreme Court of the United Kingdom, and set out its composition[2] as being made up of 12 judges, appointed by the Queen. One of

---

1   The answer begins by clearly outlining the need for a court to replace the House of Lords.
2   This demonstrates that the need to provide some description of the composition of the new court prior to attempting to evaluate the procedure for appointing new members has been recognised.

the judges is President and one Deputy President of the court. **Subsection 23(3)** provides a power to increase the number of judges. This may only be done, however, if, as set out in **subs (4)**, a draft of the Order has been laid before and approved by each House of Parliament (that is, by affirmative resolution procedure). **Subsection 23(6)** provides that the judges of the Supreme Court, apart from the President of the Supreme Court and the Deputy President of the Supreme Court, will be called 'Justices of the Supreme Court'.

Section 24 provided for the first judges of the Supreme Court to be the Lords of Appeal in Ordinary holding office at the date of commencement, i.e. the members of the former House of Lords. The senior Lord of Appeal in Ordinary prior to commencement, Lord Phillips, became the President and the second senior Lord of Appeal in Ordinary prior to commencement, Lord Hope, became the Deputy President of the Court. Thus was continuity maintained, as the members of what was the House of Lords became the first justices of the new Supreme Court when the Supreme court opened for business in the newly refurbished Middlesex Guildhall building on 1 October 2009.

In the past, criticism has been made of the way in which judges were appointed to the House of Lords, and indeed at any level in the judicial hierarchy. It was suggested that the appointments were, to say the least, lacking in transparency and subject to the control of the judiciary and the senior members of the legal profession. As a consequence of the secret nature of the 'soundings' that were taken on candidates and their perceived right of veto, it was sometimes suggested that the senior judiciary constituted a self-selecting oligarchy. In response to such criticism, the newly constituted Supreme Court has its own independent appointments system

Appointment of judges to the Supreme Court

As regards future appointments to the Supreme Court, **s 25** sets out two possible routes to qualification. These are:[3]

1.   having held high judicial office, for at least two years;
2.   having been a qualifying practitioner for at least 15 years.

Although appointment to office is by the Crown, **ss 26, 27, 28, 29, 30** and **31** and **Sched 8 CRA 2005**, set out the procedure for appointing a member of the Supreme Court.

The Lord Chancellor must convene an *ad hoc* selection commission if there is, or is likely to be a vacancy. Subsequently, the Lord Chancellor will notify the Prime Minister of the identity of the person selected by that commission, and under **s 26(4)**, the Prime Minister *must* recommend the appointment of that person to the Queen.

---

3   As the question demands evaluation of the of the procedure for appointing judges, it is important to describe the procedure before attempting any evaluation.

Schedule 8 contains the rules governing the composition and operation of the selection commission, which will consist of the President of the Supreme Court, who will chair the commission, the Deputy President of the Supreme Court and one member from each of the territorial judicial appointment commissions (see below), one of whom must be a person who is not legally qualified. The next most senior ordinary judge in the Supreme Court will take the unfilled position on the selection commission if either the President or Deputy President is unable to sit.

Section 27 sets out the process which must be followed in the selection of a justice of the Supreme Court. The commission decides the particular selection process to be applied, the criteria or competences against which candidates will be assessed, but in any event the requirement is that any selection must be made solely on merit. However, **subs 27(8)** does require that the commission must take into account the need for the Court to have among its judges, generally at least two Scottish judges and usually one from Northern Ireland. The Lord Chancellor, as provided for by **subs 27(9)**, may issue non-binding guidance to the commission about the vacancy that has arisen, for example on the jurisdictional requirements of the Court, to which the commission must have regard.

Under **subss 27(2)** and **(3)** the commission is required to consult:

❖ senior judges who are neither on the commission nor willing to be considered for selection;
❖ the Lord Chancellor;
❖ the First Minister in Scotland;
❖ the Assembly First Secretary in Wales;
❖ the Secretary of State for Northern Ireland.

Subsection 28(1) provides that after a selection has been made the commission must submit a report nominating one candidate to the Lord Chancellor, who then must also consult the senior judges (or other judges) who were consulted by the commission, the First Minister in Scotland, the Assembly First Secretary in Wales and the Secretary of State for Northern Ireland.

Section 29 sets out the Lord Chancellor's options after he has received a name from the commission and carried out the further consultation under **s 28**.

The procedure may be divided into three possible stages:

Stage 1: where a person has been selected and recommended by the appointments commission. At this stage the Lord Chancellor may:

❖ accept the nomination and notify the Prime Minister;
❖ reject the selection;
❖ require the commission to reconsider its selection.

Stage 2: where a person has been selected following a rejection or reconsideration at stage 1. In this event the Lord Chancellor can:

- accept the nomination and notify the Prime Minister;
- reject the selection but only if it was made following a reconsideration at stage 1;
- require the commission to reconsider the selection but only if it was made following a rejection at stage 1.

Stage 3: where a person has been selected following a rejection or reconsideration at stage 2. At this point, the Lord Chancellor *must* accept the nomination unless he prefers to accept a candidate who had previously been reconsidered but not subsequently recommended for a second time.

In effect this means that the Lord Chancellor's options are as follows. He can:

- accept the recommendation of the commission;
- ask the commission to reconsider; or
- reject the recommendation.

Where the Lord Chancellor requires the commission to *reconsider* its original selection, the commission can still put forward the same name with additional justifications for its selection. In such circumstance the Lord Chancellor will either accept the recommendation or reject it. Alternatively the commission can recommend another candidate, whom the Lord Chancellor can accept, reject or require reconsideration of.

However, if the Lord Chancellor *rejects* the original name provided by the selection commission, it must submit an alternative candidate giving reasons for their choice. At this point the Lord Chancellor can either:

- accept the second candidate; or
- ask the selection commission to reconsider.

On reconsideration the commission can either resubmit the second candidate or propose an alternative candidate. At this point the Lord Chancellor must make a choice. He can either accept the alternative candidate or he can then choose the reconsidered candidate.

Under **subs 30(1)**, the Lord Chancellor's right of rejection is only exercisable where in his opinion the person selected is not suitable for the office concerned. The right to require reconsideration is exercisable under three conditions:

- where he feels there is not enough evidence that the person is suitable for office;
- where he feels there is not enough evidence that person is the best candidate on merit; or

❖ where there is not enough evidence that the judges of the Court will between them have enough knowledge of, and experience in, the laws of each parts of the United Kingdom, following the new appointment.

Should the Lord Chancellor exercise either of these options he must provide the commission with his reasons in writing (s 30(3)).

Whilst it can be seen that the appointment commission for the Supreme Court will be specifically convened for its purpose, all other judicial appointments will be made under the auspices of a new independent judicial appointments commission, which it is hoped will remove the criticisms levelled at the previous appointments process, that it too lacked openness. In conclusion, whilst the proposed system of appointment certainly appears more open than the system that preceded it, how it operates in practice remains to be seen.[4]

When the Supreme Court commenced operation, in October 2009, there were only 11 justices, rather than the full complement of 12. One former member of the Judicial Committee of House, Lord Neuberger, had stepped down to take up the position of Lord of the Rolls in the Court of Appeal. At the time it was thought that the final place would be filled by Jonathan Sumption QC. Although Sumption had never held high judicial office he did qualify under the second, and perhaps surprising, criterion set out in **s. 25**, that of having 15 years qualification as a practitioner. However, it was suggested that Sumption withdrew his application, after some concern was expressed amongst the senior judiciary. Subsequently the former Court of Appeal judge Sir John Dyson was appointed to be the twelfth justice of the Supreme Court.

Following the appointment of Sir John, it was announced that he and all future holders of the office of Justice of the Supreme Court would be given the courtesy title of Lord or Lady.

In May 2011, following the retirement of Lords Saville and Collins, it was announced that Jonathan Sumption would, after all, be joining the Supreme Court together with Sir Nicholas Wilson. Lord Wilson assumed his position almost immediately, but, again rather surprisingly, Sumption's appointment was postponed to permit him to act as a barrister in several cases he was already committed to.

In July 2011, following the death of Lord Rodger and with the imminent retirement of Lord Brown in 2012, an *ad hoc* selection commission was established under **s 27** and **Sched 8** of the **Constitutional Reform Act 2005** to select candidates to replace both justices. This was followed in October by the announcement that Lord Phillips was to resign at the end of the Summer in 2012, several months before his required date of retirement. The reason

---

4   Clear evidence of evaluation of evaluation of the new procedure.

being to facilitate a smooth hand over to his subsequent replacement, during the time when the court was not actually sitting.

The Illness and subsequent death of Lord Rodger, together will the delay in Jonathan Sumption taking up his position, meant that for an extended period in 2011, the Supreme Court had to function with only ten justices.

Common Pitfalls

❖ It should be noted that the former Law Lords were members of the House of Lords, but did not normally participate in the political discourse of the second chamber, except where it concerned legal matters.
❖ The Law Lords have moved premises and become Justices of the Supreme Court. The House of Lords, as a chamber of parliament still exists.
❖ It should be remembered that there is a particular *ad hoc* process for appointment to the Supreme Court.

Aim Higher ★

❖ Look to locate the emergence of the Supreme Court in the context of the doctrine of the separation of powers.
❖ Be prepared to explain the structure/membership of the Supreme Court.
❖ Be able to explain the distinct process of appointment to the Supreme Court in some detail.

QUESTION 21
Why does the social composition of the judiciary matter?

How to Answer this Question
This question appears to be of the type that asks candidates to consider whether the particular class/race/gender background of the judges leads to a bias in their decisions. It has assumed a contemporary importance, however, given the continued increase in judicial review and the incorporation of the **European Convention on Human Rights (ECHR)** into UK law, in the form of the **Human Rights Act (HRA) 1998**. This question still requires a reference to Professor Griffith's views in *The Politics of the Judiciary*, 5th edn, 1997. A good answer might take the following form:

❖ examine the actual constitution of the judiciary, referring to any available statistics;
❖ consider why the composition of the judiciary matters, paying particular regard to judicial review and the **HRA 1998**;

❖   refer to Professor Griffith's claim as to the biased nature of the judiciary;

❖   adduce an argument to the contrary;

❖   offer some proposals as to how the perceived problems might be remedied.

| Place topic into context and examine the role of the judiciary | → | Highlight the relevance of the composition of the judiciary | → | Consider the competing arguments as to the bias, or otherwise, of the judiciary |

ANSWER

Central to the general idea of the rule of law is the specific proposition that it involves the rule of *law*, rather than the rule of *people*. From this perspective, judges are seen as subservient to, and merely the instruments of, the law; and the outcome of the judicial process is understood as being determined through the straightforward application of legal rules, both statute and precedent, to particular factual situations. In applying those rules, the judge is expected to act in a completely impartial manner, without allowing his personal preferences to affect his decision in any way. A further assumption is that in reaching a decision, the judge is only concerned with matters of law and refuses to permit politics, economics or other non-legal matters to influence his decision. The law is assumed to be distinct from, and superior to, those non-legal issues and the assumption is that the judge operates, in the words of Professor JAG Griffith, as a 'political, economic and social eunuch'. In reality, however, judges have a large measure of discretion in determining which laws to apply, what those laws actually mean and how to apply them. Equally, judges are by necessity involved in political issues when they are called upon to provide judicial review of the actions of the state and its functionaries. Although some judges have denied the political nature of such decisions, others have actually welcomed and justified the growth in judicial review, on the grounds that it permits the judiciary to protect individuals from the abuse of the power by what they perceive as an overmighty state and an otherwise uncontrolled executive. This overtly political role, which sets the courts up against the state, cannot but be increased by the enactment of the **HRA 1998**. This Act, which incorporates the **ECHR** into UK law, places the courts in the position of acting as the protectors of individual rights from incursions by the state. Although the Act expressly declines to challenge the supremacy of Parliament by denying the courts the power to strike down particular legislation as being unconstitutional, it does permit them to make declarations to the effect that such legislation is incompatible with the human rights protected under the Act. Such declarations, and there are bound to be some, if not many, will inevitably place the judiciary in a political, not to say confrontational, relationship with Parliament.[5]

5   Here the topic is put into context and the non-legal role of the judiciary is highlighted.

The potential for conflict between the judiciary and the executive arising from the **Human Rights Act** can most clearly be seen in relation to the House of Lords' decision in the *Belmarsh* case (*A v Secretary of State for the Home Department* (2004)) in which the House of Lords, by a majority of eight to one, held that the detention powers under **s 23** of the **Anti-Terrorism Crime and Security Act 2001** were not compatible with the rights provided under the **European Convention on Human Rights**. Some of the speeches delivered by the judges in the case were extremely, if not excessively, critical of the action taken by the Government in introducing the Act.

In the light of this potential creative power, it is essential to ensure that the judiciary satisfactorily represents society at large, in relation to which it has so much power, and to ensure further that it does not merely represent the views and attitudes of a self-perpetuating elite. This desideratum could be reformulated in the form of a stark question: are judges biased, and do they use their judicial positions in such a way as to give expression to that bias?[6]

Bias can operate at two levels. The first is personal bias and occurs where individual judges permit their own prejudices to influence their understanding and implementation of the law. Such bias is a serious matter and reprehensible, but the very fact that it is individual makes it more open to control and, in the long run, less serious than the accusation of corporate bias that some observers, such as Professor Griffith, level against the judiciary. Corporate prejudice involves the assertion that the judiciary, as a body, do not decide certain types of cases in a fair and unbiased way; rather that as a consequence of their shared educational experience, shared training and practical experience at the Bar, along with shared social status, they have developed a common ideology comprising a homogeneous collection of values, attitudes and beliefs as to how the law should operate and be administered. The claim is that because, as individuals, they share the same prejudices, this leads to the emergence of an in-built group prejudice which precludes the possibility of some cases being decided in a neutral way.

The essence of Griffith's argument is that judges in the UK are in the position of being required to make political choices in the many cases that come before them which require a determination of public interest. This situation will necessarily become more frequent as the judges are required, under the **HRA 1998**, to weigh individual rights against public interest. His further point is that in determining what constitutes the public interest, the judges give expression to their own values, which are in turn a product of their position in society as part of the Establishment, the group in society which is the location of established authority. The argument runs that as the judiciary are part of the machinery of authority within the state, they cannot exercise their functions

---

6   Examples are provided as a means of demonstrating the completing pressures which the judiciary may find itself under, highlighting the importance of the composition of the judiciary.

in a truly neutral way, but must, whether consciously or not – and Griffith himself suggests that it is unconscious – further the interests of that state. The consequence of this is that they decide cases in a fundamentally conservative manner, operating in such a way as to maintain the status quo and resist challenges to the established authority.

It is claimed that the most obvious examples of the judiciary's overzealous solicitude for the state's interests occur when those interests come into conflict with individual interests or the right to public information. Griffith claims that in such cases, the courts will tend to give undue preference to the state and cites various examples – such as the unilateral withdrawal of rights of trade union representation at the GCHQ – the total ban on publication of extracts from the *Spycatcher* book being simply the most recent of a number of notorious cases demonstrating the courts' readiness to promote the interests of the state and the Government above those of the individual.

With regard to the maintenance of law and order generally, but with particular reference to direct challenges to the state, Griffith cites the way in which the courts have reacted to alleged terrorists. It cannot but be admitted that the history of the trials and appeals of the Guildford Four, the Maguire Seven, the Birmingham Six and the solitary Judith Ward have resounded to the extreme discredit of the British courts, the British appeal system and British justice in general. The question has to be asked, however, do these cases reflect an inherently and inescapably conservative judiciary or are they simply unfortunate instances of errors which can occur within any system? Indeed, it could be argued that as the accused were all ultimately released, these cases actually demonstrate the neutrality and long-term validity of the British legal system. But, at the culmination of his attack on the judiciary, Griffith accuses them of actually promoting Conservative Party political views in their attitudes towards race relations, immigration and trade unions.

It is hardly surprising to find that Professor Griffith's attack on the judiciary has met with opposition.[7] One notable response (and presumed rebuttal) was provided by Lord Devlin in a review article on Griffith's book, *The Politics of the Judiciary* (1978) 41 MLR 51. Lord Devlin pointed out that in most cases, and on most issues, there tended to be plurality rather than unanimity of opinion and decision amongst judges. He also explained any apparent Conservative bias on the part of judges as a product of age rather than class and that in any case, even if the judiciary were biased, its bias was well known and allowances could be made for it. It has to be stated that Lord Devlin's response is extremely complacent and, in the light of the alleged terrorist cases mentioned previously, worryingly so.

....

7   A balanced argument is provided by considering not only Prof Griffith's arguments but also those of Lord Devlin.

It is apparent that senior judges are still being appointed from the same limited social and educational elite[8] as they always have been and that this gives rise to the accusation, if not necessarily the reality, that the decisions made by this elite merely represent the interest of a limited and privileged segment of society, rather than society as a whole. It is arguable that even if the accusations of those commentators such as Professor Griffith are inaccurate, it remains appropriate and, indeed, essential that in order to remove even the possibility of those accusations, the present structure of the judiciary be examined and altered. It is to be hoped that the establishment of the Judicial Appointments Commission, with its control over the appointment of judiciary, will open up the whole process to much welcome scrutiny in the future. There is one further point that has to be considered in relation to Griffith's attack on the judiciary, and that is the fact that, with the advent of the **Human Rights Act 1998** and the New Labour Government of 1997, many on the political left appear to see the judges as the stalwart defenders of human rights in the face of an onslaught by the authoritarian state. This is particularly the case in relation to anti-terrorist legislation, which many see as draconian in its operation and effects

QUESTION 22

Critically examine the law governing the circumstances in which judges should excuse themselves from presiding in a case because of a possible partiality.

How to Answer this Question

This question involves a consideration of the circumstances under which judges should decline to sit in a particular case. It is one of the rules of natural justice that a person should not be the judge in an action in which they have a personal interest, and the Latin expression of this rule, *nemo judex in causa sua*, goes back a long way. Answers should be able to provide an explanation of the historical context in which the question is set, but the question really demands an examination of the contemporary situation, starting with the various actions relating to the application to extradite the former Chilean dictator Augusto Pinochet and going on to consider the *Locabail* (2000) action. A good answer might adopt the following structure:

❖ an explanation of the *nemo judex* rule citing cases that show how it has been applied in the past;

❖ an explanation of how the law understands bias as it affects the judiciary considering *R v Gough* (1993);

❖ a fairly detailed explanation of the facts and law in the *Pinochet case* (1999);

❖ a consideration of the post-*Pinochet* applications and the Court of Appeal's ruling in the *Locabail* case.

---

8   The long standing argument of the judiciary being from very narrow class is discussed and the importance of not limiting selection to an elite section of society is highlighted.

Answer Structure

ANSWER --

The law in this area was, until recently, quite meagre. Judges related to parties before them, or judges with a pecuniary interest in one side of a case, were clearly required to stand down. Beyond that, in the areas of social interest, things were much less clear. However, in 1999, in *R v Bow Street Metropolitan Stipendiary Magistrate ex p Pinochet Ugarte (No 2)*, the House of Lords set aside one of its earlier decisions on the grounds that one of the Lords who delivered an opinion in the first case had a connection with Amnesty International – a body which had issued an opinion on the case.

The English legal system has a rule that no one may be a judge in their own cause, that is, they cannot judge a case in which they have an interest. This is sometimes known by the phrase *nemo judex in causa sua*. Thus, a judge who is a shareholder in a company appearing before him as a litigant must decline to hear the case: *Dimes v Grand Junction Canal* (1852). Even if a judge is unaffected by his interest in coming to a decision, it would still be wrong to preside in such a case because it might look as if the judge was improperly swayed. Thus, in the famous *dictum* of Lord Hewart, it is of fundamental importance that 'Justice must not only be done but should manifestly and undoubtedly be seen to be done' (*R v Sussex JJ ex p McCarthy* (1924), at p 259).[9]

This rule was given another dimension in *Re Pinochet Ugarte*.[10] General Pinochet, a former ruler of Chile, was in England on a visit when he was arrested for crimes of torture and mass killing allegedly orchestrated by him in Chile during the 1970s. His extradition had been requested by Spain. The legal question for the English courts was whether General Pinochet enjoyed a diplomatic immunity.

His case was eventually rejected by the House of Lords (by a 3:2 majority) in November 1998. Pinochet's lawyers then alleged that the Lords' decision was invalid as one of the majority Law Lords, Lord Hoffmann, could not be seen to be impartial, because he had a connection with the organisation Amnesty International, which had been granted leave to intervene in the proceedings and had made representations to the Lords through counsel. Lord Hoffmann, at this time, was an unpaid director of the Amnesty

---

9   The introduction places the topic into context by illustrating the traditional approach of the courts.

10   Discussion of this case places the topic into a contemporary context.

International Charitable Trust. Amnesty International was in favour of General Pinochet being brought to trial. In January 1999, on an appeal brought by Pinochet, another panel of Law Lords set aside the decision of the earlier hearing on the basis that no one should be a judge in his own cause.

Whereas previously, only pecuniary or proprietary interests had led to automatic disqualification, the House of Lords held that if the absolute impartiality of the judiciary was to be maintained, there had to be a rule which automatically disqualified a judge who was involved, whether personally or as a director of a company, in promoting the same causes in the same organisation as was a party to the suit.

Whatever one's views about the merits, sagacity or neutrality of the current judiciary, there is considerable evidence to support the proposition that historically, judges have often been biased towards certain causes and social classes. Griffith's book, *The Politics of the Judiciary*, for example, is brimming with concrete examples of judges who have shown a noted leaning towards one side of debate in cases involving workers, trade unions, civil liberties, Northern Ireland, police powers, religion and other matters. The inclusion of Lord Hoffmann on the panel was wrong because he was a director of an organisation which was represented in the case before him. Nonetheless, it is ironic that while for centuries judges have been permitted to preside in cases where their highly contentious political views have quite evidently affected their decisions (sexist, racist, anti-union, etc), the first senior judge actually to be acted against successfully for bias was someone whose agenda was nothing more than being against torture and governmental killings.

Following a number of other cases in which lawyers sought to challenge a judgment on the grounds that, through a social interest or remote financial connection, the judge was potentially biased, the Court of Appeal gave authoritative guidance on this area. The extraordinary judgment was delivered by Lord Bingham of Cornhill, Lord Chief Justice, Lord Woolf, Master of the Rolls and Sir Richard Scott, Vice Chancellor (*Locabail (UK) Ltd v Bayfield Properties Ltd and Another* (2000)). In respect of five decisions in which the judge's impartiality was questioned, the Court of Appeal ruled on general principles as follows:

(a) a judge who allowed his judicial decision to be influenced by partiality or prejudice deprived a litigant of the right to a fair trial by an impartial tribunal, and violated a most fundamental principle on which the administration of justice rested;

(b) the most effective protection of his right was, in practice, afforded by disqualification and setting aside a decision where real danger of bias was established;

(c) every such case depended on its particular facts, real doubt being resolved in favour of disqualification. It would, however, be as wrong for a judge to accede to a tenuous objection as it would be for him to ignore one of substance;

(d) in determination of their rights and liabilities, civil or criminal, everyone was entitled to a fair hearing by an impartial tribunal.

The Court of Appeal ruled that all legal arbiters were bound to apply the law, as they understood it, to the facts of individual cases, as they found them, without fear or favour, affection or ill will; that is, without partiality or prejudice. Any judge, that term embracing every judicial decision maker whether judge, lay justice or juror, who allowed any judicial decision to be influenced by partiality or prejudice deprived the litigant of his important right and violated one of the most fundamental principles underlying the administration of justice.

There was one situation where, on proof of the requisite facts, the existence of bias was effectively presumed and, in such cases, it gave rise to automatic disqualification, namely, where the judge was shown to have an interest in the outcome of the case which he was to decide or had decided: see *Dimes v Proprietors of the Grand Junction Canal* (1852), *R v Rand* (1866) and *R v Camborne Justices ex p Pearce* (1955).

In any case where the judge's interest was said to derive from the interest of a spouse, partner or other family member, the link had to be so close and direct as to render the interest of that other person, for all practical purposes, indistinguishable from an interest of the judge.

The automatic disqualification rule until recently had widely, if wrongly, been thought to apply only in cases of a judge's pecuniary or proprietary interest in the outcome of the litigation. However, *R v Bow Street Metropolitan Stipendiary Magistrate ex p Pinochet Ugarte (No 2)* (1999) made it plain that the rule extended to a limited class of non-financial interests, such as an interest in the subject matter in issue arising from the judge's promotion of some particular cause.

The law was settled in England and Wales by the House of Lords in *R v Gough* (1993) and in consequence, the relevant test was whether there was, in relation to any given judge, a real danger or possibility of bias.[11] When applying the real danger test, it would often be appropriate to inquire whether the judge knew of the matter relied on as appearing to undermine his impartiality. If it were shown that he did not, the danger of its having influenced his judgment was eliminated and the appearance of possible bias dispelled. It was for the reviewing court, not the judge concerned, to assess the risk that some illegitimate extraneous consideration might have influenced his decision.

While it would be dangerous and futile to attempt to define or list factors which might, or might not, give rise to a real danger of bias, since everything would depend on the particular facts, the court could not conceive of circumstances in which an objection could be soundly based on the religion, ethnic or national origin, gender, age, class, means or sexual orientation of the judge. Nor, at any rate ordinarily, could an objection

---

11   This case is important as it sets out the cirumstances In which a judge Is required to excuse him/herself.

be soundly based on his social, educational, service or employment background or history, nor that of any member of his family; nor previous political associations, membership of social, sporting or charitable bodies; nor Masonic associations; nor previous judicial decisions; nor extra-curricular utterances, whether in textbooks, lectures, speeches, articles, interviews, reports, responses to consultation papers; nor previous receipt of instructions to act for or against any party, solicitor or advocate engaged in a case before him; nor membership of the same Inn, circuit, local Law Society or chambers.[12]

By contrast, a real danger of bias might well be thought to arise if there were personal friendship or animosity between the judge and any member of the public involved in the case; or if the judge were closely acquainted with any such member of the public, particularly if that individual's credibility could be significant in the decision of the case; or if in a case where the credibility of any individual were an issue to be decided by the judge, he had, in a previous case, rejected that person's evidence in such outspoken terms as to throw doubt on his ability to approach such a person's evidence with an open mind on any later occasion.

In one way, the Court of Appeal was bound to come to this conclusion. Had it ruled that membership of certain societies, or a particular social background, or the previous political associations of a trial judge *were* grounds for appeal, two consequences would follow. First, there would be a rapid expansion of the use by law firms of special units that monitor and keep files on all aspects of judges' lives. Second, there would be a proliferation of appeals in all departments of the court structure, at the very time when there is such a concerted effort to reduce the backlog of appeals. What this decision leaves us with is a question of profound jurisprudential importance: how far can judges judge in an entirely neutral and socially detached manner?

Common Pitfalls

Bias or apparent bias can occur through a political association in some contexts. It is a common pitfall among poor answers to omit from discussion cases such as *Re Pinochet Ugarte (1999)*, which examine the political aspects of apparent bias.

Aim Higher ★

The Court of Appeal decision in *Locabail (UK) Ltd v Bayfield Properties Ltd and Another (2000)* added many dimensions of subtlety to the rules governing when a judge should recuse himself or herself from a case; an excellent answer will identify and explain these rules.

----

12   the question clearly asks for critical evaluation, which is provided by such discussion.

QUESTION 23

Explain how juries are constituted.

How to Answer this Question

This particular question asks for attention to be focused on the composition of the jury, rather than the jury system generally, and seeks to elicit information about how the composition is determined and how it can be interfered with. The following procedure would address those issues:

- ❖ detail the process whereby a jury is actually selected, distinguishing between 'panels of jurors' and juries;
- ❖ consider how random this process is in practice;
- ❖ consider the need for racially mixed juries and whether randomness is always fair;
- ❖ consider rights of the defence and prosecution to challenge potential jurors;
- ❖ explain the process of jury vetting and consider its general legitimacy;
- ❖ offer a conclusion as to whether randomness is fundamentally necessary or, indeed, valuable *per se*.

Answer Structure

Highlight the importance of the jury system and refer to the legal basis for selection of jury members → Consider the problems associated with jury selection and membership → Discuss the legal rules relating to jury selection and conclude as to the effectiveness of such rules

ANSWER

The procedure of deciding cases on the basis of the deliberations of a jury is an ancient one, and one that has attracted much praise within the British legal system. The implicit assumption underlying the whole jury system is that the presence of 12 ordinary lay persons, randomly introduced into the trial procedure to be the arbiters of the facts of the case, strengthens the legitimacy of the legal system. It supposedly achieves this end by introducing a democratic, humanising element into the abstract, impersonal trial process, thereby reducing the exclusive power of the legal professionals who would otherwise command the legal stage and control the legal procedure without reference to the opinion of the lay majority. A corresponding assumption is that jury service is a public duty that citizens should readily undertake, although it is made compulsory and failure to perform one's civic responsibility is subject to the sanction of a £1,000 fine. According to the Lord Chancellor's Department, around 200,000 people serve as jurors in any one year.[13]

---

13 Introduction places the topic into context by highlighting the importance of the jury system.

The procedure for determining the actual composition of the jury to hear any particular case is as follows. An officer of the court summonses a randomly selected number of qualified individuals and, from that group, draws up panels of potential jurors for various cases. The actual jurors are then randomly selected, by means of a ballot in open court.

The **Juries Act 1974**, as amended by the **Criminal Justice Act 1988**, the **Criminal Justice and Public Order Act 1994** and the **Criminal Justice Act 2003** sets out the law relating to juries.[14] It provides that any person between the ages of 18 and 70, who is on the electoral register and who has lived in the UK for at least five years, is qualified to serve as a juror. The dependency on electoral rolls to determine and locate jurors, however, raises a very real shortfall from the ideal assumptions made in relation to the jury system. The problem arises from the fact that electoral registers tend to be inaccurate. Generally, they have misreported the number of young people who are in an area, due to the fact that such people tend to have a greater degree of mobility than older people and, as a result, tend not to appear on the electoral roll of the place they currently live in. Electoral registers have also under-reported the true number of members of ethnic minorities, who have simply declined to notify the authorities of their existence.

Prior to the **Criminal Justice Act (CJA) 2003**, the general qualification for serving as a juror was subject to a number of exceptions.

For example, a number of people were deemed to be ineligible to serve on juries on the basis of their employment or vocation. Amongst this category were judges, justices of the peace, members of the legal profession, police and probation officers, and members of the clergy or religious orders. Those suffering from a mental disorder were also deemed to be ineligible. **Paragraph 2** of **Sched 33** to the **CJA 2003** removed the first three groups of persons ineligible, the judiciary, others concerned with the administration of justice and the clergy, leaving only mentally disordered persons with that status.

The provisions of the **CJA 2003** as regards eligibility to serve were challenged, as being contrary to **Art 6** of the **ECHR**, in *R v (1) Abdroikov (2) Green (3) Williamson* (2005), three otherwise unrelated cases. Each of these appellants appealed against their convictions on the grounds that the jury in their respective trials had contained members who were employed in the criminal justice system. The juries in the trials of the first and second appellants had contained serving police officers. The jury in the trial of the third appellant had contained a person employed as a prosecuting solicitor by the Crown Prosecution Service. Their proposal was that, as prior to the **CJA 2003** there would have been no doubt that the presence of such people on juries would have been unlawful, so their presence in the current cases ran contrary to the need for trials to be free from even the taint of

14 Demonstrates knowledge of the legal basis of the composition of juries and goes on to highlight important aspects of eligibility and selection.

apparent bias. The Court of Appeal rejected such arguments as spurious, holding that the expectations placed on ordinary citizens in relation to jury service had to be extended to members of the criminal justice system.[15]

The House of Lords decided that these cases did not involve the ordinary prejudices and predilections to which people were prone, but rather the possibility of bias, possibly unconscious, which flowed from the presence on the jury of people professionally committed to one side of the adversarial trial process. The expectation that each doubtful case would be resolved by the trial judge was not met if neither the judge nor counsel knew that the juror was a police officer or CPS solicitor, as appeared to be the practice. N's case was not one which turned on a contest between the evidence of the police and of N, and it would have been difficult to suggest that unconscious prejudice, if present, would have been likely to operate to N's disadvantage. The Court of Appeal had reached the right conclusion in N's case. However, in G's case, there was a crucial dispute on the evidence between G and the police officer who was the alleged victim. The victim and the police officer on the jury shared the same local service background. In those circumstances the instinct of a police officer juror to prefer the evidence of a brother officer to that of a drug-addicted defendant would be judged by the fair-minded and informed observer to be a real and possible source of unfairness, beyond the reach of standard judicial warnings and directions. G was not tried by a tribunal which was and appeared to be impartial, and his appeal was allowed. In W's case, it was clear that justice was not seen to be done where one of the jurors was a full-time, salaried, long-serving employee of the prosecutor. W's convictions were quashed. There were situations where police officers and CPS solicitors would meet the tests of impartiality. However, that did not mean they would always do so.

In an endeavour to maintain the unquestioned probity of the jury system, certain categories of persons are disqualified from serving as jurors. Amongst these is anyone who has been sentenced to a term of imprisonment, or youth custody, of five years or more. In addition, anyone who, in the past 10 years, has served a sentence, or has had a suspended sentence imposed on them, or has had a community punishment order made against them, is also disqualified. The **CJA** makes a number of amendments to reflect recent, and forthcoming, developments in sentencing legislation. Thus juveniles sentenced under **s 91** of the **Powers of Criminal Courts (Sentencing) Act 2000** to detention for life, or for a term of five years or more, will be disqualified for life from jury service. People sentenced to imprisonment or detention for public protection, or to an extended sentence under **ss 227** or **228** of the Act are also to be disqualified for life from jury service. Anyone who has received a community order (as defined in **s 177** of the Act) will be disqualified from jury service for 10 years. Those on bail in criminal proceedings are disqualified from serving as a juror in the Crown Court.

....

15   Provides discussion which illustrates the importance of jury composition.

Certain people were excused as of right from serving as jurors on account of their jobs, age or religious views. Amongst these were members of the medical professions, members of Parliament and members of the armed forces together with anyone over 65 years of age. **Paragraph 3** of **Sched 33** to the **CJA** repeals s **9(1)** of the **Juries Act 1974** and consequently no one will in future be entitled to excusal as of right from jury service.

It has always been the case that if a person who has been summoned to do jury service could show that there was a 'good reason' why their summons should be deferred or excused, **s 9** of the **Juries Act 1974** provided discretion to defer or excuse service. With the abolition of most of the categories of ineligibility and of the availability of excusal as of right, it is expected that there will be a corresponding increase in applications for excusal or deferral under s **9** being submitted to the Jury Central Summoning Bureau (see below).

Grounds for such excusal or deferral are supposed to be made only on the basis of good reason but there is at least a measure of doubt as to the rigour with which such rules are applied.

A Practice Note issued in 1988 (now *Practice Direction (Criminal: Consolidated)* [2002] 1 WLR 2870 para 42) stated that applications for excusal should be treated sympathetically and listed the following as good grounds for excusal:

(a)   personal involvement in the case;
(b)   close connection with a party or a witness in the case;
(c)   personal hardship;
(d)   conscientious objection to jury service.

The traditional procedure for determining the composition of the jury to hear any particular case is in the process of being modernised by the introduction of a central summoning bureau, based at Blackfriars Crown Court Centre in London.[16] The new bureau uses a computer system to select jurors at random from the electoral registers and issues the summonses, as well as dealing with jurors' questions and requests. It is intended to link the jury summoning system to the national police records system, to allow checks to be made against potentially disqualified individuals.

The aim of the new procedure is to ensure that all jurors are treated equally and fairly and that the rules are enforced consistently, especially in regard to requests to be excused from service and thus to reduce at least some of the potential difficulties mentioned above.

Under s **12(6)** of the **Juries Act 1974**, both prosecution and defence have a right to challenge the array, where the summoning officer has acted improperly in bringing the

----

16   Demonstrates up-to-date knowledge.

whole panel together. Such challenges are rare, although an unsuccessful action was raised in the *Danvers case* (1982).

As regards individuals, the defence until fairly recently had the right to issue peremptory challenges, that is, challenges without reason, to potential jury members, up to a maximum of three. In spite of arguments for its retention on a civil liberties basis, the right was abolished in the **Criminal Justice Act 1988**. The defence, however, still has the power to challenge any number of potential jurors for cause, that is, with reason; however, following the attempt of the defence to exclude numerous classes of people from the jury in the *Angry Brigade* trial in 1972, the Lord Chief Justice issued a Practice Direction in which it was laid down that potential jurors were not to be excluded on account of race, religion, politics or occupation.

In *Danvers*, the defence had sought to challenge the array on the basis that a black defendant could not have complete confidence in the impartiality of an all-white jury. The question of the racial mix of a jury has exercised the courts on a number of occasions. In *Ford* (1989), the trial judge's refusal to accept the defendant's application for a racially mixed jury was supported by the Court of Appeal, on the grounds that 'fairness is achieved by the principle of random selection', as regards the make-up of a jury, and that to insist on a racially balanced jury would be contrary to that principle and would be to imply that particular jurors were incapable of impartiality.

To deny people of colour the right to have their cases heard by representatives of their own race on the basis of a refusal to recognise the existence of racially discriminatory attitudes cannot but give the appearance of a society where such racist attitudes are institutionalised. Without suggesting that juries, as presently constituted, are biased, it remains arguable that if, in order to achieve the undoubted appearance of fairness, jury selection has to be manipulated to ensure a racial mix, then it should at least be considered.[17] This was apparently the view of the Runciman Commission, which suggested that in exceptional circumstances, it should be possible for either the prosecution or the defence to apply to the judge before the commencement of a trial to ensure that the jury should contain up to three people from ethnic minority communities, with at least one from the same ethnic minority as the defendant or victim. The report of Sir Robin Auld into the criminal justice system (2001) also suggested that provision should be made to enable ethnic minority representation on juries where race is likely to be relevant to an important issue in the case.

Of perhaps even more concern than challenges by the defence is the extent to which the prosecution can challenge potential jurors for, in addition to the right to challenge for cause, the prosecution also has the option of excluding particular individuals simply by

....

17 Provides examples and evaluation of the problems commonly associated with jury selection.

asking them to 'stand by' until a jury has been empanelled. The manifest unreasonableness of this procedure, in view of the limited power of the defence, led to the Attorney-General issuing a *Practice Note* ([1988] 3 All ER 1086) to the effect that the Crown should only exercise its power to stand down potential jurors in the following two circumstances:

(a)   to prevent the empanelment of a 'manifestly unsuitable' juror;
(b)   where the Attorney-General has approved the vetting of the potential jury members, and that process has revealed that a particular juror might be a security risk, and the Attorney-General has approved the use of the 'stand by' procedure.

This latter point leads, naturally, to another contentious subject, that of jury 'vetting', the process in which the Crown checks the background of potential jurors. The practice of vetting potential jurors developed after *Angry Brigade* (1972), but did not become public until the **Official Secrets Act** case, known as the *ABC Trial*, in 1978. Subsequently, the Attorney-General published the guidelines for vetting panels. The most recent guidelines were published in 1988 and, interestingly, they support the general propositions that jury members should normally be selected randomly from the panel and should be disqualified only on the grounds set out in the **Juries Act 1974**. The guidelines do, however, make reference to exceptional cases of public importance where potential jury members might properly be vetted. Such cases are broadly identified as those involving national security, where part of the evidence may be heard *in camera*, and terrorist cases. Vetting is a twofold process. An initial check in police criminal records and police Special Branch records should be sufficient to reveal whether a further investigation by the security services is required. This further investigation cannot take place without the prior approval of the Attorney-General. The purpose of the vetting is to ensure that jury members will not be likely to divulge any secrets made open to them in the course of a trial, or to ensure that jurors with extreme political views do not get the opportunity to permit those views to influence the outcome of a case.

In conclusion, therefore, it can be seen that juries are by and large random, subject to some particular and important shortcomings. However, as has been suggested above, randomness is not necessarily a virtue in itself, especially if it leads to ethnically unrepresentative juries.

QUESTION 24

Assess the impact of the **Criminal Justice Act (CJA) 2003** on who can be required to attend for jury service.

How to Answer this Question

This question requires respondents to consider the changes in requirements for jury service introduced by the **CJA 2003**, but that in turn requires a consideration of the very important case of *R v Abdroikov* (2005), in which the House of Lords used its powers under the **Human Rights Act (HRA) 1998** to effectively overturn the expressly stated will of parliament (this case may be used as an alternative source in relation to Question 50 below). A possible structure for answering the question would be as follows:

- ❖ an introduction explaining the previous system and its inherent shortcomings;
- ❖ a detailed account of the provisions introduced by the **CJA 2003**;
- ❖ in relation to eligibility, reference *must* be made to *R v Abdroikov* (2005);
- ❖ the best answers will make some comment on the use of the courts' powers under the **HRA 1988** to avoid express statutory provisions.

Answer Structure

Overview of the system prior to the enactment of the **CJA 2003** → The Auld review and changes introduced by the **CJA 2003** → The challenge to the **CJA** by *Abdroikov* (2005) under the **ECHR/HRA**

ANSWER

Prior to the **CJA 2003**, the general qualification for serving as a juror was subject to a number of exceptions and as a result it had been suggested that jury service almost amounted to a self-selecting system, under which those who did not wish to serve, were under no real compulsion to do so, just as long as they could provide a reason for not serving. Following the recommendations of the Auld review of the criminal justice system in 2001, the Government enacted the **CJA 2003** with the declared intention of not only increasing the numbers of people who would in future be required to serve as jurors, but also limiting the available excuses for not serving. However, as will be seen below, these intentions have been effectively undermined by the judges of the House of Lords.[18]

INELIGIBILITY

A variety of people were deemed to be ineligible to serve on juries on the basis of their employment or vocation. Amongst this category were: judges; Justices of the Peace; members of the legal profession; police and probation officers; and members of the clergy or religious orders. Those suffering from a mental disorder were also deemed to be ineligible. **Paragraph 2** of **Sched 33** to the **CJA 2003** removed the first three groups of ineligible persons, the judiciary, others concerned with the administration of justice, and the clergy, leaving only mentally disordered persons with that status.

---

18 Highlights the pre-**CJA** system and the background to its introduction.

The above reform came into effect in April 2005. However, the eligibility provisions of the **CJA 2003** were challenged, as being contrary to **Art 6** of the **European Convention on Human Rights**, in *R v (1) Abdroikov (2) Green (3) Williamson* (2005),[19] three otherwise unrelated cases. Each of the appellants appealed against their convictions on the grounds that the jury in their respective trials had contained members who were employed in the criminal justice system. The juries in the trials of the first and second appellants had contained serving police officers. The jury in the trial of the third appellant had contained a person employed as a prosecuting solicitor by the Crown Prosecution Service. Their proposal was that, as prior to the **CJA 2003** there would have been no doubt that the presence of such people on juries would have been unlawful, so their presence in the current cases ran contrary to the need for trials to be free from even the taint of apparent bias.

The Court of Appeal rejected such arguments as spurious, holding that the expectations placed on ordinary citizens in relation to jury service had to be extended to members of the criminal justice system. However, by a majority of three to two the House of Lords held that the appeals of Green and Williamson should succeed, but that Abdroikov's appeal must fail. Lords Rodger and Carswell, in the minority, held that all appeals should fail. In reaching its decision the majority looked at the reports of previous committees which had been tasked with examining the operation of juries. Thus they referred to the findings of the 1965 committee chaired by Lord Morris of Borth-y-Gest which recommended that the police and those professionally concerned in the administration of the law should continue to be ineligible. Then in 2001, Auld LJ reviewed the issue and recommended that everyone should be eligible for jury service save for the mentally ill. He recognised that the risk of bias could not be totally eradicated and envisaged that any question about the risk of bias on the part of any juror could be resolved by the trial judge on the facts of the case. His recommendation was given effect by the **CJA 2003 s 321**. However, as the House of Lords made clear, Auld LJ's expectation that each doubtful case would be resolved by the trial judge could not be met if neither the judge nor counsel knew that the juror was a police officer or CPS solicitor. The House of Lords recognised that there were situations where police officers and CPS solicitors would meet the tests of impartiality; however, that did not mean they would always do so or do so automatically.

However, according to Lords Rodger and Carswell in the minority, Parliament had endorsed the view that universal eligibility for jury service was to be regarded as appropriate. In reaching that conclusion Parliament had to be taken to have been aware of the test for apparent bias. It must, therefore, be taken to have considered that the risk of bias in the case of serving police officers or CPS solicitors was manageable within the system of jury trial. The consequence of the House of Lords' majority decision was pointed out by Lord Rodger in the clearest of terms:

---

19 Consideration of the challenge to the changes introduced by the **CJA** made under the **ECHR/HRA**.

I can see no reason why the fair-minded and informed observer should single out juries with police officers and CPS lawyers as being constitutionally incapable of following the judge's directions and reaching an impartial verdict. It must be assumed, for instance, that the observer considers that there is no real possibility that a jury containing a gay man trying a man accused of a homophobic attack will, for that reason alone, be incapable of reaching an unbiased verdict, even though the juror might readily identify with a fellow gay man. Despite this – if Mr Green's appeal is to be allowed – the observer must be supposed to consider that there is, inevitably, a real possibility that a jury will have been biased in a case involving a significant conflict of evidence between a police witness and the defendant, just because the witness and a police officer juror serve in the same borough or the juror serves in a force which commits its work to the trial court in question. Similarly, if Mr Williamson's appeal is allowed, the observer must be taken to consider that the same applies to any jury containing a CPS lawyer whenever the prosecution is brought by the CPS. In my view, an observer who singled out juries with these two types of members would be applying a different standard from the one that is usually applied. For no good reason, the observer would be virtually ignoring the other 11 jurors ... your Lordships' decision to allow two of the appeals will drive a coach and horses through Parliament's legislation and will go far to reverse its reform of the law, *even though the statutory provisions themselves are not said to be incompatible with Convention rights.* Moreover, any requirement for police officers and CPS lawyers balloted to serve on a jury to identify themselves routinely to the judge would discriminate against them by introducing a process of vetting for them and them alone. Parliament cannot have considered that such a requirement was necessary since it did not impose it. The rational policy of the legislature is to decide who are eligible to serve as jurors and then to treat them all alike.

DISQUALIFICATION

In an endeavour to maintain the unquestioned probity of the jury system, certain categories of persons are disqualified from serving as jurors. Amongst these are anyone who has been sentenced to a term of imprisonment, or youth custody, of five years or more. In addition, anyone who, in the past 10 years, has served a sentence, or has had a suspended sentence imposed on them, or has had a community punishment order made against them, is also disqualified. The **CJA 2003** makes a number of amendments to reflect recent and forthcoming developments in sentencing legislation. Thus, juveniles sentenced under **s 91** of the **Powers of Criminal Courts (Sentencing) Act 2000** to detention for life, or for a term of five years or more, will be disqualified for life from jury service. People sentenced to imprisonment or detention for public protection, or to an extended sentence under **s 227** or **s 228** of the Act are also to be disqualified for life from jury service. Anyone who has received a community order (as defined in **s 177** of the Act) will be disqualified from jury service for 10 years. Those on bail in criminal proceedings are disqualified from serving as a juror in the Crown Court.

EXCUSAL

Certain people were excused as of right from serving as jurors on account of their jobs, age or religious views. Amongst these were members of the medical professions, Members of Parliament and members of the armed forces, together with anyone over 65 years of age. **Paragraph 3** of **Sched 33** to the **CJA 2003** repeals **s 9(1)** of the **Juries Act (JA) 1974** and consequently no one will in future be entitled to excusal as of right from jury service.

It has always been the case that if a person who has been summoned to do jury service could show that there was a 'good reason' why their summons should be deferred or excused, **s 9** of the **JA 1974** provided discretion to defer or excuse service. With the abolition of most of the categories of ineligibility and of the availability of excusal as of right, it is expected that there will be a corresponding increase in applications for excusal or deferral under **s 9** being submitted to the Jury Central Summoning Bureau (see below).

Grounds for such excusal or deferral are supposed to be made only on the basis of good reason, but there is at least a measure of doubt as to the rigour with which such rules are applied.

A Practice Note issued in 1988 (now *Practice Direction (Criminal: Consolidated)* (2002), para 42) stated that applications for excusal should be treated sympathetically and listed the following as good grounds for excusal:

(a) personal involvement in the case;
(b) close connection with a party or a witness in the case;
(c) personal hardship;
(d) conscientious objection to jury service.

However, a new **s 9AA**, introduced by the **CJA 2003**, places a statutory duty on the Lord Chancellor, in whom current responsibility for jury summoning is vested, to publish and lay before Parliament guidelines relating to the exercise by the Jury Central Summoning Bureau of its functions in relation to discretionary deferral and excusal.

The aim of the guidelines should be to ensure that all jurors are treated equally and fairly and that the rules are enforced consistently, especially in regard to requests to be excused from service, and thus to reduce at least some of the potential difficulties mentioned above.

The Criminal Process

INTRODUCTION

The official purpose of the criminal justice system (CJS) is 'to deliver justice for all, by convicting and punishing the guilty and helping them to stop offending, while protecting the innocent'. It is responsible for detecting crime and bringing offenders to justice; and carrying out the orders of court, such as collecting fines, and supervising community and custodial punishment.

The key goals for criminal justice were stated in 2010 as being:

❖ to improve the effectiveness and efficiency of the CJS in bringing offences to justice;
❖ to increase public confidence in the fairness and effectiveness of the CJS;
❖ to increase victim satisfaction with the police, and victim and witness satisfaction with the CJS;
❖ to consistently collect, analyse and use good quality ethnicity data to identify and address race disproportionality in the CJS; and
❖ to increase the recovery of criminal assets by recovering £250 million of assets acquired through crime by 2009–10.

Not all parts of the CJS are working well. In November, 2011 a National Audit Office (NAO) report into financial management at the Ministry of Justice (which is responsible for the CJS) revealed that Courts in England and Wales were owed £413 million in unpaid fines and £388 million in un-collected confiscation orders. The amount in outstanding fines has increased by 25 per cent since 2006–2007. The NAO observed that in 2011–2012 the Ministry of Justice was asked to make savings of £500 million in order to achieve the required funding cut of 23 per cent by 2014 and will therefore need to make significant efficiency savings. While finding that the financial management of the Ministry of Justice has improved since the audit in November 2010, the NAO nevertheless stated that in some important areas, 'the Ministry still has a great deal to do'.

The CJS is designed to operate as a coherent whole. It is comprised of: the National Criminal Justice Board, 42 Local Criminal Justice Boards across England and Wales, and the Office for Criminal Justice Reform.

The scale of activity is large. In 2012, government statistics revealed that in the 12 months ending September 2011, there were 230,700 police cautions in England and Wales and 1.32 million offenders were convicted and sentenced.

The Ministry of Justice was created in 2007 to provide a stronger focus on the criminal justice system, and to reduce re-offending. Many changes have been made since by the **Criminal Justice and Immigration Act 2008**. Among other things, the Act:

- ❖ introduces a minimum tariff of two years for prisoners serving indeterminate public protection sentences;
- ❖ ends automatic discounts for offenders given an indeterminate sentence after the initial sentencing decision has been judged unduly lenient;
- ❖ gives powers for courts to make dangerous offenders given a discretionary life sentence serve a higher proportion of their tariff before being eligible for parole;
- ❖ creates a presumption that trials in magistrates' courts will proceed in the event the accused fails to appear;
- ❖ provides for non-dangerous offenders who breach the terms of their licence to be recalled to prison for a fixed 28-day period;
- ❖ creates a Youth Rehabilitation Order – a generic community sentence for children and young offenders – this will target the causes of offending behaviour and will simplify the current sentencing framework;
- ❖ creates the Youth Conditional Caution for children and young offenders;
- ❖ brings compensation for those wrongly convicted broadly into line with compensation for victims of crime.

Checklist ✔

In particular, you should be familiar with the following recommendations and changes in the law.

Appeals
- The work of the Criminal Cases Review Commission.
- The powers for the Court of Appeal.
- The Court of Appeal's decision in *Secretary of State for the Home Department ex p Hickey and Others* (1995).

Trial by jury
- The provisions of the **Criminal Justice Act 2003, ss 43–50** and **321**.

Right to silence
- **Sections 34–37** of the **Criminal Justice and Public Order Act (CJPOA) 1994**, which explain what inferences may now be drawn in what circumstances from the silence of the accused.

Confessions
- **Sections 32–33** of the **CJPOA 1994**, which abolish the rules requiring the court to give the jury a warning about convicting the accused on the uncorroborated evidence of a person who is an accomplice or, in sexual cases, the victim.

Plea bargaining
Limited introduction was recommended by Runciman – reduced sentences for guilty pleas.

In general, you will need to know the major provisions of the Police and Criminal Evidence Act (PACE) 1984 and other provisions relating to criminal procedure:

- the general powers of arrest – **s 24** of **PACE**;
- the general arrest conditions – **s 25** of **PACE**;
- the common law powers of arrest;
- procedure on arrest;
- information on arrest;
- stop and search – **ss 1** and **2** (and revised Code A) of **PACE**;
- search of arrested person – **s 32** of **PACE**;
- search on detention – **s 54** of **PACE**;
- search of premises – **ss 17, 18** and **32** of **PACE**;
- search warrants – **ss 8, 15** and **16** of **PACE**;
- interrogation, confession and admissibility of evidence;
- bail – the **CJPOA 1994** changes;
- plea bargaining.

QUESTION 25
Critically evaluate the use of civil law by citizens who seek justice from it as an alternative to the criminal law.

How to Answer this Question
In your answer you should:

❖ explain the differences between the civil law and the criminal law;

❖   explain the basic nature of the private prosecution;
❖   give examples of citizens resorting to civil action where the criminal justice system has been judged by them to have failed;
❖   identify the legal difficulties concerning the appropriate standard of proof in civil trials about criminal matters;
❖   draw conclusions about the implications of the rising phenomenon for the legal system at large

Answer Structure

Whereas the main purpose of the criminal law is for the start, on behalf of society, to condemn and punish serious wrongs, the purpose of civil law is to allow citizens to gain compensation or court orders if someone else has broken a civil law and caused them loss or harm. Sometimes, however, the civil law is used by citizens because the criminal law has been ineffective.

A private prosecution is a prosecution started by a private individual who is not acting on behalf of the police or any other prosecuting authority such as the Health and Safety Executive or the Inland Revenue. The right to bring private prosecutions is preserved by the **Prosecution of Offences Act 1985 s 6(1).** There are, however, some controls: under the **Prosecution of Offences Act 1985 s 6(2)** the DPP has the power to take over private prosecutions. In some cases, the private prosecutor must seek the consent of the Attorney General or of the DPP before the commencement of proceedings.

At just after 3 pm on 15 August, 1998, in a busy shopping street in Omagh, Northern Ireland, 29 people were murdered in a terrorist car-bomb atrocity. Most of the people blown up were women and children. The murder victims were both Protestant and Roman Catholic, and included a woman celebrating her 65th birthday with her pregnant daughter and 20-month-old granddaughter.

No one was convicted for this crime (Colm Murphy was sentenced to 14 years in prison in January 2002 for conspiracy to cause the explosion, but the conviction was overturned on appeal and in 2010 he was still awaiting a retrial). Years later, as the criminal law was seen to be ineffective in condemning the guilty, relatives of the victims brought a civil action. In 2009, four men and the Real IRA were held liable in civil law for the homicides (*Breslin & Ors v McKenna & Ors (Omagh Bombing case)* (2009)). Mr Justice Declan Morgan awarded more than £1.6 million in damages to 12 relatives of 29 people but the compensation is unlikely ever to be paid and, in any event, the action was not motivated by money but by a quest for court justice.

Victor Barker, whose 12-year-old son, James, was killed in the attack said:

> We've finally achieved some justice for the families. I will never get over the loss of my son, but I have done what I could for him and I'm proud that I stood up for him.

He noted that in 1998 the Prime Minister had pledged to convict the killers, leaving not one stone unturned, and added 'Well, he clearly did because the families had to pick up all those stones and bring them to court' (*The Times*, 9 June, 2009).[1]

The Omagh litigation is part of a growing use of the *civil* process to pin a legal judgment of liability on culprits who have not, but arguably should have been, convicted by the criminal law. That is not an index of a healthy legal system. The courage and perseverance of those who brought the Omagh civil action, and their legal win, are noteworthy but the victory is a limited one. The criminal law and the civil law have different purposes.

The purpose of the criminal law, according to Blackstone's elegant encapsulation, is to condemn and punish acts which 'strike at the very being of society'. He said that civil wrongs were wrongs that affected 'individuals, considered merely as individuals' whereas crimes were wrongs which struck at the whole community 'in its social aggregate capacity' (*Commentaries on the Laws of England*, IV, 1, 5).

If the civil justice system is being used in a makeshift way only because the criminal justice system has failed, the result is unsatisfactory. A civil suit does not really fit these circumstances.

It has been suggested that the Omagh case will promote a wider belief that civil actions can succeed against perpetrators when the traditional use of a criminal prosecution has failed ('Families of victims triumph in civil lawsuit over Omagh bombings', *The Times*, 9 June 2009). If that is so, there is likely to be a reduction, not an enlargement, of legal justice over time. The registration on the public record of some serious crimes will be hidden in the files of civil judgments. Another possibility is that some serious crimes will result in prosecutions and convictions but only after a civil suit. Thus the civil action becomes a sort of rough rehearsal for a prosecution. I shall mention some cases like that below but they just raise the question why citizens should bear a burden of

---

1   The use of appropriate examples affords the opportunity to provide clear explanation of how crimes may be both persecuted using both criminal and civil means. It also allows the answer to move on, seamlessly and logically, to the failings of the criminal system and the value of civil prosecutions in attaining justice.

evidence-gathering and argument formulation that could have been carried out by police officers or prosecutors.

An early use of the civil process to get a law court to condemn what was essentially a serious crime came in the case of Michael Brookes. In a civil case in 1991, a High Court judge ruled that Michael Brookes had killed Lynn Siddons, a 16-year-old stabbed 40 times in 1978. Her family were awarded £10,641 damages (*The Times*, 1 October, 12 December, 1991). Mr Justice Rougier, however, applied the criminal standard of proof (that the case must be proven beyond a reasonable doubt) saying that a civil action for murder demanded no less (*Halford v Brookes and another* (1991)). The original police investigation and case against another defendant were found to have been completely bungled, but, after the civil case, Brookes was later convicted following a fresh criminal investigation of the murder (*The Times*, 9 October, 1998).

In 1995, Linda Griffiths went to the civil courts in an action alleging that she had been raped by Arthur Williams, a former chef at the Dorchester, while working for him in 1991 as a dishwasher. The Crown Prosecution Service (CPS) had decided not to prosecute Mr Williams. In the civil case against Mr Williams for trespass against the person, Ms Griffiths won and was awarded £50,000 damages (*The Times*, 5 November 1997).

In 1997, not long before OJ Simpson was found liable in a Californian civil court for the homicide of his former wife Nicole and her friend Ronald Goldman, a civil summons relating to homicide was issued in London by the father of a murdered doctor, Joan Francisco. The following year, Mr Justice Alliott identified Tony Diedrick as the killer of Dr Francisco (*Francisco v Diedrick* (1998)). He awarded her family £50,000. Diedrick was later convicted of the killing and sentenced to life imprisonment.

Mr Justice Alliott decided the issue of liability (in an allegation of assault causing death) by reference to the balance of probabilities 'while bearing in mind that the allegation is of utmost gravity and can only be established by truly cogent evidence'.

He cited the decision of the House of Lords in *Re H and R (Child Sexual Abuse: Standard of Proof)* (1996) and, in particular the speech of Lord Nicholls of Birkenhead in these terms (at page 96B):

> ... The balance of probability standard means that a court is satisfied an event occurred if the court considers that, on the evidence, the occurrence of the event was more likely than not. When assessing the probabilities the court will have in mind as a factor, to whatever extent is appropriate in the particular case, that the more serious the allegation the less likely it is that the event occurred and, hence, the stronger should be the evidence before the court concludes that the allegation is established on the balance of probability. Fraud is usually less likely than negligence. Deliberate physical injury is usually less likely than accidental physical injury ...

... The more improbable the event, the stronger must be the evidence that it did occur before, on the balance of probability, its occurrence will be established. Ungoed-Thomas J. expressed this neatly in *In re Dellow's Will Trusts* [1964] 1 WLR. 451, 455: 'The more serious the allegation the more cogent is the evidence required to overcome the unlikelihood of what is alleged and thus to prove it.'

That subtlety is important when a High Court judge comes to direct himself as to the standard of proof required in a civil case arising from an alleged crime. But, from a public perspective, put simply, the difference between the burden of proof in civil and criminal cases is that the burden of proof is lower in civil courts than in criminal courts. It is easier to prove a tort than a crime. This gives some opportunity for people successfully sued for alleged crimes to protest that just because their conduct is certified by the civil system as a civil wrong does not mean that a crime has been committed.

In *The Devil's Dictionary* Ambrose Bierce famously described a lawsuit as 'a machine which you go into as a pig and come out of as a sausage'. Never an enjoyable experience for litigants, litigation is especially harrowing when it is being taken by desperate victims of very serious wrongs who are doing so only because the state has evidently failed in its duty. Suing is a notoriously expensive and protracted experience so the fact that an apparently growing number of crime victims are disposed to fight their cases in the civil courts is a token of grave dissatisfaction with the ordinary prosecution process.

In some cases, prosecutors have been, are, and will be absolutely justified in declining to prosecute because there is insufficient credible and admissible evidence to satisfy the Code for Crown Prosecutors criterion requiring there to be a 'realistic prospect of conviction'. There might be circumstances in which the acquisition of sufficiently good evidence to build a prosecution case is impossible. More troubling, though, are those cases in which inadequate police investigations effectively rule out a prosecution. That some police investigations are inadequate is strongly suggested where privately garnered evidence enables a civil win, and, thereafter, a public prosecution and conviction. British policing is, as you might expect from the world's earliest professionalised service, about the best in the world; but any unprosecuted serious crime leaves an enduring scar on the body politic.[2]

> **Common Pitfalls**
> A candidate who does not exhibit a clear understanding of the different purposes and processes of civil and criminal law will make a poor impression.

2   The provision of this conclusion provides the opportunity to highlight/emphasise the value of civil law in circumstances that would normally be dealt with under the criminal system. Re-reading the question before attempting a conclusion can often be valuable, as it allows the conclusion to be directed towards the specific question set.

Aim Higher ★

High ability will be demonstrated by showing a knowledge of *Shah v Gale* (2005).

Demonstrating a good knowledge of the reasoning in *Re H and R (Child Sexual Abuse: Standard of Proof)* (1996) will be highly creditable.

QUESTION 26

After a shop has been set on fire late one night, Detective Constables Whistle and Cuff, in a nearby road, hear about the incident on their car radio. They then see two youths, Gas and Spark, running down the road away from the area of the shop. The officers stop the youths, who smell of petrol, and ask them some questions. Gas and Spark are then arrested for arson and taken to the police station.

Before questioning, the officers untruthfully told Gas that his fingerprints had been discovered on a discarded bottle of petrol found in the burnt out shop. The solicitor, unaware of the deceit, advised Gas to disclose any involvement he had had in the incident and Gas admitted having taken part.

Spark declined to accept any legal advice after the proper notices about its availability had been given to him. Spark was a drug addict and after a session of relentless questions being fired at him for over two hours, he asked whether the police would agree to bail if he admitted to being involved in the incident. The officer in the room agreed and Spark made a statement, in which he said he was at the shop at the time the fire was just becoming serious, and had gone in to see if any property could be salvaged, but he had not started the fire.

▶ **Advise Gas and Spark on the admissibility of their statements.**

How to Answer this Question

Advice to Gas

In your advice to Gas, you should:

- ❖ explain the significance of **s 82(1)** of the **Police and Criminal Evidence Act (PACE) 1984**;
- ❖ explain the relevance of **ss 76** and **78** of **PACE**;
- ❖ explain and apply *Sang* (1980);
- ❖ explain and apply *Mason* (1988).

Advice to Spark

When advising Spark, include discussion of:

- ❖ the rule in *Zavekas* (1970);

- ❖   s **76** of **PACE**, Code C and *Sharp* (1988);
- ❖   *Goldenberg* (1988) and the drug issue;
- ❖   three possible arguments on appeal, ss **76, 78** and **82** of **PACE**;
- ❖   precedent on 'oppressive', for example, *Miller* (1986).

Answer Structure

ANSWER

ADVICE TO GAS

A confession is defined[3] in **s 82(1)** of **PACE** as a statement 'wholly or partly adverse to the party who made it'. Gas, within these terms, appears to have made a confession. The admissibility of a confession is governed by several sections of **PACE**. **Section 76(2)** states that in relation to confessions which have allegedly resulted from 'oppression', or in consequence of anything said or done which was likely, in the circumstances existing at the time, to render unreliable any confession made, the court shall not admit the evidence unless the prosecution proves that the confession was not obtained in such a manner.

Section 78 allows a court to refuse to admit evidence if it appears, having regard to all the circumstances including the circumstances in which the evidence was obtained, that admission of the evidence would have such an adverse effect on the fairness of the proceedings that the court ought not to admit it. It was held by the Court of Appeal in *Mason* (1988) that regardless of whether the admissibility of a confession falls to be considered under **s 76(2)**, a judge has the discretion to deal with it under **s 78**.

Section 82 states that 'nothing in this part of the Act [**Pt VIII**, dealing with evidence] shall prejudice any power of a court to exclude evidence'. The general view is that **s 82** preserved the whole of the common law existing prior to **PACE**, so that a confession could also be excluded under decisions like that of the House of Lords in *Sang* (1980). That

---

3   Always consider providing definitions of legal terminology relevant to the question. Remember that an examiner is unlikely to give you marks for such knowledge unless you specifically provide it.

case permitted exclusion of evidence where its prejudicial effect outweighs its probative value. Lord Diplock thought that a discretion only existed at common law with regard to admissions and confessions and 'generally with regard to evidence obtained from the accused after commission of the offence'. One observation of Lord Diplock's which is especially helpful to Gas (although *obiter dicta*) is that the purpose of such judicial discretion is to ensure that an accused was not induced to incriminate himself by deception.

It would be possible for Gas to argue for the exclusion of his admission on all three of the above sections (**ss 76, 78** and **82**).

In *Mason* (1988), on facts similar to those in question, the defendant was tricked into making an admission of instigating an arson attack on the car of an enemy, after a police officer had told both him and his solicitor that the defendant's fingerprints had been found on a bottle of inflammable liquid used in the attack. Following the solicitor's advice to give an explanation, the defendant then admitted his role in the arson. The Court of Appeal quashed the defendant's conviction as having such an adverse effect on the fairness of the proceedings (**s 78**) that the court should have excluded it. It is not certain, however, that this case would assist Gas. In *Mason*, the trial judge had admitted the evidence of the defendant's admission, but, in saying the trial judge wrongly exercised his discretion, the Court of Appeal said he had omitted one 'vital factor' from his considerations: that of the deceit practised on the defendant's solicitor. Evidently, a deceit practised only upon the defendant – as in our case – would not in itself warrant discretionary exclusion of the admission.[4]

ADVICE TO SPARK

Zavekas (1970) was a case decided using the old Judges' Rules, which held that admissions, to be admissible, had to be voluntary in the sense of being obtained without 'fear of prejudice or hope of advantage, exercised or held out by a person in authority'. The Court of Appeal quashed a conviction, because the trial judge had admitted a confession made after the defendant asked the police whether he could have bail if he made a statement and, receiving an affirmative reply, proceeded to confess. Such law has, however, been effectively overruled by **s 76(2)(b)** of **PACE** and Code C, which give a much narrower compass to the notion of unreliability in respect of confessions. Spark's admission is 'mixed', in that it contains parts which are incriminating (he was at the scene of the crime and he did go into the shop) and

4   While it is important to clearly set out relevant law, don't forget that examiners will also be looking for evidence of your ability to apply the law to a given scenario. You will not necessarily be expected to come to a definite conclusion but, instead, to argue the various possibilities based largely on how the courts have dealt with cases in the past, where the material facts were sufficiently similar to the scenario provided. (Thus not only is the legislation important but case law too!)

parts which are self-serving and self-exculpatory (he did not start the fire). The combination of the provisions of **PACE** and the decisions of the House of Lords in *Sharp* (1988) and *Aziz* (1996) appear to have put the law on this subject beyond doubt. Their Lordships in both *Sharp* and *Aziz* specifically approved the judgment of Lord Lane in *Duncan* (1981), which held that the simplest method and, therefore, the one most likely to produce a just result is for the jury to consider the whole statement, both the incriminating parts and the excuses and explanations, in deciding where the truth lies. **Section 82(1)** of **PACE** defines 'confession' as including 'any statement wholly or partly adverse to the person who made it'. Accordingly, statements of 'mixed' content count as confessions and are admissible in evidence, subject to **s 76** of **PACE** being satisfied.

The Code says that if a suspect asks an officer a 'direct question' as to what action will be taken in the event of his answering questions, making a statement or refusing to do either, 'the officer may inform him what action he proposes to take in that event provided that the action itself is proper and warranted' (Code C, para 11.3).

Provided that the police officer, in stating that the police would agree to bail in consequence of an admission, was answering a direct question from Spark, then the police conduct is lawful and the evidence not rendered inadmissible or vulnerable to exclusion.

The fact that Spark was a drug addict and might have been sufficiently desperate for more drugs to have admitted to anything in order to get bail would not, on current case law, appear to affect the matter provided, of course, that his confession was not prompted by any other factor of police conduct in breach of the Act or the Codes. In *Goldenberg* (1988), the defendant, a heroin addict, requested an interview five days after his arrest and, during this interview, he allegedly gave information about someone whom he claimed had supplied him with heroin. At trial, counsel for the defendant argued that the evidence of the interview might be unreliable under **s 76**:

(a)   because the admissions were made in an attempt to get bail; and
(b)   because of his addiction, it might be expected that the defendant would do or say anything – however false – to get bail and thus be able to feed his addiction.

This latter argument was rejected both at trial and on appeal. There was no argument that the interviewing officer had said or done anything improper, and the words 'in consequence of anything said or done' in **s 76(2)(b)** meant said or done by someone other than the suspect.

If it can be shown that the police interview with Spark was 'oppressive', then the argument for the exclusion of the confession could be run in any or all of three ways: (a) that it should be excluded by virtue of **s 76(2)(a)**, as the police conduct was oppressive *simpliciter*, or that in conjunction with the fact of Spark's addiction and in view of the *ratio* of *Goldenberg* (where the appeal was dismissed because of no evidence of police misconduct), it was a confession gained by oppression; or (b) that it should be excluded by virtue of **s 78** (see advice to Gas, above); or (c) that it should be excluded by virtue of **s 82**, as its prejudicial effect greatly outweighs its probative value and it is within Lord Diplock's formula from *Sang* (1980) of protecting a suspect's right not to incriminate himself.

It will be difficult to show that the police interview was 'oppressive', as the courts have been very reluctant to make such findings. In *Fulling* (1987), the Court of Appeal gave 'oppression' its dictionary meaning, which involves 'the exercise of power or authority in a burdensome, harsh or wrongful manner'. *Fulling* was applied in *Emmerson* (1991). Questioning that was 'rude and discourteous', with a raised voice and some bad language and which gave the impression of 'impatience and irritation', was not considered oppressive. *Paris* (1994) produced a different result. The police were held to have behaved oppressively after shouting at a suspect what they wanted him to say over 300 times, after he had denied involvement in the offence charged. However, in *L* (1994), tactics similar to those employed in *Paris* appear to have been regarded as acceptable. The length of the interviews and the nature of the questioning are, of course, the important considerations.

Rules in Code C govern how interviews should be conducted. It is provided (Code C, para 12.7) that breaks from interviewing shall be made at recognised meal times and that 'short breaks for refreshment shall also be provided at intervals of approximately two hours'. An officer has the discretion to delay a break, but only where there are reasonable grounds for believing that the break would:

(a)   involve a risk of harm to persons or serious loss or damage to property; or
(b)   unnecessarily delay the suspect's release from custody; or
(c)   otherwise prejudice the outcome of the investigation.

It thus seems unlikely that Spark's interview, which lasted 'for over two hours' (but, presumably, nearer to two than three hours), was oppressive, unless he can show that it was deliberately aimed at producing a state of confusion, or that it transgressed the fairly wide Code rules.

One final consideration is that Spark is described as a 'youth'. Code C, para 1.5 says that if anyone appears to be under the age of 17, then he shall be treated as a juvenile. Code C, para 11.14 states that a juvenile, whether suspected or not, must not be interviewed or asked to provide or sign a written statement in the absence of an appropriate adult (unless para 11.1 or Annex C applies, allowing an interview to take place if a delay in interviewing the suspect would lead to interfering with evidence or witnesses).

QUESTION 27 -

After a series of burglaries in Grimtown, Pat and Billy were arrested by police and taken to the local police station. Pat and Billy were taken to separate rooms for interrogation.

Pat asked to see a solicitor. A police officer wrote something down, went out of the room and came back saying that there would need to be a little delay, as: 'We would not want word to get out to the wrong people that you're in here.' The officer then said: 'You know the ropes, Pat, we would just like to ask you a few simple questions.' Pat then made some confessions which were admitted in court and he was convicted for offences of burglary.

In the other room, Billy also asked about a lawyer. 'We can arrange for one or you can have your own', he was told. Billy thought for a moment and then replied that it would probably be too expensive, so he would not opt for legal advice. Billy asked the police to inform the president of the Civil Freedom League of his arrest. A senior officer told Billy that would not be possible. Billy has now also confessed to certain burglaries and has been tried and convicted.

▶ **Advise Pat and Billy on the possibility of appealing against their convictions.**

How to Answer this Question

Advice to Pat

In your advice to Pat, you should:

- ❖ give the meaning of **s 58** of the **Police and Criminal Evidence Act (PACE) 1984**;
- ❖ explain the significance of **s 116**, 'serious arrestable offence';
- ❖ state whether burglary falls within this category – see **s 24(1)(b)**;
- ❖ explain and apply *McIvor* (1987);
- ❖ explain and apply *Smith (Eric)* (1987), *Samuel* (1988) and *Parris* (1989);
- ❖ explain and apply Code C, Annex B, Note B4.

Advice to Billy

In your advice to Billy, you should examine:

- ❖ his entitlement to free advice: revised Code C, para 3.1;
- ❖ the meaning of 'friend or relative' (**s 56(6)**);
- ❖ the application of *Beycan* (1990);
- ❖ the relevance of **s 76(2)(b)**.

Answer Structure

ANSWER

ADVICE TO PAT

PACE came into effect in 1986 and, since that time, the access a suspect in a police station has to a lawyer has been governed by the Act. **Section 58(1)** of **PACE** states that a person arrested and held in custody in a police station shall be entitled, if he so requests, to consult a solicitor at any time. The request must be recorded in the custody record and the request must be granted 'as soon as is practicable', except to the extent that delay is permitted by the section. Delay in compliance with Pat's request is only permitted by the section if he is being held in connection with a 'serious arrestable offence' and an officer of at least the rank of superintendent authorises it. 'Serious arrestable offences' are defined in **s 116** and **Sched 5**. The term includes named offences such as murder and rape and also any arrestable offence which has, *inter alia*, led to 'substantial financial gain to any person' (**s 116(6)(e)**) or 'serious financial loss to any person' (**s 116(6)(f)**).

Burglary is an 'arrestable offence' by virtue of **s 24(1)(b)** of **PACE** as someone over 21 (without previous convictions) could, upon conviction for it, be sentenced to a term of imprisonment of five years. It is arguable whether Pat has been arrested in connection with a 'serious arrestable offence'.[5] It would depend on the value of the stolen goods and on the respective financial positions of:

(a) those who were burgled; and
(b) Pat.

It was held in *McIvor* (1987)[6] that the theft of 28 beagles worth £880 from a hunt was not a serious arrestable offence. The theft of the dogs, which were owned collectively by the hunt, did not cause 'serious financial loss'. In *Smith (Eric)* (1987), a robbery from Woolworths involving two video recorders (valued at £800) plus cash of £116 was

5   Relevant law is stated before any conclusions can be drawn as to whether Pat has grounds for appeal. Once stated, the law can then be applied to the facts of the scenario and possible outcomes considered.
6   Discussion of relevant case law such as this is important, as it is through decided cases that the courts provide their interpretation of legislation.

regarded by the trial judge as probably not a serious arrestable offence: the loss to such a large national store would be small and the gain to the robbers would not necessarily be substantial.

Under Code C, Annex B, Note C1, an officer of at least the rank of superintendent may only delay Pat's access to a solicitor on the grounds stated in **s 58** of **PACE**. He must have 'reasonable grounds' for believing that such access will:

(a)   lead to interference with, or harm to, evidence connected with a serious arrestable offence, or interference with, or physical injury to, other persons; or
(b)   lead to the alerting of other persons involved in the offence but not yet arrested; or
(c)   hinder the recovery of any property obtained as a result of the offence.

The words used by the officer to Pat, 'We would not want word to get out to the wrong people that you're in here', are consistent with any of the statutory reasons in (a) to (c) above. The Act says, however, that if the delay is authorised, then the suspect must be told the reason for the delay and the reasons must be recorded on the custody sheet. The officer's words here are quite vague, so neither of the requirements (the explanation to Pat and the recording of the reason) appear to have been complied with.

Moreover, it was held in *Samuel* (1988) that it was insufficient for an officer simply to believe that giving a suspect access to a solicitor might lead to the alerting of accomplices: the defendant was being questioned about offences of burglary and robbery. His request to see a solicitor was refused, on the grounds that the offences were serious and that there was a risk of accomplices being inadvertently alerted. The defendant subsequently made confessions which were admitted at trial. The Court of Appeal quashed his conviction, stating that access to a solicitor was a 'fundamental right' of a citizen and that a police officer who sought to refuse access had to justify the refusal by reference to the specific circumstances of the case. The court noted that 'solicitors are intelligent professional people', whereas most suspects were 'not very clever', so the likelihood of the latter being able to hoodwink the former into inadvertently passing on a coded message to fellow criminals was very low. This would probably only be a sustainable point in very few cases.

In *Parris* (1989), it was held that where the lawyer called was the duty solicitor, there would usually be no grounds for the police fearing that he would alert other parties to the crime. Here, the court quashed a conviction for armed robbery because of breaches of **s 58**. In *Davidson* (1988), it was held by the Court of Appeal that the police had to be 'nearly certain' that a solicitor granted access to the suspect would warn another criminal or get rid of the proceeds of the crime. The power to delay access to a solicitor could not be exercised until the suspect had nominated an actual solicitor. This was not the case here; the court excluded the confessions given by the suspect without legal advice and, as a result, the prosecution's case collapsed.

The revised Code of Practice (Code C, Annex B, Note B4) clarifies the position further. This says that the officer may only authorise a delay if he has reasonable grounds to believe that the specific solicitor in question will, inadvertently or otherwise, pass on a message from the detained person which will lead to the alerting of accomplices, or interference with evidence. It is uncertain from the question whether Pat is asking to see a specific solicitor. Unless this is the case and the officer has reasonable grounds for the relevant suspicions, then he will be in breach of the Code and **s 58**. Such a breach, though, does not entail automatic exclusion by the court of any resulting statement made by the suspect. The court will evaluate all the circumstances.

In *Dunford* (1990)[7] the defendant had a record and was aware of his right not to answer any questions put by the police. Before reaching the police station, he had refused to answer questions and had, thereafter, answered several questions with the phrase 'no comment'. In such circumstances, the Court of Appeal ruled that the judge had been entitled to allow the confession made in the police station. Moreover, the Court of Appeal ruled in *Walsh* (1990) that an 'adverse effect on the fairness of proceedings' within the meaning of **s 78** would no doubt follow from a 'significant and substantial breach' of **s 58**, but that did not necessarily mean that the evidence thus obtained had to be excluded. The court had to decide, not simply whether there had been an adverse effect on the fairness of proceedings, but whether it had been such an adverse effect that justice required the evidence to be excluded.

In sum, Pat's appeal could succeed if he could persuade the Court of Appeal that **s 78** should have been used to exclude evidence of his confessions because of significant breaches of **s 58** and Code C, which had such an adverse effect on the fairness of proceedings that justice requires they be excluded. Pat's access to a lawyer is delayed, but was **s 58** of **PACE** complied with? The officer 'wrote something down', but was this the required entry on the custody sheet? He went out of the room, but was it to get the required permission of the superintendent? Was the vague reason given to Pat for the delay sufficient to exclude Pat's 'fundamental right'? There are also significant doubts about whether the offence was a 'serious arrestable offence' and whether, if so, the police had reasonable grounds to believe that any of the criteria in **s 58(8)** were applicable. Overall, this gives a strong case to Pat, only slightly counterposed by virtue of Pat's possible criminal record (that is, '... you know the ropes, Pat . . .') by the decisions in *Dunford* and *Walsh*.

ADVICE TO BILLY

The duty solicitor schemes at police stations, set up under **PACE**, are run by the Legal Aid Board. The provision of legal advice to suspects at police stations is not means tested; it is

....

7 Once more discussion of relevant case law is appropriate as, where the material facts of the decided case are sufficiently similar to the facts of the scenario, this will provide a strong indication/argument as to how the court are likely to apply the law in Pat's situation.

paid for by the state. Research has shown that many suspects who previously did not take up the opportunity for legal advice abstained because they were unaware that it was free. The revised Code of Practice (April 1995) dealt with this problem by requiring the police to inform the suspect that the advice is free (Code C, para 3.1(ii)). The Code also requires (para 6.3) that a poster advertising the right to have free legal advice must be displayed prominently in the charging area of every police station.

We are not told whether there is a poster for Billy to see, but in not informing Billy that advice is free, the officer is in breach of the Code.

Under **s 56** of **PACE**, an arrested person held in custody, like Billy, has the right to have someone informed of his arrest. The person to be informed must be a 'friend or relative or other person who is known to him or who is likely to take an interest in his welfare'. Whether the president of the Civil Freedom League is within this category is a moot point. He would be if he was a friend or associate of Billy's and even, possibly, in his capacity as someone publicly concerned with civil liberties but, if the only link was the latter one, it is uncertain whether this would be sufficient. A circular issued to police to assist them with the operation of **s 56**'s forerunner (**s 62** of the **Criminal Law Act 1977**) excluded public figures, like pop stars and football players, from the sorts of person who could be notified. Those groups, however, are of course not related to civil liberties.

The only other reasons given in the Act to justify a delay in notifying a specified person are when, in a case of a serious arrestable offence (see under advice to Pat), an officer of at least the rank of superintendent authorises it for any of the reasons in **s 56(5)**, which are the same as those dealt with in Pat's case under **s 58(8)**. **Section 56(6)** states that the suspect must be told of the reason for the delay and it must be recorded on the custody sheet, neither of which appear to have been done in this case.

It seems more likely that there has been a breach of Code C (in respect of the notification of free legal advice) than of **s 56**, but, even if there were only such a breach of the Code, it is quite possible that the Court of Appeal would quash Billy's conviction, as he was deprived of his fundamental right to legal advice as a result of the breach. In *Beycan* (1990), the Court of Appeal quashed a conviction based on a confession when the suspect had been arrested, taken to the station and asked: 'Are you happy to be interviewed in the normal way we conduct these interviews without a solicitor, friend or representative?' Billy's case is arguably stronger, as he has actually expressed a desire for advice and only proceeded reluctantly without it.

It may be possible to construe these events, in respect of Billy, in a way which shows him 'changing his mind' about taking legal advice. Thus, there could also be a possible breach of Code C, para 6.6(d):

When the person who wanted legal advice changes his mind, the interview may be started without further delay provided the person has given his agreement in writing or on tape to being interviewed without receiving legal advice and that an officer of the rank of inspector or above has given agreement . . .

In *Wadman* (1996), the defendant, having initially declined legal advice, changed his mind and then, while arrangements were being made, reverted to saying that he did not wish to have a solicitor. The police failed to comply with para 6.6(d) of Code C. The judge held that the Code was not 'mandatory' and admitted the evidence. On appeal, the conviction was quashed. The court ruled that the judge's approach to the Code was flawed; he confused the discretion he had on the *voir dire* – whether to admit the evidence – with the absence of discretion for police officers when complying with the Code: it was a disciplinary offence not to do so. It was not a case where the court should exercise its own discretion.

The appeals of both Pat and Billy could also be argued under **s 76(2)(b)**, which permits the court not to allow the confession if it was gained in consequence of:

. . . anything said or done which was likely, in the circumstances existing at the time, to render unreliable any confession which might be made by him in consequence thereof.

The basis of the argument would be the same as for **s 78**.

QUESTION 28

After a serious assault on an old woman by a group of youths, PCs East and Wood stopped Peter in the street late at night. He had blood on his hands. When asked some simple routine questions, Peter became abusive and very hostile to the officers. He told the officers that his name was 'Mickey Mouse' and refused to answer any questions.

The following day, Mary and Paul are arrested for taking part in the assault. During questioning by police, Mary sat with her boyfriend, who is a law student. Before being cautioned, she answered some questions, but not others and, at her trial, the judge suggested to the jury that she 'might have remained silent to avoid incriminating herself'.

Paul remained silent after being cautioned, refusing to answer police questions and, at trial, the judge invited the jury to consider whether an innocent man would have behaved in such a manner.

Peter has been convicted of obstructing the police officers in the execution of their duty. Mary and Paul have now been convicted of the assault. Advise Peter, Mary and Paul about their possible grounds of appeal.

How to Answer this Question

Advice to Peter

When advising Peter:

- ❖ apply *Rice v Connolly* (1966) – consider what constitutes 'obstruction';
- ❖ apply *Ricketts v Cox* (1982) – 'the manner of a person together with his silence';
- ❖ consider whether the decisions are distinguishable.

Advice to Mary

When advising Mary:

- ❖ apply *Davis* (1959) – improper directions to a jury;
- ❖ consider the rule in *Parkes* (1976), where people are speaking on equal terms;
- ❖ discuss the decision in *Chandler* (1976);
- ❖ evaluate which case is closer to the facts of the problem.

Advice to Paul

Your advice to Paul should include:

- ❖ the basis for an appeal – the **Criminal Appeal Act 1968**;
- ❖ application of *Chandler* (1976).

Answer Structure

For each party in turn:

Introduction to relevant law in regard to each parties rights in terms of their treatment by police and their consequent convictions

Application of relevant law (legislation and case law) to each of the three scenarios, together with reasoned advice on possible grounds, and likely success, of any appeal

ANSWER

ADVICE TO PETER

Peter might have an appeal against his conviction for obstructing the police officers in the execution of their duty if he was not legally obliged to answer the questions put to him by the officers. Normally, the citizen is entitled to remain silent in the face of police questions, without this either being the subject of a charge of obstructing the police in the execution of their duties, or being commented on adversely by the prosecution or judge at trial.

This rule is established by the important Divisional Court decision in *Rice v Connolly* (1966). The appellant was seen by officers at night in an area where burglaries had been committed. He refused to tell the police where he had come from or where he was going. He identified himself only by his surname and a street name where he said he lived. He refused to accompany the police to a police box to further verify his identity. His conviction for an offence under **s 51(3)** of the **Police Act 1964** (resisting or wilfully obstructing a police officer in the execution of his duty) was quashed, as the Divisional Court said he had the right not to answer the questions. Lord Parker CJ stated that a proper conviction would require proof that the action was 'wilful', which means not only done intentionally, but also done without lawful excuse. Citizens, he said, had a moral duty and perhaps a social one to help the police with their inquiries, but there was no such legal duty.[8]

The decision in *Rice v Connolly* was unanimous, but James J noted that he would not go so far as to say that silence combined with conduct could not amount to an obstruction. It would be a matter for the courts to decide on the facts of any particular case. In *Ricketts v Cox* (1982), on facts similar to those in question here, the defendant's appeal against a conviction under **s 51(3)** was dismissed. Two police officers questioned the defendant and another man in the early hours of the morning, following a serious assault. The defendant was uncooperative and shouted in obscene language at the officers, and then tried to walk away without answering any questions. The court found that this was an instance where 'the manner of a person together with his silence' could amount to obstruction. This decision probably accounts for Peter's conviction, in view of his obstreperous conduct coupled with the evidently false name he gave.

The decision in *Ricketts v Cox* has been widely criticised (Glanville Williams; Smith and Hogan; and Bailey, Harris and Jones) as flawed and at odds with *Rice v Connolly*. If a refusal to answer questions is lawful, which it clearly is, then how can this important constitutional right be cancelled merely because the questioned party is abusive? Peter's appeal could be based upon this point, inviting the Court of Appeal to deal with the confusion promoted by the two Divisional Court decisions by overruling *Ricketts v Cox*. Peter could possibly be acquitted if the facts of his case were governed simply by the decision in *Rice v Connolly*. Even though, unlike the appellant in the 1966 case, Peter had gone beyond simple reticence and told the officers his name was 'Mickey Mouse', this could perhaps be argued to be so self-evidently false as tantamount to saying, 'I shall not tell you my name'. The court agreed, in *Rice v Connolly*, that to tell a 'cock and bull' story to the police would obviously be an obstruction. This would clearly cover Peter had he said his name was Tom Smith and misled the police as to his true identity, but his sarcastic reference to a cartoon character could be regarded as not seriously misleading, and lawful, as he is not legally obliged to reveal his name.[9] It does not look like Peter was

....

8   This discussion demonstrates knowledge of relevant legislation, together with an understanding of the manner in which it has been applied by the courts in a decided case, both of which are equally important when providing advice relevant to a particular scenario.

9   This is an excellent example of how case-law can be used to illustrate a variety of possible outcomes, of how to argue different perspectives and how to provided reasoned advice.

under caution when he refused to answer police questions. If he was, then his failure to answer could be made the subject of comment (see below, under 'Advice to Mary') by the trial judge under **s 34** of the **Criminal Justice and Public Order Act (CJPOA) 1994**.

ADVICE TO MARY

Mary's conviction could be quashed if it can be shown that the trial judge's words to the jury amounted to a misdirection. Before the **CJPOA 1994**, the 'right to silence' was regarded as a well entrenched principle of law. The common law position is that everyone still has the right to remain silent in the same circumstances as they did before the **1994 Act**; what has changed is the entitlement of the judge or prosecuting counsel to make adverse comment on such a silence. There are many reasons why a suspect might remain silent when questioned (for example, fear, confusion, reluctance to incriminate another person) and, generally, failure or refusal to answer questions does not amount to evidence against the person concerned, unless it can be said that the defendant was on 'equal terms' with the questioner. In *Parkes* (1976), the Privy Council ruled that a judge could invite the jury to consider the possibility of drawing adverse inferences from silence from a tenant who had been accused by a landlady of murdering her daughter. The landlady and tenant, for this encounter, were regarded as having parity of status, unlike a person faced with questions from the police. Failure to answer questions put by a police officer, or someone in a similar position, is unlikely to lead to adverse inferences being drawn at any trial. In *Chandler* (1976), the suspect, in the company of his solicitor, refused to answer some questions asked by a police officer before the caution. The judge told the jury that they should decide whether the defendant's silence was attributable to his wish to exercise his common law right, or because he might incriminate himself. The Court of Appeal thought the presence of Chandler's solicitor meant that the parties were on 'even terms' but, on the facts, quashed Chandler's conviction, since the judge had gone too far in suggesting that silence before a caution could be evidence of guilt.

The alleged advantage of the change of law[10] is that **ss 34–38** of the **CJPOA 1994** help convict criminals who, under the old law, used to be acquitted because they took advantage of the right to keep quiet when questioned, without the court or prosecution being able to comment adversely upon that silence. However, the dangers entailed in undermining the right of silence are most acute in respect of police questioning scenarios. In *R v Condron* (1997), the Court of Appeal said that the guidelines set out in *R v Cowan* (1996), regarding the drawing of adverse inferences where the accused fails to testify, are equally applicable where the accused fails to answer questions when being interviewed by the police. More detailed guidance was given in *R v Argent* (1997), where the Court of Appeal set out the conditions which have to be satisfied before adverse

---

10   Where law is about to be, or has recently been, amended, consideration of both positions can provide an opportunity to gain extra marks. (However, do not spend too much time on this unless it is specifically required by the question.)

inferences can be drawn from a person's failure to answer police questions (**s 34** of the **CJPOA 1994**). The conditions include:

(a)   the failure to answer has to occur before a defendant was charged;
(b)   the alleged failure must occur during questioning under caution;
(c)   the questioning must be directed at trying to discover whether and by whom the offence has been committed;
(d)   the failure must be a failure to mention any fact relied on in the person's defence; and
(e)   the fact that the defendant failed to mention has to be one which this particular defendant could reasonably be expected to have mentioned when being questioned, taking account of all the circumstances existing at that time (for example, the time of day, the defendant's age, experience, mental capacity, state of health, sobriety, personality and access to legal advice).

Therefore, **s 34(1)** only applies in respect of questioning under caution. If no caution is administered, no inference can be drawn from the failure to mention a fact in response to such questioning. A person must be cautioned where there are grounds to suspect him of an offence, before any questions are put to him regarding involvement or suspected involvement in that offence (Code C, para 10.1 of the **Police and Criminal Evidence Act (PACE) 1984**) and a person must normally be cautioned on being arrested (Code D, para 10.3). A caution need not be administered if the questions are put for other purposes. **Section 34** permits adverse inferences to be drawn from silence in situations that do not amount to 'interviews', as defined by Code C of PACE, and thus which are not subject to the safeguards of access to legal advice and of contemporaneous recording, which exist where a suspect is interviewed at a police station. An 'interview' is defined by Code C, para 11.1(a) as being:

> ... the questioning of a person regarding his involvement or suspected involvement in a criminal offence or offences which by virtue of para 10.1 of Code C is required to be carried out under caution.

Sections 36 and **37** of the **CJPOA 1994** permit inferences to be drawn from the failure of an arrested person to account for an object, substance or mark, etc, or to account for his presence at a particular place where he is found. The main differences between **s 34** and **ss 36** and **37** are that **s 34** applies where the suspect has been cautioned, but **ss 36** and **37** only apply where the suspect has been arrested; **ss 36** and **37** apply whether or not a fact is relied upon in a person's defence, whereas **s 34** applies only in respect of failure to mention a fact relied upon in a person's defence.

Mary could appeal against her conviction if prosecution evidence is obtained as a result of unfair or unlawful police conduct under **ss 76** and **78** of **PACE**. The questioning of Mary at the station prior to a caution being given may be in contravention of **s 34** of the **CJPOA 1994** and the Codes of Practice in **PACE** (Code C, para 10 and

Code D).[11] Cautions need not be given if the questions put did not constitute an 'interview' and were 'questions put for other purposes', but these considerations would not be applicable here, as Mary was already arrested at the material time of being questioned. If Mary failed to answer questions subsequently, under caution or on being charged, **s 34** applies only to facts which she later relies on in her defence. The section has no function if she makes no attempt to put previously undisclosed facts forward at trial.

The common law position continues to apply where the new statutory provisions do not apply. Mary could appeal against her conviction on the grounds that she was not on 'equal terms' with the officer who interviewed her as, unlike the defendant in *Chandler*, she was not accompanied by a lawyer, but merely a law student.

ADVICE TO PAUL

Prior to 1996, the Court of Appeal would allow an appeal if they thought that: (a) the conviction was unsafe and unsatisfactory; (b) the judgment of the court trial should be set aside on a wrong decision on any question of law; and (c) there had been a material irregularity in the course of the trial. The **Criminal Appeal Act 1995** abolishes the three grounds of appeal, replacing them with a single test, namely, that the court thinks the conviction is unsafe. The Act does not contain any definition of the word 'unsafe'. Much of the former law will therefore be relevant in deciding what is liable to render a conviction unsafe. In particular, the court may still apply the 'lurking doubt' test enunciated in *R v Cooper* (1969):

> . . . whether we are content to let the matter stand as it is, or whether there is not some lurking doubt in our minds which makes us wonder whether an injustice has been done.

As noted above, **ss 34–38** of the **CJPOA 1994** constitute a major curtailment of the 'right of silence'. Thus, although Paul retains his 'right' to remain silent both at the trial and the interrogation, 'proper' inferences may be drawn from his failure to mention certain facts when questioned under caution or on being charged (**s 34**).

Paul's appeal could succeed if he can show that **s 78** of **PACE** should have been used to exclude adverse inferences of his silence because of significant breaches of **s 34** of the **CJPOA 1994**. If he simply contends that there is no case to answer, that he has no fact which he could have contributed and he does not rely on a particular defence, **s 34** can have no effect. There can be no conviction on silence alone. **Section 38** applies to all four provisions of the **1994 Act** which operate to permit the drawing of inferences, and

11   Don't worry that you always have to come to a definite conclusion. If the law were that certain, there would be no need for trials: where the outcome is unclear, embrace the opportunity to demonstrate your knowledge by considering all possibilities.

stipulates that a defendant cannot be convicted or have a case to answer solely on the basis of an inference drawn from silence. There must, therefore, be some other evidence in addition to any inference to be drawn.

QUESTION 29

After an armed robbery at the Upland Bank in Oldcastle, the police arrested Karl for his involvement in the crime. An hour later, having interviewed Karl at the police station, the police went to his parents' home to remove for forensic examination a car parked in the driveway. Tony, Karl's father, resisted the police attempts to remove the vehicle and punched PC Grit. Tony was eventually overpowered and PC Grit then searched the garage and found a collection of plastic bank cards with different names and a pile of correspondence about crimes, including some letters bearing advice from Karl's solicitor.

Karl has been charged with involvement in the bank robbery and crimes relating to the stolen bank cards. Tony has been charged with assaulting an officer in the execution of his duty. Advise Karl and Tony.

How to Answer this Question

Advice to Karl
You should include:

❖ an explanation and application of **s 78** of the **Police and Criminal Evidence Act (PACE) 1984**;
❖ an explanation and application of **s 18** of **PACE**;
❖ an explanation and application of **s 32** of **PACE**;
❖ an application of *Badham* (1987);
❖ consideration of Code B (revised) on searches and **s 67(11)** on exclusions;
❖ discussion of the ambit of **s 19** of **PACE**.

Advice to Tony
Include:

❖ an explanation of the effect of **s 117** of **PACE** in the context of the legality of the searches under **s 18** or **s 20**;
❖ discussion of **s 51** of the **Police Act 1964**.

Answer Structure

For each party provide: → Consideration of relevant legislation, together with discussion on how the law has previously been interpreted and applied by the courts (case law). → Application of the law to the facts of the scenario, including argument in regard to potential outcomes where more than one is possible.

ANSWER

ADVICE TO KARL

The police appear to have had sufficient evidence on which to arrest Karl before any examination of the car in his driveway. Nevertheless, the car seems to be very significant evidence as the police went back to get it. It is important to discover, therefore, whether the police were legally entitled to act as they did. If not, then the evidence obtained might be excluded under **s 78** of **PACE**, if it is likely to have, in all of the circumstances, an adverse effect on the trial.

The answer to this particular question – whether the police search was lawful – will also determine whether Tony was legally justified in acting as he did, so this matter shall be returned to again later.

Karl has been arrested for robbery, which is an arrestable offence by virtue of the fact that Karl, if he was over 21 (even without previous convictions), could be sentenced to a term of imprisonment for five years or more upon conviction (**s 24** of **PACE**). **Section 18** of **PACE** empowers an officer to enter premises 'occupied or controlled by a person arrested for an arrestable offence' to search for evidence related to that or connected offences. He must, however, have 'reasonable grounds' for believing that there is evidence on the premises that relates to the offence in question or to some offence 'which is connected with or similar to that offence'. Searching for the vehicle suspected of being used in the armed robbery would be within the section's ambit, provided that Karl was an occupant of the address in the sense that he lived or stayed there. We know that letters to Karl from his solicitor were found in his father's garage, which suggests that Karl lived at that address. The search of the garage, which results in the discovery of the cards and letters, would also be within the section's scope, if crimes relating to stolen bank cards can be regarded as 'similar to' the crime of bank robbery. The element of violence or its threat involved in robbery would probably, however, put it in a different class from matters of deception and fraud.

The section also states that any officer making such a search must have prior authorisation in writing from a fellow officer of at least the rank of inspector, or subsequent approval, if such is necessary for the 'effective investigation of the offence'. The authorising officer must make a record of the search and, if the search was authorised in advance, it must show the nature of the evidence that was sought, in order to avoid 'fishing expeditions'. Failure to conform with these rules courts the risk that evidence, thus obtained, will not be admissible in court. Many searches of this type are conducted some time after arrest, so the lapse of an hour before the police come to search Tony's premises and take the evidence does not appear to affect the lawfulness of the conduct.

It may be[12] that Karl did not live with or stay with his parents, in which case the search would not be lawful under s 18. There is, however, the possibility that the search could have been lawful under s 32, which authorises the search, *inter alia*, of any premises on which the arrest took place. The search can be for anything relating to the offence for which a person has been arrested. If the search was made under this power, then it would be lawful in respect of the car (allegedly, used in the robbery), but not in respect of the bank cards or letters. We do not know where Karl was arrested, but, if he was arrested at his parents' home, then s 32 would legitimise the police search. The delay, however, might be more significant here. According to the decision in *Badham* (1987), a search of the home where the defendant lived with his father, which took place three hours after the defendant's arrest was not lawful. The Act gave no time-limit, but the section was headed 'Search upon arrest' and the power was an immediate one. The Crown Court held that it would be wrong to permit an open-ended right to go back to the premises where the arrest had taken place. Here, PC Grit goes to Tony's house only an hour after Karl's arrest, but the *ratio decidendi* of *Badham* would apply just as much to this shorter, but still considerable, delay. **Section 32** might perhaps permit an officer escorting an arrested suspect back to the station to turn around after two minutes' walking and return to search the premises where the arrest was made, but not after an hour.

It is a requirement of the revised Code B (April 1995) that when conducting a search, the police shall give to the occupier a written notice of powers and rights showing which powers have been exercised. This applies to searches made under several powers, including those under ss 18 and 32. The notice must specify under which power the search is being made. The notice must also explain the rights of the occupier and the owner of any property seized. The Codes of Practice are not technically 'law'. If Karl can show that evidence (that is, relating to the car) has been obtained in breach of the Code, then the trial judge or Appeal Court can be invited to exclude that evidence (s 67(11)).

There is no common law power to enter and search premises after an arrest, so any search not lawful under ss 18 or 32 would be unlawful.

Under s 19, an officer who is lawfully searching any premises is authorised to seize any article (if it is not covered by legal professional privilege) if he reasonably believes that it is evidence relating to the offence which he is investigating, or 'any other offence', and that it is necessary to seize it in order to prevent it from being 'concealed, lost, damaged, altered or destroyed'. It would be possible for the police to make a convincing case for the car (if there was evidence connecting it to the robbery) and the bank cards to be seized. It seems likely, however, that the solicitor's letters would be protected within the status of

---

12 Evidence that a thoughtful approach has been taken. More than just the obvious has been considered
    – but take care not to go too far in this respect, as you will not impress an examiner by making up your
    own facts to suit your argument.

professional legal privilege, as **s 10(1)(a)** defines items 'subject to legal privilege' as including 'communications between a professional legal adviser and his client made in connection with giving legal advice to the client'.

In sum, Karl might be able to show that any evidence obtained relating to the car should be excluded by **s 78**. The search might not be lawful under **s 18** if:

(a)   Karl was not an occupant of his father's house; or
(b)   the search was not properly authorised in writing by an inspector; or
(c)   there were no reasonable grounds to believe that there was evidence at Tony's address which related to the robbery.

Additionally, the search might not be lawful under **s 32** if it was not the site of Karl's arrest. Furthermore, Karl might be able to show that the conduct of the search was not in accordance with Code B if, for example, the written notice of rights and powers was not given to Tony.

ADVICE TO TONY

If the search of Tony's premises is lawful under either **s 18** or **s 32**, then **s 117** of **PACE** confers power on the police to use force in order to carry out their search, provided that the force used is reasonable and necessary. In such circumstances, PC Grit would have been acting in the execution of his duty and Tony would be guilty of an assault under **s 51** of the **Police Act 1964**. If, however, PC Grit's search was unlawful, so that he was not acting in the execution of his duty, then Tony would be entitled to use force to resist the intrusion onto his premises. There are many decisions to vindicate Tony's actions if the search was unlawful. The convictions of *Badham* (1987) and *Churchill* (1989), for obstructing a police officer in the execution of his duty and assault occasioning actual bodily harm respectively, were quashed on appeal, because the searches in both cases were not justifiable within the provisions of **PACE**. If the search was unlawful for the reasons discussed in the advice to Karl, then the prosecution of Tony for the assault might fail.

QUESTION 30

Ben was walking home in the early hours of the morning. He was approached by two constables, PC Blue and PC Green, and asked to stop. He then, reluctantly, answered some questions about who he was and where he had been. By now fed up, he started to walk away as PC Blue was checking his details over the radio. PC Green tried to stop Ben and was punched in the face.

Later, but before dawn, PC Blue saw Dodger, who appeared scruffy and panicked and whom he suspected was carrying a set of 'skeleton keys' to fit various types of household door. He stopped Dodger and asked, 'Okay if we have a look at what you have got on you?' and then, receiving no reply, searched him very thoroughly. Dodger then protested and PC Blue replied: 'Look, this is quite legal, I am PC Blue of Fenwick Street station and I think you are up to no good.' PC Blue found 'skeleton keys' on Dodger, who has, as a result, now been convicted of 'going equipped to steal'.

Ben has been charged with assaulting a constable in the execution of his duty and Dodger wishes to appeal against his conviction. Advise Ben and Dodger.

How to Answer this Question

Advice to Ben
Consider:

- ❖ whether PC Green was acting in the course of his duty;
- ❖ the *de minimis* rule;
- ❖ any application of *Bentley v Brudzinski* (1982).

Advice to Dodger
You should:

- ❖ explain the statutory setting: **ss 1, 67** and **78** of the **Police and Criminal Evidence Act (PACE) 1984** and revised Code A;
- ❖ apply this to the facts;
- ❖ discuss **s 2** of **PACE** and the legality of the search;
- ❖ apply *Fennelley* (1989).

Answer Structure

ANSWER

ADVICE TO BEN

In order to discover whether Ben has assaulted the constable in the execution of his duty, we need to determine whether PC Blue was acting 'in the course of his duty'.[13] If not, then

---

13 In typical 'problem' style, the answer immediately moves to the heart of the question. (Compare this to 'essay' type questions, where a more general approach may be appropriate, with the provision of an introduction which places the topic(s) into context before specific issues are directly addressed.)

Ben cannot be convicted of the crime charged, although it is worthy of note that had he been charged with common assault,[14] he could have been found guilty, according to *obiter dicta* of Donaldson LJ in *Bentley v Brudzinski* (1982).

In *Kenlin v Gardiner* (1967), a police officer took hold of the arm of a boy whom he wanted to question about the latter's suspicious conduct. The boy did not believe the man was a policeman; despite having been shown a warrant card, he punched the officer in order to escape. Another boy who he was with behaved similarly and their convictions for assaulting an officer in the execution of his duty were quashed by the Divisional Court. The court held that the boys were entitled to act as they did in self-defence, as the officer's conduct in trying to physically apprehend them had not been legal. There is no legal power of detention short of arrest. As Lawton LJ observed in *Lemsatef* (1977), the police do not have any powers to detain somebody 'for the purposes of getting them to help with their enquiries'. This reasoning would assist Ben, assuming that PC Green was not in fact trying to stop Ben in order to arrest him.

It is important, however, to examine the precise circumstances of the detaining officer's conduct, because there are cases to suggest that if what the officer does amounts to only a *de minimis* interference with the citizen's liberty, then forceful 'self-defence' by the citizen will not be justified. In *Donnelly v Jackman* (1970), an officer approached a suspect to ask some questions. The suspect ignored the request and walked away from the officer. The officer followed and made further requests for the suspect to stop and talk. He tapped the suspect on the shoulder and the suspect reciprocated by tapping the officer on the shoulder and saying, 'Now we are even, copper'. The officer tapped the suspect on the shoulder again, which was replied to with a forceful punch. Mr Donnelly's conviction was upheld and the decision in *Kenlin v Gardiner* was distinguished as, in the earlier case, the officers had actually taken hold of the boys and detained them. The court stated that:

> . . . it is not every trivial interference with a citizen's liberty that amounts to a course of conduct sufficient to take the officer out of the course of his duties.

In *Bentley v Brudzinski* the facts were very close to those in question.[15] A constable stopped two men who had been running barefoot down a street in the early hours. He questioned them about a stolen vehicle, as they fitted the description of suspects in an

---

14 Mention of the potential alternative charge demonstrates knowledge and is therefore likely to gain a candidate a few extra marks. It is, however, worth noting that the question does not require discussion of any alternative and any more than a mention would be excessive and rather a waste of time.

15 This is important as, where material facts of a scenario are sufficiently similar to the material facts of a decided case (precedent), this provides a strong indication of how the court would be likely to decide the issue in the scenario.

earlier incident. They waited for about 10 minutes while the officer checked their details over a radio and then they began to leave. Another constable, who had just arrived on the scene, then said, 'Just a minute', and put his hand on the defendant's shoulder. The defendant then punched that officer in the face. Unlike the decision in *Donnelly v Jackman*, the Divisional Court held here that the officer's conduct was more than a trivial interference with the citizen's liberty and amounted to an unlawful attempt to stop and detain him. The respondent was thus not guilty of assaulting an officer in the execution of his duty. We know that PC Green 'tried to stop Ben'. If this attempt involved physical restraint, then the authorities suggest that Ben's resistance would not have amounted to the crime of assaulting an officer in the execution of his duty, because the officer would not have been acting within his powers. Conversely, if the attempt amounted to nothing more than a tap on the shoulder, Ben would probably be guilty as charged.[16]

ADVICE TO DODGER

Under **s 1** of **PACE**, PC Blue is entitled to stop and search someone whom he reasonably suspects of carrying certain items, including an article 'made or adapted for use in the course of or in connection with . . .' (**s 1(7)(b)(i)**) '. . . burglary' (**s 1(8)(a)**). 'Skeleton keys' would fall within such a category. It might be, however, that PC Blue is in breach of the rules in the Codes of Practice, in particular, Code A for the exercise by police officers of statutory powers of stop and search. The Codes are not technically law[17] although they were mistakenly labelled as having 'statutory authority' by Russell LJ in *McCay* (1991). A judge may, however, exclude evidence which has been obtained in breach of the rules and an appeal court may quash a conviction where the judge failed to do so (**s 67(11)**). Additionally, **s 78** of **PACE** allows the exclusion of evidence which has been obtained in breach of the Act. The court, after considering all the circumstances, including the circumstances in which the evidence was obtained, will not admit evidence which would have 'an adverse effect on the fairness of the proceedings that the court ought not to admit it'.

What, if anything, has PC Blue done wrong? Did he have reasonable grounds for suspecting that Dodger was carrying 'skeleton keys'?[18] Reasonable suspicion requires an objective basis. In favour of PC Blue's case is the fact that it was in the early hours and Dodger was 'panicked'. Code A states that reasonable suspicion may exist where 'a person is seen acting covertly or warily'. It would perhaps be difficult to bring 'panic' within the categories cited by the Code. The Code specifically states that 'hairstyle',

---

16 Thoughtful approach taken with alternative arguments effectively considered. Demonstrates strong evaluative and analytical skills.

17 A good point to make, as it demonstrates an understanding of the difference between 'law' and other 'rules' and adds to the general feeling of confidence in the answer provided.

18 Clear indication that the question has been well analysed and that the issue at the very heart of the question has been recognised.

'manner of dress' and knowledge of 'previous convictions' cannot alone or in combination give grounds for suspicion.

The current Code A (May 1997) was amended to provide some clarification of police powers in relation to groups and gangs. The additional sections (Code A, para 1.6(a) and Code A, para 1.7(aa)) state that where there is reliable information that members of a group or gang who habitually carry knives, weapons or controlled drugs and wear a distinctive item of clothing or other means of identification to indicate membership of it, then police officers may use that identifying item as the basis of their suspicion.

We are not informed as to what basis PC Blue thinks he has for his suspicions, but as he suspects Dodger to be carrying 'skeleton keys', in particular, we might infer that PC Blue knows Dodger from a previous encounter, perhaps one which resulted in Dodger's arrest and subsequent conviction. Even this, coupled with Dodger's scruffiness, would not suffice as a reasonable ground.[19] 'Time and place' and 'behaviour' are factors which can constitute the necessary reasonable grounds and it is just possible that the panic of Dodger in the early hours in the street would lend support to the officer's case, but he would still have to address the question of why he suspected Dodger of carrying 'skeleton keys'.

Under s 2 of **PACE**, the police officer who proposes to carry out a search must state his name and police station (which PC Blue does, but only after the search has begun), the purpose of the search and the grounds for the search. PC Blue fails to comply with these latter rules. A failure to give grounds, as required by s 2(3)(c), will render the search unlawful (*Fennelley* (1989)) and, in view of the very generalised explanation given by PC Blue, 'I think you are up to no good', it seems that the officer is in breach of the Act. The *Fennelley* decision shows that the courts are prepared to be quite strict in their interpretation of the rules. The defendant (F), a heroin addict, was seen by plain clothes police officers in the street. They believed they witnessed him selling drugs on the street. F was stopped, questioned and asked what he had in his pockets. He was searched and no drugs were found but, during a later strip search at the police station, some heroin was found in his underpants. F was charged with possession with intent to supply the drug, but the Crown Court decided that the evidence found by the police officers during the search should be excluded, using s 78 of **PACE**, as the police officers had failed to abide by the Act and the Codes in a number of respects. Significantly for our concerns here, they had failed to comply with the mandatory requirements of s 2(3), in that they had not informed F about their grounds for suspicion, nor about the purpose of their search. It was argued that these breaches affected the fairness of the trial, because F had not been given the chance to answer the suspicions of the police at the earliest opportunity. If he

---

19 Discussion of the 'rules' followed by application of the rules to the facts of the scenario has produced sound, logical argument.

had, he might have been able to give an explanation which would have resulted in his being charged with mere possession, rather than possession with intent to supply.

The Act also requires that a search in the street must be limited to outer clothing and gloves (**s 2(9)**). We know that Dodger has been searched 'very thoroughly' and if that has entailed the removal of more than a coat, jacket or gloves in the street, then the rule has been broken.

The Act, however, does not apply to voluntary searches. If Dodger 'consents' to be stopped and searched, then PC Blue is not exercising any power. Dodger's protests come only towards the end of the search, so his acquiescence at the outset could be construed as consent. The revised Code A now states that juveniles or mentally handicapped people should not be subject to voluntary searches. If Dodger was in either category, then even a voluntary search would be in breach of the rules.

Thus, Dodger might be able to succeed on appeal if he can show that key evidence leading to his conviction should have been excluded as having been obtained in breach of the Act or the Codes and in a way that had an adverse effect on the proceedings. The weak grounds for his original suspicions, the failures properly to inform Dodger about the grounds for, and the purpose of, the search and the nature of the search itself are all in question and could separately, or together, form the basis of an appeal. This is provided that the search was not by consent.[20]

QUESTION 31

Dozy went shopping at his local supermarket. He picked an apple from the shelf and ate it while doing his other shopping in the store. Dozy then paid for the items in his trolley and walked towards the exit. Before he left, Dozy was apprehended by Peter, a store detective, who said, 'You cannot leave this store'. Dozy asked why not and was informed that he was not being arrested, but that the store manager wished to see him. Dozy was then taken by force to the manager's office where he was made to wait for an hour until the manager returned from his lunch. When the manager arrived, he told Dozy that the store's policy was to always prosecute shoplifters and that the police would now be called to take Dozy away.

Dozy has now been acquitted on a charge of stealing the apple and he wishes to sue the supermarket. Advise Dozy.

....

20 Strong conclusion which helpfully sums up the various arguments put forward in the main body of the answer. (Note that a conclusion should not introduce new information or be repetitive: it should be brief and no more than a quick reminder of what has been argued in the main body.)

How to Answer this Question

You should consider:

- ❖ grounds for Dozy's civil action;
- ❖ the legal definition of an 'arrest';
- ❖ the lawfulness of the arrest;
- ❖ *Walters v WH Smith & Son Ltd* (1914);
- ❖ *Self* (1992);
- ❖ *John Lewis & Co Ltd v Tims* (1952).

Answer Structure

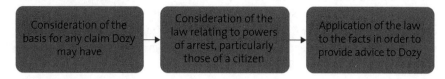

| Consideration of the basis for any claim Dozy may have | → | Consideration of the law relating to powers of arrest, particularly those of a citizen | → | Application of the law to the facts in order to provide advice to Dozy |

ANSWER

Dozy might have an action for damages against Peter or the store (if vicarious liability applies) for false imprisonment. The answer to this question would largely depend upon whether the action of Peter was lawful.[21]

There is no legal power to detain a suspect without arrest. 'Arrest', however, is a matter of fact, not a legal concept. In *Spicer v Holt* (1977), Lord Dilhorne said that:

> Whether or not a person has been arrested depends not on the legality of the arrest, but on whether he has been deprived of his liberty to go where he pleases.

Thus, Dozy may have been arrested if he was prevented from leaving (the use of force on him to take him back to the manager's office helps support such an argument), but whether the arrest was lawful will depend on other matters, namely, the conditions specified in **s 24** of the **Police and Criminal Evidence Act (PACE) 1984**.[22] Aside from the technicalities of whether there has been an arrest, there seems clear *prima facie* evidence of false imprisonment. Having been forcibly taken to the manager's room, it seems likely that force or its threat was used to keep Dozy there, but, even if not, an action for false imprisonment would still exist. The claimant need not even know he has been restrained. In *Meering v Grahame White Aviation Co Ltd* (1919), Lord Atkin stated that a person could be 'imprisoned' within the terms of the tort, even if they were asleep or drunk at the time and thus remain unaware of their captivity.

---

21 Immediately gets to the heart of the issue, demonstrating good analysis of question.

22 Demonstrates appropriate knowledge by directly referring to relevant legislation.

Peter, though, may have arrested Dozy. If this was so, the question remains whether the arrest was lawful.

Dozy was evidently not informed of why he was being arrested. **Section 28(3)** of **PACE** states that an arrest is not lawful unless the person arrested is informed of the ground for the arrest at the time of, or as soon as practicable after, the arrest. It was, however, recognised in *Christie v Leachinsky* (1947), and remains good law today, that the rule does not apply where the arrest is by a private citizen and the ground of arrest is obvious.[23] If Peter's actions, despite his words, do amount to an arrest, then it could be regarded as having taken place in circumstances which made it obvious why it was being carried out. Even if the arrest is regarded as unlawful for failure to inform of the relevant ground, the illegality will not operate retrospectively to vitiate the whole arrest. It will, according to the Divisional Court in *DPP v Hawkins* (1988), render the arrest unlawful, as from the moment when it would have been practicable for the arrestor to have given a reason. Thus, any damages which Dozy could claim would be limited to those reflecting his experience during the time in the office, from when he should have been informed about why he had been arrested, until the time he was told of the reason for his arrest by the police.[24]

An arrestable offence is one for which the sentence is fixed by law or for which a person over 21 may be sentenced on the first occasion to at least five years' imprisonment (**s 24** of **PACE**). Theft, fitting in the second category, is an arrestable offence and **ss 24** and **25** of **PACE** give a general power of arrest without warrant for 'arrestable offences'. The Act, however, preserves an old common law distinction in respect of the powers of constables and private individuals when making such arrests. Where an arrest is being made *after* an offence is thought to have been committed, then **PACE** confers narrower rights upon the private individual than on the police officer.

In *Walters v WH Smith & Son Ltd* (1914), the defendants had reasonably suspected that Walters had stolen books from a station bookstall. At his trial, Walters was acquitted as the jury believed his statement that he had intended to pay for the books. No crime had therefore been committed in respect of any of the books. Walters sued the defendants, *inter alia*, for false imprisonment, a tort which involves the wrongful deprivation of personal liberty in any form, as he had been arrested for a crime which had not in fact been committed. The Court of Appeal held that to justify the arrest, a private individual had to show, not only reasonable suspicion, but also that the offence for which the arrested person was given over into custody had in fact been committed, even if by someone else. A police officer making an arrest in the same circumstances could legally

---

23 Importantly, the differing rights of police officers and citizens in regard to the power of arrest has been recognised.

24 Good use of case law, demonstrating knowledge and supporting arguments put forward.

justify the arrest by showing 'reasonable suspicion' alone, without having to show that an offence was in fact committed.

This principle is now incorporated into **PACE** and Peter appears to have fallen foul of the provision, because the *de facto* arrest takes place after the alleged crime of shoplifting but, as events fall, the criminal courts have acquitted Dozy of any crime. If there was no crime, then Peter could not rely on **s 24(5)**, which only allows an individual to arrest a suspect whom he has reasonable grounds to believe has committed the offence 'where an arrestable crime has been committed'.

It is worthy of note that the less prudent arrestor who acts against a suspect when the latter is suspected of being in the act of committing an arrestable offence (**s 24(4)**) can justify his conduct simply by showing that there were 'reasonable grounds' on which to base the suspicion. He need not show that an offence was in fact being committed.

This analysis is supported by the decision in *Self* (1992), on facts very similar to the question's.[25] The defendant was seen by a store detective in Woolworth's to pick up a bar of chocolate and leave the store without paying. The detective followed him out into the street and, with the assistance of a member of the public, she arrested the suspect under the powers of **s 24(5)** of **PACE**. The suspect resisted the arrest and assaulted both his arrestors. He was subsequently charged with theft of the chocolate and with offences of assault with intent to resist lawful apprehension or detainer, contrary to **s 38** of the **Offences Against the Person Act 1861**. At his trial, he was acquitted of theft (apparently, for lack of *mens rea*), but convicted of the assaults. These convictions were quashed by the Court of Appeal on the grounds that as the arrest had not been lawful, he was entitled to resist it. The power of arrest conferred upon a citizen (**s 24(5)**) in circumstances where an offence is thought to *have been committed* only applies when an offence *has* been committed and, as the jury decided that Mr Self had not committed any offence, there was no power to arrest him.

We know that Dozy has been acquitted of any crime, so it looks as if any arrest made by Peter (*de facto* and, therefore, in law) would be invalidated by virtue of **s 24(5)** of **PACE**, which provides that the offence must have 'been committed'. However, despite Dozy's acquittal, it might be possible to contend that a crime had still 'been committed'. Such a contention was not possible in *Walters v WH Smith*, because there Mr Walters had denied the *mens rea* of the offence of theft, a vital ingredient of the crime, and the jury had accepted this version, thus denying that a crime had taken place. In different circumstances, perhaps, than those in the question, it might be that the defendant in any criminal proceedings (Dozy) was acquitted by way of a successful 'excusatory defence', for example, insanity, which would not deny that a crime had occurred, simply that the

---

25 Good use made of decided case (precedent) with sufficiently similar material facts for those of the scenario.

defendant could not be legally responsible. In such circumstances, the arrest would be lawful, as a crime would have 'been committed'.

A question would then arise as to the period of detention for over an hour. In *John Lewis & Co v Tims* (1952), Mrs Tims and her daughter were arrested by store detectives for shoplifting four calendars from the appellant's Oxford Street store. It was a regulation of the store that only a managing director or a general manager was authorised to institute any prosecution. After being arrested, Mrs Tims and her daughter were taken to the office of the chief store detective. They were detained there until a chief detective and a manager arrived to give instructions whether to prosecute. They were, eventually, handed over to police custody within an hour of arrest. In a claim by Mrs Tims for false imprisonment, she alleged that the detectives were obliged to give her into the custody of the police immediately upon arrest. The House of Lords held that the delay was reasonable in the circumstances, as there were advantages in refusing to give private detectives a 'free hand' and leaving to a superior official the determination of such an important question as whether to prosecute.

Dozy's case may be distinguishable (although the distinction is not a compelling one) as here, the reason for the delay is concerned with the comfort the manager will enjoy by not interrupting his lunch, rather than any matter of company business.[26] The evidence in the *John Lewis* case was that the manager came without any delay and listened to the evidence; any delay (which was evidentially in doubt) occurred while the accounts of the store detectives were being given in the presence of the suspects.

It is true that Dozy has not suffered any real damage to his person but, as Lord Porter observed in the *John Lewis* case, when 'the liberty of the subject is at stake, questions of the damage sustained become of little importance'

QUESTION 32

On the one hand, English law rightly presumes that everyone is innocent until proven guilty, so it would be wrong to keep anyone in custody (normally a punishment) unless they have been convicted. On the other hand, some of those charged with serious crimes are likely to try to abscond or interfere with witnesses or evidence unless they are kept secure until trial. Framing rules to govern this conflict is a question of balance.

In the light of recent changes to the principles of bail in the English legal system, discuss whether current law has the balance right.

....

26 Importantly, the possibility that the facts of the decided case are distinguishable from those of the scenario has been highlighted, demonstrating strength in terms of application of the law.

How to Answer this Question

Answers should incorporate:

- ❖ discussion of the background to key legal changes in 1993–94;
- ❖ explanation of the current legal framework;
- ❖ s 27 of the **Criminal Justice and Public Order Act (CJPOA) 1994** – extension of police powers in relation to bail;
- ❖ the **Bail Act 1976** and the presumption of bail;
- ❖ s 25 of the **CJPOA 1994** and the denial of bail where there has been earlier conviction for murder, etc;
- ❖ appeals and repeated applications;
- ❖ the **Bail (Amendment) Act 1993**;
- ❖ conclusions.

Answer Structure

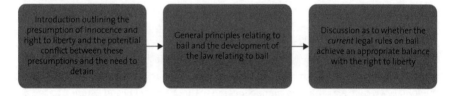

Introduction outlining the presumption of innocence and right to liberty and the potential conflict between these presumptions and the need to detain → General principles relating to bail and the development of the law relating to bail → Discussion as to whether the *current* legal rules on bail achieve an appropriate balance with the right to liberty

ANSWER

There is in most circumstances a strong legal presumption that for an unconvicted suspect, liberty must prevail over incarceration. In *Hurnam v State of Mauritius* (2005), the Privy Council held that the seriousness of an offence cannot be treated as a conclusive reason for refusing bail to an unconvicted suspect. The right to personal liberty is an important constitutional right, and a suspect should remain at large unless it is necessary to refuse bail in order to serve one of the ends for which detention before trial was permissible.[27]

In the early 1990s, the UK Government took the view that bail was too easily granted and that too many crimes were being committed by those on bail who deserved to be in custody while awaiting trial. The **Bail (Amendment) Act 1993** and the **CJPOA 1994** (ss 25–30) emanate from that philosophy, their aim being to restrict the granting of bail. A case which caught public sympathy for this view involved a young man who had many convictions for car crime and joyriding. Whilst on bail, he was joyriding in a vehicle when he smashed into a schoolgirl. She clung to the bonnet but he shook her off and thus killed her. The Home Secretary commented publicly that the new legislative measures would prevent such terrible events.

....

27 Introduction demonstrates a sound understanding of why liberty should *normally* prevail over incarceration.

Each year, about 50,000 offences are committed by people on bail. A study by the Metropolitan Police in 1988 indicated that 16 per cent of those charged by that force were already on bail for another offence. Another study in 1993 from the same force showed that of 537 suspects arrested in one week during a clampdown on burglary, 40 per cent were on bail. Some had been bailed 10 or 15 times during the preceding year.[28]

Before examining how recent legislation changes the law, it is appropriate to set out the general principles of bail. In the criminal process, the first stage at which bail is raised as an issue is at the police station. If a person is arrested on a warrant, this will indicate whether he is to be held in custody or released on bail. If the suspect is arrested without a warrant, then the police will have to decide whether to release the suspect after he has been charged. After a person has been charged, **s 38(1)(a)** of the **Police and Criminal Evidence Act (PACE) 1984** states that a person must be released unless: (a) his name and address are not known; or (b) the custody officer reasonably thinks that his detention is necessary for his own protection, or to prevent him from injuring someone or damaging property; or (c) because he might abscond or interfere with the course of justice. Most arrested people are bailed by the police. In 1990, 83 per cent of those arrested in connection with indictable offences and 88 per cent of those arrested for summary offences (other than motoring offences) were released. This area has been amended by **s 28** of the **1994 Act**. A custody officer can now, in the case of an imprisonable offence, refuse to release an arrested person after charge if the officer has reasonable grounds for believing that the detention of that person is necessary to prevent him from committing *any* offence. Previously, many cases were caught by (b) above, and the police officer was able to keep a dangerous person in custody, but some sorts of conduct that the arrested person was likely to go out and commit (for example, drink driving) were not the sort of thing that the police were entitled to use to refuse bail.

Section 27 of the **1994 Act** amends **ss 38** and **47** of **PACE** so as to allow the police to grant conditional bail to persons charged. The conditions can be whatever is required to ensure that the person surrenders to custody, does not commit an offence while on bail, or does not interfere with witnesses or otherwise obstruct the course of justice. The new powers of the custody officer, however, do not include a power to impose a requirement to reside in a bail hostel. By amending **Pt IV** of **PACE, s 29** of the **1994 Act** gives the police power to arrest without warrant a person who, having been granted conditional police bail, has failed to attend at a police station at the appointed time.

The **Bail Act 1976** created a statutory presumption of bail. It states (**s 4**) that subject to **Sched 1** and amendments made by **s 25** of the **1994 Act** about murder, manslaughter, etc (see below), bail shall be granted to a person accused of an offence in a magistrates' court

---

28 Good introduction to the opposing argument in terms of refusing the right to bail.

or a Crown Court and to convicted people who are being remanded for reports to be made. The court must therefore grant bail (unless one of the exceptions applies), even if the defendant does not make an application. **Schedule 1** provides that a court need not grant bail to a person charged with an offence punishable with imprisonment if it is satisfied that there are substantial grounds for believing that if released on bail, the defendant would:

(a)   fail to surrender to custody;

(b)   commit an offence while on bail; or

(c)   interfere with witnesses, or otherwise obstruct the course of justice.

The court can also refuse bail if it believes that the defendant ought to stay in custody for his own protection, or if it has not been practicable 'for want of time to obtain sufficient information to enable the court to make its decision on bail'.

When the court is considering the grounds stated above, all relevant factors must be taken into account, including the nature and seriousness of the offence, the character, antecedents, associations and community ties of the defendant and his record for satisfying his obligations under previous grants of bail.

If the defendant is charged with an offence not punishable with imprisonment, **Sched 1** provides that bail can only be withheld if he has previously failed to surrender on bail and if the court believes that in view of that failure, he would fail again to surrender if released on bail.

Section 25 of the **CJPOA 1994** provides that in some circumstances, a person who has been charged with or convicted of murder, attempted murder, manslaughter, rape or attempted rape must not be granted bail. The circumstances are simply that the conviction must have been within the UK and that in the case of a manslaughter conviction, it must have been dealt with by way of a custodial sentence. The term 'conviction' is given a wide meaning and also includes anyone found 'not guilty by way of insanity.'[29]

There has been debate[30] about whether the changes wrought by **s 25** are justifiable. A Home Office minister, defending the section, stated that it would be worth the risk if it prevented just one murder or rape, even though there might be a few 'hard cases', that is, people eventually acquitted of crime who were remanded in custody pending trial. As

---

29 The preceding paragraphs provide knowledgeable consideration of the principles of bail, the original law and its development.

30 Discussion of academic debate of an issue such as bail not only demonstrates knowledge but also encourages an evaluative approach and informs and supports any argument put forward. (Remember that unsupported argument is unlikely to attract particularly high marks.)

Card and Ward have remarked in a commentary on the Act (**Criminal Justice and Public Order Act 1994**), the Government, when pushed, was unable to cite a single case where a person released on bail in the circumstances covered by **s 25** reoffended in a similar way. There is no time-limit on the previous conviction and there is no requirement of any connection between the previous offence and the one in question. Card and Ward suggest that there is a world of difference between a person who was convicted of manslaughter 30 years ago on the grounds of complicity in a suicide pact and who is now charged with attempted rape (of which he must be presumed innocent), and the person who was convicted of rape eight years ago and now faces another rape charge. The first person is not an obvious risk to society and it is, they argue, regrettable that bail will be denied to him. There is also argument to be had with the contents of the **s 25** list. Why should some clearly dangerous and prevalent crimes like robbery be omitted from it? In any case, it may have been better had the offences in the list raised a strong presumption against bail as opposed to an absolute ban, as the former could be rebutted in cases where there was, on the facts, no risk.

The **Criminal Justice Act 2003** made a number of changes to the law in respect of bail. It enables action to be taken to reduce breaches of bail by introducing a new presumption against bail in certain circumstances. The Act enables the immediate grant of bail at the scene of arrest ('street bail') if there is no immediate need to deal with the arrested person at a police station. It gives police the discretion to decide when and where an arrested person should attend a police station for interview. It also enables reviews of the continuing need for detention without charge to be conducted over the telephone rather than in person at the police station as was previously the case.

Part II (ss 13–21) of the **2003 Act** gives effect to the Law Commission's recommendation that minor amendments needed to be made to the **Bail Act 1976** to ensure that its compliance with the **European Convention on Human Rights** is beyond dispute. The earlier law which purported to make it an exception to the right to bail that an offence appears to have been committed while the defendant was on bail for another offence was repealed, and replaced with a presumption that bail will not be granted in these circumstances to a defendant aged 18 or over unless the court is satisfied that there is no significant risk of his reoffending on bail. There is also a presumption that a defendant aged 18 or over who, without reasonable cause, has failed to surrender to custody will not be granted bail, unless the court is satisfied that there is no significant risk that he would so fail if released.

This Act also gives effect to recommendations of Lord Justice Auld in his *Review of the Criminal Courts of England and Wales* for simplifying the bail appeals system, including the removal of the High Court's bail jurisdiction where it was concurrent with that of the Crown Court. The right of the prosecution to appeal to the Crown Court against a decision by magistrates to grant bail is extended to cover all imprisonable offences (and not just, as earlier, those carrying a maximum penalty of five years or more).

The **2003 Act** creates a presumption that bail will not be granted for a person aged 18 or over who is charged with an imprisonable offence, and tests positive for a specified Class A drug, if he refuses to undergo an assessment as to his dependency or propensity to misuse such drugs, or following an assessment, refuses any relevant follow-up action recommended unless the court is satisfied that there is no significant risk of his reoffending on bail.

Bail can be granted as conditional or unconditional. Where it is unconditional, the accused must simply surrender to the court at the appointed date. Failure to appear without reasonable cause is an offence under **s 6** of the **Bail Act 1976** and can result, if tried in a Crown Court, in a sentence of up to 12 months' imprisonment or a fine. Conditions can be attached to the granting of bail where the court thinks that it is necessary to ensure that the accused surrenders at the right time, does not interfere with witnesses or commit further offences. There is no statutory limit to the conditions the court may impose and the most common include requirements that the accused reports daily or weekly to a police station, resides at a particular address, surrenders his passport or does not go to particular places or associate with particular people.

Section 7 of the **1976 Bail Act** gives the police power to arrest anyone on conditional bail whom they reasonably suspect is likely to break the conditions, or who has already done so. Anyone arrested in these circumstances must be brought before a magistrate within 24 hours. The magistrate may then reconsider the question of bail.

Personal recognisances, by which the suspect agreed to pay a sum if he failed to surrender to the court, were abolished by the **1976 Act**, except in cases where it is believed that he might try to flee abroad. The Act did retain the court's right to ask for sureties as a condition of bail. By putting sureties in a position where they can have large sums of money 'estreated' if the suspect does not surrender to the court, a significant pressure (not using the resources of the criminal justice system) is put on the accused. The proportion of those who do not answer to bail is very small – consistently about 4 per cent of those given bail. **Section 9** of the Act strengthens the surety principle by making it a criminal offence to agree to indemnify a surety. This sort of thing could happen, for example, if the accused agreed to reimburse the surety in the event that the accused skipped bail and the surety was requested to pay.

The rules which govern how someone who has been refused bail might re-apply and appeal have also been framed with a view to balancing the interests of the accused with those of the public and justice. The original refusal should not be absolute and final but, on the other hand, it is seen as necessary that the refusals are not reversed too easily.

If the court decides not to grant the defendant bail, then **s 154** provides that it is the court's duty to consider whether the defendant ought to be granted bail at each subsequent hearing. At the first hearing after the one at which bail was first refused, he may support an application for bail with any arguments, but at subsequent hearings, the court need not hear arguments as to fact or law which it has heard before. The **Criminal Justice Act 1982** enables a court to remand an accused in his absence for up to three successive one week remand hearings, provided that he consents and is legally represented. Such repeated visits are costly to the state and can be unsettling for the accused, especially if he has to spend most of the day in a police cell only to be told the case has been adjourned again without bail. If someone does not consent, they are prevented from applying for bail on each successive visit if the only supporting arguments are those that have been heard by the court before (*R v Nottingham Justices ex p Davies* (1980)).

To avoid unproductive hearings, that is, to promote courts being able to adjourn a case for a period within which reasonable progress can be made on a case, **s 155** of the **Criminal Justice Act 1988** allows for adjournments for up to 28 days, provided that the court sets the date for when the next stage of the proceedings should take place. What began as an experiment under this section has now, by statutory order (**SI 1991/2667**), been extended to all courts.

The interests of the accused are also served by the variety of appeals he may make if bail has been refused. If bail has been refused by magistrates, then, in limited circumstances, an application may be made to another bench of magistrates. Applications for reconsideration can also be made to a judge in chambers (through a legal representative) or to the Official Solicitor (in writing). Appeal can also be made to the Crown Court in respect of bail for both pre-committal remands and where a defendant has been committed for trial or sentence at the Crown Court.

Section 3 of the **Bail Act 1976** allows for an application to vary the conditions of court bail to be made by the person bailed, the prosecutor or a police officer. Application may also be made for the imposition of conditions on unconditional court bail. As amended by the **CJPOA 1994, s 3** of the **Bail Act 1976** now[31] allows for the same thing in relation to police bail, although the new provisions do not allow the prosecutor to seek reconsideration of the decision to grant bail itself. Under the **Bail (Amendment) Act 1993**, however, the prosecution does now have a right to appeal against the grant of bail by a court. This right applies to offences which carry a maximum sentence of imprisonment of five years, or more, and to offences of taking a vehicle without consent (joyriding). When this right of appeal is exercised, the defendant will remain in custody until the appeal is heard by a Crown Court judge, who will decide whether to grant bail or remand the defendant in custody within 48 hours of the magistrate's decision. Parliament was concerned that this power could be abused and has stated that it should be reserved 'for cases of greatest

---

31 Helpful comparison of 'old' and 'new'.

concern, when there is a serious risk of harm to the public' or where there are 'other significant public interest grounds' for an appeal.

Although this area of law was subject to a comprehensive revision after a Home Office special working party reported in 1974, and has been legislatively debated and modified five times since the **1976 Act**, it is still a matter of great importance, both to those civil libertarians who consider the law too tilted against the accused, and to the police and some commentators who believe criticism of the law from both sides to the debate might indicate a desirable state of balance reached by the current regulatory framework.[32]

QUESTION 33

What difficulties are involved in designing rules to govern plea bargaining and how successful is the English system in this respect?

How to Answer this Question

Any answer on this theme should take account of the research findings presented to the Royal Commission on Criminal Justice and the recommendations made by the Commission:

- ❖ definition of terms;
- ❖ explanation of the guidelines in *Turner* (1970);
- ❖ difficulties in applying the *Practice Direction (Turner Rules)* (1976);
- ❖ discussion of the points in *Pitman* (1991);
- ❖ whether the Court of Appeal can attract proper guilty pleas whilst not engaging in injudicious disclosure of the possible sentence;
- ❖ recommendations of the Runciman Commission and the Auld Report;
- ❖ conclusion.

Answer Structure

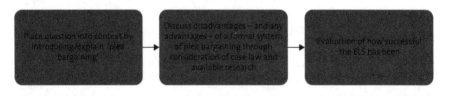

ANSWER

'Plea bargaining' has been defined as 'the practice whereby the accused enters a plea of guilty in return for which he will be given some consideration that results in a sentence

---

32 Recognises the importance of providing a conclusion which 'sums up' and succinctly answers specific question set.

concession' (Baldwin and McConville, *Negotiated Justice*, 1977). In practice, this can refer to a situation either where there has been a plea arrangement for the accused to plead guilty to a lesser charge than the one with which he is charged (charge bargaining), or where there is simply a sentencing discount available on a plea of guilty by the accused (sentence bargaining).

For a guilty defendant and for the prosecution, such a negotiated settlement represents a mutually valuable compromise, because the prosecution has gained a guilty plea and the defendant a sentence concession. Additionally, there will have been a significant saving to the state in the cost of a trial. Such bargains, however, are fraught with legal difficulties, chiefly because they can be construed as circumstances where undue pressure has been put on the accused to plead guilty. Many convictions have been quashed for just such a reason.[33]

There is a limited way in which 'plea bargaining' is already part of the English legal system. The **Serious Organised Crime and Police Act 2005** introduced a formalised system of plea bargaining. The current general system of judges giving indications of how they might sentence if the court were given a guilty plea, and judges giving sentence discounts for early pleas, is not affected by the Act. Such a system, though, is open and controlled by a judge. The **2005 Act** gives power to prosecutors to grant full and conditional immunities to putative or actual defendants. It is possible for the agreements to be supported by formal contracts. Thus, if a witness granted immunity from prosecution subsequently fails to testify as agreed against his or her co-conspirators, the contract is repudiated, and that defendant is again liable to prosecution.[34]

A commitment to implement such principles was announced in 2007 (*The Times*, 15 March, 2007) as part of reforms to the handling of large-scale fraud cases. Lord Goldsmith, QC, the Attorney-General, cited such agreements among measures aimed at tackling fraud, now estimated to be costing Britain £20 billion a year. Other plans include tougher jail terms, the maximum term expected to be increased to 14 years' imprisonment.

Research conducted by Professor Zander for the Royal Commission on Criminal Justice (Runciman Report, Cm 2263, 1993)[35] found that in a study of 900 Crown Court cases, 90 per cent of barristers and two-thirds of judges were in favour of formalising plea bargaining based on sentence discounts. The study suggests that 11 per cent of those who pleaded guilty in fact maintained their innocence, but wanted to secure a reduction in sentence.

....

33 Introductory paragraphs provide helpful clarification of 'plea bargaining' and its value.

34 Good overview of the use of plea bargaining in the ELS at present.

35 The ability to be able to refer to such reliable research is likely to impress any examiner. Use it to inform and support arguments put forward.

A plea of guilty by the accused must be made freely. He must only be advised to plead guilty if he has committed the crime in question. In *Turner* (1970), Lord Parker CJ set out guidelines on plea bargaining. He stated that:

(a) it may sometimes be the duty of counsel to give strong advice to the accused that a plea of guilty with remorse is a mitigating factor which might enable the court to give a lesser sentence;

(b) the accused must ultimately make up his own mind as to how to plead;

(c) there should be open access to the trial judge and counsel for both sides should attend each meeting, preferably in open court; and

(d) the judge should never indicate the sentence which he is minded to impose, nor should he ever indicate that on a plea of guilty, he would impose one sentence, but that on a conviction following a plea of not guilty, he would impose a more severe sentence. The judge could say what sentence he would impose on a plea of guilty (where, for example, he has read the depositions and antecedents), but without mentioning what he would do if the accused were convicted after pleading not guilty. Even this would be wrong, however, since the accused might take the judge to be intimating that a more severe sentence would follow upon conviction after a guilty plea. The only exception to this rule is where a judge says that the sentence will take a particular form, following conviction, whether there has been a plea of guilty or not guilty.

These guidelines were subsequently embodied in the Court of Appeal's *Practice Direction (Turner Rules)* (1976). A number of difficulties have been experienced in applying these principles. Perhaps the greatest problem has resulted from the fact that although the principles state in (d) that a judge should never say that a sentence passed after a conviction would be more severe than one passed after a guilty plea, it is a generally known rule that, guilty pleas lead to lesser sentences. In *Cain* (1976), it was stressed that, in general, defendants should realise that guilty pleas attract lesser sentences. Lord Widgery said: 'Any accused person who does not know about it should know about it.' The difficulty is that the trial judge must not mention it, otherwise he could be construed as exerting pressure on the accused to plead guilty.

In *Turner*, the defendant pleaded not guilty on a charge of theft. He had previous convictions and, during an adjournment, he was advised by counsel in strong terms to change his plea; after having spoken with the judge, which the defendant knew, counsel advised that in his opinion, a plea of guilty would result in a non-custodial sentence, whereas if he persisted with a not guilty plea and thereby attacked police witnesses, there was a real possibility of receiving a custodial sentence. The defendant changed his plea to guilty and then appealed on the ground that he did not have a free choice in changing his plea. His appeal was allowed on the basis that he might have formed the impression that the views being expressed to him by his counsel were those of the judge, particularly as it was known by the accused that counsel had just returned from seeing the judge when he gave his advice to the accused.

The advantages for the prosecution in gaining a guilty plea are obvious but, as the *Code for Crown Prosecutors* notes, administrative convenience in the form of a rapid guilty plea should not take precedence over the interests of justice. Justice demands that the court should be able to pass a proper sentence, consistent with the gravity of the accused's actions and, if a plea is accepted, then the defendant can only be sentenced on the basis of the crime that he has admitted. It is noteworthy that the judge is not bound to accept a plea arrangement made between the sides. The Farquharson Committee on the Role of Prosecuting Counsel thought that there is a general right for the prosecution to offer no evidence in respect of any particular charge, but that where the judge's opinion is sought on whether it is desirable to reassure the public at large that the right course is being taken, counsel must abide by the judge's decision. Where the judge thinks that counsel's view to proceed is wrong, the trial can be halted until the Director of Public Prosecutions (DPP) has been consulted and given the judge's comments. In the notorious case of *Sutcliffe* (1981) (the 'Yorkshire Ripper' case), the prosecution and defence had agreed that Sutcliffe would plead guilty to manslaughter on the grounds of diminished responsibility, but the trial judge rejected that agreement and, after consultations with the DPP, Sutcliffe was eventually found guilty of murder.

The extent of the difficulties in framing rules on plea bargaining which achieve clarity and fairness can be judged by the remark of Lord Lane CJ in the case of *Pitman* (1991):

> There seems to be a steady flow of appeals to this court arising from visits by counsel to the judge in his private room. No amount of criticism and no amount of warnings and no amount of exhortation seems to be able to prevent this from happening.

In this case, on counsel's advice, the appellant pleaded not guilty to causing death by reckless driving. On cup final day in 1989, he had driven, having been drinking all afternoon, in a car without a rear view mirror. He had crashed into another car, killing one of its passengers, whilst having double the permitted level of alcohol in his blood.

During the trial, the judge called both counsel to his room and stated that he did not think there was a defence to the charge. Counsel for the appellant explained that although the appellant had admitted that his carelessness caused the accident, the advice to plead not guilty was based on the fact that the prosecution might not be able to prove the necessary recklessness. The trial judge replied that the appellant's plea was a matter for the appellant himself and not counsel and that if the appellant accepted responsibility for the accident, he ought to plead guilty and if he did so, he would receive 'substantial credit' when it came to sentencing.

Counsel for the appellant then discussed this with the appellant, who changed his plea to guilty and was sentenced to nine months' imprisonment and was disqualified for four years. His appeal was allowed, as the judge had put undue pressure on the appellant and his counsel to change his plea to guilty and his remarks had suggested that his chances of acquittal were slight if he pleaded not guilty and that if he was found guilty, having pleaded not guilty, he would certainly be sentenced to imprisonment. Lord Lane CJ emphasised that a judge should not initiate discussions in private and that where, at the behest of counsel, they are absolutely necessary, they should be recorded by shorthand or on a recording device.

Another problem[36] here concerns framing the guidelines so that they are sufficiently permissive to allow counsel access to the judge in his private room in cases in deserving instances, but avoiding the problems of confidentiality. As Mustill LJ said in *Harper-Taylor and Bakker* (1988):

> The need to solve an immediate practical problem may combine with the more relaxed atmosphere of the private room to blur the formal outlines of the trial.

There is a risk that counsel and solicitors may hear something said to the judge which they would rather not hear, putting them into a state of conflict between their duties to their clients and their obligations to maintain the confidentiality of the private room. Reviewing the current state of the law, Curran (see [1991] Crim LR 79) has written that the effect of cases like *Bird* (1977) and *Agar* (1990) (the latter not a plea bargaining case, but one which hinged on a judge's ruling in his private room as complied with by counsel to the appellant's detriment) is that defence counsel has a duty to disclose to his client any observations made by the judge in his room which significantly affect the client's case, whether or not the judge expresses them to be made confidentially.

The Royal Commission on Criminal Justice, chaired by Viscount Runciman, reported in July 1993. It recommended (pp 156–159) a clearly articulated system of sentence discounts, with earlier pleas attracting higher discounts. Lord Runciman pointed out that this was not 'plea bargaining' in the American sense, in which the prosecution can suggest the appropriate sentence. The proposal was supported by law enforcement officers, like the DPP, who regard it as a way to tackle 'cracked trials': those which abort at the last minute through a change of plea to guilty. In 1994, 83 per cent of defendants who elected for trial at the Crown Court changed their plea to guilty. The proposal was, however, opposed by groups like Liberty and Justice, who believe that these changes might pressurise innocent people, intimidated by the system, into a guilty plea. It can be seen as subtly undermining the presumption of innocence and the requirement that the prosecution proves its case.

....

36 As the question specifically asks for consideration of 'difficulties', highlighting such problems is vital in achieving good marks.

Further recommendations have been put forward by the Auld Report (2001), which proposed (para 12) the introduction of a scheme of discounts on sentencing on a graduated scale, so that the earlier the plea of guilty is entered, the higher the discount for it. Such a scheme should be coupled with a system of advance indication of sentence for a defendant who is considering pleading guilty.

Sanders and Young (*Criminal Justice*, 1994) have argued that it is artificial and unrealistic for the law to encourage guilty pleas through the sentence discount, whilst simultaneously denying the defence the opportunity to discover exactly what, if anything, is on offer from the judge in a particular case. They contend that, in practice, both defence counsel and judges have abused their right to meet in private and have, despite the Court of Appeal's guidance, engaged in sentence bargaining on a wide scale.

The Court of Appeal has consistently indicated that the information should not be given to defendants, because that might put undue pressure on them to plead guilty, but sentence discounts are legally recognised (see Thomas, in *Current Sentencing Practice*, para A8 2(b)); a guilty plea attracts a lighter sentence, and the extent of the reduction is usually between one-quarter and one-third of what would have otherwise been the sentence. Moreover, Lord Widgery has stated (above) that defendants should know about them. The pressure could scarcely be increased by informing a defendant with details, rather than leaving it to his general knowledge. If anything, Zander has argued, it would diminish the pressure by making it clear that the defendant's fears about the penalty for pleading not guilty are exaggerated.

There is, however, reason for anxiety with such a call for more openness. Sanders and Young regard it as 'an idealistic notion' that one can improve the effectiveness of the system in convicting the guilty without also increasing its effectiveness in convicting the innocent (*Criminal Justice*, 1994). In one Home Office study (1992), Hedderman and Moxon found that 65 per cent of those pleading guilty in Crown Court cases said that their decision had been influenced by the prospect of receiving a discount in sentence. Even the Royal Commission recognised that not all those pleading guilty are, in fact, guilty; some may have just capitulated to the pressure of taking the reduced sentence, rather than run the risk of the full sentence. As Sanders and Young contend, this issue goes to the heart of constitutional principles. Only if the state acts properly in collecting and presenting evidence can punishment be justified, according to commonly accepted principles. Even the guilty are entitled to due process of law. A system of plea bargaining may undermine such principles, since it allows the state to secure convictions based on unproven allegations.[37]

....

37 Conclusion demonstrates thoughtfulness.

QUESTION 34

How far should the law allow witnesses to be prepared by the advocates who will examine them in criminal courts?

How to Answer this Question

Your answer should:

- ❖ explain the importance of witnesses to the court process;
- ❖ introduce the important case of *Momodou* (2005), and the Bar Code provisions;
- ❖ mention civil case rules, just to help set the scene for the criminal case issues which are the main focus of this essay;
- ❖ differentiate lawful 'witness familiarisation' from improper 'witness coaching';
- ❖ explain the dangers of witness coaching to the legal process;
- ❖ explain the Court of Appeal's test to distinguish the acceptable forms of witness preparation from the unacceptable forms;
- ❖ explain the Attorney-General's 2005 proposals for change;
- ❖ explain the objections to his proposals.

Answer Structure

Introduction providing an overview of the present system (in criminal trials) → Consideration of problems associated with present system and argument for and against change → Balanced and logically argued conclusion

ANSWER

This question concerns matters central to the way the English legal system deals with evidence. Witnesses are integral parts of criminal and civil cases in the English legal system. They are arguably the most important feature of the process by which courts aim to get to the truth in a dispute. Can and should court witnesses be prepared by their advocate before giving their testimony?

These issues were recently addressed by the Court of Appeal in *R v Momodou* (2005). The legal background to this case is in a rule of the Bar Code of Conduct: Part VII – Conduct of Work.[38] It explains (rule 705) that:

A barrister must not:

(a) rehearse, practise or coach a witness in relation to his evidence;

....

38 Helpful and knowledgeable introduction which sets the scene in terms of the extent of 'witness preparation', well supported by case law and professional code.

(b)   encourage a witness to give evidence which is untruthful or which is not the whole truth.

In civil cases a barrister can 'give general advice to a witness about giving evidence, for example, speak up, speak slowly, answer the question, keep answers as short as possible, ask if a question is not understood, say if you cannot remember and do not guess or speculate . . .' (Miscellaneous Guidance, Part F, para 9). In criminal cases a barrister can have contact with a witness before the case 'with a view to introducing himself to the witness, explaining the court's procedure . . . and answering any questions on procedure which the witness may have'. Barristers are also permitted to put a witness through some questions before the case in order to test his recollection and the quality of his evidence.

In *Momodou*, the Court of Appeal criminal division clearly defines the difference, in a *criminal case* context, between the proper process of 'witness familiarisation' and the improper use of 'witness training or coaching'. The case concerned defendants who had been convicted of violent disorder during a serious disturbance at the Yarls Wood Detention Centre, in Bedfordshire, in 2002. The Court rejected claims that unlawful pre-trial coaching of security guard prosecution witnesses had led to the wrongful conviction of two asylum-seekers involved in the riot at the detention centre.

The Court of Appeal held that, although two key security guard witnesses had attended a programme operated by a legal training firm, the safety of the convictions had not been undermined.

Lord Justice Judge observed that the dangers[39] in witness coaching included that a dishonest witnesses might learn, during a rehearsal, how to 'improve' his testimony. The danger augmented if the coaching was not one-to-one but conducted collectively because prospective witnesses might 'bring their respective accounts into what they believe to be better alignment with others'. Pre-trial arrangements to familiarise a witness with the layout of the court, court processes, and the way evidence should be given, will be fine provided the trainers, preferably lawyers, have no knowledge of the actual issues in the forthcoming trial. Lord Justice Judge explained the core of the reasoning of the Court of Appeal on this issue. He said there is a dramatic distinction between witness training or coaching, and witness familiarisation. Training or coaching for witnesses in criminal proceedings (whether for prosecution or defence) is not permitted. This is the logical consequence of the well-known principle that discussions between witnesses should not take place, and that the statements and proofs of one witness should not be disclosed to any other witness. He noted: 'The witness should give

---

39 Discussing such 'dangers' highlights the problem of 'witness coaching'.

his or her own evidence, so far as practicable uninfluenced by what anyone else has said, whether in formal discussions or informal conversations' (para 61).

The rule reduces, indeed hopefully avoids, any possibility that one witness may tailor his evidence in the light of what anyone else said, and equally, avoids any unfounded perception that he may have done so. These risks are inherent in witness training.

Lord Justice Judge also said: 'An honest witness may alter the emphasis of his evidence to accommodate what he thinks may be a different, more accurate, or simply better remembered perception of events. A dishonest witness will very rapidly calculate how his testimony may be "improved"' (para 61).

The Court ruled that this familiarisation process should normally be supervised or conducted by a solicitor or barrister, or someone who is responsible to a solicitor or barrister with experience of the criminal justice process, and preferably by an organisation accredited for the purpose by the Bar Council and Law Society. None of those involved should have any personal knowledge of the matters in issue. Records should be maintained of all those present and the identity of those responsible for the familiarisation process, whenever it takes place. The programme should be retained, together with all the written material (or appropriate copies) used during the familiarisation sessions. None of the material should bear any similarity whatever to the issues in the criminal proceedings to be attended by the witnesses, and nothing in it should play on or trigger the witness's recollection of events.

In December 2004, not long before the Court of Appeal's February 2005 decision, the Attorney-General, Lord Goldsmith QC, issued a statement in which he advocated the case for prosecutors being able to speak with witnesses privately, and off the record before the trial.[40] This is an utterance not in perfect harmony with the views expressed by the Court of Appeal in *Momodou*.

The Attorney-General said that many people would be surprised to learn that prosecutors in England and Wales are not entitled to interview witnesses before trial, even when they are key prosecution witnesses whose credibility may be critical to whether a prosecution should go ahead or not. He said the practice should change, arguing that: 'It is striking that it is only in England and Wales that prosecutors do not have direct access to witnesses even in order to assess their credibility and reliability.'

The conclusions reached by the Attorney-General included that prosecutors should be permitted to speak to witnesses – including children and vulnerable witnesses – about

....

40 By providing consideration of the arguments for 'witness preparation', a more balanced argument can be provided.

matters of evidence. He said prosecution witness interviews should be conducted for the purpose and the extent that, in the view of the prosecutor, such an interview is necessary in order to assess the reliability of or clarify a witness's evidence.

Where possible, he argued, an interview should generally take place once the prosecutor considers that he/she has sufficient information and evidence for an interview to be of value, but before the prosecutor reaches a decision to proceed.

However, prosecutors should, he said, be permitted to hold witness interviews *at any stage of the proceedings* including, therefore, just before trial. He argued that this was particularly so if further evidence or material, casting doubt on the reliability of a witness's evidence, came to light at a later stage in the proceedings or if further witnesses came to light after a decision to prosecute has been reached.

The Attorney-General contended that interviews should be conducted informally with the prosecutor, the witness, where possible a police officer, and independent support if the witness so wishes. He suggested that interviews should be conducted in the absence of the defence, and that police officers should be permitted to be present at interviews.

One sharply expressed objection to this came during a House of Lords' debate. The eminent lawyer Lord Thomas of Gresham said (Lords' *Hansard* text for 17 January 2005 (250117–22) Column 626):

> In subtle ways, the complainant in a criminal case is beginning to be treated as the client of the prosecutor. The essential impartiality of prosecuting counsel is, in my view, being undermined. He is being asked to take sides and to become involved in the emotions and personalities of complainants and their families. Achieving justice, objectively, between the state and the individual should be at the heart of the criminal justice system – not, as the Government so often states, victims and witnesses.[41]

He argued that justice cannot be done if a witness is so intimidated that he does not come forward or if his account is incomplete. But that, he said, is a matter for the police to investigate and not counsel. Similarly, the voluntary witness service does a great deal to ease the fears of complainants and witnesses where the court proceedings are in themselves intimidating. The prosecutor should not be involved at all in some kind of calming and comforting role.

He contended that, generally, the American experience shows how undesirable witness coaching is. Prosecutors have the ability, consciously or unconsciously, to strengthen the

---

41 An important point which demonstrates an understanding of matters at the very heart of the debate on this issue.

case by questions and suggestions that cause the witness to fill gaps in memory, eliminate ambiguities or contradictions, sharpen language, create emphasis, and alter demeanor. He asked 'Do we in this country really want to get involved in suspicions of horse shedding?'

The expression 'horse shedding' is a nineteenth-century American expression and refers to the practice whereby lawyers would coach witnesses in the horse sheds near the court houses in rural parts of the United States.

How far we do now go down that road is a political decision to be taken in the legislature on behalf of society at large, and it is clear that this apparently technical legal issue is in fact quite a contentious political issue of balancing the interests of the state and the individual.

Common Pitfalls

A failure to differentiate clearly between (i) advice related to the presentation of evidence and (ii) coaching about the content of testimony is a common feature of poor answers.

Aim Higher

High credit can be gained by exhibiting a good knowledge of the 2005 governmental reform proposals and their rationale: Lords' *Hansard* text for 17 January 2005 (250117–22) Col 626.

Civil Process and Legal Services

INTRODUCTION

The purpose of the Civil Justice Council is that of 'ensuring that this country retains a fair and effective justice system'. How far that system is fair and effective is the key theme of this chapter.

The county courts are the main platform on which the civil law rights and duties of British citizens are played out. If something goes badly wrong here, as the evidence suggests is happening now, then the rights of British citizens are prejudiced on a significant scale.

There are 216 county courts in England and Wales, dealing with claims for matters such as personal injury, debt, house repossessions and breaches of contract. All but the most complicated and momentous civil cases are dealt with by the county courts.

In February 2007, Judge Paul Collins, London's most senior county court judge, told BBC Radio 4's *Law in Action* programme that low pay and high turnover amongst administrative staff mean that serious errors are commonplace and routinely lead to incorrect judgments in court. Judge Collins said:

> We are operating on the margins of effectiveness and with further cuts looming we run the risk of bringing about a real collapse in the service we're able to give to people using the courts.

According to Judge Collins, the lack of resources is causing mistakes. A common problem is one in which someone who is being sued files a defence but the papers are not passed on to the judge by overburdened court staff. The judge will automatically award damages to the person who brought the claim, assuming that the person being sued does not want to defend it. According to Judge Collins:

> This happens on a regular basis and although these errors can be put right it takes work to put them right, producing more to do for already hard pressed court staff and judges.

Staff in the court service are amongst the poorest paid of all government departments. In Judge Collins' own court in Central London, the number of people employed had been cut from 125 in 1992 to just 80 at the time he spoke out. The quantity of work, however, had not diminished. Roughly speaking, therefore, the remaining staff were having to cover between them about a third more work than when there were 125 staff. It is no wonder that county court staff are becoming stressed and losing files.

The position had not improved by 2010. Judge Monty Trent, President of the Association of District Judges, noted that:

> Many of our courts are old, many are dilapidated. We can expect more court closures, impeding access to local justice.
>
> The Times, 1 April, 2010

County courts are no longer subsidised through general taxation. Instead, they are expected to generate all their income from fees charged to court users. This was intended to protect the courts from having to compete with other public services for government funds.

Problems in the administration of the courts have, in Judge Collins' experience, been further exacerbated by cuts in the availability of legal aid. He stated that:

> There is plenty of anecdotal evidence that this has led to an increase in the number of people representing themselves without the help of a qualified lawyer. These cases inevitably take up more time and as a result court proceedings last longer to the detriment of others using the courts.

One clear way in which the system has improved in recent times has been in respect of the accessibility of its information. The website of the Ministry of Justice contains links to all the most recent judgments of the court and to the relevant **Civil Procedure Rules (CPR)**. Another useful website is that of the Civil Division of the Court of Appeal, where details on case progression, available advice and support and contact details are provided: www.justice.gov.uk/courts/rcj-rolls-building/court-of-appeal/civil-division.

Since 1999, the civil process and the provision of legal services have undergone a major change. The **Civil Procedure Rules (CPR)**, the most fundamental changes in civil process for over a century, have radically altered the operation of civil justice. Part of the rationale of the rules was to expedite the way cases were dealt with and to allow more cases to be settled early, through negotiation between the parties or alternative dispute resolution (ADR). In this respect, there is some evidence of success.

The overriding objective of the **CPR** is to enable the court to deal justly with cases. The first rule reads:

> 1.1(1) These rules are a new procedural code with the overriding objective of enabling the court to deal with cases justly.

This objective will include ensuring that the parties are on an equal footing and saving expense. When exercising any discretion given by the **CPR**, the court must, according to **r 1.2**, have regard to the overriding objective and a checklist of factors, including the amount of money involved, the complexity of the issue, the parties' financial positions, how the case can be dealt with expeditiously and by allotting an appropriate share of the court's resources, while taking into account the needs of others. As a result, as Judge John Frenkel observes ('On the road to reform' (1998)): 'The decisions of the Court of Appeal are more likely to illustrate the application of the new rules to the facts of a particular case, as opposed to being interpretative authorities that define the meaning of the rules.'

Another area of change concerns conditional fee arrangements (CFAs). In the first version of CFAs, only people who expected to win money from their case could benefit from conditional fees. This was the only way that most people could afford to pay the success fee, but it meant that a successful litigant would not receive all the money he had been awarded. So, in 2000, the Government took the power, in the **Access to Justice Act 1999**, to make it possible for the winning party to recover the success fee and any insurance premium from the losing party. This ensures that it is the person or organisation that has committed the legal wrong who pays, and it will allow defendants and claimants (other than in family law cases), whose case is not about money, to use CFAs.

Legal services have also undergone very significant change in recent times. Expanded rights of advocacy for solicitors and others (including patent agents) have changed the traditional picture of the courts as the domain of barristers. There are currently approximately 4000 qualified solicitor-advocates. The introduction of the Legal Services Commission (LSC) and the Community Legal Service (CLS) marked a sea-change in the delivery of publicly funded law and the impending change, to a public defender system, carrying the potential for far-reaching implications for both the legal system and for the public, as consumers of its services. The cuts to the public funding of these bodies will present even greater challenges to their provision of services going forward.

Checklist ✔

You should be familiar with:

- the main provisions of the 1996 Woolf Report on Civil Justice;
- the purpose and main provisions of the new **CPR**;
- the arguments both for and against the proposition that the reforms can work and have worked well in practice;
- the main provisions of the **Legal Services Act 2007**;
- the main provisions of the **Access to Justice Act 1999**;
- the role and purpose of the LSC and the CLS;

- CFAs;
- the nature and purpose of the proposed Salaried Defence Service and critical commentary on this system;
- changes concerning rights of audience and legal liability of the legal professions.

QUESTION 35

Explain the process of judicial review, and state how the process is different from an appeal.

How to Answer this Question

❖ Set the structure of the answer by outlining the basic difference between a judicial review and an appeal.

❖ Turn to an example of a judicial review case and expound it: *The Queen on the Application of Greenpeace Ltd v Secretary of State for Trade and Industry* (2007).

❖ Explain the basic mechanics (prerogative remedies) of the judicial review.

❖ Cite and explain *Associated Provincial Picture Houses Ltd v Wednesbury Corporation* (1948).

❖ Explain the case's significance in respect of the 'reasonableness' principle.

Answer Structure

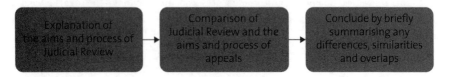

Explanation of the aims and process of Judicial Review → Comparison of Judicial Review and the aims and process of appeals → Conclude by briefly summarising any differences, similarities and overlaps

ANSWER

The process of judicial review is a part of the civil process categorised as administrative law. It is the process whereby the High Court can check that public bodies make their decisions using only legal and fair procedures. This process is different from an appeal, because the bodies that the High Court finds are in violation of the requirements of legal and fair decision making cannot be ordered to come to *different* decisions, but merely to reconsider the issue in question acting within the legal rules and fairly. Unlike a successful appeal, a successful judicial review does not result in the original decision being reversed, but merely invalidated.[1]

---

1 Answer immediately demonstrates knowledge by highlighting the differences between Judicial Review and appeals.

A recent example can be found in the decision *The Queen on the Application of Greenpeace Ltd v Secretary of State for Trade and Industry* (2007).[2] The High Court decided that a consultation process carried out by the Government on the future production of electricity was inadequate. Mr Justice Sullivan ruled that in attempting to canvass public opinion about the use of nuclear power plants, having said in a White Paper (a governmental proposal and discussion document) that it would allow 'the fullest public consultation', the Government's subsequent consultation exercise was procedurally unfair. There was a breach of the 'legitimate expectation' that there would be a full public consultation. The exercise was too rushed and confined by a tight deadline. The Government had later stated that as a result of its consultation, 'The Government believes that nuclear has a role to play in the future UK generating mix alongside other low carbon generating options'. The judicial review was brought by Greenpeace Ltd, which wanted to make a considered response to the consultation. The Court did not rule that the Government's decision to build another nuclear power plant was 'wrong as a matter of policy'; it ruled simply that a political decision that condoned the development of further nuclear plants had not been made in an appropriate way. Mr Justice Sullivan held that (para 120):

> [T]here was a breach of the claimant's legitimate expectation to fullest public consultation; that the consultation process was procedurally unfair; and that therefore the decision in the Energy Review that nuclear new build 'has a role to play . . .' was unlawful.

The essence of successful judicial review like this is not that a court says that a public body made a *wrong* decision but that it made a decision in a *wrong way*. Here, the Government had, in July 2006, come out in favour of new nuclear power stations without fulfilling its earlier documented promise to carry out 'the fullest consultation'. Whether the UK opts for new nuclear power stations is a *political* decision which the people (via our Government), not the law courts, will make. But in making the decision, proper process must be followed, so even mighty politicians must obey the rules of decision making. If they promise to consult fully then they must do just that.

Consulting the public is an important governmental activity. The people are an intrinsic part of government in the modern European setting. The European Court of Justice in 1980 referred to: '. . . the fundamental democratic principle that the peoples [of democratic countries in Europe] should take part in the exercise of power . . .' (Case 138/79, *SA Roquette Frères v Council* (1980) ECR 3333, 3360, para 33).[3]

---

2 The use of examples demonstrates deeper knowledge, aids explanation and provides support and legal authority.
3 In addition to demonstrating broad knowledge, reference to this European Union case assists in illustrating the importance of the availability of Judicial Review.

Judicial review is the procedure by which *prerogative* remedies (coming from the inherent power of the court) have been obtainable in the High Court against lower courts, tribunals, and administrative authorities from which there is no formal appeal process. So, where there is no procedure for an appeal to reconsider the merits of a decision (like the decision to approve new nuclear power stations), it is very important that the decision-making panel's approach to its task is impeccably fair. The primary purpose of judicial review is to control any actions of public authorities that might be made in excess of their proper powers (*ultra vires*) or on the basis of some unreasonable way of coming to a decision.

Judicial review, part of administrative law, has expanded dramatically as a part of law in recent history. In 1981, 552 applications for judicial review were made at the High Court, whereas in 2008, a total of 7,169 applications were made. We have come a long way since 1935 when Lord Chief Justice Hewart dismissed administrative law as worthless 'Continental jargon'.

The foundational precedent for modern cases of judicial review is *Associated Provincial Picture Houses Ltd v Wednesbury Corporation* (1948).[4] This concerned a local authority, in Wednesbury, central England, which had, under the **Sunday Entertainments Act 1932**, granted a licence to a company for it to open its Gaumont cinema on Sundays. The Act allowed for a licence to be granted with 'such conditions as the authority thinks fit'. The authority imposed the condition that children under 15 were not to be allowed into cinemas on Sundays. The company argued that the provision was 'unreasonable' and therefore *ultra vires*, that is, 'beyond the powers' of the local authority. It argued that the court should be the arbiter of whether a condition was reasonable.

In the Court of Appeal, the reasoning of Lord Greene, the Master of the Rolls, soon crystallised into a hallowed legal proposition. He said that where Parliament had entrusted discretionary powers to another body, like a local authority, the courts could declare that some decisions were 'unreasonable', and therefore beyond what the authority was authorised to do.

In a key passage of his judgment, the Master of the Rolls said:

> The court is entitled to investigate the action of the local authority with a view to seeing whether they have taken into account matters which they ought not to take into account, or, conversely, have refused to take into account or neglected to take into account matters which they ought to take into account. Once that question is answered in favour of the local authority, it may be still possible to say that,

---

4   Use of older cases provides background and demonstrates understanding of the development of the action.

although the local authority have kept within the four corners of the matters which they ought to consider, they have nevertheless come to a conclusion so unreasonable that no reasonable authority could ever have come to it. In such a case, again, I think the court can interfere. The power of the court to interfere in each case is not as an appellate authority to override a decision of the local authority, but as a judicial authority which is concerned, and concerned only, to see whether the local authority have contravened the law by acting in excess of the powers which Parliament has confided in them.

The courts, though, could not simply substitute their own opinion for that of the public body.[5] To be unreasonable, the decision would have to be one where an authority had 'taken into account matters which it ought not to take into account, or, conversely, has refused to take into account or neglected to take into account matters which it ought to take into account'. Applying the principles in this case, the court held that that the local authority had not acted unreasonably or *ultra vires* in imposing the condition that those under 15 could not attend the cinema on a Sunday.

Even if the way a decision was made passes that test, the decision could still be challenged in the courts if it was one which 'no reasonable body could have come to'. In other words, if it is a patently mad decision. An example given in an earlier case was if a teacher had been dismissed 'because she had red hair, or for some equally frivolous and foolish reason'.

The principles have since become the touchstone of the courts when deciding judicial review cases, and the legal phrase '*Wednesbury* unreasonable' is shorthand for a decision of a public body or official that violates the criterion of necessary reasonableness established in this case. The judicial control of governmental power is an essential element of democracy.

Common Pitfalls

The definition of 'reasonableness' according to the *Wednesbury* case decision is subtle and multifaceted. It is a common among poor answers for the definition to be inadequately recounted, so learn it well.

Another common pitfall is the failure to explain the legal consequence of a successful judicial review, i.e. that the matter is remitted to the original decision-maker to look at again in a legally proper way.

---

5   Demonstrates an appreciation of the fact that Judicial Review is not about *what* was decided by the public body but, instead, *how* the decision was reached.

Aim Higher ★

It is highly creditable to include some European context or cases, for example: *SA Roquette Frères v Council* (1980).

The demonstration of an appreciation of the political context of judicial review is also highly creditable. This can be done, for example, by reference to cases in which the tension between judicial and governmental power is manifest; see, e.g. *The Queen on the Application of Greenpeace Ltd v Secretary of State for Trade and Industry* (2007).

QUESTION 36

What pressures have been found to encourage litigants to settle claims, even against their best interests, and what approach to this issue is taken by the **CPR**?

How to Answer this Question

You should consider the following:

❖   the nature of settlement;
❖   fear of costs and uncertainty of outcome;
❖   Part 36 payments;
❖   the **Civil Procedure Rules (CPR)** and limiting costs;
❖   active case management.

Answer Structure

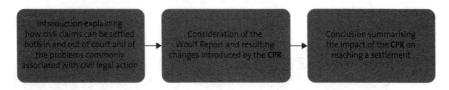

ANSWER

A settlement is a compromise. In the context of litigation, it involves the parties deciding to resolve their dispute out of court, rather than go to a full hearing and have the matter decided by a judge, or even a civil jury. If a litigant is being pushed into giving in when he has a sound legal case and his rights should be vindicated, then a compromise is undesirable. Where, however, a dispute is evenly balanced and would involve a great deal of time, anxiety and resources to resolve in a full trial, then a compromise might well represent a trilateral relief: relief for both sides and the taxpayers who support the legal system.

Most civil disputes are settled out of court.[6] Less than 10 per cent of cases where a claim form is issued actually go to court and, even of those which do go to trial, many are settled before judgment. Evidence presented by the London Passenger Transport Board to the Winn Committee on Personal Injury Litigation (1968), for example, showed that of about 5,000 claims made against it per year, about 4,900 were settled without proceedings. Of the 100 or so cases which were commenced, only about one-quarter were taken to full judgment.

The largest study of this sort was conducted by the Oxford Centre for Socio-Legal Studies (Harris *et al, Compensation and Support for Illness and Injury*, 1984), which examined a random sample of 1,711 accident victims who had been incapacitated for a minimum of two weeks.[7] Of this group, only 26 per cent had considered claiming damages, only 14 per cent had consulted a solicitor and only 12 per cent were awarded damages. The study looked at the level of damages obtained by the small group (8 per cent) who gained them without the use of solicitors, and concluded that these people appeared to be under-compensated. In the 182 cases (from 1,711 in the sample) in which damages were obtained, the claimant accepted the first offer made in 104 cases (see Genn, *Hard Bargaining: Out of Court Settlements in Personal Injury Claims*, 1987).

Many factors combine to persuade disputants to settle out of court[8] and the fear of prohibitive costs can be a serious deterrent to bringing proceedings. This is particularly so when it is remembered that the basic rule is that 'costs follow the event', that is, the successful party can expect the judge to order the loser to pay some or all of his solicitor's bill. Costs,[9] however, are a discretionary matter, so the whole process is beset with uncertainties. Another gamble the claimant is faced with is the procedure of 'payment into court' (now known as a 'Part 36 payment') where, at any stage after the commencement of proceedings, the defendant may make a payment into court in satisfaction of the claimant's claim. The claimant may accept the payment or continue the action. If the claimant chooses to continue and the damages obtained are not greater than the amount paid in by the defendant, the claimant will be liable for the defendant's taxed costs (that is, costs which are authorised by a court official – a taxing master) from the time of payment in, even though he has won the action. When the judge makes an award of damages, he will not know the amount of any payment into court, so he cannot influence the matter of whether the claimant has to suffer under the rule.

....

6   Such discussion demonstrates understanding of the fact that civil disputes, unlike criminal prosecutions, may – and are – settled without reference to the courts.

7   Reference to reliable research such as this demonstrates knowledge and understanding and strengthens argument. Where possible, provide a balanced argument by considering opposing or more contemporary research findings.

8   This introduces thoughtful consideration of *why* claimants settle out of court

9   Fear of the costs is one of the main barriers to accessing justice.

There were 80 cases in the Oxford study which involved abandoned claims and, of these, 16 per cent were abandoned because of fear of legal expenses. Where a claimant is not legally aided, the lawyer may try to persuade him to accept a settlement offer, plus costs, rather than risk a legal action which could fail. This is better for the lawyer, as it assures the payment of costs but, arguably, is not in the best interests of many claimants, because settlement awards are generally lower than damages awarded by courts for the same types of case.[10]

A study of High Court personal injury cases by Zander (1973–74) ((1975) *Law Soc Gazette*, 25 June, p 680) showed that while costs were a relatively low proportion of damages in large claims, they were proportionately very high in small claims. Where the damages were under £1,000, 86 per cent of cases had claimed costs for one side amounting to three-fifths of the damages or more. In 33 per cent of cases, the total costs of both sides amounted to more than the amount in dispute. The CJR found that the average cost to the claimant in High Court personal injury actions in 1984 was £6,830 in London and £2,480 outside London. In the county court, costs were an average of 99 per cent of the claimant's damages recovered, as opposed to about one-quarter in the High Court.

Research conducted for the Woolf Report on the civil justice system threw further light on this area. The Final Report (*Access to Justice*, 1996) includes a survey of Supreme Court Taxing Office taxed bills conducted by Professor Hazel Genn of University College, London. Genn found alarming data on costs (*Hard Bargaining: Out of Court Settlement in Personal Injury Claims*, 1987). Her findings indicate that the average costs among the lowest value claims consistently represented more than 100 per cent of the claim value. They also showed that in cases worth between £12,500 and £25,000, average costs ranged from 40 per cent to 95 per cent of the value of the claim. The system provided higher benefits to lawyers than to their clients.

In the Oxford study, delay[11] was another significant factor influencing people to discontinue claims; 6 per cent of those who abandoned their actions cited it as affecting their decision. Cane (in Atiyah's *Accidents, Compensation and the Law*, 1993) has shown evidence that delay and its attendant anxiety can cause a recognisable state of 'litigation neurosis', a complaint which ceases upon the resolution of the dispute. Delay generally assists the defendant and is sometimes used as a deliberate tactic against weaker opponents, or to alleviate the cashflow problems of the smaller insurance companies.

Another factor putting pressure on litigants to settle is that of the risks and uncertainties entailed in the claim. If the case goes to trial, then the claimant will, to succeed, have to

---

10 Discuss addresses the central question of whether settlement out of court is *always* in the best interests of the claimant.

11 Delay is a further obstacle to justice as claims can take many years to get to court.

prove his case on the balance of probabilities. The process is beset with legal uncertainties. Is the defendant liable at law for the claimant's loss or injury? Even where the law is clear, there may be evidential difficulties. Genn has presented material to suggest that in many cases, a claimant's solicitor either does not have sufficient resources to undertake proper factual investigations, or does not seek out all available reports. It is also very difficult to contact all relevant witnesses and to assess how persuasive their courtroom evidence would be. Defendants, including or assisted by insurance companies, will often have resources which place them in a good position to fully investigate the circumstances of accidents. Assessing the quantum of damages is another very problematic part of litigation. In an American experiment, 20 pairs of practising lawyers were given identical information about a case and were instructed to negotiate a settlement. Their resultant settlements ranged from the highest of US $95,000 to the lowest of US $15,000, with an average of just over US $47,000.

The Oxford study found that many other factors contributed to the discontinuation of claims, including the fear of affecting a continuing relationship and arguments that the victim's own fault caused the accident. The most cited reason (mentioned by 45 per cent of respondents) was problems over obtaining evidence. There have been some legal changes since the Oxford study in 1984, and it will be interesting to see if future studies detect any significant consequential changes in claimants' behaviour.

The LCD committed itself (in the CJR's General Issues Paper) to the use of new technology, especially for improving the system of county court debt business. The Production Centre has operated since early 1990, since when, relying on new technology, it has issued over 1.5 million summonses. Dealing more expeditiously with this sort of work could free the courts and thus reduce delays for other types of case.

The courts have made some progress in this area since 1996,[12] although the challenges in the UK are considerable. Lord Justice Brooke, a leading proponent of the use of information and communications technology (ICT) in the courts, has noted that in England at the time, there was no Ministry of Justice with masses of resources at its command, and the LCD, which supports the courts, is a small department and, over the last 10 years, its credibility with the Treasury was damaged because of the way that unbudgeted legal aid expenditure went on soaring. Lord Justice Brooke believes that expenditure on ICT has suffered as a result:

> We have certainly not seen any of the imaginative forward investment in IT which other comparable countries have experienced. In America, for instance, the federal

---

12 Heralds discussion of the nature of reforms that have been introduced.

judiciary run the federal courts, and, in 1990, the Senate voted them US 70 million to undertake a programme of computerisation in the court process.

Lord Justice Brooke, *The Changing Jurisdiction, IT and the English and Welsh Courts: The Next 10 Years*, keynote speech to the 13th Bileta Conference, Dublin, 28 March 1998

In 2001, there were only about 140 judges using computers in court, but the number is rising steadily, with consequential improvements in the efficiency of the courts.

Under the **CPR**, there is a greater incentive for parties to settle their differences. The court now takes into account any pre-action offers to settle when making an order for costs. Thus, a side which has refused a reasonable offer to settle will be treated less generously in the issue of how far the court will order their costs to be paid by the other side. For this to happen, the offer, however, must be one which is made to be open to the other side for at least 21 days after receipt (to stop any undue pressure being put on someone with the phrase: 'Take it or leave it, it is only open for one day, then I shall withdraw the offer'). Also, if the offer is made by the defendant, it must be an offer to pay compensation and to pay the claimant's costs.

Several aspects of the new rules encourage litigants to settle rather than take risks in order (as a claimant) to hold out for unreasonably large sums of compensation, or to try to get away (as a defendant) with paying nothing, rather than some compensation. The system of Part 36 payments or offers does not apply to small claims, but, for other cases, it seems bound to have a significant effect. Thus, if at the trial, a claimant does not get more damages than a sum offered by the defendant in what is called a Part 36 payment (that is, an offer to settle or a payment into the court), or obtain a judgment more favourable than a Part 36 offer, the court will order the claimant to pay any costs incurred by the defendant after the latest date for accepting the payment or offer. The court now has a discretion to make a different order for costs from the normal order.

District Judge Frenkel has given the following example: claim, £150,000 – judgment, £51,000 – £50,000 paid into court. The 'without prejudice' correspondence shows that the claimant would consider nothing short of £150,000. The claimant may be in trouble. The defendant will ask the judge to consider overriding principles of **Pt 1**: 'Was it proportional to incur the further costs of trial to secure an additional £1,000?' **Part 44.3** confirms the general rule that the loser pays, but allows the court to make a different order to take into account offers to settle, payment into court, the parties' conduct, including pre-action conduct and exaggeration of the claim ((1999) 149 NLJ 458).

Similarly, where at trial a defendant is held liable to the claimant for more money than the proposals contained in a claimant's Part 36 offer (that is, where the claimant has made an offer to settle), the court may order the defendant to pay interest on the award, at a rate not exceeding 10 per cent above the base rate, for some or all of the period starting with the date on which the defendant could have accepted the offer.

Active case management imposes a duty on the courts to help parties settle their disputes. A 'stay' is a temporary halt in proceedings and an opportunity for the court to order such a pause arises at the stage when the defence to a claim has been filed. Parties can indicate that they have agreed on a stay to attempt to settle the case and, provided the court agrees, can have an initial period of one month to try to do this. In order to avoid the stay being used as a delaying tactic, the order granting the stay will require the parties to report back to the court within 14 days of the end of the period of the stay to:

(a)   inform the court if the matter has been settled either wholly or partly; or

(b)   ask for more time for settlement; or

(c)   report that the attempt to settle hasqaal failed, so that the process of allocation of court track can take place.

The court will always give the final decision about whether to grant the parties more time to use a mediator, or arbitrator, or expert[13] to settle, even if the parties are agreed that they wish to have more time. A stay will never be granted for an indefinite period.

In the Final Report on *Access to Justice*, Lord Woolf recognised the importance of witness statements in cases, but observed that they had become problematic, because lawyers had made them excessively long and detailed in order to protect against leaving out something which later proved to be relevant. He said, 'witness statements have ceased to be the authentic account of the lay witness; instead, they have become an elaborate, costly branch of legal drafting' (para 55). Under the new rules, witness statements must contain the evidence that the witness will give at trial, but they should be briefer than those drafted under the previous rules; they should be drafted in lay language and should not discuss legal propositions. Witnesses are now allowed to amplify on the statement, or deal with matters that have arisen since the Report was served, although this is not an automatic right and a 'good reason' for the admission of new evidence will have to be established.

Overall, it seems likely that as a result of the introduction of the new **CPR**,[14] fewer of the annually settled cases will have been settled for the 'wrong reasons' (that is, because parties are frightened of the possible delays, costs, and uncertainties of proceeding to a full judgment) and more disputants will settle in the truer spirit of compromise, facilitated by an improved legal system.

---

13   Consideration of alternative means of resolving disputes (known as ADR) is important as it demonstrates understanding of the alternatives open to potential litigants.

14   Always try and access up-to-date research which will allow you to support any conclusions reached (see the suggested answer to the next question).

NOTE

Inordinate delay also raises questions of human rights. Consider this case from the European Court of Human Rights. In *Jose da Conceicao Guerreiro v Portugal* (2002) App No 00045560/99 (G Ress P), 31 January, the applicant complained of a violation of **Art 6(1)** of the **European Convention on Human Rights**, on the basis that civil proceedings to which he was a party had lasted 14 years and two months and had therefore exceeded the 'reasonable time' requirement of the Article. The Court held unanimously that there had been a violation of **Art 6(1)** and the applicant was awarded 5,500 euros (about £3,500) for non-pecuniary and pecuniary damages. Most civil cases in the UK do not last that long, but a great many do endure for longer than five years, with all the attendant cost and the stress that such a period of uncertainty entails.

QUESTION 37

The **Civil Procedure Rules (CPR)** introduced in 1999 have been an unqualified success in changing the legal system.

▶ **Discuss.**

How to Answer this Question

You will need to consider the following:

- ❖ the background to the new rules;
- ❖ Burton J's criticisms;
- ❖ the assessment of Burns J;
- ❖ concealed delays under the new system;
- ❖ the Eversheds study;
- ❖ judges and lawyers struggling with the new system.

Answer Structure

Introduction highlighting the pre-1999 position (see previous answer) → Provide an overview of the main changes introduced by the CPR → Evaluate the impact of the CPR referring to appropriate research and concluding as to their success

ANSWER

The new **CPR**, the most fundamental changes in civil process for over 100 years, have radically altered the operation of civil justice. Since the new rules came into force (26 April 1999), they have been regularly reformed. The 52nd update was completed in March 2010.

Part of the rationale of the new rules was to expedite the way cases were dealt with and to allow more cases to be settled early through negotiation between the parties or alternative dispute resolution (ADR). In this respect, there is some evidence of success.

Between May and August 1999, there was a 25 per cent reduction in the number of cases issued in the county courts, compared with the same period the previous year. By the end of January 2000, there was a further fall of 23 per cent. There is also evidence (in a speech by David Lock MP, Parliamentary Secretary to the Lord Chancellor's Department (LCD), 15 October 1999) that changes to pre-action behaviour, as a result of the pre-action protocols, have been partly responsible for the reduction in the number of cases going all the way through to trial.[15]

An interesting assessment of the new rules was presented by Mr Justice Burton of the Queen's Bench Division. Speaking at the city law firm Kennedys, he outlined five benefits of the reforms and five problems ((2000) *Law Soc Gazette*, 10 February).

The five problems with the reforms were: the courts' inflexibility in not allowing parties to agree extensions of time between themselves; the danger of the judiciary pushing time guillotines onto parties; the risk that lawyers and clients could exploit 'standard' disclosure to conceal important documents; single joint experts possibly usurping the role of judges; and summary assessments of costs, leading to judges making assumptions replacing detailed costs analyses. He itemised the benefits as: pre-action protocols; emphasis on encouraging settlement; judicial intervention; Part 24 strike-out provisions; and Part 36 offers to settle.

Mr Justice Burton said that there had been three options for reforming appeals: (1) to extend the present system in order to discourage more than one appeal; (2) to refuse appeals without leave; or (3) to abolish the present system, giving no right to rehearings, only appeals. He said that he regretted that all three had been adopted (in the **Access to Justice Act 1999**). The consequence will be pressure on judges 'to get it right first time' and higher costs for parties.

Richard Burns, a barrister and recorder sitting in the county court, and thus someone who has experienced the new rules from both sides of the Bench, has made some interesting observations about the new system ('A view from the ranks' (2000) 150 NLJ 1829, pp 1829–1830). On the positive side, Judge Burns says that 'the transition has been far smoother than many had anticipated and there have been a number of very worthwhile gains'. He notes, however, that set against the ambitious aims Lord Woolf had set for the reforms, they were a 'relative failure'. Among the gains, the judge lists the unified system of procedure in all civil courts; awareness that the costs of litigation should bear a 'passing resemblance to the value of the claim'; vastly improved pre-action co-operation; more sensible and open pleadings which force the parties to define the issues at an early

---

15 Where progress – or otherwise – has been made over a number of years, ensure that you also research to up-to-date information, which will help attain top marks.

stage; the wider use of jointly instructed (and, therefore, impartial) experts; and in **Part 36** of the **CPR**, rules cunningly devised to encourage the parties to settle.

One way in which the system is not working properly, according to Richard Burns, is in relation to costs. He argues that the system is, in fact, proving more expensive than the old system for many litigants, as the timetable imposed usually compels the parties 'to spend time and money progressing claims to trial whether or not they expect to settle. Paradoxically, the procedures encouraging, as they do, the front-end loading of expenditure on cases may lead to more trials – certainly, this appears to have been happening in some of the court centres where I appear'.

Another difficulty concerns the system of case management, which Lord Woolf envisaged would be the engine to drive forward the litigation cheaply and expeditiously. Burns regards this as a system which is 'excessively bureaucratic and makes too many demands on the parties'. It is also, he argues, very poorly resourced, as the Court Service received very little extra money to finance the sort of increases in judicial staffing and information technology that Woolf had seen as essential.

Concealed delays are also blighting the system, according to Judge Burns. While recognising that on the whole, cases come to trial more quickly than they did, he notes that:

> The overall delay experienced by litigants is much the same as it ever was. This is because solicitors, feeling daunted by the demands made on them by the **CPR** and lacking the time and resources to manage more than a certain quota of cases through the system, are delaying the issue of proceedings. The delay frequently runs into years.

Eversheds, the corporate law claims firm, has conducted an 'access to justice' survey for five years. It canvassed the opinions and experiences of lawyers and those using the legal system. Results published in 2000, after one year of the Woolf reforms, showed that of its respondents, 54 per cent said that the civil litigation process had improved in the past year, a big increase on 1998's 15 per cent. Some 52 per cent of respondents believed that litigation was quicker, but only 22 per cent thought costs were lower.

John Heaps, head of litigation at Eversheds, has stated (*The Times*, 2 May, 2000) that: 'The UK legal system historically has been plagued by unsatisfactory delays and expense. The style of dispute resolution is changing as a result of the Woolf reforms; people no longer seek aggressive uncompromising lawyers, but those who look for commercial solutions.'

The survey sought the views of heads of legal departments of UK companies and public sector bodies; 70 per cent of respondents were in the private sector, with 30 per cent in London. The replies suggest that a change in culture is emerging. Nearly two-thirds of respondents did not think that the reforms would make them less likely to start proceedings, but 43 per cent said that they were settling cases earlier and almost half said that their lawyers were handling disputes differently. Mediation, or ADR, is also becoming more popular: 41 per cent have used it, compared with 30 per cent in 1998.

There is, however, concern that while judges are managing cases more effectively, the courts do not have adequate resources (this was expressed by 50 per cent of respondents). Only 24 per cent believed that litigants were now getting better justice; 44 per cent said that they were not.

On the matter of costs, opinions were sharply divided. Nearly half did not believe costs to have been affected by the introduction of the new rules. Disturbingly, however, 19 per cent said that costs had risen, particularly in the regions. But a conference on Woolf held by CEDR found that although costs had increased at the start of litigation (front-loading), overall, they were down, as settlements came sooner.

Conditional or 'no win, no fee' work is attractive in principle, but little used: 48 per cent of respondents said that they would pay lawyers a higher fee for winning, if they could pay a lower fee, or none, if the case was lost, but only 24 per cent had discussed such a deal.

Litigation may be quicker and less likely to go to court, but 52 per cent of respondents expected to have the same number of business disputes in the following year, with as many being resolved through litigation. One in five were more optimistic and thought fewer disputes would be resolved in court.

John Heaps argues that overall the findings are positive. He has said: 'Over half the respondents feel the speed of resolving disputes has improved. But there are concerns that the aims and aspirations are not matched by court resources.'

A survey carried out by the City Research Group of the firm Wragge & Co obtained similar findings (*The Times*, 2 May, 2000). It suggests that among in-house lawyers from FTSE 1,000 companies, a lack of resources has become 'a major stumbling block'. Some 81 per cent of respondents thought that courts did not have the resources to process claims quickly enough and some complained of 'inconsistent interpretation' between courts; however, 89 per cent of respondents backed the changes and said that litigation was quicker, with fewer 'frivolous claims'. Some 41 per cent thought that costs had been cut and there was strong backing for ADR, with 80 per cent saying that it had proved popular. Nine out of 10 lawyers thought that clients were more involved in the management of the dispute, but 38 per cent believed that the reforms had compromised justice at the expense of cost-cutting. As with the CEDR survey, the change singled out for the biggest impact is that which allows either party to make a formal settlement offer at any stage, or potentially face cost penalties.

A senior litigation partner at Wragge & Co, Andrew Manning Cox, observed that the survey mirrored the firm's experiences. Among surprise findings was the low awareness of Woolf among businesses. Their lawyers were apparently not using the new rules to the best tactical advantage of their companies.

Another City law firm, Lovells, found 71 per cent of respondents were now treating litigation as a last resort, with 72 per cent willing, voluntarily, to exchange documents with the other side. Where litigation is unavoidable, it is quicker, with 66 per cent saying that judges now set tighter timetables. Two-thirds found that the court 'rubber stamped' joint requests by the parties to move back dates in the timetable, but this flexibility did not extend to trial dates.

One of the findings that will be very disappointing for many involved with the project of the Woolf reforms is the apparently low use of a jointly appointed expert. According to the survey, only 7 per cent of respondents were involved in cases with such an expert.

The survey also highlights a low level of case management. Only 9 per cent found that the court monitored case progress and chased lawyers to meet deadlines; 42 per cent found the court had sought to narrow the issues as early as it could. The commercial court, Lovells found, was managing cases better than other High Court divisions. Moreover, courts did not penalise parties who failed to comply with the new rules. This certainly ties in with the experience of the barrister and county court judge Richard Burns. He has noted that the burden of work on many civil judges is so heavy that they cannot properly manage each case:

> Their burden in the busier courts is so huge that all they can do is skim the surface of files that cross their desks. It is rare, in my experience, for the same judge to be able to deal with all the interlocutory stages of even the bigger cases and so there is little or no continuity.

(2000) 150 NLJ 1830

Asked for the worst aspect of the reforms, respondents chose the rule on summary assessment of costs in preliminary hearings, criticised as a lottery. In fact, the main deficiency in the new system seems to be one of variable application according to the style or interpretation of them favoured in any given court or region. This, though, may well become more uniform over time and, if that occurs, then the new rules really can claim to have radically and successfully altered the civil process in England and Wales.[16]

---

16 Try and provide as balanced a conclusion as possible by weighing up both the positives and the negatives of any changes. This demonstrates that you posses skills such as evaluation and synthesis.

NOTES

THE CIVIL PROCEDURE (AMENDMENT) RULES 2010 SI 2010 No 621 (L3)

This instrument amends the **CPR**, in particular by making amendments concerning a new procedure for personal injury claims in road traffic accidents valued at between £1,000 and £10,000, which is set out in the Pre-Action Protocol for Low Value Personal Injury Claims in Road Traffic Accidents (the 'RTA Protocol'). This instrument inserts a new **Section VI** in **Part 45** of the **CPR** which sets out the fixed costs that will apply in claims that have, or should have, followed the RTA Protocol, where the amount of damages are not agreed and proceedings are started under the **CPR**. This instrument also inserts a new section in **Part 36** of the **CPR** which deals with offers to settle made by the parties under the Pre-Action Protocol.

QUESTION 38

What is meant by legal professional privilege, and what purpose does it serve in the English legal system?

How to Answer this Question

The question calls for an explanation of the doctrine, and then a description of why the privilege is a part of the system. The part of the answer dealing with the purpose of the privilege can be enhanced by an evaluative element.

- ❖ Introduce the theme with an example.
- ❖ Explain the principle and its origin.
- ❖ Provide some case law support for the doctrine.
- ❖ Explain the social benefits of client–lawyer confidentiality.
- ❖ Illustrate the limitation of the privilege *R v Cox and Railton* (1884).
- ❖ Conclusion – evaluation of doctrine.

Answer Structure

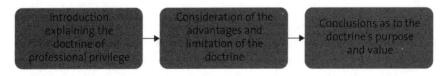

Introduction explaining the doctrine of professional privilege → Consideration of the advantages and limitation of the doctrine → Conclusions as to the doctrine's purpose and value

ANSWER

A special set of rules controls the confidentiality of communications between lawyers and their clients. It is a very important part of the legal system.

The issue of secretly recorded conversations between the lawyer Simon Creighton and his imprisoned client (*The Times*, 5 February, 2008) raised for public debate the question: why do we have the principle of 'professional privilege' that protects the lawyer–client relationship?

In essence, the privilege means that communications between a lawyer and client are confidential, and can only be revealed to a law court or the police at the option of the client. The same protection of confidentiality does not extend to doctor–patient, priest–penitent, or accountant–client relationships so it is easier for the legal system to acquire information from those professional communications.[17]

The word 'privilege' comes from the Latin (*privilegium*) for 'private law': a law applying to an individual or small group. Under general law, what citizens say to each other can be used in evidence in law courts. A 'private law' though, applies to lawyers, and gives lawyer-client communications a specially guarded confidentiality.

The justification is simple and compelling. Citizens do not want to live in anarchy, they want to live in a society of laws and rules. As there are hundreds of thousands of laws, citizens do not want to have to become expert themselves on them all, anymore than they want to learn medicine just so they can be their own doctor. People want experts on the laws: lawyers. So, a society should encourage citizens to go to its lawyers for advice whenever they are in difficulties. To ensure the lawyer–client relationship works well, there must be complete trust, and, in order for that to happen, the client must feel assured that client–lawyer communications are completely private and confidential.[18]

It might be argued that 'if a client has done nothing wrong, they've got nothing to worry about if their chats with their lawyer are recorded and later played to a court'. That, though, misses an important point. To be full and frank with lawyers in criminal, family, civil, and commercial cases, many clients have to mention secret, embarrassing or compromising things that are incidental to their main stories but more social good is served by those things remaining confidential, and the law taking its proper course guided by lawyers, than if clients were deterred from telling the bigger truths of their situations to lawyers for fear of the incidental compromising facts being open to be made public.

The rule of privilege is long established. In *Greenough v Gaskell* (1833), Lord Chancellor Brougham said (at 621) that the rule was important to uphold 'the interests of justice'. He said if the rule did not exist, people would be mistrustful of consulting legal experts, and so would end up worsening their own positions with do-it-yourself law. He said 'every one would be thrown upon his own legal resources'.

....

17 Clear and succinct explanation of the doctrine of legal professional privilege sets the scene and provides a helpful introduction.
18 Highlights the rationale behind the doctrine allowing, and encouraging, in-depth consideration of its value and limitations.

More recently, in 2003, the Privy Council (the highest appeal court for many commonwealth countries) ruled that lawyer–client privilege is fundamental to the operation of justice and should not be overridden unless the law has specifically said so in a particular circumstance: *B v Auckland District Law Society* (2003). The Privy Council held that the power of a district law society in New Zealand to require the production of documents by legal practitioners when investigating complaints against them under **s 101(3)(d)** of the **Law Practitioners Act 1982**, did not override legal professional privilege, and privilege was not waived by voluntarily making the documents available for limited purposes. The privilege is also protected under European law: Case 155/79 *AM&S Europe Ltd v EC Commission* (1983), and European human rights law: *Campbell v UK* (1992).[19]

The privilege against disclosure does not, however, cover all communications. In a case in 1884, an English appeal confirmed that if a client asks a lawyer for information in order to be guided on how to commit a crime, the lawyer can testify about that to a court despite the client's protests: *R v Cox and Railton* (1884).

Henry Muster, who had been libelled in *The Brightonian*, was awarded damages. But the publisher of the paper, Richard Railton, conspired with a business partner to make a property transaction in order to avoid paying the damages. Railton had asked his solicitor some questions in preparation to do something unlawful. Informed by his solicitor, for example, that he was not allowed to sell property to his own business partner, Railton asked the solicitor 'Does anyone know about the partnership except for you?' After the scam was exposed, the solicitor was called as a prosecution witness and Railton and his partner were convicted.

Allowing client–lawyer privilege does not, as is sometimes said, amount to allowing criminals to thrive. Legally, a lawyer must not assist in the commission of a crime or say to a court anything he knows is untrue – those are very serious offences. Moreover, it is a lawyer's positive duty to disclose information that he knows or suspects relates to particular crimes such as terrorism (under the **Terrorism Act 2000**) or money laundering (under the **Proceeds of Crime Act 2002**).

Sometimes, of course, deciding whether the obligation to report something wrongful to a court puts lawyers in a difficult position. The barrister Rayner Goddard (who became Lord Chief Justice in 1946) asked his first client, during their initial cell interview at the Old Bailey: 'Now, my man, what is your story?' The client replied 'Well, that's rather up to you, guv'nor.'

19 The provision of appropriate, supporting legislation and case law aids explanation, demonstrates knowledge and also adds credibility to the discussion.

It might be that the privilege rule means that lawyers get to hear of some immoral or shocking non-criminal aspects of the lives of certain clients, and that those remain secret. That, though, is a small price to pay for a population knowing that the state does not have its eye and an ear in the very offices to which its citizens go when they need help.

QUESTION 39

Explain the circumstances in which an advocate can be held liable for courtroom negligence and assess the public policy arguments in this area.

How to Answer this Question

Look at:

- ❖   the decision in *Arthur JS Hall & Co v Simons* (2000);
- ❖   the brief historical background;
- ❖   the advocate's divided loyalty;
- ❖   the 'cab rank' rule;
- ❖   the witness analogy;
- ❖   collateral attack;
- ❖   the need for public confidence in the system.

Answer Structure

Introduction which sets out the old position in regard to an advocate's liability → Evaluation of the old position together with consideration of *Hall v Simons*, highlighting the issue of public interest → Conclusion which sums up the present position

ANSWER

In *Arthur JS Hall & Co v Simons* (2000), the House of Lords made a bold change in this area of law. It imposed a duty of care upon courtroom advocates that had not been previously supported in law.

Lawyers are, for the general public, the most central and prominent part of the English legal system. They are, arguably, to the legal system what doctors are to the health system. For many decades, a debate has grown about why a patient injured by the negligence of a surgeon in the operating theatre can sue for damages, whereas a litigant whose case is lost because of the negligence of his advocate cannot sue. It all seemed very unfair. Even the most glaringly obvious courtroom negligence was protected against legal action by a special advocates' immunity. The claim that this protection was made by lawyers (and judges who were lawyers) for lawyers was difficult to refute. In this House of Lords' decision, the historic immunity has been abolished in respect of both barristers and solicitor-advocates (of whom there are now over 2,000 with higher courts' rights of audience) and for both civil and criminal proceedings.[20]

In three cases, all conjoined on appeal, a claimant raised a claim of negligence against a firm of solicitors and, in each case, the firms relied on the immunity attaching to barristers and other advocates from actions in negligence. At first instance, all the claims were struck out. Then, on appeal, the Court of Appeal said that claims could have proceeded. The solicitors appealed to the Lords and two key questions were raised: should the old immunity rule be maintained and, in a criminal case, what was the proper scope of the principle against 'collateral attack'? A 'collateral attack' is when someone convicted in a criminal court tries to invalidate that conviction outside the criminal appeals process by suing his trial defence lawyer in a civil court. The purpose of such a 'collateral attack' is to win in the civil case, proving negligence against the criminal trial lawyer, and thus by implication, to show that the conviction in the criminal case was unfair.

The House of Lords held (Lord Hope, Lord Hutton and Lord Hobhouse dissenting in part) that in the light of modern conditions, it was now clear that it was no longer in the public interest in the administration of justice that advocates should have immunity from suit for negligence for acts concerned with the conduct of either civil or criminal litigation.

Lord Hoffmann (with Lord Steyn, Lord Browne-Wilkinson and Lord Millett delivering concurring opinions) said that over 30 years had passed since the House had last considered the rationale for the immunity of the advocate from suit, in *Rondel v Worsley* (1969). Public policy was not immutable and there had been great changes in the law of negligence, the functioning of the legal profession, the administration of justice and public perceptions. It was, once again, time to re-examine the whole matter.[21] Interestingly, Lord Hoffmann chose to formulate his opinion in a creative mode to reflect public policy, rather than in the tradition of what can be seen as slavish obedience to the details of precedent:

> I hope that I will not be thought ungrateful if I do not encumber this speech with citations. The question of what the public interest now requires depends upon the strength of the arguments rather than the weight of authority.

The point of departure was that, in general, English law provided a remedy in damages for a person who had suffered injury as a result of professional negligence. It followed that any exception which denied such a remedy required a sound justification. The arguments relied on by the court in *Rondel v Worsley* as justifying the immunity had to be considered. One by one, these arguments were evaluated and rejected.

....

20 Highlights the basis of the debate.
21 Demonstrates understanding that the law cannot remain static as society develops.

ADVOCATE'S DIVIDED LOYALTY

There were two distinct versions of the divided loyalty argument.[22] The first was that the possibility of being sued for negligence would actually inhibit the lawyer, consciously or unconsciously, from giving his duty to the court priority over his duty to his client. The second was that the divided loyalty was a special factor that made the conduct of litigation a very difficult art and could lead to the advocate being exposed to vexatious claims by difficult clients. The argument was pressed, most strongly, in connection with advocacy in criminal proceedings, where the clients were said to be more than usually likely to be vexatious.

There had been recent developments in the civil justice system designed to reduce the incidence of vexatious litigation. The first was **r 24.2** of the **CPR**, which provided that a court could give summary judgment in favour of a defendant if it considered that 'the claimant had no real prospect of succeeding on the claim'. The second was the changes to the funding of civil litigation introduced by the **Access to Justice Act 1999**, which would make it much more difficult than it had been in the past to obtain legal help for negligence actions which had little prospect of success.

There was no doubt that the advocate's duty to the court was extremely important in the English justice system. The question was whether removing the immunity would have a significantly adverse effect. If the possibility of being held liable in negligence was calculated to have an adverse effect on the behaviour of advocates in court, one might have expected that to have followed, at least in some degree, from the introduction of wasted costs orders (where a court disallows a lawyer from being able to claim part of a fee for work which is regarded as unnecessary and wasteful). Although the liability of a negligent advocate to a wasted costs order was not the same as a liability to pay general damages, the experience of the wasted costs jurisdiction was the only empirical evidence available in England to test the proposition that such liability would have an adverse effect upon the way advocates performed their duty to the court, and there was no suggestion that it had changed standards of advocacy for the worse.

THE 'CAB RANK'

The 'cab rank' rule provided that a barrister could not refuse to act for a client on the ground that he disapproved of him or his case. The argument was that a barrister, who was obliged to accept any client, would be unfairly exposed to vexatious actions by clients whom any sensible lawyer with freedom of action would have refused to act for. Such a claim, however, was in the nature of things intuitive, incapable of empirical verification and did not have any real substance.

---

22 Knowledge of the arguments both for and against is central to the question.

THE WITNESS ANALOGY

The argument started from the well established rule that a witness was absolutely immune from liability for anything that he said in court. So were the judge, counsel and the parties. They could not be sued for libel, malicious falsehood or conspiring to give false evidence. The policy of the rule was to encourage persons who took part in court proceedings to express themselves freely. However, a witness owed no duty of care to anyone in respect of the evidence he gave to the court. His only duty was to tell the truth.

There was no analogy with the position of a lawyer who owed a duty of care to his client. The fact that the advocate was the only person involved in the trial process who was liable to be sued for negligence was because he was the only person who had undertaken such a duty of care to his client.

COLLATERAL ATTACK

The most substantial argument was that it might be contrary to the public interest for a court to retry a case which had been decided by another court. However, actions for negligence against lawyers were not the only cases that gave rise to a possibility of the same issue being tried twice. The law had to deal with the problem in numerous other contexts. So, before examining the strength of the collateral challenge argument as a reason for maintaining the immunity of lawyers, it was necessary to consider how the law dealt with collateral challenge in general.

The law discouraged relitigation of the same issues, except by means of an appeal. The Latin maxims often quoted were *nemo debet bis vexari pro una et eadem causa* and interest *rei publicae ut finis sit litium*. The first was concerned with the interests of the defendant: a person should not be troubled twice for the same reason. That policy had generated the rules which prevented relitigation when the parties were the same: *autrefois acquit* (someone acquitted of a crime cannot be tried again for that crime[23]), *res judicata* (a particular dispute decided by a civil court cannot be retried) and issue estoppel (a person cannot deny the fact of a judgment previously decided against him).

The second policy was wider: it was concerned with the interests of the state. There was a general public interest in the same issue not being litigated over again. The second policy could be used to justify the extension of the rules of issue estoppel to cases in which the parties were not the same, but the circumstances were such as to bring the case within the spirit of the rules. Criminal proceedings were in a special category because, although they were technically litigation between the Crown and the defendant, the Crown prosecuted on behalf of society as a whole. So, a conviction had some of the quality of a judgment *in rem*, which should be binding in favour of everyone.

---

23 Commonly referred to as 'double jeopardy'.

Not all relitigation of the same issue, however, would be manifestly unfair to a party, or bring the administration of justice into disrepute. Sometimes, there were valid reasons for rehearing a dispute. It was, therefore, unnecessary to try to stop any relitigation by forbidding anyone from suing their lawyer. It was, in Lord Hoffmann's words, 'burning down the house to roast the pig; using a broad-spectrum remedy without side effects could handle the problem equally well'.

The scope for re-examination of issues in criminal proceedings was much wider than in civil cases. Fresh evidence was more readily admitted. A conviction could be set aside as unsafe and unsatisfactory when the accused appeared to have been prejudiced by 'flagrantly incompetent advocacy': see *R v Clinton* (1993). After conviction, the case could be referred to the Court of Appeal if the conviction was on indictment, or to the Crown Court if the trial was summary, by the Criminal Cases Review Commission.

It followed that it would ordinarily be an abuse of process for a civil court to be asked to decide that a subsisting conviction was wrong. That applied to a conviction on a plea of guilty, as well as after a trial. The resulting conflict of judgments was likely to bring the administration of justice into disrepute. The proper procedure was to appeal, or if the right of appeal had been exhausted, to apply to the Criminal Cases Review Commission. It would, ordinarily, be an abuse because there were bound to be exceptional cases in which the issue could be tried without a risk that the conflict of judgments would bring the administration of justice into disrepute.

Once the conviction has been set aside, there could be no public policy objection to an action for negligence against the legal advisers. There could be no conflict of judgments. On the other hand, in civil, including matrimonial, cases, it would seldom be possible to say that an action for negligence against a legal adviser or representative would bring the administration of justice into disrepute. Whether the original decision was right or wrong was usually a matter of concern only to the parties and had no wider implications.[24] There was no public interest objection to a subsequent finding that, but for the negligence of his lawyers, the losing party would have won.

But, again, there might be exceptions. The action for negligence might be an abuse of process on the ground that it was manifestly unfair to someone else. Take, for example, the case of a defendant who published a serious defamation which he attempted, unsuccessfully, to justify. Should he be able to sue his lawyers and claim that if the case had been conducted differently, the allegation would have been proved to be true? It seemed unfair to the claimant in the defamation action that any court should be allowed to come to such a conclusion in proceedings to which he was not a party. On the other

....

24 Good example of 'public interest'.

hand, it was equally unfair that he should have to join as a party and rebut the allegation for a second time. A man's reputation was not only a matter between him and the other party. It represented his relationship with the world. So, it might be that in such circumstances, an action for negligence would be an abuse of the process of the court.

Having regard to the power of the court to strike out actions which had no real prospect of success, the doctrine was unlikely, in that context, to be invoked very often. The first step in any application to strike out an action alleging negligence in the conduct of a previous action had to be to ask whether it had a real prospect of success.

Lord Hope, Lord Hutton and Lord Hobhouse delivered judgments in which they agreed that the immunity from suit was no longer required in relation to civil proceedings, but dissented to the extent of saying that the immunity was still required in the public interest in the administration of justice in relation to criminal proceedings.

This decision is of major and historic importance in the English legal system for several reasons. It can be seen as a bold attempt by the senior judiciary to drag the legal profession (often a metonymy for the whole legal system) into the 21st century world of accountability and fair business practice. In his judgment, Lord Steyn makes this dramatic observation:

> . . . public confidence in the legal system is not enhanced by the existence of the immunity. The appearance is created that the law singles out its own for protection no matter how flagrant the breach of the barrister. The world has changed since 1967. The practice of law has become more commercialised: barristers may now advertise. They may now enter into contracts for legal services with their professional clients. They are now obliged to carry insurance. On the other hand, today we live in a consumerist society in which people have a much greater awareness of their rights. If they have suffered a wrong as the result of the provision of negligent professional services, they expect to have the right to claim redress. It tends to erode confidence in the legal system if advocates, alone among professional men, are immune from liability for negligence.[25]

The case raises and explores many key issues of the legal system, including the proper relationship between lawyers and the courts, the proper relationship between lawyers and clients, the differences between criminal and civil actions, professional ethics, the nature of dispute resolution and the circumstances under which the courts should make new law. Above all, however, the case has one simple significance: 'It will', in the words of Jonathan Hirst QC, Chairman of the Bar Council, 'mean that a claimant who can prove

---

25 Quote has been used to highlight the need for change and support argument.

loss, as the result of an advocate's negligence, will no longer be prevented from making a claim. We cannot really say that is wrong' ((2000) *Bar News*, August, p 3).

NOTES

The case of *Moy v Pettmann Smith (a firm)* (2005) gives some comfort to advocates regarding advice provided to clients at the door of the court, that is when, at the last moment before a case begins, an offer to settle the case is made by the other side and a lawyer has to advise his or her client under some pressure of time whether to accept it. The House of Lords decided that advice given by lawyers in such circumstances does not have to be absolutely perfect in order to be avoid being safe from an action for negligence by a dissatisfied client.

QUESTION 40

Evaluate the role of the expert witness in the English legal system.

How to Answer this Question

Various approaches could be used in answer to this question. Provided that a structured response is given, and that it provides what the question asks for, it will be satisfactory. The answer here has been structured as follows:

- ❖   Explain the historical setting of expert witnesses.
- ❖   Identify the potential danger of unreliable expert evidence.
- ❖   The challenges posed in the field of costs: *Webster & Ors v Ridgeway Foundation School* (2010).
- ❖   The recommendations of the Jackson Review.
- ❖   The challenges of esoteric information and theories.
- ❖   The Law Commission paper (2009).
- ❖   Conclusion – the inherent difficulties of partisan evidence.

Answer Structure

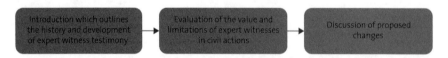

Introduction which outlines the history and development of expert witness testimony → Evaluation of the value and limitations of expert witnesses in civil actions → Discussion of proposed changes

ANSWER

Historically, witnesses in court cases were called to give evidence as they had personal knowledge of the particular facts of the case before the court. In the nineteenth-century, the courts established the role of experts who were called to assist the court about recondite matters that the court would not be expected to know about or understand. Where experts appeared as witnesses about scientific or artistic matters, as opposed to lawyers reading parts from books, the quality of their testimony could be tested through cross questioning. The role of the expert witness, though, has not developed in an entirely unproblematic way.

In 2007, Gene Morrison, a conman from Hyde, in Cheshire, was convicted of 22 crimes, including deception offences and perjury, after having posed in court for years as a forensic psychologist. He had used the title 'Dr' but when asked by police from which university he gained that qualification, he replied (on film) 'I have forgotten that.' Worryingly, he was able to have given testimony in over 700 cases without being exposed by lawyers or judges as a fake.

Many legal disputes need the evidence of experts. Expert opinion is much more than what an American judge once condemned as 'only an ordinary guess in evening clothes'. Every week thousands of specialists like consultant doctors, accountants, authorities on art, and shipping experts, deliver testimony. Such expertise makes the discovery of truth much easier. But it does present occasional problems.[26]

An incompetent expert can cause more misery than a psychotic gang member. When justice is miscarried because someone has given sham evidence from the witness box, the repercussions can be catastrophic: people get imprisoned, companies collapse, and children can be taken from parents.

The relatively unregulated nature of expert evidence also presents problems in the field of costs. In *Webster & Ors v Ridgeway Foundation School* (2010)[27] a minor celebrity headmistress claimed £200,000 for appearing as an expert witness for a school being sued by a pupil left brain damaged in a hammer attack by classmates. Marie Stubbs, who won acclaim for her teaching of inner-city children, and whose career was dramatised in a television drama starring Julie Walters, charged the enormous fee for writing a 30-page report assessing the school's health and safety policies and for a three-day court appearance (Lois Rogers, *The Sunday Times*, 28 February, 2010).

Henry Webster, now 18, was left for dead with a fractured skull on a tennis court at the Ridgeway school in Wroughton, near Swindon in Wiltshire, three years ago, after being repeatedly beaten with the claw end of a hammer. Webster had been hoping to win compensation from the school for its failure to protect him from the unprovoked attack by strangers who had entered school premises. Gus John, the expert witness recruited on behalf of the Websters, produced a 374 page report and charged about £70,000 for his time. Mr Webster's claim failed because the judge found no evidence the school could

....

26 This paragraph provides a helpful link between the value of expert witnesses and the possible problems associated with their use.
27 The use of examples such as this can make explanation easier, demonstrates knowledge and adds additional weight to arguments.

have foreseen the attack or prevented it. His family was told their insurance would not cover the costs of the six-week court case, which, including Stubbs's £200,000 fee, will exceed £800,000.

Stubbs's fee has yet to be formally approved at a costs hearing. The claim highlighted the unregulated nature of the expert witness industry. There is no limit to the fees that can be claimed and no requirement for experts to be vetted or trained.

Gus John and Marie Stubbs were both criticised by the trial judge, Mr Justice Nicol. He stated (para 13):

> I was not greatly assisted by either witness. Neither had experience of giving expert evidence in High Court proceedings before this case. The task is not an easy one. It is to provide assistance to the Court on matters which may be outside the Court's general knowledge and within the area of the witness' own expertise. It is not the role of the witness simply to become an extra advocate for the party which calls him or her.

In his *Review of Civil Litigation Costs* (December 2009) Lord Justice Jackson asks for improved control of costs and the use of experts (Part 6, section 38). He notes (p 43) that experts' reports can generate 'excessive costs'. Jackson recommends (p 385) that:

> CPR Part 35 or its accompanying practice direction should be amended in order to require that a party seeking permission to adduce expert evidence [furnishes] an estimate of the costs of that evidence to the court.

An abiding challenge in the field of expert evidence is that a judge or a jury has to evaluate intricate testimony to do with science, technology, or finance, and to conclude which side of a case is supported by stronger evidence. Sometimes a trial does not get as much expertise as is later seen to be helpful. In February 2007, in a retrial, Ian and Angela Gay were acquitted of having killed the three-year-old Christian Blewitt, by poisoning him with salt. In this second trial, a new medical expert witness presented an alternative theory about Christian's fatally high sodium level. He showed how the boy's blood–salt concentration could have been attributable to osmoreceptor dysfunction – a medical condition that results in the body not being able properly to regulate its sodium levels.

In civil cases, one problem has sometimes been a profusion of specialist testimony, leaving the court, as one judge said adapting a line of Milton, 'dark with excessive brightness'. To avoid a trial becoming overborne by an abundance of obscure expertise, a court now has the power under the **Civil Procedure Rules**[28] to direct that evidence is given

---

28 Reference to the **CPR**, both Civil and Criminal (below), demonstrates knowledge of the changes introduced in regard to the use of expert witnesses.

by a single expert to serve 'both sides' of the case. **Rule 35.7(3)** states that where the parties cannot agree who should be the expert, the court may select the expert from a list provided by the parties, or chosen in another manner 'as the court may direct'.

It is also important that when technical evidence is adduced (brought forward and offered) in court, that it can be understood by people outside of whatever discipline it comes from. Medical evidence, for example, however abstruse must be able to be explained in non-medical terms. And arguments about whether something is good practice must be such as could persuade a court, not just a panel of doctors. In a House of Lords' decision in 1997, Lord Browne-Wilkinson said that medical evidence must be 'capable of withstanding logical analysis' (i.e. from a non-doctor) and that if it was not, 'a judge is entitled to hold that the body of opinion is not reasonable or responsible' (*Bolitho v City and Hackney Health Authority* (1997)).

Another point about expert evidence is that those giving it have a duty to justice above their duty to the person paying for their services. In criminal cases, expert witnesses have an obligation to assist the court, and they must remain objective and express only genuinely held opinions which are not biased in favour of either party.

Experts should ensure that developments in scientific thinking and techniques are not kept from the court, even where they remain at the stage of a mere hypothesis. This duty is facilitated by the **Criminal Procedure Rules** which enable opposing experts to consult together before the trial and, if possible, to settle their points of agreement or disagreement with a summary of their reasons.

Similarly, in civil trials, experts must be more than hired proponents of their side's case. The Practice Direction on **Civil Procedure Rule 35** states that 'it is the duty of an expert to help the court' and that this duty 'is paramount and overrides any obligation to the person from whom the expert has received instructions or by whom he is paid'. The rules are strict and demand that an expert should provide objective, unbiased opinion, and should not assume 'the role of an advocate.'

In its paper *The Admissibility of Expert Evidence in Criminal Proceedings in England and Wales, Consultation Paper No 190* (2009) the Law Commission expresses concern that defendants are at risk of being wrongly convicted on the evidence of 'charlatan' and 'biased' expert witnesses. A series of notorious cases in which convictions have been overturned after concerns over 'flawed' expert evidence 'represent the tip of the iceberg'. It canvasses views on the suggestion that expert evidence is sometimes admitted into court too readily and there is a 'pressing danger of wrongful convictions'. In recent years, miscarriages of justice such as the cases of Sally Clark and Angela Cannings, both convicted of killing their babies and then cleared on appeal, have highlighted the difficulties.

The commission says there is a danger that juries sometimes have little option but to defer to the views of a particular expert witness. The problem is particularly pronounced with scientific evidence which is said to have an 'aura of infallibility'; jurors might assume that just because it was scientific, it is reliable.

The Commission recommends that magistrates and judges act as gatekeepers and screen expert witnesses by applying a list of criteria, to be encapsulated in a new statutory test, before they can give evidence in court. The purpose of the test would be to ensure that juries are not exposed to unreliable experts.

The report says:

> ... 6.6 Accordingly, as a general rule, and bearing in mind the provisional assumption of reliability, the trial judge would first need to determine whether the tendered expert evidence satisfies the following admissibility requirements:
>
> (1)   Is the evidence logically relevant to a disputed matter?
> (2)   Would the evidence provide the jury with substantial assistance?
> (3)   Does the witness qualify as an expert in the field, and would he or she be able to provide an impartial opinion?
>
> 6.7 The party tendering the evidence would therefore need to explain at the outset how the expert's testimony is logically relevant to a matter in issue and demonstrate that it 'is sufficiently tied to the facts of the case that it will aid the jury in resolving' it. If the evidence fails this preliminary test it will be inadmissible.

The commission concludes (1.2, p 4):

> We believe that our proposals, if adopted, would ensure that convictions and acquittals would be founded on expert evidence only if the hypothesis and methodology underpinning that evidence can be shown to be trustworthy.

And it adds: 'We believe that the 'orthodoxy' that cannot be shown to be trustworthy should not be admissible.' The absence of any effective screening test risked convictions of the innocent or the acquittal of the guilty.

A major danger to be averted is the problem of the partisan expert witness; the person hired to put a particular slant on the evidence as opposed to giving entirely professional neutral testimony. That sort of witness has been highlighted by Lord Justice Leveson who has referred (*The Times*, 17 November, 2009) to an orthopaedic surgeon who was known by the initials NWA – 'never work again' (because that was the evidence he always gave about the impact of an injury on a litigant) and his frequent opponent in cases, another surgeon known by the initials BTW – 'back to work' – because his expert evidence was always that the injured party was well enough to return to work.

Common Pitfalls

The word 'forensic' means related to a court, though it is often wrongly used as if it has something to do with science. Forensic science is science related to court cases. It is a common pitfall to restrict discussion in questions such as this to expert evidence related only to science.

The way that costs issues affect justice, i.e., the question of whether it is necessary to pay for a range of potentially very expensive experts in each case, is an important issue and is commonly omitted in poor answers.

Aim Higher

Highly creditable answers will introduce some good case illustrations that exemplify the relevant theoretical points, for example: *Webster & Ors v Ridgeway Foundation School* (2010) and will display a sound knowledge of recent reform proposals such as *The Admissibility of Expert Evidence in Criminal Proceedings in England and Wales, Consultation Paper No 190* (2009).

Alternative Dispute Resolution

INTRODUCTION

This part of the English legal system has undergone significant development in recent times. English legal system courses tend to focus too much attention on the operation of the traditional court system. Whilst the courts are of fundamental importance, one should not overlook the increasing importance of alternative methods of deciding disputes. It should never be forgotten that tribunals actually deal with more cases than the county courts and High Court combined. The use of specialist tribunals to decide problems has a long history in England, but it has to be realised that the huge growth in the number of tribunals is a product of the growth of the interventionist welfare state and represents, at one level, an attack on the traditional legal system. These alternative mechanisms may also be seen as highlighting the weaknesses in the adversarial court system, in that they emphasise conciliation over conflict and, to that extent at least, they may well represent an advance on the traditional system of dispute resolution. It should also be borne in mind, however, that such informal procedures themselves are not without weaknesses.

Litigation is an extremely costly procedure. This is so not just for the parties concerned in any action who have to pay the costs of their legal representatives, but also for the state which has to provide the legal framework within which the action is taken, that is, courts, judges and other staff. This has been a great impetus for potential litigants to resort to alternative dispute resolution (ADR) and, in particular, to mediation – the use of a neutral third party to assist the disputants to reach a compromise. Most civil cases are settled at the door of the court, but by the time they arrive there, most parties have spent much time and money. Mediation aims to encourage disputants to reach such an agreement earlier. One private mediation company, Mediation UK, already mediates in over 5,000 neighbour disputes a year.

Checklist ✔

You should:

- have at least a minimal understanding of the social historical process that has seen the substantial development of tribunals;
- have particular knowledge of the operation of a substantial number of tribunals;
- be able to compare the advantages and disadvantages of alternative dispute resolutions, as against traditional court mechanisms;
- be able to distinguish and write about arbitration, mediation and conciliation;
- be prepared to answer a specific question relating to the **Arbitration Act 1996**;
- be prepared to answer a question on the county court small claims procedure (this may stand you in good stead for questions on court structure or civil procedure as well).

QUESTION 41

Explain the operation of tribunals as alternatives to the court system and assess the need for the proposed reforms included in the **Tribunals, Courts and Enforcement Act (TCEA) 2007**.

How to Answer this Question

This question invites a relatively straightforward comparison of tribunals and courts, but also requires some knowledge of the proposals to reform the operation of tribunals. The answer should include at least some of the following points:

- ❖ consideration of the usual advantages cited for tribunals – cheapness, speed and informality;
- ❖ consideration of the foregoing in the light of the disadvantages of the system;
- ❖ some note of the fact that the same areas can be cited as advantages and disadvantages, at one and the same time;
- ❖ comparison of the operation of tribunals with that of the courts;
- ❖ a conclusion suggesting whether, and if so how, the operation of tribunals can be improved (mention should be made of the review of tribunals conducted by Sir Andrew Leggatt);
- ❖ a consideration of the proposals contained in the **TCEA 2007** as far as they relate to tribunals.

Answer Structure

The establishment of a tribunal system alongside the court system → The advantages and disadvantages of the original tribunal system and the need for change → The changes introduced by enactment of the **TCEA 2007**

ANSWER

The reason generally put forward for the establishment and growth of tribunals in Britain since 1945 is the need to provide a specialist forum to deal with cases involving conflicts between an increasingly interventionist welfare state, its functionaries, and the rights of private citizens.[1] It is arguable, however, that the large-scale development of this special area of dispute resolution marks a diminishment in the general rule of law, to the extent that it has led to a transfer of power from the ordinary courts. A number of advantages are usually cited in favour of the use of tribunals, rather than the ordinary court system. These advantages relate to the cost, speed, efficiency, privacy and the lack of formality involved in such proceedings. It is important, however, that these supposed advantages are not simply taken at face value for, although they do no doubt represent significant improvements over the operation of the ordinary court system, it is at least arguable that some of them are not necessarily as advantageous as they appear at first sight and that others represent potential (if not actual) weaknesses in the tribunal system.

The ordinary system of courts, with the important exception of the magistrates' courts, are staffed by people who have had a specifically legal education and training, as may be seen from the requirement for judges to be qualified legal practitioners of some standing. With regard to the tribunal system, however, this is not the case.

Tribunals are usually made up of three members, only one of whom, the chair, is expected to be legally qualified. The other two members require no specific legal qualification or expertise. The lack of legal training is not considered a drawback, given the technical administrative, as opposed to specifically legal, nature of the provisions they have to consider. Indeed, the fact of there being two lay representatives on tribunals provides them with one of their perceived advantages over courts, for, to the extent that the non-legal members may provide specialist knowledge, they enable the tribunal to base its decision on actual practice as opposed to abstract legal theory, and thus enable decisions to be taken on practical grounds rather than on the basis of mere legal formalism.

An example of this can be seen in respect of the tribunals responsible for deciding matters relating to employment under the **Employment Rights Act 1996**. In practice, such tribunals are normally made up of a legally qualified chairperson, a representative of employers and a representative of employees. As a consequence, the tribunal has access to the practical experience of the lay members, together with knowledge of the circumstances involved in any particular dispute from both sides of the employment relationship. Such practical experience and expertise provides a basis for the decisions of the tribunal and gives such decisions a degree of pragmatic legitimacy.

---

1   Background to the establishment of a tribunal system.

A lack of formalism is also evident in the general procedure of tribunals, with the intention of making them less intimidating than full-blown court cases. Informality is shown in the fact that the strict rules relating to evidence, pleading and procedure, which apply in courts, are not binding or applied in tribunal proceedings. An example of this relaxation of strict court procedure is evident in the fact that tribunals are not bound by the strict rules of precedent. Of equal importance is the perhaps conflicting, if not contradictory, need for consistency of treatment, which is one of the major justifications of the system of precedent.

When these matters relating to the lack of formality are linked with the fact that tribunal proceedings tend not to be accusatorial, they generally lead to the conclusion that complainants do not need to be represented by a lawyer in order to present their grievance. They may represent themselves or be represented by a more knowledgeable associate, such as a trade union representative or a friend.

The fact that complainants do not have to rely on legal representation, in turn, makes the tribunal procedure less expensive than using the traditional court system, and this reduction in expense is further enhanced by the additional facts that there are no court fees involved in relation to tribunal proceedings and that costs are not normally awarded against a party who loses the case.

A further perceived advantage of the tribunal system is the speed of its operation, together with the certainty that a dispute will be heard on a specific date.

The final advantage usually cited is the fact that proceedings can be taken before a tribunal without necessarily triggering the publicity that might follow from a court case.

All of these factors, making the use of the tribunal system less intimidating as well as much less expensive than using the normal court system, serve to encourage individuals to pursue their grievances in circumstances where they might not be willing to take action in the courts and, thus, they can be seen as serving the praiseworthy function of increasing access to the law and legal remedies.

Having examined the supposed advantages of the tribunal system, its shortcomings remain to be considered.[2] The first of these arises with regard to the uncertainty and lack of uniformity that exists in relation to appeals from tribunals. Rights of appeal from decisions of tribunals and the route of such appeals depend on the provision of the statute under which a particular tribunal operates and, where they exist, may be exercised variously, to a further tribunal, a minister or a court of law. Prior to the Franks Committee Report (Cmnd 218, 1957), tribunals were not required to provide reasons for their decisions and this

2   Consideration of both the advantages *and* disadvantages of the tribunal system.

prevented appeals in most cases. Subsequent to the Franks Report, however, most tribunals, although still not all of them (and this remains a major bone of contention), are required to provide reasons for their decisions under **s 12** of the **Tribunals and Inquiries Act 1971**. The importance of this provision is that in cases where a tribunal has erred in its application of the law, the claimant can appeal to the High Court for an application for judicial review, to have the decision of the tribunal set aside for error of law on the face of the record.

Second, it has generally been accepted that the lack of publicity in relation to the majority of tribunal proceedings is an advantage, but the alternative possibility has to be considered: that such lack of publicity is, in fact, a distinct disadvantage, because it has the effect that cases involving issues of general public importance are not given the publicity and consideration that they might merit.

The major weakness as regards the operation of tribunals, however, is that except for Land Tribunals and the Commons Commissioners, people pursuing cases before tribunals were not entitled to legal aid to finance their cases. The effect of the replacement of legal aid by the Community Legal Service fund under the **Access to Justice Act 1999** remains to be seen. It is probably accurate to say, however, that in this particular area, it certainly cannot make matters worse and that the establishment of Community Legal Service Partnerships may well improve the availability of quality advice for those with problems to be decided by tribunals.

The foregoing has stated that the major advantages of the tribunal system are to be found in its lack of formality and its non-legal atmosphere, but research has shown that individual complainants fare better where they are, in fact, represented by lawyers. Additionally, it is, perhaps, one of the unintended consequences of the Franks Report that the appointment of legally qualified chairpersons has led to an increase in the formality of tribunal proceedings. As a consequence, non-law experts find it increasingly difficult in practice to represent themselves effectively. This difficulty is compounded when the body which is the object of the complaint is itself legally represented, for although the parties to hearings do not have to be legally represented, equally, there is nothing to prevent them from being so represented, no doubt to their advantage.

If tribunals are becoming increasingly important in determining individual rights and are, at the same time, becoming formalistic, then the refusal of assistance to fund legal representation to those seeking to use tribunals is tantamount to refusing them access to justice.

In August 2001, Sir Andrew Leggatt published his review of the tribunal system and after commenting on the lack of coherence in the system, his most important recommendations were as follows:[3]

---

3   Proposals for change to the tribunal system.

❖ to make the present 70 separate tribunals into one Tribunals System;

❖ to ensure that the tribunals operate independently of their sponsoring departments by having them administered by one Tribunals Service. Sir Andrew felt that tribunals neither appeared to be independent, nor were independent in fact, from their department of state;

❖ to improve the training of chairpersons and members in the interpersonal skills peculiarly required by tribunals;

❖ to clarify the appeals procedure. At present, routes of appeal from tribunal decisions are extremely confusing;

❖ Leggatt recommended that there should be a right of appeal on a point of law, by permission, on the generic ground that the decision of the tribunal was unlawful:

   (a) from the first-tier tribunals in each Division to its corresponding appellate tribunal;

   (b) from appellate tribunals to the Court of Appeal;

❖ to consider the effectiveness of lay members. It was felt that there is no justification for any members to sit, whether expert or lay, unless they have a particular function to fulfil, as they do in Employment Tribunals. In all other Divisions, the President (or Regional or District Chairmen) should have a discretion concerning whether lay members should sit in any particular case or category of cases.

Subsequently, in March 2003, the Lord Chancellor's Office announced the Government's intention to follow Sir Andrew Leggatt's recommendations and to institute a new unified Tribunals Service. The new organisation formally came into being in April 2005 and was launched operationally in April 2006 and was followed by new legislation in the following year.

The Tribunals, Court and Enforcement Act (TCEA) 2007

In pursuance of the Leggatt review, the stated intention of this piece of legislation (**TCEA 2007**) was the creation of a new, simplified, statutory framework for tribunals, which was to be achieved not just by the bringing together of existing tribunal jurisdictions but by the provision of a new structure of jurisdiction and new appeal rights.

❖ *Unified structure*
   The Act provides for the establishment of a new unified structure to subsume all tribunals, except for the Employment and Asylum and Immigration tribunals which will remain independent. This unification is to be achieved through the creation of two new tribunals, the First-tier Tribunal and the Upper Tribunal and in pursuit of that end the Act gives the Lord Chancellor power to transfer the jurisdiction of existing tribunals to the two new tribunals. The Act also provides for the establishment within each tier of 'chambers' so that exiting jurisdictions may be grouped together appropriately.

Chambers at the first-tier level will hear cases initially and the role of the upper chambers will be mainly, but not exclusively, to hear appeals from the first tier. Each chamber will be headed by a Chamber President and the tribunals' judiciary, as the legal members of tribunals will now be entitled, will be headed by a Senior President of Tribunals.

❖ *Appeals*

The Act specifically recognises and attempts to deal with the previous unclear and unsatisfactory routes of appeal in relation to tribunals' decisions. Under its provisions, in most cases, a decision of the First-tier Tribunal may be appealed to the Upper Tribunal and a decision of the Upper Tribunal may be appealed to a court. However, it also provides that any such appeal must relate to a point of law and may only be exercised with permission from the tribunal being appealed from or the tribunal or court being appealed to.

❖ *Administration*

The Act restate-dthe role of the Tribunal Service, subsequently replaced by the amalgamated HM CTS, in the successful operation of the new unified system.

❖ *Supervision*

Whereas the previous tribunals had come under the purview of the Council of Tribunals, the new act replaced that body with the Administrative Justice and Tribunals Council (AJTC) an important new institution with responsibility, not just for tribunals as was the remit of the previous body, but with a wider overview and input into the operation of the administrative justice system as a whole.

❖ *Enforcement*

In relation to enforcement, at present, tribunals have no enforcement powers of their own. Consequently if a monetary award is not paid then the claimant must register the claim in the county court before seeking enforcement. Under **TCEA 2007** claimants will be able to go directly to the county court or High Court for enforcement.

Progress on the TCEA 2007

Sir Robert Carnwath, a Court of Appeal Judge, was appointed as the first Senior President of Tribunals. He has responsibility for representing the views of the tribunal judiciary to Ministers, Parliament and for training, guidance and welfare. In addition to the powers under the Act, the Lord Chief Justice has delegated to the Senior President some of his powers under the Constitutional Reform Act, particularly in relation to judicial discipline of most tribunal judges and members.

The following **Chambers within the First-tier** are operational:

❖ **General Regulatory Chamber**

The General Regulatory Chamber (GRC) was established within the First-tier Tribunal on 1 September 2009. The GRC brings together tribunals that hear appeals on regulatory issues relating to the following specific areas:

(a) Charity: the role of this tribunal is to hear appeals against the decisions of the Charity Commission and to consider references from the Attorney General or the Charity Commission on points of law.

(b) Claims Management Services: the role of this tribunal is to hear appeals from businesses and individuals who provide claims management services in areas including:

- ❖ personal injury;
- ❖ criminal injuries compensation;
- ❖ employment matters;
- ❖ housing disrepair;
- ❖ financial products and services;
- ❖ industrial injury disablement benefits.

The Tribunal considers cases where the Claims Management Regulator has refused them authorisation or imposed sanctions on them.

(c) Consumer Credit: this tribunal hears appeals against decisions of the Office of Fair Trading relating to:

- ❖ licensing decisions of the Office of Fair Trading made under the **Consumer Credit Act 1974**;
- ❖ the imposition of requirements or a civil penalty on licensees under the **Consumer Credit Act 1974**;
- ❖ the refusal to register, cancellation of registration, or imposition of a penalty under the **Money Laundering Regulations 2007**.

(d) Estate Agents: this tribunal hears appeals against decisions made by the Office of Fair Trading relating to, for example, orders prohibiting a person from acting as an estate agent where a person has been convicted of an offence involving fraud or other dishonesty.

(e) Gambling: this tribunal hears appeal on issues such as the granting of operating licences by the Gambling Commission.

(f) Immigration Services: this tribunal hears appeals against decisions made by the Office of the Immigration Services Commissioner and considers disciplinary charges brought against immigration advisors by the Commission.

(g) Information Rights: this tribunal hears appeals from notices issued by the Information Commissioner under:

- ❖ **Freedom of Information Act 2000**;
- ❖ **The Environmental Information Regulations 2004**;
- ❖ **INSPIRE Regulations 2009** (these are the result of an EU Directive to establish an infrastructure for spatial information in Europe);
- ❖ **Data Protection Act 1998**;
- ❖ **Privacy and Electronic Communications Regulation 2003**;
- ❖ **Data Protection Monetary Penalty Regulations 2010**.

(h) Local Government Standards in England: established to decide references and appeals about the conduct of members of local authorities.

(i)   Transport Functions: this tribunal decides appeals against decisions of the Registrar of Approved Driving Instructors. These appeals concern approved driving instructors, trainee driving instructors, and training provider appeals. It can also hear appeals for London service permits against decisions of Transport for London and resolve disputes over postal charges.

❖   **Social Entitlement Chamber**

The SEC Chamber deals with the following areas:

(a)   Asylum Support (it does not deal with asylum claims or other immigration matters).

(b)   Criminal Injuries Compensation.

(c)   Social Security and Child Support.

❖   **Health, Education and Social Care Chamber**

(a)   Care Standards (i.e. appeals from people who have received a decision issued by organisations concerned with children and vulnerable adults, and those which regulate the provision of social, personal and health care).

(b)   Special Education Needs and Disability.

(c)   Mental Health Review.

(d)   Primary Health Lists: this tribunal hears appeals/applications resulting from decisions made by Primary Care Trusts as part of the local management of such lists, which medical practitioners must be on in order to function.

❖   **Tax Chamber**

This chamber has two specific areas of competence:

(a)   Tax, where it hears appeals against decisions relating to tax made by Her Majesty's Revenue and Customs (HMRC).

(b)   MP Expenses, where it hears appeals against certain decisions made by the Compliance Officer. The Compliance Officer is appointed by the Independent Parliamentary Standards Authority (IPSA) and is responsible for determining and paying MP Expenses. Appeals can be made by MPs, under the **Parliamentary Standards Act 2009.**

❖   **War Pensions and Armed Forces Compensation Chamber**

As its title suggests this Chamber hears appeals from ex-servicemen or women who have had their claims for a war pension rejected by the Secretary of State for Defence.

The following is a list of the **Chambers within the Upper Tribunal** already operating:

❖   **Administrative Appeals Chamber**

This chamber hears appeals from the present First-tier Tribunals; the General Regulatory Chamber, the Health, Education and Social Care Chamber, Social Entitlement Chamber, and the War Pensions and Armed Forces Compensation Chamber.

❖ **Tax and Chancery Chamber**
This chamber hears appeals from the First-tier Tax Chamber Tribunal. This brought together the four existing tax tribunals to hear the full range of direct and indirect tax cases.

❖ **Lands Chamber (Lands Tribunal)**
In June 2009 the Lands Tribunal joined the tribunal system established by the TCEA when it became the Lands Chamber of the Upper Tribunal. As its functions have not changed, for the time being the Lands Chamber of the Upper Tribunal is still known as the Lands Tribunal.

❖ **Immigration and Asylum Chamber**
In February 2010, Immigration and Asylum Chambers were established in both tiers of the Unified Tribunals framework. The Upper Tribunal is a superior court of record dealing with appeals against decisions made by the First-tier Immigration and Asylum Chamber Tribunal.

The Employment Tribunals and the Employment Appeal Tribunal continue largely unchanged as a separate 'pillar' of the new system. They are subject to the authority of the Senior President for training and welfare purposes and are treated as having the same status as Chambers in the First-tier and Upper Tribunals.

Common Pitfalls

❖ This question should not be treated as general question about tribunals, as it requires some close attention to be focussed on the TCEA 2007.
❖ This topic is currently in flux and students should be aware of any future changes.

Aim Higher ★

❖ Marks will be available for a consideration of the implementation of the TCEA 2007.

QUESTION 42

Explain the operation of the ombudsman system.

How to Answer this Question

The Parliamentary Commissioner for Administration (hereon the Commissioner) is better known as the ombudsman, whose function under the **Parliamentary Commissioner Act 1967 (PCA)** is to investigate complaints relating to maladministration. The Commissioner deals with problems in relation to central government and the health service, but other ombudsmen have been appointed under the **Local Government Act (LGA) 1974** to oversee the administration of local government in England and Wales. In dealing with this question, the following points should be addressed:

- ❖ a brief history of the concept of ombudsmen;
- ❖ the statutory basis of the Commissioner's powers;
- ❖ the meaning of maladministration;
- ❖ the filter role of MPs;
- ❖ the powers of the Commissioner;
- ❖ criticisms/limitations of the system;
- ❖ the spread of the system to other areas;
- ❖ case studies should be provided to support analysis.

Answer Structure

Introduction to the ombudsman system, in particular origins and history → Consideration of modern-day ombudsfolk, their role, processes and powers

ANSWER

The actual concept of the ombudsman is Scandinavian in origin and the function of the office holder is to investigate complaints of maladministration: that is, situations where the performance of a government department has fallen below acceptable standards of administration.

As with tribunals, so the institution of the ombudsman reflects the increased activity of the contemporary state. The ombudsman procedure, however, is not just an alternative to the court and tribunal system; it is based upon a distinctly different approach to dealing with disputes. Indeed, the **PCA 1967**, which established the position of the first ombudsman, provides that complainants with rights to pursue their complaints in either of those arenas will not be able to make use of the ombudsman procedure. This prohibition is subject to the discretion of the ombudsman and, in practice, it is interpreted in a generous manner in favour of the complainant, so as to allow investigations.

The first ombudsman, appointed in 1967 under the aforementioned legislation, operated – and the present Commissioner, Ann Abraham, still operates – under the title of the Parliamentary Commissioner for Administration and was empowered to consider central government processes only. Since that date, under the **LGA 1974** a number of other ombudsmen have been appointed to oversee the administration of local government in

England and Wales.[4] Scotland and Northern Ireland have their own local government ombudsmen fulfilling the same task. Initially a separate ombudsman was appointed to oversee the operation of the health service but that role has subsequently been assumed by the Parliamentary Commissioner. In 1994, an ombudsman for the Prison Service was appointed to cover that area. Additionally, the ombudsman role has proved popular in commercial areas and ombudsmen have been appointed in relation to legal services, banking, building societies, insurance and pensions.[5] This proliferation of ombudsmen has led to some confusion about which one any particular complaint should be taken to. This can be especially problematic where the complaint concerns more than one public body. In order to remedy this potential difficulty, a Cabinet Office review recommended in April 2000 that access be made easier through the establishment of one new Commission, bringing together the ombudsmen for central government, local government and the health service. The body subsequently established is the Commission of Local Administration, although the Parliamentary and Local Government ombudsmen still operate independently.

The procedure for making use of the various ombudsmen and their powers differs according to the particular field they cover and the manner in which they were established, that is, whether under statutory authority or purely as a voluntary procedure under commercial codes of conduct. As regards the Parliamentary Commissioner for Administration, the following points are worthy of mention.

Although maladministration is not defined in the **PCA 1967**, it has been taken to refer to an error in the way a decision was reached, rather than an error in the actual decision itself. Indeed, **s 12(3)** of the **PCA 1967** expressly precludes the Commissioner from questioning the merits of particular decisions taken without maladministration. Maladministration, therefore, can be seen to refer to a procedure used to reach a result, rather than the result itself. In an illuminating and much-quoted speech introducing the **1967 Act**, Richard Crossman, the then leader of the House of Commons, gave an indicative, if non-definitive, list of what might be included within the term maladministration, and included within it: bias, neglect, inattention, delay, incompetence, ineptitude, perversity, turpitude and arbitrariness.

Members of the public do not have the right to complain directly to the Commissioner, but must channel any such complaint through an MP. Complainants do not have to provide precise details of any maladministration; they simply have to indicate difficulties they have experienced as a result of dealing with an agency of central government. It is the function of the Commissioner to discover whether the problem arose as a result of

....

4   This discussion clearly indicates knowledge of the expansion of the use of ombudsmen.
5   Importantly, this demonstrates understanding that the utilisation of ombudsmen are not limited to the public sector.

maladministration. There is a 12-month time limit for raising complaints, but the Commissioner has discretion to ignore this.

The powers of the Commissioner to investigate complaints are similar to those of a High Court judge: to require the attendance of witnesses and the production of documents; wilful obstruction of the investigation is treated as contempt of court. On conclusion of an investigation, the Commissioner submits reports to the MP who raised the complaint and to the principal of the government office which was subject to the investigation. The Commissioner has no enforcement powers, but, if his recommendations are ignored and existing practices involving maladministration are not altered, he may submit a further report to both Houses of Parliament, in order to highlight the continued bad practice. The assumption is that on the submission of such a report, MPs will exert pressure on the appropriate minister of state to ensure that any necessary changes in procedure are made. Annual reports are laid before Parliament and a Parliamentary Select Committee exists to oversee the operation of the Commissioner.

Two reports from the Commissioner are worthy of particular consideration.[6] The first one, issued in February 1995, related to the effect of the delays in determining the route for the Channel Tunnel rail link. As a consequence of the four-year delay on the part of the Department of Transport in deciding on a route, the owners of properties along the various possible routes found the value of their properties blighted and the properties themselves even unsaleable. The situation was not finalised until the Department announced its final selection in 1994. According to the Commissioner:

> The effect of the Department of Transport's policy was to put the project in limbo, keeping it alive when it could not be funded.

As a consequence, he held that the Department:

> . . . had a responsibility to consider the position of such persons suffering exceptional or extreme hardship and to provide redress where appropriate.

The unusual thing about this case, however, was the reaction of the Department of Transport, which rejected the findings of the Commissioner and refused to provide any compensation. It was this refusal which led the Commissioner to issue his special report, consequent upon a situation where an 'injustice has been found which has not or will not be remedied'. Even then, the Department of Transport did not give way, until pressured to do so by the Parliamentary Select Committee on the Parliamentary Commissioner for Administration. Eventually, payments of £5,000 were made to those owners whose houses had suffered from property blight.

---

6   The value of reference to real-life examples of the work of ombudsmen should not be underestimated.

The second report, entitled *Equitable Life: a decade of regulatory failure*, came out in July 2008 and set out ten specific findings of maladministration: one against the former Department of Trade and Industry, four against the Government Actuary's Department, and five against the Financial Services Authority, in relation to their regulation of Equitable Life Assurance Society, whose financial mismanagement had led to the loss of pension for a substantial number of people. Included in findings were that:

❖ during the period before mid-1998, the regulators failed to verify the financial position of Equitable Life, even though they were duty-bound to do so and that such failure 'permitted misleading information . . . to be provided to policyholders and potential policyholders';

❖ the company's financial position was further obscured by the publication in 1999 of misleading regulatory returns showing a solvency position that was boosted by a 'worthless' reinsurance arrangement;

❖ after Equitable closed to new business in late 2000, the regulators 'provided misleading information to policyholders and the public, saying that Equitable had always been solvent for regulatory purposes. The regulators also gave assurances that the company had always met its other regulatory requirements. Neither was the case.'

On the basis of those findings the Ombudsman recommended, first, that, in recognition of the justifiable sense of outrage felt by those who had complained, the public bodies concerned should apologise for their failures. More importantly, however, her second recommendation was that the Government should establish and fund a compensation scheme, with the aim of putting those who had suffered in the position they would have been in had they not invested in Equitable Life policies. Effectively this would have meant paying compensation to remedy any financial losses, which would not have been suffered had those people invested elsewhere than with Equitable.

In February 2009 the then Treasury minister, Yvette Cooper, apologised on behalf of regulators and successive Governments for the maladministration found by the Ombudsman. However, she rejected the recommendation that compensation should be provided to all Equitable members and announced that a payment scheme for policyholders would focus on helping those investors who had been 'disproportionately affected' by the maladministration. The retired judge, Sir John Chadwick, was nominated to determine who was actually to be counted in that category, with of course a consequent further delay in any payment. One of the first measures announced by the new coalition Government, in May 2010, was that a scheme would be established to pay the claims in line with the Ombudsman's recommendations. It was expected that the total could amount to £5 billion. However, following Chadwick's conclusion that, even although people had lost £4.8 billion in the debacle, compensation payments should only be between £400 million and £500 million, the coalition Government was seen to withdraw from its original promise to the Equitable Life claimants and in October 2010 it announced that it would limit payments to £1.5 billion.

In offering an evaluation of the ombudsman procedure, it may be claimed that, all in all, the system appears to work fairly well within its restricted sphere of operation, but there are major areas where it could be improved. The more important of the criticisms levelled at the Parliamentary Commissioner for Administration relate to:

(a) the retention of MPs as filters for complaints. It is generally accepted that there is no need for such a filter mechanism;

(b) the restrictive nature of the definition of maladministration. It is possible to argue that any procedure that leads to an unreasonable decision must involve an element of maladministration and that, therefore, the definition as currently stated is not overly restrictive. However, even if such reverse reasoning is valid, it would still be preferable for the definition of the scope of the Commissioner's investigations to be clearly stated and be stated in wider terms than at present;

(c) the lack of publicity given to complaints. If more people were aware of the procedure and what it could achieve, then more people would make use of it, leading to an overall improvement in the administration of governmental policies;

(d) the reactive role of the ombudsmen. This criticism refers to the fact that the ombudsmen are dependent upon receiving complaints before they can initiate investigations. It is suggested that a more proactive role, under which the ombudsmen would be empowered to initiate investigation on their own authority, would lead to an improvement in general administration, as well as an increase in the effectiveness of the activity of the ombudsmen.

Common Pitfalls ✗

The Parliamentary Commissioner should be the focus of any answer and should not be confused with other 'ombudsmen' if they are considered.

Aim Higher ★

Case studies will support analysis and the more up-to-date the case the better. The *Equitable Life* case will get good marks.

QUESTION 43

Explain the content and effect of the **Arbitration Act 1996**.

How to Answer this Question

This question is very straightforward and simply tests the candidate's knowledge of this important piece of legislation. In answering it, candidates should be aware of the changes introduced by the Act; essentially, the shift from a court-based system to a voluntary, party-based system, and should be able to provide a clear analysis of the major statutory provisions. An explanation of the reasons for the change and its origin would also be beneficial. The following structure would provide a framework for answering the question adequately:

- ❖ introduction – principles behind and reasons for the Act;
- ❖ freedom of the parties to choose what suits them best;
- ❖ arbitrators and their powers;
- ❖ role and powers of the court.

Answer Structure

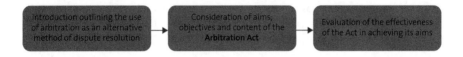

ANSWER

The **Arbitration Act 1996** was given Royal Assent in June 1996, and the majority of its provisions were brought into force by January 1997. The Act repeals **Pt I** of the **Arbitration Act 1950** and the whole of the **Arbitration Acts** of **1975** and **1979**. The Act follows the Model Arbitration Law adopted in 1985 by the United Nations Commission on International Trade Law (UNCITRAL).

Section 1 of the Act states that it is founded on the following principles:

(a) the object of arbitration is to obtain the fair resolution of disputes by an impartial tribunal without necessary delay or expense;

(b) the parties should be free to agree how their disputes are resolved, subject only to such safeguards as are necessary in the public interest;

(c) in matters governed by this part of the Act the court should not intervene except as provided by this part.

This statement of general principles, which should inform the reading of the later detailed provisions of the Act, is unusual for UK legislation, but may be seen as reflecting the purposes behind the Act. One major purpose was to ensure that London did not lose its place as a leading centre for international arbitration. As a consequence of the demand-driven nature of the new legislation, it would seem that court interference in the arbitration process has had to be reduced to a minimum and replaced by party autonomy. Under the Act, the role of the arbitrator has been increased and that of the court has been reduced to the residual level of intervention where the arbitration process either requires legal assistance, or else is seen to be failing to provide a just settlement.

In analysing the operation of the Act, and contrasting it with the way in which the previous legislation operated, it is useful to consider it in three distinct parts:

(a)   autonomy of the parties;
(b)   powers of the arbitral panel;
(c)   court powers.

AUTONOMY

As has been stated already, the main thrust of the Act is to empower the parties to the dispute and to allow them to decide how the matter is best decided. In pursuit of this aim, the mandatory parts of the Act only take effect where the parties involved do not agree otherwise. It is even possible for the parties to agree that the dispute should not be decided in line with the strict legal rules, but rather in line with commercial fairness, which might be a completely different thing.

Whilst it is possible for there to be an oral arbitration agreement at common law, **s 5** provides that **Pt I** of the Act only applies to agreements in writing. What this means in practice, however, has been extended by **s 5(3)**, which provides that where the parties agree to an arbitration procedure which is in writing, that procedure will be operative, even though the agreement between the parties is not itself in writing. An example of such a situation would be where a salvage operation was negotiated between two vessels at sea on the basis of Lloyd's standard salvage terms. It would be unlikely that the actual agreement would be reduced to written form, but nonetheless, the arbitration element in those terms would be effective.

Section 6 provides that an arbitration agreement means an agreement to submit to arbitration present or future disputes, whether contractual or not.

ARBITRATORS AND THEIR POWERS

The arbitration tribunal may consist of a single arbitrator, or a panel, as the parties decide (**s 15**). If one party fails to appoint an arbitrator, then the other party's nominee may act as sole arbitrator (**s 17**).

Under **s 20(4)**, where there is a panel and it fails to reach a majority decision, then the decision of the chair shall prevail.

Section 28 expressly provides that the parties to the proceedings are jointly and severally liable to pay the arbitrators such reasonable fees and expenses as appropriate. Previously, this was only an implied term. And **s 29** provides that arbitrators are not liable for anything done or omitted in the discharge of their functions, unless the act or omission was done in bad faith.

It is also for the tribunal to decide all procedural and evidential matters. **Section 30** provides that unless the parties agree otherwise, the arbitrator can rule on questions relating to its own jurisdiction, that is, in relation to:

(a) whether there actually is a valid arbitration agreement;
(b) whether the arbitration tribunal is properly constituted;
(c) what matters have been submitted to arbitration in accordance with the agreement.

Parties may be represented by a lawyer or any other person, and the tribunal may appoint experts or legal advisers to report to it. **Section 33** provides that the tribunal has a general duty:

(a) to act fairly and impartially between the parties, giving each a reasonable opportunity to state their case; and
(b) to adopt procedures suitable for the circumstances of the case, avoiding unnecessary delay or expense.

Section 35 provides that, subject to the parties agreeing to the contrary, the tribunal shall have the following powers:

(a) to order parties to provide security for costs (previously, a power reserved to the courts);
(b) to give directions in relation to property subject to the arbitration;
(c) to direct that a party or witness be examined on oath and to administer the oath. The parties may also empower the arbitrator to make provisional orders (**s 39**).

Section 46 states that the arbitral tribunal must decide the dispute:

(a) in accordance with the law chosen by the parties; or
(b) in accordance with such other considerations as the parties have agreed.

Section 48 again states that, unless agreed otherwise, the tribunal shall have the following powers:

(a) to make a declaration about any matter to be determined in the proceedings;
(b) to order payment of money;
(c) to order a party to refrain from doing anything;
(d) to order specific performance of a contract;
(e) to order rectification, setting aside or cancellation of a deed or any other document.

Section 49 empowers the awarding of interest, either simple or compound, and **s 50** allows for the extension of the time for making an award. **Section 58** provides that any award made is final and binding on the parties, and **s 66** provides that any such award can be enforced in the same manner as a court judgment.

ROLE OF THE COURT

Where one party seeks to start a court action, in contradiction to a valid arbitration agreement to the contrary, then the other party may request the court to stay the litigation in favour of the arbitration agreement under ss 9–11 of the Act. Where, however, both parties agree to ignore the arbitration agreement and seek recourse to the litigation, then, following the party consensual nature of the Act, the original agreement may be ignored.

Under s 12, the courts may grant an extension to any set time limit for starting proceedings, but only on the limited exceptions stated, that is, what is reasonable and in the interests of justice.

The courts may order a party to comply with an order of the tribunal, and may also order parties and witnesses to attend and to give oral evidence before tribunals (s 43).

Under s 18, the court has power to revoke the appointment of an arbitrator, on application of any of the parties, where there has been a failure in the appointment procedure, and it also has powers to revoke authority under s 24, on the application of one of the parties, where the arbitrator:

(a)   has not acted impartially;

(b)   does not possess the required qualifications;

(c)   does not have either the physical or mental capacity to deal with the proceedings;

(d)   has refused or failed:

    (i)   to conduct the proceedings properly; or

    (ii)   has been dilatory in dealing with the proceedings or in making an award, to the extent that it will cause substantial injustice to the party applying for their removal.

Section 32 allows any of the parties to raise in court preliminary objections to the substantive jurisdiction of the arbitration tribunal, but provides that they may only do so on limited grounds, which requires either the agreement of the parties concerned, or the permission of the arbitration tribunal and the agreement of the court. Leave to appeal will only be granted where the court is satisfied that the question involves a point of law of general importance.

Under s 45, the court may, on application by one of the parties, decide any preliminary question of law arising in the course of the proceedings.

APPEALS

Once the decision of the arbitral panel has been made, there are only limited grounds for appeal to the court. The first ground arises under s 67, in relation to the substantive jurisdiction of the arbitral panel, although this right may be lost if the party attempting to make use of it took part in the arbitration proceedings without objecting to the alleged lack of jurisdiction.

The second ground for appeal to the courts is on procedural grounds, under **s 68**, on the basis that some serious irregularity affected the operation of the tribunal. By serious irregularity is meant:

(a) failure to comply with the general duty set out in **s 33**;
(b) failure to conduct the tribunal as agreed by the parties;
(c) uncertainty or ambiguity as to the effect of the award;
(d) failure to comply with the requirement as to the form of the award.

Under **s 69**, parties may also appeal on a point of law arising from the award. However, the parties can agree beforehand to preclude such a possibility and, where they agree to the arbitral panel making a decision without providing a reasoned justification for it, they will also lose the right to appeal.

The issue of rights to appeal under **s 69** has been considered in a number of cases by the Court of Appeal. In 2002 in *North Range Shipping Ltd v Seatrams Shipping Corporation* (2002) it confirmed that there was no further right of appeal against a judge's refusal to grant permission for an appeal against an arbitrator's decision, except on the grounds of unfairness. In *CMA CGM SA v Beteiligungs KG* (2002) it insisted that judges in the High Court should not be too hasty in allowing appeals. In the case in point, the Court of Appeal decided that the present appeal should not have been allowed. In reaching this decision the court set out the new standard that had to be met to justify an appeal, that 'the question should be one of general importance and the decision of the arbitrators should be at least open to serious doubt'. This standard was higher than that applied under the previous test as stated in *Antaios Compania Naviera SA v Salen Redereierna AB* (1985).

In *BLCT Ltd v J Sainsbury plc* (2003) the Court of Appeal held that the case not only had no real prospect of succeeding in its appeal but also rejected the argument that by curtailing the right of appeal, **s 69** was incompatible with **Art 6** of the **European Convention on Human Rights**.

The foregoing sets out the main provisions of the **Arbitration Act 1996** in such a way as to demonstrate the shift from a court-based system to a voluntaristic arbitration-based system, in line with the expressed wishes of commercial enterprises.[7]

....

7   Conclusion sums up the effect of the **Arbitration Act** as supporting the move away from the courts as a
    means of resolving civil disputes and, importantly, also emphasises that the Act does so in a manner
    which satisfies the needs of its 'customers' (i.e. businesses).

QUESTION 44

'For most people most of the time, litigation in the civil courts, and often in tribunals too, should be the method of dispute resolution of last resort.'

▶ Consider what alternatives to the court system are available and why they should be used.

How to Answer this Question

This question is more general than the previous ones, but it still requires a consideration of arbitration as well as mediation and conciliation. Detail is necessarily less, but the question still requires a substantial understanding of the processes. The following structure might prove satisfactory:

❖   consider the operation of arbitration as compared to the ordinary courts (refer specifically to the **Arbitration Act 1996**);

❖   consider the distinction between mediation and conciliation, as well as detailing how and when they are likely to be used;

❖   consider especially how the courts will use costs awards to ensure that the Alternative Dispute Resolution (ADR) is used;

❖   conclude by placing these various ADR mechanisms within the framework of the general legal system.

Answer Structure

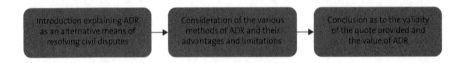

Introduction explaining ADR as an alternative means of resolving civil disputes → Consideration of the various methods of ADR and their advantages and limitations → Conclusion as to the validity of the quote provided and the value of ADR

ANSWER

As the question suggests there are a number of valuable alternatives to using the courts. These Alternative Dispute Resolution mechanisms have many features that make them preferable to the ordinary court system in many areas. For one thing they tend to be much less formal and less stressful that the court system. However, perhaps their main advantages are that they are less antagonistic than the ordinary legal system, being designed to achieve agreement between the parties involved and they are, by and large much cheaper than the courts.

ARBITRATION

It is generally recognised that the formal atmosphere of the ordinary courts is not necessarily the most appropriate one in which to determine all disputes which might need adjudication. In recognition of this fact, various alternatives have been developed specifically to avoid the perceived shortcomings of court procedure.

The first and oldest of these alternative procedures is arbitration. Arbitration is the procedure whereby parties in dispute refer the issue under contention to a third party for resolution, rather than institute legal proceedings in the courts. This practice is well established in commerce and industry;[8] its legal effectiveness has long been recognised by the court. In contemporary business usage, it is a matter of common practice for commercial contracts to contain express clauses referring any future disputes to arbitration.

Arbitration proceedings are now governed by the **Arbitration Act 1996**, which repeals previous legislation. This Act (which is dealt with in detail in Question 43, above) significantly alters the relationship between the parties, the arbitrator and the courts. Whereas, previously, the courts ultimately dominated the procedure, now their role has been reduced to providing safeguards against improper actions on the part of the arbitrator, and the determination of points of law. So, now the parties to any dispute are at liberty to provide their procedures for resolving it.

It is possible for arbitration agreements to specify in advance who will act as arbitrator in the event of any dispute. Such a person may be a legal practitioner, or an expert in the particular field of commerce to which the contract relates. There are also specialist institutions which deal with arbitration, and it is quite common for the agreement simply to refer the dispute to such an institution to select an appropriate arbitrator.

There are numerous advantages to be gained from using arbitration rather than the court system.[9] First, arbitration tends to be a private procedure and this has the twofold advantage that outsiders do not get access to any potentially sensitive information and, further, that the parties to the arbitration do not run the risk of any damaging publicity arising out of reports of the proceedings.

Second, the use of arbitration lessens the likelihood of protracted litigation, although it has to be admitted that where one of the parties makes use of the available grounds to challenge an arbitration award, the prior costs of the arbitration will have been largely wasted.

This previous point leads to a consideration of the actual costs of the arbitration process. It is generally asserted that arbitration is a much cheaper procedure than taking a case to the normal courts, but the costs of arbitration and the use of specialist arbitrators should not be underestimated, for they can in themselves be considerable.

....

8   This emphasises that arbitration is most used by commerce rather than individual litigants.

9   It is important to explain both the advantages and limitations of ADR, in order to be able to draw conclusions as to the worth of the various options for resolving disputes.

Cost is usually in direct proportion to the time taken to decide a case and, here again, the arbitration procedure has distinct advantages over the usual court procedure, for it is distinctly quicker in delivering a decision on the case in point.

A further point which follows from the use of a specialist arbitrator is that the parties to the arbitration can rely on that person having an expert knowledge of the actual practice within the area that constitutes the ground of the dispute, and can count on the arbitrator delivering a decision in line with accepted practice.

SMALL CLAIMS

The type of arbitration scheme considered above tends to relate to large business contracts, but it should be noted that, since 1973, an arbitration service has been available within the county court specifically for the settlement of small claims.[10] Any dispute involving a sum of £3,000 or less was automatically referred to this procedure and claims involving more than £3,000 could be referred to the procedure with the approval of the parties involved. As with arbitration, the aim of this procedure was to provide a cheap, informal mechanism for dealing with small claims and, specifically, consumer complaints, usually under the supervision of a district judge. In pursuit of those ends, the county court rules actually provided that, in relation to the arbitration process, any such hearing should be informal and that the strict rules of evidence should not apply.

This previous procedure has been replaced, following **Pt 27** of the **Civil Procedure Rules 1998**. Under the new rules, the concept of an 'arbitration' disappears and is replaced by a small claims hearing, although there is no longer any 'automatic' reference to the small claims track. Other consequential changes to the handling of small claims include:

❖ an increase in the jurisdiction from £3,000 to no more than £5,000, with the exception of claims for personal injury and for housing disrepair where the limit remains at £1,000;

❖ where a judge thinks that paper adjudication may be appropriate, that is, without the parties having to attend, then they will be asked to say whether or not they have any objections within a given time period. If a party does object, the matter will be given a hearing in the normal way;

❖ parties need not attend the hearing, but the court will take into account any written evidence that a party has sent to the court;

❖ parties, with the court's approval, can consent to use the small claims track, even if the value of their claim exceeds the normal value for that track;

❖ parties will also be restricted to a maximum one day hearing.

---

10 Although not strictly a form of ADR, as it comes within the remit of the Anglo-Welsh court system, the 'small claims track' provides many of the features associated with ADR, such as minimum formality.

Aspects of the old small claims procedure which are retained include their informality, the interventionist approach adopted by the judiciary, the limited costs regime and the limited grounds for appeal (misconduct of the district judge, or an error of law made by the court).

Although the use of legal representation is not forbidden, it is effectively discouraged by the fact that the normal rule as to costs following the event is not applicable under the arbitration process; this 'no costs' rule provides that expenses are not awarded to the successful party in such a case. The general attempt to provide an informal atmosphere is further encouraged by the wide discretion afforded to the courts as to the manner in which they pursue the arbitration procedure, to the extent that they can assume an inquisitorial approach to the hearings before them in order to elicit information on which to base their decisions.

MEDIATION

Mediation and conciliation are the most informal of all ADR procedures. Mediation is the process where a third party acts as the conduit through which two disputing parties communicate and negotiate in an attempt to reach a common resolution of a problem. Mediation has an important part to play in family matters, where it is felt that the adversarial approach of the traditional legal system has tended to emphasise, if not increase, existing differences of view between individuals and has not been conducive to amicable settlements.[11] Thus, in divorce cases, mediation has traditionally been used to enable the parties themselves to work out an agreed settlement, rather than having one imposed on them from outside by the courts. It is important to realise that there are potential problems with mediation. The assumption that the parties freely negotiate the terms of their final agreement in a less than hostile manner may be deeply flawed, to the extent that it assumes equality of bargaining power and knowledge between the parties to the negotiation. Mediation may well ease pain, but, unless the mediation procedure is carefully and critically monitored, it may gloss over and perpetuate a previously exploitative relationship, allowing the more powerful participant to manipulate and dominate the more vulnerable, and force an inequitable agreement. Establishing entitlements on the basis of clear legal advice may be preferable to apparently negotiating those entitlements away in the non-confrontational, therapeutic atmosphere of mediation.

CONCILIATION

Conciliation takes mediation a step further and gives the mediator the power to suggest grounds for compromise and the possible basis for a conclusive agreement. Both mediation and conciliation have been available in relation to industrial disputes, under

11   An important point which highlights the failings of the court system in maintaining a positive relationship between disputing parties.

the auspices of the Government-funded Advisory Conciliation and Arbitration Service (ACAS).[12] and have an important part to play in family matters. The essential weakness in these two procedures, however, lies in the fact that although they may lead to the resolution of a dispute, they do not necessarily achieve that end. Where they operate successfully, they are excellent methods of dealing with problems, as essentially the parties to the dispute determine their own solutions and, therefore, feel commitment to the outcome. The problem is that they have no binding power and do not always lead to an outcome.

The foregoing has considered a variety of alternative mechanisms for dealing with legal problems which have been developed in response to particular shortcomings in the ordinary court system and, perhaps, they point to a fundamental need to reform the operation of those law courts and to regularise the whole provision of dispute resolution devices under the law.

As part of the civil justice reforms, the general requirement placed on courts to actively manage cases includes 'encouraging the parties to use an alternative dispute resolution procedure if the Court considers that to be appropriate and facilitating the use of such procedure'. **Rule 26.4** of the **Civil Procedure Rules (CPR) 1998**[13] enables judges, either on their own account or at the agreement of both parties, to stop court proceedings where they consider the dispute to be better suited to solution by some alternative procedure, such as arbitration or mediation. **CPR 44.3(2)** provides that 'if the court decides to make an order about costs (a) the general rule is that the unsuccessful party will be ordered to pay the costs of the successful party; but (b) the court may make a different order'. **CPR 44.3(4)** provides that 'in deciding what order (if any) to make about costs, the court must have regard to all the circumstances, including (a) the conduct of the parties'. **Rule 44.3(5)** provides that the conduct of the parties includes '(a) conduct before, as well as during, the proceedings and in particular the extent to which the parties followed any relevant pre-action protocol.' If, subsequently, a court is of the opinion that an action it has been required to decide could have been settled more effectively through ADR, then under r 44.5 of the **CPR**, it may penalise the party who insisted on the court hearing by awarding them reduced or no costs should they win the case.

The potential consequences of not abiding by a recommendation to use ADR may be seen in *Dunnett v Railtrack plc* (2002).[14] When Dunnett won a right to appeal against a previous court decision, the court granting the appeal recommended that the dispute should be put to arbitration. Railtrack, however, refused Dunnett's offer of arbitration and insisted

---

12 Helpful use of an example, demonstrating knowledge and providing clarity of explanation.
13 Demonstrates knowledge and understanding of the means though which the state promote and support ADR.
14 Reference to this decided case provides powerful evidence of the value of ADR.

on the dispute going back to a full court hearing. In the subsequent hearing in the Court of Appeal, Railtrack proved successful. The Court of Appeal, however, held that if a party rejected ADR out of hand when it had been suggested by the court, they would suffer the consequences when costs came to be decided. In the instant case, Railtrack had refused to even contemplate ADR at a stage prior to the costs of the appeal beginning to flow.

It is possible to refuse to engage in mediation without subsequently suffering in the awards of costs. The test, however, is an objective rather than a subjective one, and a difficult one to sustain, as was shown in *Hurst v Leeming* (2002). Hurst, a solicitor, started legal proceedings against his former partners and instructed Leeming, a barrister, to represent him. When the claim proved unsuccessful, Hurst sued Leeming in professional negligence. When that claim failed, Hurst argued that Leeming should not be awarded costs, as he, Hurst, had offered to mediate the dispute, but Leeming had rejected the offer. Leeming cited five separate justifications for his refusal to mediate. These were:

❖   the heavy costs he had already incurred in meeting the allegations;
❖   the seriousness of the allegation made against him;
❖   the lack of substance in the claim;
❖   the fact that he had already provided Hurst with a full refutation of his allegation;
❖   the fact that, given Hurst's obsessive character, there was no real prospect of a successful outcome to the litigation.

In *Halsey v Milton Keynes General NHS Trust* (2004), the Court of Appeal emphasised that the criterion was the reasonableness of the belief.

Common Pitfalls
Avoid the temptation either to ignore arbitration or, alternatively, just to focus on that aspect of ADR?

Aim Higher
Higher marks may be gained by reference to any contemporary reports on mediation which tend to appear regularly. Also reference to how the courts use cost awards to ensure people do use ADR will be advantageous.

The Rule of Law, Judicial Review and Human Rights

INTRODUCTION

The questions in this chapter may not appear in all English Legal System syllabuses. It is true that this chapter touches on material that will, traditionally, be considered more fully in other courses, such as public or constitutional and administrative law, civil liberties options, or, indeed, some legal theory courses. The fact is, however, that the English legal system simply cannot be fully understood or placed in its contemporary context without a consideration of the points raised hereafter, and many syllabuses look to students to have at least a passing acquaintance with the matters that are considered in this chapter.

The English legal system cannot be treated as static; it is continuously responding to changes that take place in society as a whole. As was stated in the introduction to Chapter 1 of this text, to deny the relevance of European law in an English Legal System course would not only be restrictive, it would be wrong, to the extent that it ignores an increasingly important factor in the formation and determination of UK law. The same can be said of the change in the form and content of law that took place in the course of the twentieth century and which can be linked to the emergence of the interventionist state. Equally, the same can be said with regard to the increase in applications for judicial review. Arguably, this may be seen as the judges fighting a reactionary rearguard action against the forces of the all-encompassing state, or it can be seen as the judges valiantly endeavouring to curtail excesses of that state in the defence of individual liberties. In either case, it represents a political struggle between the judiciary and the executive and one that has fundamental implications for not only the English legal system, but also the constitution of the UK.

The incorporation of the **European Convention on Human Rights (ECHR)** into UK law through the **Human Rights Act (HRA) 1998** has had profound implications for the operation of the English legal system and the relationship of the judiciary to the legislature and executive. Although how it finally works out remains to be seen, it can already be seen to have had a substantial effect since its implementation in October 2000.

Checklist ✔

- What is actually meant by the term 'the rule of law'?
- Does everyone agree as to the meaning?
- To what extent has the meaning changed over time?
- Is there an identifiable core meaning to 'the rule of law'?
- What is judicial review and what remedies does it offer?
- Why have applications for judicial review increased so remarkably?
- Is law an end in itself, or simply a means to an end?
- What does the **HRA 1998** provide?
- What are the implications of the **HRA 1998**?

QUESTION 45

Section 1 of the **Constitutional Reform Act 2005** specifically provides that it 'does not adversely affect the existing constitutional principle of the rule of law . . .'.

▶ **Explain what is meant by the 'rule of law' and its relevance in contemporary society.**

How to Answer this Question

This question asks for a general consideration of the rule of law and, importantly, questions its relevance in contemporary times. Candidates must know what is understood by the concept and must offer an opinion as to its continued relevance; but they must be careful to substantiate any opinion and not resort to mere assertion and amorphous waffle. One way (and it is only one of many ways) to answer this question is as follows:

- ❖ offer a general definition of the rule of law, before going on to examine particular versions of the idea;
- ❖ explain AV Dicey's understanding of the concept;
- ❖ outline historical criticisms of Dicey;
- ❖ give an account of Friedrich von Hayek's view of the rule of law;
- ❖ describe Raz's critique of Hayek and his version of the rule of law;
- ❖ conclude by considering the possibility of there being some core meaning within the idea of the rule of law.

Answer Structure

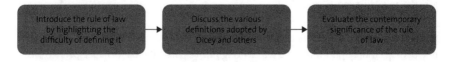

Introduce the rule of law by highlighting the difficulty of defining it → Discuss the various definitions adopted by Dicey and others → Evaluate the contemporary significance of the rule of law

ANSWER

The rule of law has been described by DM Walker, in *The Oxford Companion to Law* (1980), as a 'concept of the utmost importance but having no defined, nor readily definable, content'. Although there is certainly an element of truth in what Walker states, it is suggested that it is possible to establish a core meaning in relation to the idea of the rule of law, although the complete meaning of the concept does tend to be more ambiguous and subject to change, depending on the political outlook of the person using the term and the time period in which it is being considered.

In considering the meaning of the concept 'the rule of law', one is immediately drawn into a consideration of the work of the nineteenth-century writer on the English constitution, AV Dicey, whose *Law of the Constitution* was first published in 1885. According to the chauvinistic Dicey, the rule of law was one of the key features which distinguished the English constitution from its continental counterparts. (The other essential element in the English constitution was the sovereignty of Parliament, an idea not completely compatible with the rule of law, for the idea that Parliament is sovereign and recognises no restraint is in conflict with a notion of the rule of law which sees it as primarily about controlling executive power.)

Whereas foreigners were subject to the exercise of arbitrary power, the Englishman was secure within the protection afforded him by the rule of law. In setting out what was actually meant by the rule of law, Dicey considered three distinct elements. First, it involved an absence of arbitrary power on the part of the Government. Under the rule of law, the extent of the state's power and the manner in which it exercises such power is limited and controlled by law. This control is aimed at preventing the state from acquiring and using wide discretionary powers, because Dicey recognised that inherent in discretion is the possibility of its being used in an arbitrary manner.

The second of Dicey's elements related to equality before the law; the fact that no person is above the law, irrespective of rank or class, together with the related fact that functionaries of the state are subject to the same law and legal procedures as private citizens. Thus, the law, as represented in Dicey's version of the rule of law, ignores substantive differences and treats everyone as formally equal. In other words, the law is blind to real, concrete differences between people, in terms of wealth or power or connection, and treats them all the same as possessors of abstract rights and duties.

The third component of the rule of law for Dicey related to the fact that the rules of the English constitution were the outcome of the ordinary law of the land and were based on the provision of remedies by the courts, rather than on the declaration of rights in the form of a written constitution.

It is essential to recognise that Dicey was writing not just at a particular historical period but, perhaps more importantly, he was writing from a particular political perspective. He was a committed believer in the free operation of the market and was opposed to any increase in state activity, particularly with regard to any attempt by the state to regulate the economy. It is at least arguable that at the time Dicey wrote his *Law of the Constitution*, he was misrepresenting changes that had already occurred in the UK polity, in a desire to curtail the burgeoning activity of the state and, at the same time, to justify that political stance on the basis of a spurious constitutional history. Certainly, by 1933 and in the light of the increased role that the state had assumed in organising society[1] in general and the economy in particular, Sir Ivor Jennings, in his book *The Law and the Constitution* (5th edn, 1959), could express the view that if Dicey's version of the rule of law:

> ... means that the state exercises only the functions of carrying out external relations and maintaining order, it is not true. If it means that the state ought to exercise these functions only, it is a rule of policy for Whigs (if there are any left) [Whigs were a former political party].

If there were no Whigs as such, their attitudes towards the free market lived on in the work of such social thinkers as Friedrich von Hayek. Although Hayek's work has become increasingly influential with the coming to power of the Thatcher Conservative government in 1979, it has to be said that in 1944, when his *The Road to Serfdom* was first published, he was almost a lone voice crying in the wilderness. As regards the rule of law, it is not surprising that Hayek followed Dicey in emphasising its essential component as the absence of arbitrary power in the hands of the state. According to Hayek:

> Stripped of all technicalities, the rule of law means that government in all its actions is bound by rules fixed and announced beforehand.

Hayek, however, went further than Dicey in setting out the actual form and, at least in a negative way, the actual content of legal rules, in order for them to be considered as compatible with the rule of law. As Hayek expressed it in *The Road to Serfdom*:

> The Rule of Law implies limits on the scope of legislation, it restricts it to the kind of general rules known as formal law; and excludes legislation directly aimed at particular people.

Nor should law be aimed at particular goals. In other words, the Government has no place in usurping the authority of individuals by deciding their course of action for them. Within clearly defined and strictly controlled legal parameters, individuals should be left to act as they choose. The job of law is to set the boundaries of personal action, not to dictate the course of such action. Laws should not be particular in content or application, but should be general in nature, applying to all and benefiting no one in particular.

---

1   An important point, as it highlights that, as society changes, the law must also develop in response.

It is important to note that Hayek did not suggest that rules are not laws; they are legal, as long as they are enacted through the appropriate and proper mechanisms; they simply are not in accord with the rule of law. Hayek may very well have agreed with Karl Mannheim, whom he quoted, that the rule of law only operated during the classical liberal competitive phase of capitalism, but he certainly regretted and condemned the change that had taken place in the form and function of law. His regret and condemnation arose from two sources. First, from the economic perspective, as only the particular individual concerned can fully know all the circumstances of his situation, the state should, *as a matter of efficiency*, leave that individual to make his own decisions. Second, from the moral perspective, to the extent that the all-encompassing interventionist/welfare state leaves individuals less room to make decisions as to their actions, it reduces their freedom.

Other legal philosophers have recognised the need for, and have come to terms with, state intervention in the pursuit of substantive as well as merely formal justice and have provided new ways of understanding the rule of law as a means of controlling discretion, without attempting to eradicate it completely. Joseph Raz, for example, took Hayek to task for disguising a socio-economic argument as a legal one, in order to strike at policies of which he did not approve as being contrary to the rule of law, and he suggested that such reasoning was in danger of identifying the 'rule of law' with the rule of 'good law', that is, law/policy of which Hayek approved.

If both Dicey and Hayek laid great emphasis on government by law, rather than by men, Raz[2] recognises the need for the government of men as well as of laws and that the pursuit of social goals may require the enactment of both general *and particular* laws. Indeed, he suggests that it is actually inconceivable for law to consist solely of general rules. Raz claims that the basic requirement from which the wider idea of the rule of law emerges is the requirement that the law must be capable of guiding the individual's behaviour. On that basis, he lists some of the most important principles that may be derived from the general idea. These are as follows:

(a) laws should be prospective rather than retroactive, for the reason that people cannot be guided by and expected to obey laws which have not as yet been introduced. The laws should also be open and clear, in order to enable people to understand/guide their actions in line with them;

(b) laws should be relatively stable and should not be changed too frequently, as this might lead to confusion as to what actually is covered by the law;

(c) there should be clear rules and procedures for making laws;

(d) the independence of the judiciary has to be guaranteed, to ensure that it is free to decide cases in line with the law and not in response to any external pressure;

---

2   In addition to considering Dicey, Hayek and Raz, reference to the contemporary debate could be introduced by consideration of the views of Lord Bingham, which are discussed in Question 46.

(e)   the principles of natural justice should be observed, requiring an open and fair hearing to be given to all parties to proceedings;

(f)   the courts should have the power to review the way in which the other principles are implemented, to ensure that they are being operated as demanded by the rule of law;

(g)   the courts should be easily accessible, as they remain at the heart of the idea of making discretion subject to legal control;

(h)   the discretion of the crime prevention agencies should not be allowed to pervert the law.

Raz recognises the validity of, and the need to use, discretionary powers and particular goal-oriented legislation in contemporary society and, to that extent, he differs from both Dicey and Hayek. Yet, he also sees the rule of law as essentially a negative value, acting to minimise the danger that can be consequent upon the exercise, in an arbitrary manner, of such discretionary power. In seeking to control the exercise of discretion, he shares common ground with Dicey and Hayek.[3]

QUESTION 46

Assess Lord Bingham's contribution to the contemporary debate as to the meaning and content of the concept of 'the rule of law'.

How to Answer this Question

This question clearly requires the respondent to have a detailed knowledge of Lord Bingham's *Sir David Williams Lecture* on the rule of law, but as this is likely to form a central component of any English Legal System module dealing with the rule of law, the specific nature of the question is not unexpected.

A structure for answering the question would be as follows:

❖   introduce the concept with a brief reference to the context in which the lecture was delivered;

❖   deal with each of Lord Bingham's sub-rules in some detail, but being careful to précis the content so as to keep the answer within the necessary limitations of length;

❖   provide a critical analysis/commentary on each of the points made in the lecture;

❖   finish with a general conclusion as to the relevance and success of the lecture.

---

3   Don't underestimate the value of a conclusion which summarises your views and provides a brief answer to the specific question asked. (You may find it useful to re-read the question before beginning your conclusion.)

Answer Structure

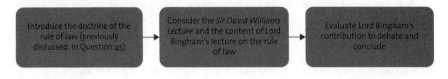

Introduce the doctrine of the rule of law (previously discussed in Question 45) → Consider the *Sir David Williams Lecture* and the content of Lord Bingham's lecture on the rule of law → Evaluate Lord Bingham's contribution to debate and conclude

ANSWER

The **Constitutional Reform Act 2005** provides, in **s 1**, that the Act does not adversely affect 'the existing constitutional principle of the rule of law'. That provision is further reflected in the oath to be taken by Lord Chancellors under **s 17(1)** of the Act, to respect the rule of law and defend the independence of the judiciary. However, as Lord Bingham has pointed out, the Act does not actually define what is meant by the rule of law, or indeed the Lord Chancellor's role in relation to it. Whilst he recognised the difficulty[4] in fixing a single meaning to the principle, citing various different academic references to it, Lord Bingham nonetheless felt it appropriate to offer his own understanding of the rule of law in the sixth *Sir David Williams Lecture* delivered at the Centre for Public Law at the University of Cambridge.

According to Lord Bingham, at the core of the concept of the rule of law is the idea that:

> all persons and authorities within the state, whether public or private, should be bound by and entitled to the benefit of laws publicly and prospectively promulgated and publicly administered in the courts.

However, the vital element is the detail that Lord Bingham introduces through his consideration of the eight implications, or sub-rules, that he holds are particular aspects of the general principle of the rule of law. These sub-rules are:

❖ *The law must be accessible and so far as possible intelligible, clear and predictable*

The reasoning behind this requirement is that if everyone is bound by the law they must be able without undue difficulty to find out what it is, even if that means taking advice from their lawyers. Equally the response should be sufficiently clear that a course of action can be based on it. However, for this to be achieved there has to be an end to what Lord Bingham refers to as the legislative hyperactivity which appears to have become a permanent feature of our governance. This excessive legislation, exacerbated by baffling parliamentary draftsmanship, is particularly problematic in relation to the 'torrent of criminal legislation', not all of which is 'readily intelligible'.[5]

---

4   As previously highlighted in the answer to Question 45.
5   This is a valuable example of the importance of not only providing relevant factual information but of also being prepared to evaluate the relevance and/or effect of that information – which is bound to impress an examiner!

❖ *Questions of legal right and liability should ordinarily be resolved [...] law and not the exercise of discretion*

Lord Bingham does not share Dicey's complete antipathy to the ex[...] and cites immigration law as an example where it has been advan[...] he does believe that the essential truth of Dicey's insight stands a[...]

> the broader and more loosely-textured a discretion is, *whether conferred on an official or a judge*, the greater the scope for subjectivity and hence for arbitrariness, which is the antithesis of the rule of law.

However, he is satisfied of the need for discretion to be narrowly defined, and its exercise to be capable of reasoned justification are requirements which UK law almost always satisfies.

❖ *The laws of the land should apply equally to all, save to the extent that objective differences justify differentiation*

However, if the law is to apply to all, then governments should also accept the converse, that the rule of law does not allow for any distinction between British nationals and others. Unfortunately, the second part of the reciprocal link did not appear to have been considered when parliament passed **Pt 4** of the **Anti-Terrorism, Crime and Security Act 2001**, which was held to be incompatible with the **Human Rights Act 1998** in the *Belmarsh* case (*A v Secretary of State for the Home Department* (2004)).[6]

❖ *The law must afford adequate protection of fundamental human rights*[7]

This sub-rule goes beyond the formalistic approaches of both Dicey and Raz to insist that the rule of law does in fact connote a substantive content, although Lord Bingham is less certain as to the particular detail of that content. However, he still maintains that:

> within a given state there will ordinarily be a measure of agreement on where the lines are to be drawn, and in the last resort (subject in this country to statute) the courts are there to draw them.

Consequently the rule of law must require the legal protection of such human rights as are recognised in that society.

❖ *Means must be provided for resolving, without prohibitive cost or inordinate delay, bona fide civil disputes which the parties themselves are unable to resolve*

....

6   This paragraph demonstrates the helpful use of specific legislation and case law in highlighting and/or strengthening argument.
7   As protection of human rights came to the fore following the end of WWII, it is a good example of the contemporary significance of the rule of law, as specifically highlighted in the question.

corollary of the principle that everyone is bound by and entitled to the benefit of the law is the requirement that people should be able, in the last resort, to go to court to have their rights and liabilities determined. In stating this sub-rule Lord Bingham makes it clear that he is not seeking to undermine arbitration, which he sees as supremely important, rather he is looking to support the provisions of a properly funded legal aid scheme,[8] the demise of which he clearly regrets, as may be seen from the following:

❖ *Ministers and public officers at all levels must exercise the powers conferred on them reasonably, in good faith, for the purpose for which the powers were conferred and without exceeding the limits of such powers*

As Lord Bingham saw it:

> The historic role of the courts has of course been to check excesses of executive power, a role greatly expanded in recent years due to the increased complexity of government and the greater willingness of the public to challenge governmental (in the broadest sense) decisions. Even under our constitution the separation of powers is crucial in guaranteeing the integrity of the courts' performance of this role.

This judicial role has of course been met through judicial review.

❖ *Adjudicative procedures provided by the state should be fair*

In Lord Bingham's view decisions must be taken by adjudicators who are:

> independent and impartial: independent in the sense that they are free to decide on the legal and factual merits of a case as they see it, free of any extraneous influence or pressure, and impartial in the sense that they are, so far as humanly possible, open-minded, unbiased by any personal interest or partisan allegiance of any kind.

However, a second element is involved, which relates to the presumption that any issue should not be finally decided against a person until they have had an adequate opportunity for their response to the allegation to be heard. In effect this means that:

> a person potentially subject to any liability or penalty should be adequately informed of what is said against him; that the accuser should make adequate disclosure of material helpful to the other party or damaging to itself; that where the interests of a party cannot be adequately protected without the benefit of professional help which the party cannot afford, public assistance

---

8   Further reference to the contemporary significance of the rule of law.

should so far as practicable be afforded; that a party accused should have an adequate opportunity to prepare his answer to what is said against him; and that the innocence of a defendant charged with criminal conduct should be presumed until guilt is proved.

❖ *The existing principle of the rule of law requires compliance by the state with its obligations in international law*

This particular section of Lord Bingham's lecture is interesting for the indirect way in which he examined the involvement of the UK in the ongoing war in Iraq whilst, as he said:

> not for obvious reasons touch[ing] on the vexed question whether Britain's involvement in the 2003 war on Iraq was in breach of international law and thus, if this sub-rule is sound, of the rule of law.

The way he achieved this was through a comparison between the procedures followed in 2003 and those followed at the time of the Suez invasion of 1956. Whilst he concluded that the comparison suggests that over the period the rule of law has gained ground in the UK it also allowed him to make some pointed comments in relation to the way the current war was initiated.

In conclusion, Lord Bingham correlated the rule of law with a democratic society based on[9]

> an unspoken but fundamental bargain between the individual and the state, the governed and the governor, by which both sacrifice a measure of the freedom and power which they would otherwise enjoy. The individual living in society implicitly accepts that he or she cannot exercise the unbridled freedom enjoyed by Adam in the Garden of Eden, before the creation of Eve, and accepts the constraints imposed by laws properly made because of the benefits which, on balance, they confer. The state for its part accepts that it may not do, at home or abroad, all that it has the power to do but only that which laws binding upon it authorise it to do. If correct, this conclusion is reassuring to all of us who, in any capacity, devote our professional lives to the service of the law. For it means that we are not, as we are sometimes seen, mere custodians of a body of arid prescriptive rules but are, with others, the guardians of an all but sacred flame which animates and enlightens the society in which we live.

....

9   Very relevant conclusion, which allows Lord Bingham himself to summarise the contemporary debate on the significance of the rule of law. (In an examination, you may find it difficult to provide a verbatim quote: don't be afraid to paraphrase but ensure that you make it clear whether you are providing a quote or paraphrasing.)

QUESTION 47

In relation to the **European Convention of Human Rights** and the European Court of Human Rights explain the following concepts

(i)   derogation;
(ii) margin of appreciation;
(iii) proportionality;
(iv) the convention as a living text.

How to Answer this Question

Answer Structure

Introduction providing a brief overview of the Council of Europe, the **Convention** and Court of Human Rights and their influence in the UK → Discussion on each specific issue listed in the question

ANSWER

(i) *Derogation*

The rights listed in the **European Convention on Human Rights** are not all treated in the same way. Some rights are absolute and inalienable and cannot be interfered with by the signatory state to the **Convention**. Others rights, however, are merely contingent and are subject to derogation. This means that, in particular circumstances and to a limited and controlled degree, states can effectively opt out of those provisions they do not wish to comply with. For example and in particular, the UK **Humans Right Act**,[10] which implements the **ECHR**, provides that **Arts 8, 9, 10** and **11** are subject to legal restrictions such as are:

> . . . necessary in a democratic society in the interests of national security or public safety, for the prevention of crime, for the protection of health or morals or the protection of the rights and freedoms of others [**Art 11(2)**].

The UK entered such a derogation in relation to the extended detention of terrorist suspects without charge, under the **Prevention of Terrorism (Temporary Provisions) Act 1989**, subsequently replaced and extended by the **Terrorism Act 2000**. Those powers had been held to be contrary to **Art 5** of the **Convention** by the ECtHR in *Brogan v UK* (1989).

---

10 Wherever possible, refer to legal authority in support of argument and to provide examples.

The UK also entered a derogation with regard to the **Anti-Terrorism, Crime and Security Act 2001**, which was enacted in response to the attack on the World Trade Center building in New York on 11 September of that year. The Act allowed for the detention without trial of foreign citizens suspected of being involved in terrorist activity.

In deciding the legality of any derogation, courts are required not just to be convinced that there is a need for the derogation, but they must also be sure that the state's action has been proportionate to that need. In other words, the state must not overreact to a perceived problem by removing more rights than is necessary to effect the solution.

(ii) *The Margin of Appreciation*

This refers to the fact that the ECtHR recognises that there may well be a range of responses to particular crises or social situations within individual states, which might well involve some legitimate limitation on the rights established under the **ECHR**. The Court recognises that in such areas, the response should be decided at the local level, rather than being imposed centrally. The most obvious, but by no means the only, situations that involve the recognition of the margin of appreciation are the fields of morality and state security. For example, *Wingrove v UK* (1997)[11] concerned the refusal of the British Board of Film Classification to give a certificate of classification to the video film, *Visions of Ecstasy*, on the grounds that it was blasphemous, thus effectively banning it. The applicant, the director of the film, claimed that the refusal to grant a certificate of classification to the film amounted to a breach of his rights to free speech under **Art 10** of the **ECHR**. The Court rejected his claim, holding that the offence of blasphemy, by its very nature, did not lend itself to precise legal definition. Consequently, national authorities 'must be afforded a degree of flexibility in assessing whether the facts of a particular case fall within the accepted definition of the offence'. In reaching its decision, the Court clearly set out how the doctrine was to operate and its justifications. It also explained the different ranges of the margin of appreciation that will be allowed in different areas. Thus:

> Whereas there is little scope under **Article 10, para 2** of the **Convention (Art 10(2))** for restrictions on political speech or on debate of questions of public interest a wider margin of appreciation is generally available to the Contracting States when regulating freedom of expression in relation to matters liable to offend intimate personal convictions within the sphere of morals or, especially, religion. Moreover, as in the field of morals, and perhaps to an even greater degree, there is no uniform European conception of the requirements of 'the protection of the rights of others' in relation to attacks on their religious convictions. What is likely to cause substantial offence to persons of a particular religious persuasion will vary significantly from time to time and from place to place, especially in an era characterised by an ever growing array of faiths and denominations. By reason of their direct and continuous

---

11   Again the use of a relevant example can demonstrate understanding and aid explanation.

contact with the vital forces of their countries, State authorities are in principle in a better position than the international judge to give an opinion on the exact content of these requirements with regard to the rights of others as well as on the 'necessity' of a 'restriction' intended to protect from such material those whose deepest feelings and convictions would be seriously offended.

In *Civil Service Unions v UK* (1988), it was held that national security interests were of such paramount concern that they outweighed individual rights of freedom of association. Hence, the unions had no remedy under the **ECHR** for the removal of their members' rights to join and be in a trade union.

It should also be borne in mind that states can enter a derogation from particular provisions of the **ECHR**, or the way in which they operate in particular areas or circumstances. The UK entered such derogation in relation to the extended detention of terrorist suspects without charge under the **Prevention of Terrorism (Temporary Provisions) Act 1989**, subsequently replaced and extended by the **Terrorism Act 2000**. Those powers had been held to be contrary to **Art 5** of the **ECHR** by the ECtHR in *Brogan v UK* (1989). The UK also entered a derogation in relation to the **Anti-Terrorism, Crime and Security Act 2001**, which was enacted in response to the attack on the World Trade Center in New York on 11 September of that year. The Act allows for the detention without trial of foreign citizens suspected of being involved in terrorist activities (see *A v Secretary of State for the Home Department* (2002)).

One point to note in relation to the operation of the margin of appreciation is that, by definition, it is a rule of international law, in that it recognises the different approaches of distinct states. Consequently, it is limited in operation to the supranational ECtHR and not to national courts. The latter may follow precedents based on the doctrine, but it is difficult to see how they could themselves apply it in a national context, although it would appear that the domestic courts' development of the doctrine of deference achieves similar ends to those allowed under the margin of appreciation.

(iii) *Proportionality*

Even where states avail themselves of the margin of appreciation, they are not at liberty to interfere with rights to any degree beyond what is required, as a minimum, to deal with the perceived problem within the context of a democratic society. In other words, there must be a relationship of necessity between the end desired and the means used to achieve it.

As the ECtHR stated in *Chorherr v Austria* (1994):

The margin of appreciation extends in particular to the choice of the reasonable and appropriate means to be used by the authority to ensure that lawful manifestation can take place peacefully.

Proportionality may also be considered in relation to judicial review, where it has been suggested that it might infiltrate the English legal. However, in relation to the **HRA**, proportionality is central to the jurisprudence of the ECtHR and as such is now central to the jurisprudence of the UK courts in relation to human rights issues. It is suggested that it will not be restricted to this limited sphere for long and that it will expand into judicial review and other areas as the **HRA** becomes increasingly understood and used.

(iv) *The living instrument*

It also has to be recognised that the **ECHR** as a legal document is not fixed text. As Luzius Wildhaber, the former president of the Court, stated:

> On the question of evolutive interpretation, it is precisely the genius of the **Convention** that it is indeed a dynamic and a living instrument, which has shown its capacity to evolve in the light of social and technological developments that its drafters, however far sighted, could never have imagined. The **Convention** has shown that it is capable of growing with society; and in this respect its formulations have proved their worth over five decades. It has remained a live and modern instrument.

The 'living instrument' doctrine is one of the best known principles of Strasbourg case law, the principle that the **Convention** is interpreted 'in the light of present day conditions', that it evolves, through the interpretation of the Court.

The recognition of this approach may be seen in the Court's legal recognition of transsexuals' new sexual identity in *Goodwin v UK* (2002). Until that decision, the Court had found that there was no positive obligation for the states to modify their civil status systems so as to have the register of births updated or annotated to record changed sexual identity. However, in *Goodwin*, the Court finally reached the conclusion that the fair balance now favoured the recognition of such rights, and ruled accordingly.

QUESTION 48

Consider the development of judicial review in the light of the judiciary's attempt to control the exercise of administrative discretion, and assess the likely impact of the **Human Rights Act (HRA) 1998** on this process.

How to Answer this Question

This is a much more subtle and searching question than the previous one. It requires a consideration of modern forms of law, the rule of law, the constitutional role of the judiciary, as well as a knowledge of the procedure for judicial review. Consideration of the following will cover the above points well:

- ❖ the development of administrative law;
- ❖ the tension between the exercise of discretionary power and the rule of law;
- ❖ judicial review as the courts' means of curtailing abuse of discretion;
- ❖ the grounds for judicial review;
- ❖ the possibility of the doctrine of 'proportionality' as the means of extending judicial review in the area of substantive administrative decisions;
- ❖ judges' competence to make policy decisions;
- ❖ the constitutional situation of the judiciary.

Answer Structure

Introduction briefly explaining the function of Judicial Review → Consideration of the increased role of the state, the rule of law and the use of Judicial Review → Discussion of the **Human Rights Act** and conclusion as to its impact

ANSWER

According to AV Dicey, in *Law of the Constitution*, published in 1885, the UK knew no such thing as administrative law as distinct from ordinary law. In Dicey's exposition, it was essential that all activities be open to the ordinary law of the land for the maintenance of the rule of law. Whether or not he was correct when he expressed this opinion, and there are substantial grounds for doubting the accuracy of his claim even at the time he made it, it can no longer be denied that there is now a large area of law that can be properly called administrative, that is, related to the pursuit and application of particular policies, usually within a framework of statutory powers, although the powers under question may be derived from the common law. The lack of a more precise definition reflects the extent to which the state and state-appointed bodies intervene in contemporary life and the multiplicity of areas in which they act. It is certainly true that the twentieth century saw a large scale increase in the power of the state – both central and local – and its various functionaries and appointed bodies to intervene in the day-to-day lives of its citizens.[12] The question that arises is whether such activity is subject to judicial control and, if it is, how such control is to be exercised.

Dicey described the concept of the rule of law as one of the two fundamental elements of the English polity, the other being Parliamentary sovereignty, or, in other words, the undisputed supremacy of central government. The former was aimed at controlling arbitrary power, but the latter could, within this constitutional structure, make provision for the granting of such arbitrary power by passing appropriate legislation. The historical

---

12 An important point, as the increasing intervention of the state in the lives of the citizen has highlighted an increased need to control the powers of public bodies.

reality is that in the course of the twentieth century, with the emergence and development of the interventionist welfare state, the Government increasingly took over the regulation of many areas of social activity and delegated wide-ranging discretionary powers to various people and bodies, in order to implement its policies and to deal with particular problems as they arose. It has been suggested by some that in fact, the rule of law has been reduced to a matter of procedure, to the mere requirement that legislation be passed in the prescribed manner and that the most arbitrary of party political decisions can, thus, be readily cloaked with legality.[13]

Dicey did not resolve the potential conflict between the rule of law, as represented by the decisions of the ordinary courts of the land, and the sovereignty of Parliament, nor can it be claimed, as yet, that such tensions have been resolved. Indeed, it might be argued that the tension between the two principles has not only continued, but has intensified with the growth in state activity. There are significant indications that the higher judiciary may well be attempting to reassert at least a measure of control over the executive, but, if this is the case, it is not, in itself, unproblematic and has important constitutional implications for the UK. The importance of this process was not lost on the former Master of the Rolls, Sir Thomas Bingham, who described it in an interview (*The Observer*, 9 May 1993) as follows:

> Slowly, the constitutional balance is tilting towards the judiciary. The courts have reacted to the increase in powers claimed by the Government by being more active themselves.

Judicial review may be seen as one of the ways in which the courts have attempted to maintain a measure of control over such activity, in an endeavour to reassert the dominance of the rule of law ideal. Of all areas of law, judicial review is the one in which most growth was apparent, before the enactment of the **Human Rights Act 1998**, as can be seen from the fact that in 1980, there were only 525 applications for judicial review, but in 2007, there were 6,690 such applications, more than a twelvefold increase in 27 years.[14]

Judicial review may be seen, therefore, as the means to curtail the power of the executive and as a counter to the use of discretionary forms of regulation. The grounds of application can be considered under two traditional heads: *procedural ultra vires* and *substantive ultra vires*. Procedural *ultra vires*, as its name suggests, relates to the failure of a person, or body provided with specific authority, to follow the procedure established for using that power, or to follow the requirements of natural law. Substantive *ultra vires*

....

13 Such discussion demonstrates an understanding of the subtleties of state power.
14 Demonstrate your research skills and an ability to stay up-to-date by adding contemporary references and statistics where possible.

occurs where someone does something that is not actually authorised by the enabling legislation, and its most interesting area of operation relates to areas where it is sought to challenge the substance of a decision.

In *Associated Provincial Picture House v Wednesbury Corp* (1947),[15] which concerned a local authority's decision to impose a condition on a licensing of a cinema, Lord Greene MR established the possibility of discretionary decisions being challenged on the basis of their being unreasonable. As Lord Greene pointed out:

> ... the decision of the local authority can be upset if it is proved to be unreasonable in the sense that the court considers it to be a decision *that no reasonable body could have come to.*

Lord Greene's approach was endorsed and refined by Lord Diplock in *Council of Civil Service Unions v Minister for the Civil Service (the GCHQ case)* (1984), where he established the three grounds for judicial review to be:

(a) illegality;
(b) irrationality; and
(c) procedural impropriety.

In delivering his judgment, however, Lord Diplock, intriguingly, introduced the possibility of a much wider-ranging reason for challenging administrative decisions. The additional ground for applying for judicial review was based on the doctrine of 'proportionality', which looks at the substance of a decision, rather than simply the way in which it is reached.

The applicability of the concept of proportionality was at least uncertain under judicial review, but it has been given direct relevance under the **HRA 1998**. Under that Act, the courts have been given the power to intervene in situations where public authorities have acted in such a way as to breach any of the rights provided to individuals under the **European Convention on Human Rights**. However, not all the rights provided under the HRA are absolute, and in some situations the state can interfere with them, as long as it acts in a proportionate manner. In other words, the courts are given the power to decide whether the state has taken more action than is necessary to deal with a particular problem. Thus, the doctrine of proportionality requires the courts to engage in what are essentially political decisions. Similarly, under the **HRA**, the courts have the power to declare secondary legislation, such as statutory instruments, invalid and although they cannot exercise the same power with regard to primary legislation, they can make a declaration that such legislation is incompatible with the **European Convention**. Once

---

15 Such discussion demonstrates the development of judicial review.

again, this can be seen as introducing the judiciary into the political arena in a much more direct way than was possible under the restricted approach of judicial review.[16]

The increased participation of the judiciary in the socio-political arena raises a number of important issues.

First, there is the question of the competency of the judiciary to overrule substantive decisions. Judges are experts in law; they are not expert in the questions of policy that come before them in the guise of legal cases. They may disagree with particular decisions, but it has to be, at least, doubted that they are qualified to take such policy decisions. A classic example of this arises from the infamous 'fares fair' case, *Bromley LBC v GLC* (1982), in which the courts held that a policy to subsidise transport within London was not legal. When an amended scheme came before the court in *London Transport Executive ex p GLC* (1983), it was decided that the Greater London Council could instruct the London Transport Authority to implement policies that would effectively reduce its revenues. Thus, the courts could reject schemes, but could not replace them with other ones.

There is also the wider question that in interfering with substantive decisions, the judiciary involves itself in political matters and, therefore, exceeds its constitutional powers. It has to be remembered that judges are unelected and unaccountable. The question as to their suitability to take such essentially political decisions cannot but be brought into question. As Farquharson LJ commented in *The Observer* interview:

> We have to be very careful: the executive is elected. We have a role in the constitution, but if we go too far, there will be a reaction.

In conclusion,[17] if judicial review has firmly placed the judiciary in the political arena, the introduction of the **HRA 1998** can only increase that process of overt politicisation, in that it expressly gives judges the duty and power to protect individuals' rights from attack from public authorities. The question that remains to be answered, especially in the light of criticisms directed at the conservative nature of the judiciary, levelled by some commentators on the political left, is whether the judiciary are the right people to be given such power.

QUESTION 49
Explain the background and content of the **Human Rights Act (HRA) 1998**.

---

16 This paragraph provides clear evidence of how Judicial review and human rights are linked.
17 Note that Question 49 also contains insights on human rights which may be relevant in answering this question.

How to Answer this Question

This question asks candidates to provide a brief consideration of the incorporation of the **European Convention on Human Rights (ECHR)** into UK law, through the mechanism of the **HRA 1998**. It requires a basic knowledge of the content and effect of the **HRA 1998**. The following points should be covered:

❖   explain what the **ECHR** is;
❖   explain the disadvantages of the UK's relationship to the **Convention** prior to the **HRA 1998;**
❖   list the various Articles that have been incorporated by the Act;
❖   consider the effect of the Act on public bodies;
❖   explain what is meant by a declaration of compatibility in relation to legislation;
❖   assess the role of the courts in relation to the Act;
❖   explain fast-track remedial action for legislation that is found to be incompatible.

Answer Structure

Introduction to the Council of Europe, the ECHR and its aims → Consideration of the pre-HRA impact of the ECHR in the UK → Discussion on the content of the HRA and its impact

ANSWER

The UK was one of the initial signatories to the **European Convention on Human Rights (ECHR)** in 1950, which was created in post-war Europe as a means of establishing and enforcing essential human rights. In 1966, the UK recognised the power of the European Commission on Human Rights to hear complaints from individual UK citizens and, at the same time, recognised the authority of the European Court of Human Rights to adjudicate in such matters. It did not, however, at that time incorporate the **ECHR** into UK law.

The consequence of non-incorporation was that the **Convention** could not be directly enforced in English courts. In *R v Secretary of State for the Home Department ex p Brind* (1991), the Court of Appeal decided that ministerial directives did not have to be construed in line with the **ECHR**, as that would be tantamount to introducing the **Convention** into English law without the necessary legislation. UK citizens were therefore in the position of having to pursue rights, which the state endorsed, in an external forum, rather than through their own court system and, in addition, having to exhaust the domestic judicial procedure before they could gain access to that external forum. Such a situation was expensive, time consuming and extremely unsatisfactory, and not just for complainants under the **Convention**. Many members of the judiciary, including the former Lord Chief Justice, Lord Bingham, were in favour of incorporation, not merely on general moral grounds, but equally on the ground that they resented having to make decisions in line with UK law which they knew full well would be overturned on appeal to the European Court. Equally, there was some discontent that the decisions in the European Court were being taken, and its general jurisprudence was being developed, without the direct input of the UK legal system.[18]

The **HRA 1998** corrected this anomalous situation by incorporating the rights enshrined in the **ECHR**, together with the protocols to it, into UK law. The Act received Royal Assent on 9 November 1998, but was only brought fully into force on 2 October 2000. The reason for the delay was so that the courts, from the magistrates all the way up to the House of Lords, could be adequately trained in the consequences of the Act.

The rights incorporated are listed in **Sched 1** to the Act, and cover the following matters:[19]

❖ a general commitment to human rights (**Art 1**);
❖ right to life (**Art 2**);
❖ freedom from torture and inhuman or degrading treatment or punishment (**Art 3**);
❖ freedom from slavery and forced or compulsory labour (**Art 4**);
❖ right to liberty and security of person (subject to a derogation applicable to Northern Ireland) (**Art 5**);
❖ right to a fair and public trial within a reasonable time (**Art 6**);
❖ freedom from retrospective criminal law and no punishment without law (**Art 7**);
❖ right to respect for private and family life, home and correspondence (**Art 8**);
❖ freedom of thought, conscience and religion (**Art 9**);
❖ freedom of expression (**Art 10**);
❖ freedom of assembly and association (**Art 11**);
❖ right to marry and found a family (**Art 12**);
❖ prohibition of discrimination in the enjoyment of the **Convention** rights (**Art 14**);
❖ right to peaceful enjoyment of possessions and protection of property (**Art 1, Protocol 1**);
❖ right to education (subject to a UK reservation) (**Art 2, Protocol 1**);
❖ right to free elections (**Art 3, Protocol 1**);
❖ right not to be subjected to the death penalty (**Arts 1** and **2, Protocol 6**).

The above rights can be relied on by any person, non-governmental organisation or group of individuals. Importantly, it also applies where appropriate to companies which are incorporated entities and, hence, legal persons and other bodies. It cannot be relied on by governmental organisations, such as local authorities.

....

18 Sets out the original impact of the **ECHR** in the UK and the problems associated with non-incorporation.
19 Don't panic if you can't remember all of the rights contained within the legislation. Examples of the most important would be acceptable.

The general list of rights are not all seen in the same way. Some are absolute and inalienable and cannot be interfered with by the state, or, at least, only to a limited and tightly circumscribed degree. Others are merely contingent and are subject to derogation, that is, signatory states can opt out of them in particular circumstances. The absolute rights are those provided for in **Arts 2, 3, 4, 7** and **14.** All the others are subject to potential limitations; and, in particular, the rights provided for under **Arts 8, 9, 10** and **11** are subject to legal restrictions, such as are:

> . . . necessary in a democratic society in the interests of national security or public safety, for the prevention of crime, for the protection of health or morals or the protection of the rights and freedoms of others [**Art 11(2)**].

In deciding the legality of any derogation, courts are required not just to be convinced that there is a need for the derogation, but they must also be sure that the state's action has been proportionate to that need. In other words, the state must not overreact to a perceived problem by removing more rights than is necessary to effect the solution. With further regard to the possibility of derogation, **s 19** of the Act requires a minister, responsible for the passage of any Bill through Parliament, either to make a written declaration that it is compatible with the **Convention** or, alternatively, to declare that although it may not be compatible, it is still the Government's wish to proceed with it.

The **HRA 1998** has profound implications for the operation of the English legal system.[20] **Section 2** of the Act requires future courts to take into account any previous decision of the European Court of Human Rights. It was at first thought that this provision would have a major impact on the operation of the doctrine of precedent within the English legal system, as it was thought effectively to sanction the overruling of any previous English authority that was in conflict with a decision of the European Court of Human Rights. However, in *Price v Leeds City* (2006) the House of Lords distinguished between decisions of the European Court of Justice and those of the European Court of Human Rights: the former are binding, while the latter are not.[21] As Lord Bingham put it:

> The mandatory duty imposed on domestic courts by **s 2** of the **1998 Act** is to take into account any judgment of the Strasbourg Court and any opinion of the Commission. Thus they are not strictly required to follow Strasbourg rulings, as they are bound by **s 3(1)** of the **European Communities Act 1972** and as they are bound by the rulings of superior courts in the domestic curial hierarchy.

---

20 Although the question does not specifically ask for discussion of the impact of the **HRA**, it is implicit that consideration of its effect should be provided.

21 This distinction in very important. Students often confuse the **ECHR** with the law of the EU and, although the EU recognise and apply principles contained in the **Convention**, demonstrating that you understand the difference can only impress.

As a consequence the House of Lords decided that the normal rules of precedent should apply, and lower courts should follow the House of Lords, even when their decisions have been overturned by the ECtHR. This does not apply, however, where the previous authority had been set without reference to the **Human Rights Act**.

Also, **s 3**, requiring all legislation to be read so far as possible to give effect to the rights provided under the Convention, has the potential to invalidate previously accepted interpretations of statutes which were made, by necessity, without recourse to the Convention. Thus, in *Mendoza v Ghaidan* (2002), the Court of Appeal used **s 3** to extend the rights of same-sex partners to inherit a statutory tenancy under the **Rent Act 1977**. In *Fitzpatrick v Sterling Housing Association Ltd* (1999), the House of Lords had extended the rights of such individuals to inherit the lesser assured tenancy by including them within the deceased person's family. However, it declined to allow them to inherit statutory tenancies, on the grounds that they could not be considered to be the wife or husband of the deceased as the Act required. In *Mendoza*, the Court of Appeal held that the **Rent Act**, as it had been construed by the House of Lords in *Fitzpatrick*, was incompatible with **Art 14** of the **ECHR** on the grounds of its discriminatory treatment of surviving same-sex partners. The court, however, decided that the failing could be remedied by reading the words 'as his or her wife or husband' in the Act as meaning 'as if they were his or her wife or husband'. The Court of Appeal's decision and reasoning was subsequently confirmed by the House of Lords in 2004.

Section 6 declares it unlawful for any public authority to act in a way which is incompatible with the Convention, and **s 7** allows the 'victim of the unlawful act' to bring proceedings against the public authority in breach. **Section 8** empowers the court to grant such relief or remedy against the public authority in breach of the Act, as it considers just and appropriate. However, where a public authority is acting under the instructions of some primary legislation, which is itself incompatible with the **Convention**, the public authority will not be liable under **s 6**.

It can be seen that the Act reflects a move towards the entrenchment of rights recognised under the **Convention**, but the Act expressly states that the courts cannot invalidate any primary legislation, essentially Acts of Parliament, which are found to be incompatible with the **Convention**. The courts can only make a declaration of such incompatibility and leave it to the legislature to remedy the situation through new legislation (**s 4**). The Act requires that the Crown be given notice of a case where a declaration might be given, and the Crown is given a right to intervene in the case. This will enable the Crown to argue that the provision can be interpreted compatibly with the **Convention** rights. It also ensures that the Crown is in a position to respond quickly where a declaration of incompatibility is made. In this respect, the Act provides for the provision of remedial legislation through a fast-track procedure. This fast-track procedure gives a minister of the Crown the power to alter primary legislation by way of statutory instrument. This power is also available to implement judgments of the Strasbourg Court against the UK which are made after the coming into force of the **HRA 1998**. It is also available in urgent cases, where subordinate legislation has been quashed or declared invalid.

QUESTION 50

Assess the impact of the **Human Rights Act (HRA) 1998** on the separation of powers.

How to Answer this Question

This question requires an examination of the way in which the courts have made use of the powers extended to them under the **HRA 1998** within the context of the separation of power, which should briefly be explained at the outset. Although many other cases and examples could be used to answer the question, the suggested answer focuses on the specific area of anti-terrorist legislation, which has highlighted the issue most clearly.

A possible structure could take the following form:

- ❖ briefly explain what is meant by the separation of powers;
- ❖ set out the courts' powers under the **HRA 1998**, making specific reference to the duty under **s 3** to interpret legislation in line with the **European Convention on Human Rights (ECHR)**, and **s 4** declarations of incompatibility;
- ❖ consider the doctrine of proportionality;
- ❖ consider case examples where the courts have made use of these powers;
- ❖ conclude with an assessment of the effect of the provisions in the **HRA 1998**.

Answer Structure

Introduction outlining the doctrine of the separation of powers → Overview of the content of the HRA and discussion of its impact on the doctrine, in particular its effect on the roles of the judiciary, executive and legislators → Conclusion summarising impact of the HRA

ANSWER

Although the idea of the separation of powers can be traced back to ancient Greek philosophy, it was advocated in early modern times by the English philosopher Locke and the later French philosopher Montesquieu, and found its practical expression in the constitution of the US. The idea of the separation of powers is posited on the existence of three distinct functions of government (the legislative, executive and judicial functions) and the conviction that these functions should be kept apart in order to prevent the centralisation of too much power (essentially a system of checks and balances). Establishing the appropriate relationship between the actions of the state and the legal control over those actions crucially involves a consideration of whether there is any absolute limit on the authority of the Government of the day.[22] Answering that question inevitably involves an examination of the general constitutional structure of the UK and, in particular, the inter-relationship of two doctrines: parliamentary sovereignty and judicial independence, in that although the courts have always operated free from direct interference from either parliament or the Government, nonetheless it has always retained the right to make such laws as it considers fit, without limit and without the interference of the courts. However, it is at least arguable that this historical relationship has been altered by the implementation of **HRA 1998**, which has caused no little friction between the judiciary and the executive, but which has also increased the powers of the courts *vis à vis* the legislature.

Section 3 of the **HRA** requires all legislation to be read so far as possible to give effect to the rights provided under the **Convention**. This section provides the courts with new and extended powers of interpretation. Where a court cannot interpret a piece of primary legislation in such a way as to make it compatible with the **Convention**, it cannot declare the legislation invalid but, under **HRA s 4**, it can make a declaration that the legislation in question is not compatible with the rights provided by the **Convention**. In deciding whether or not a piece of legislation is compatible with the **ECHR** the courts will assess whether or not it represents a proportionate response to the particular problem that it is intended to address. Without doubt the clearest and sharpest conflict between the judiciary and the executive and Parliament, in relation to the powers given to the courts under the **HRA 1998**, has arisen in connection with anti-terrorist legislation and the treatment of those suspected by the authorities of being terrorists. This conflict highlights not only the tensions between these branches of the constitution but also the way in which the courts will use the powers previously mentioned under the **HRA 1998** and their willingness to use those powers in the face of political opposition.

ANTI-TERRORISM, CRIME AND SECURITY ACT 2001[23]

Following the terrorist attack on the World Trade Center on 11 September 2001, the UK Parliament introduced the **Anti-Terrorism, Crime and Security Act (ACSA) 2001**. This Act allowed for the detention, without charge, of non-UK citizens suspected of terrorist activities, but who could not be repatriated to their own countries because of fear for their well-being.

Under **s 21(1)**, the Home Secretary was given the power to issue a detention certificate in respect of a person if he reasonably:

....

22 Helpful discussion which not only sets our the doctrine of the separation of powers but also demonstrates understanding by the provision of an explanation of the role it fulfils.

23 The provision of an example such as **ACSA** demonstrates not only knowledge but also assists in providing a clear illustration of the impact of the **HRA** on the separation of powers.

(a)   believes that person's presence in the UK is a risk to national security; and

(b)   suspects that the person is a terrorist.

While a person who would otherwise be detained was free to leave the UK, the Act provided that a person certificated as a suspected international terrorist under s 21 might be detained in circumstances where their safe removal or departure from the UK was not practical (s 23(1)). Such a provision was clearly contrary to Art 5 of the ECHR. Consequently, the Government was required to enter a derogation from the **Convention** by virtue of the **Human Rights Act 1998 (Designated Derogation) Order 2001**, the justification for the derogation being that the prospect of terrorism following 11 September 2001 threatened the life of the nation. As a result of the **HRA 1998** and the limited derogation, the Home Secretary's power under the **ACSA 2001** could only be exercised in relation to individuals who were suspected of being a risk to national security because of their connection to the public emergency cited in the derogation – namely the threat posed by Al Qa'ida and its associated networks. Consequently, it was not enough that the detained person might have had connections with a terrorist organisation. It must be a terrorist organisation that had links with Al Qa'ida.

In July 2002, the Special Immigration Appeals Commission, SIAC, held that the **ACSA 2001** was not in compliance with the anti-discriminatory provisions of **Art 14** of the **ECHR**, to the extent that it treated non-nationals differently from UK nationals. When the case eventually came before the House of Lords (*A & Ors v Secretary of State for the Home Department* (2004)), it resulted in a crushing judgment against the Act, the Court holding, by a majority of eight to one, that the **ACSA 2001** was incompatible with the provisions of the **ECHR**. Although the House of Lords recognised the deference due to the Government and Parliament and accepted that the Government had been entitled to conclude that there was a public emergency, it nonetheless concluded that the response to the perceived threat had been disproportionate and incompatible with the rights under the **ECHR**. It held that the prohibition on grounds of nationality or immigration status under **Art 14** had not been the subject of derogation. Further, it held that the decision to detain one group of suspected international terrorists, defined by nationality or immigration status, and not another, could not be justified, and violated **Art 14** of the **ECHR**. The House of Lords also held that ss 21 and 23 of the Act were disproportionate for the general reason that the provisions did not rationally address the threat to the security of the UK presented by Al Qa'ida terrorists and that consequently s 23 of the **ACSA 2001** was incompatible with **Arts 5** and **14** of the **ECHR**. The House of Lords appropriately quashed the derogation order, as it was secondary rather than primary legislation.

PREVENTION OF TERRORISM ACT (PTA) 2005

This Act, which replaced the **ACSA 2001**, dealt with one of the shortcomings of the earlier Act by widening the provisions of the previous legislation to control all terrorist-related activity, *irrespective of nationality* and replaced the detention without trial regime under the **ACSA 2001** with a new system of 'control orders'. These control orders were to be of two distinct types: derogating and non-derogating, in relation to the **ECHR**.

Derogating control orders require derogation from **ECHR** because they deprive the person affected of their liberty by requiring them to remain in a particular place at all times. It is equivalent to house arrest and consequently it clearly infringes the person's rights under **Art 5** of the **ECHR**. Non-derogating control orders, however, allow the Home Secretary to impose a range of controls over people's activities, such as the imposition of curfews and the use of tagging for the purposes of monitoring those curfews. They also allow for the restriction and control of the movement of the individuals concerned, or restrictions on association with other named individuals. They also provide for the possibility of a ban on the use of mobile phones or the Internet. The Government claimed that, even if the non-derogational control orders affected other **Convention** rights, such as the right to private and family life (**Art 8**), the right to freedom of expression (**Art 10**), or the right to freedom of association (**Art 11**), as they very well might, nonetheless they would not require derogation because they did not engage the right to liberty (**Art 5**).

The **PTA 2005** retains the role of the *special advocate*, who is expected to support the interests of the suspect in regard to material to which neither the accused nor his chosen legal representatives is allowed access.

The legal effect of non-derogation control orders issued under the **PTA 2005** was considered by the House of Lords in four related appeals, the decisions in which were delivered in three judgments at the end of October 2007.

In the first (*Secretary of State for the Home Department v JJ and others* (2007)) the majority of the House of Lords held that a control order imposing an 18-hour curfew amounted to a deprivation of liberty contrary to **Art 5**. Subsequently, in *Secretary of State for the Home Department v MB & AF* (2007) the House of Lords unanimously held that a curfew of 14 hours did not amount to a deprivation of liberty. However, the majority also held that the reliance on undisclosed material could not be supported in cases where the accused had no possibility of responding to allegations charged against them, and that the special advocate system did not validate such a system. Rather than issue a declaration of incompatibility the majority preferred to interpret the provisions of the **PTA 2005** to ensure the provision of a fair trial, but in complete contradiction to the actual wording of the Act.

Whether one approves of the House of Lords' decisions in the above cases probably depends on one's political perspective, and that is specifically the point, for it emphasises that the judges were engaged in taking essentially political decisions. In using their powers under the **HRA 1998**, it is arguable that the House of Lords did not just subvert the policy of the executive, but rewrote the express provisions of parliament. In doing so it is also arguable that they may have overstepped their limited role within the UK constitution. Such a possibility was not lost on Lord Bingham who, in *A v SSHD* (2004), justified the courts' new status thus:

> ... Parliament has expressly legislated in **section 6** of the **1998 Act** to render unlawful any act of a public authority, including a court, incompatible with a Convention right, has required courts (in **section 2**) to take account of relevant Strasbourg jurisprudence, has (in **section 3**) required courts, so far as possible, to give effect to **Convention** rights and has conferred a right of appeal on derogation issues. The effect is not, of course, to override the sovereign legislative authority of the Queen in Parliament, since if primary legislation is declared to be incompatible the validity of the legislation is unaffected (**section 4(6)**) and the remedy lies with the appropriate minister (**section 10**), who is answerable to Parliament. The **1998 Act** gives the courts a very specific, wholly democratic, mandate.

Index

Abraham, Ann 228

advocates: advice given under pressure
212; basic issues 206; cab rank rule 208;
collateral challenge 209–12; divided
loyalty 208; duty of care 206–7; negligence
68, 206–12; solicitors as 187; witness
analogy 209

alternative dispute resolution 218–19;
basic issues 219, 232–3, 238; conciliation
241–2; cost awards 243; mediation 241;
recommendation to use 242–3; small
claims 240–1; tribunals see tribunals, see
also arbitration; ombudsman system;
tribunals

anti-terrorism legislation 60–3, 267–70

appeals: accessibility 67–8; arbitration 236–7;
civil see civil appeals; criminal see criminal
appeals; finality 67; orality 67; principles
66; recommendations/changes 133, 199;
statistics 45–6, 66–7; structure 66–8

appellate process 47–8

arbitration: advantages 239; agreements 234;
appeals 236–7; autonomy 234; costs 240;
powers 234–5; role of court 236; specialist
arbitrator 240; statutory principles 233–4, 239

Aristotle 14

armed robbery 155, 156

arrest: access to solicitor 145, 146–9; arrestable
offences 145–6, 148, 156, 165–6; definition
164–5; false imprisonment 163–7;
lawfulness 164–5; right to silence 134,
149–50, 152–5; searching of premises 155–8

arson 139

assault 149

Auld Report 71–2, 128, 171, 179

bail 134, 139–42, 167–74; basic issues
168; conditional/unconditional 172,
173–4; general principles 169; personal
recognisances 172; presumption of
liberty 168; reapplication/appeal 172–3;

refusal 170–1; statistics 169; statutory
presumptions 169–70, 171, 172

balancing of interests: basic issues 58–9;
excluded evidence 103–4; human rights 62;
litigation control 59–60; terrorism 60–3

bank robbery 155, 156

Bentley, Derek 71

Bierce, Ambrose 138

bills, procedures 20–2

binding precedent: advantages/disadvantages
84; analogous cases 88; basic issues 80;
criminal/civil appeals 82; distinguished 86,
87–8; effect on common law 85–9; EU law
82; exceptions 81–2; hierarchical structure
80–1, 82–3, 86; overruled 86–7; ratio
decidendi/obiter dicta, distinction 83, 86–7,
see also precedent

Bingham, Lord 249–53

Blackstone's Commentaries 8, 136

Bowman Review 72–3

Bracton, H de 8

Brodrick Committee 54–5

Brookes, Michael 137

burglary 144, 145–6

Burns, Richard 199–200

Burton, Mr Justice 199

bylaws 26

Carson, Sir Edward 65

CCRC see Criminal Cases Review Commission
(CCRC)

Chancery, origins 15–18

civil appeals 68, 72–75; Direction 74–5;
discretionary decision 73; rationalisation
74; reduction recommendations 72–3;
statistics 72

civil law system 184–8; basic issues 187–8;
conditional work 201; courts see county
courts; CPR see Civil Procedure Rules (CPR);
as criminal law alternative 134–9; legal
services, changes 187; litigation 218

Civil Procedure Rules (CPR): amendment 203; basic issues 198; costs 200, 201; effect 198–9; gains/problems 199–202; jointly appointed expert 202; objectives 186–7; settlements incentives 196–7

CJEU *see* Court of Justice of the European Union (CJEU)

Clarke, Kenneth 76

Cobb, Stephen 76

Coke, Sir E 8

Collins, Judge Paul 76, 185

common law 1, 7–8; alteration 96; binding precedent, effect 85–9; emergence 9–13; equity, distinction 15–16

conciliation 241–2

conditional fee arrangements (CFAs) 187

confessions: admissibility 140–1; basic issues 139–40; juvenile 143; mixed content 141–2; obtained by oppression 142–3; uncorroborated 134

Cooper, Yvette 231

coroners' courts: basic issues 53; history 53–4; juries 54–5; reorganised system 54, 55–6, 57; statistics 54; types/circumstances of deaths 54, 55–6

Council of Ministers (EU) 30–1

county courts: resource issues 185–6; statistics 46

Court of First Instance (EU) 33, 35

Court of Justice of the European Union (CJEU) 34–8; basic issues 34; domestic courts, distinction 37–8; functions 35–6; personnel 34–5; procedure 36; referral to 36–7

court rule committees 26

courts: basic system 45; ICT use 195–6; statistics 45–7

CPR *see* Civil Procedure Rules (CPR)

criminal appeals 68–72; Criminal Cases Review Commission (CCRC) 71; fresh evidence 70; grounds for 68–9; juries 68, 72; safe/unsafe verdicts 69–70, 154

Criminal Cases Review Commission (CCRC) 71

criminal justice system (CRS): appeals *see* appeals; arrest *see* arrest; bail *see* bail; changes 133; civil law, as criminal law alternative 134–9; confessions 134; financial management 132; goals 132; institutions 132; plea bargaining 134; plea bargaining *see* plea bargaining; procedure 134; right to silence 134, 149–50, 152–5; standard of proof 137–8; statistics 133; trial by jury *see* juries

criminal law, civil law, as alternative 134–9

criminal offences, mental element 96–7

cross-examination 63–6

Crossman, Richard 229

Crown application 97

crown courts, statistics 47

Crown Prosecution Service 76, 138

Curia Regis 10–13

Curtis-Bennett, Sir Henry 65

custom 8–9

de minimis **interference** 160–1

defamation, convicted person 68

delegated legislation 1, 6–7; advantages/disadvantages 27–8; basic issues 25; judicial control 28; types 25–6

Devlin, Lord 116

Dicey, AV 245, 246–7, 258–9

Diedrick, Tony 137–8

directives (EU) 30

domestic violence 42

ECHR (European Convention on Human Rights), incorporation 254, 262

economic recession 75–8

Edward I 11

ejusdem generis **rule** 98

Equitable Life case 231, 232

equity 1; common law, distinction 15–16; emergence/development 14–18

European Convention on Human Rights (ECHR), incorporation 254, 262

European Council 33

European Court of Human Rights 33, 38

European Court of Justice 32–3

European Parliament 31–2

European Union (EU): basic issues 28–9; Civil Service Tribunal 33; Commission 32; competencies 30; Council of Ministers 30–1; General Court 33, 35; law 5–6, 34; origins 29; President/High Representative for Foreign Affairs 30–1; regulations/directives 30; treaties 29–30

evidence, children's 101

excluded evidence 98–104; balancing of interests 103–4; basic issues 98–9; hearsay evidence 101–2; previous convictions 99–100; public interest 102–3; types 99; unreliable 101

expert witnesses 212–17; basic issues 212; costs 213–14; duty to justice 215–16; esoteric information/theories 214–15; historical setting 212–13; partisanship 216–17;

recommendations 216; unreliable evidence 212–13, 216
expressio unius exclusio alterius rule 98

fairness issues 77–8
false imprisonment 163–7
family justice system 76
forensic evidence 217
Francis, R 17

General Court (EU) 33, 35
Glanvill, R 8
Goddard, Rayner 205
Griffiths, JAG 113–17, 119
guilty plea 176–7

Hansard 92, 96, 183, 184
Hart, Herbert 77
Hayek, F von 245, 247–8
health system 59
Heaps, John 201
hearsay evidence 101–2
Henry II 10–11
High Representative for Foreign Affairs (EU) 30–1
Hirst, Jonathan 211–12
homicide 42
Human Rights Act: background 244; balancing of interests 62; basic issues 261–2; delegated legislation 28; derogation 254–5, 264; and English legal system 264–5; incorporation of ECHR 254, 262; and judiciary 114–15; list of rights 263–4; living instrument doctrine 257; margin of appreciation 255–6; and primary legislation 265–6; primary/secondary legislation, distinction 23–4; proportionality 256–7, 260–1; separation of powers 266–70; settlements 198; statutory interpretation 93

interests *see* balancing of interests
international law obligations 97
Isaacs, Sir Rufus 64–5

Jennings, Sir Ivor 247
judges: basic issues 107; conflict with executive 114–15; ICT use 195–6; judicial precedent *see* precedent; judicial reasoning 79; juryless trials 107; and legislation *see* statutory interpretation; medieval 11–12; partiality 117–21; personal bias 115–16; social composition 105, 113–17; threaten industrial action 76–7

Judicial Appointments Commission 112, 117
judicial review 28, 41, 46, 113, 114, 188–92, 257–61; administrative discretion 257–61; background 244; basic issues 188, 257–8; political context 189, 192; prerogative remedies 190; proper process 188–9; reasonableness 190–1, *see also* rule of law
juries: attendance requirement changes 127–31; basic issues 105–6, 107, 122; composition 122–7; coroners' courts 54–5; defence challenges 126–7; disqualification 123–4, 124–5, 130; excusal/deferral 125–6, 131; fairness 106; ineligibility 128–30; juryless trials 106–7; rationale 122; trial provisions 133; vetting 127

Kafka, Franz 59

Law Commission: aims 39; basic issues 38–9, 44; implementation 42–3; process 39–40; programme projects 40–1
legal aid system 77
legal professional privilege: basic issues 203; basic rules 203–4; exceptions 205–6; meaning of privilege 204; rationale 204–5
legal textbooks 8
Leggatt Review 222–3
legislation: delegated *see* delegated legislation; interpretation *see* statutory interpretation; parliamentary 6–7; primary/secondary, distinction 23–4; process 20–3; proposals for 19–20; types 23
liberty deprivation 97
litigation 218

Macpherson Inquiry 41
magistrates' courts: criminal appeals 72; statistics 46–7
Maitland, FW 10, 11
mediation 241
Ministry of Justice 132, 133
Mortimer, Sir John 64
murder 42

negligence action against lawyers 68, 206–2012
Nichomachaen Ethics (Aristotle) 14
no fee, no win work 201
noscitur a sociis rule 98

Omagh case 135–7
ombudsman system: basic concept 228; basic issues 227–8; development 228–9;

evaluation 232; maladministration 229–30; Parliamentary Commissioner for Administration 227–32; reports 230–1, 232
Osborne, George 77–8
Oxford Centre for Socio-Legal Studies 193

Parliamentary Commissioner for Administration (PCA) 227–32
parliamentary legislation 6–7
Pinochet case 118–19, 121
plea bargaining 134, 174–9; basic issues 174; definition 174–5; formalisation 175; guidelines 176, 178; guilty plea 176–7; sentence discounts 178–9
police: assault on 158–61; interviews 142–3, 144–9; obstruction of 149–52, 155–8; stop and search 161–3
Pollock, F 10, 11
Popplewell, O 65–6
precedent: CJEU/domestic courts, distinction 37; judicial 7–8, see also binding precedent
President (EU) 30–1
primary/secondary legislation, distinction 23–4
privilege see legal professional privilege
privity of contract 41
professional bodies 26
public interest 102–3

rape within marriage 40, 84, 87
ratio decidendi/obiter dicta, distinction 83
Raz, J 248–9
regulations (EU) 30
retrospective effect 97
right to silence 134, 149–50, 152–5
Royal Assent 22–3
rule of law: background 244; basic issues 245; Bingham on 249–53; concept 246; Dicey on 245, 246–7, 258–9; Hayek on 245, 247–8; principles 250–3; Raz on 248–9, see also judicial review
Runciman Commission 178

searching: of premises 155–8; stop and search 161–3
Selden, J 17
separation of powers 266–70
settlements: basic issues 192; CPR incentives 196–7; factors 193–5; human rights 198; meaning 192–3; statistics 193, 194
sex discrimination 37–8

shoplifting 163–7
silence, right to 134, 149–50, 152–5
small claims 240–1
solicitors: access to 145, 146–9; advocacy 187
sources of law: basic issues 4–5; common law 1, 7–8; custom 8–9; European law 5–6; legal textbooks 8; parliamentary legislation 6–7
stare decisis see binding precedent
statutory instruments 26
statutory interpretation: alteration of common law 96; basic issues 89, 94; Crown application 97; extrinsic assistance 95–6; golden rule 91; human rights 93; international law obligations 97; intrinsic assistance 95; liberty deprivation 97; literal rule 90–1; mental element for criminal offences 96–7; mischief rule 91–2; presumptions 96–8; purposive approach 92–3; retrospective effect 97; role of judges 89–90; rules 90, 94; secondary aids 94; words' meaning in context 98
Stephen Lawrence case 41
stop and search 161–3
suicide 57
Supreme Court 8; access to 68; appointment process/requirements 109–18; basic issues 108; binding precedents 81–3, 84, 85; composition 108–9; overruling of previous judgments 48–53; separation of powers 108

terrorism legislation 60–3, 267–70
Thatcher government 247
theft 163–7
treasure troves 54
tribunals: advantages/disadvantages 220, 221–2; basic issues 219; composition 220; informality/formality 221, 222; legal aid 222; Leggatt Review 222–3; statutory framework 223–4; tier/chamber structure 224–7
trusts, origins 15–16, 18

vexatious litigants 58, 59

Wakley, Dr Thomas 53–4
witness preparation 180–4
Woolf Report 14, 77, 187, 197, 199, 200–2
words' meaning in context 98

Zander, M 175
Zuckerman, A 14